Advance Reviews of Lake Carriers' Association History 1880-2015

George Ryan's book on the history of the Lake Carriers' Association shines a light on how the Maritime Industry evolved and became not only an important part of Great Lakes economy, but America's economy. The contributions of the Lake Carriers Association and its members have been and continue to play a critical role for America's Manufacturing. Without the role of the Lake Carrier's Presidents and its membership bringing the issues of the day regarding marine transportation on the Inland Sea forward to our nation's leaders, the Great Lakes would have not been able to develop the modern efficient marine navigation system that our country enjoys today. George Ryan brings that important story to life in "Lake Carrier's Association History 1880-2015".
Mark Barker, President, Interlake Steamship Company

George Ryan's Lake Carriers' Association History adds an important document to the rich history of the Great Lakes. His exhaustive work is beautifully organized and masterfully written and will be referenced for decades to come. The Lake Carriers' Association has been and is a significant driver of policy and economic development in the Midwest and now its role is recorded for all who are interested in Great Lakes maritime heritage. Thank you, George, for your book and for your contribution to the industry.
Michelle Cortright, Publisher, Great Lakes/Seaway Review

"Little known and perhaps less understood, the Lake Carriers' Association has been at the center of economic development on the Great Lakes for almost 140 years. George Ryan's masterful narrative of this critical organization is arguably the most important contribution to Great Lakes historical research in the past quarter century. It is hard to imagine the economic success of the Great Lakes without the Lake Carriers' Association but it is equally hard to imagine any future research on any Great Lakes

topics that does not consult Lake Carriers' Association History 1880-2015 by George Ryan."
Christopher Gillcrist, Executive Director, National Museum Great Lakes, Great Lakes Historical Society

"George Ryan's Lake Carriers' Association History 1880-2015 represents a major contribution to the maritime history of the Great Lakes region. It belongs in every library throughout the region and on the shelf of every historian hoping to understand the complex history of one of the region's most significant organizations."
Robert R. Graham, Archivist, Historical Collections of the Great Lakes Bowling Green State University

"Maritime professionals, boat nerds and armchair historians will find a special place in their libraries for this exhaustively researched book. More than a history of the Lake Carriers' Association, it is packed with profiles of the shipowners and other industry leaders and the struggles they encountered in developing safe, profitable and efficient waterborne transportation on the Great Lakes."
Davis Helberg spent 45 years in Great Lakes shipping and retired in 2003 after 24 years as Duluth Port Director.

Having grown up near Cleveland and then embarking on a Coast Guard career that brought me into contact with the Great Lakes, I have gained insight and appreciation for the history and uniqueness of this trade on our northern maritime border. A history and importance to our nation that most Americans do not understand much less appreciate. George has brought this history to life and provided insight critical to the future of the industry. All who are interested in this region must read this book!
Vice Admiral James D. Hull, USCG, (Ret.), 2002 operational commander of Coast Guard Atlantic Area, 1999 Commander of the Ninth Coast Guard District and prior to that many other challenging assignments ashore and afloat.

"Throughout the annals of Great Lakes History the Lake Carriers Association has embodied the ideals of its leaders and membership to serve as the binding force for our industry's sustainability past, present, and future. With that, there is no more fitting a person to tell this story of steadfast resolve and prosperity than one of its longest serving Presidents, George Ryan. The Great Lakes maritime industry's future will be well served by reflecting on the LCA's storied past."
Paul C. LaMarre III, Port Director, Port of Monroe, MI & Director, Col James M. Schoonmaker Museum Ship

A fascinating read that led me to a much deeper appreciation of the history and accomplishments of the Lake Carriers' Association. LCA is a success story; it's a story of a tight band of vessel owners working together on common issues, developing a groundbreaking method of working with industry end users, political groups, ship owners and government to make great strides in a safety of navigation and efficiency of Great Lakes waterborne traffic.
Tom Wiater, President, Central Marine Logistics

Lake Carriers' Association History 1880-2015

Lake Carriers' Association History 1880-2015

To my Irish Family,
God Bless,
George J. Ryan

George J. Ryan
President, Lake Carriers' Association
1983-2002

Copyright © 2017 by George J. Ryan.
Cover design by Marek Mutch, Bay Village, OH

Library of Congress Control Number: 2017910238
ISBN: Hardcover   978-1-5434-3333-3
         Softcover   978-1-5434-3332-6
         eBook   978-1-5434-3331-9

All rights reserved. No part of this book may be reproduced or transmitted in any form or by any means, electronic or mechanical, including photocopying, recording, or by any information storage and retrieval system, without permission in writing from the copyright owner.

Any people depicted in stock imagery provided by Thinkstock are models, and such images are being used for illustrative purposes only. Certain stock imagery © Thinkstock.

Print information available on the last page.

Rev. date: 11/06/2017

To order additional copies of this book, contact:
Xlibris
1-888-795-4274
www.Xlibris.com
Orders@Xlibris.com
760075

Table of Contents

Introduction xv
Personal Reflection xvii
Acknowledgements xix

**Chapter 1   Lake Carriers' Association History,
              1880 to 1902** 1
  Political/Social Climate 1880-1902 1
  Cleveland Vessel Owners' Association and Lake Carriers'
    Association, Buffalo 3
  1892 Reorganization of Lake Carriers' Association 15
  Legislative Action of the Lake Carriers' Association 17

**Chapter 2   The Livingstone Presidency and the
              Reorganization of 1903** 31
  William Livingstone (1844-1925) Shipowner and
    President of the Lake Carriers' Association 32
  The Livingstone Presidency 1902-1925 42
  LCA Organization and Offices 45
  Rationale lobbying congress and the administration 48
  LCA Interaction with the Canadian Government and
    Ship Owners 49
  LCA Communications 50
  LCA and the Great Lakes Protective Association 53
  Vessel Losses and Crew casualties 54
  The Great War-The European War- Impact upon the
    growth of the Lake Carriers' Association 57
    • Operation of ships carrying grain in the fall and
      winter of 1917 58
    • Selective Service and LCA 60
    • War Regulations at the Soo 62
    • Wartime Mobilization Committee Activities in
      1918-1919 62
    • Ore and Coal Exchange, born of the Great War 64

- Maritime Union Grievances and Actions during the War 64
- Other Wartime Actions Impacting Lake Shipping 66

Water Pollution by Ships 67
LCA Involvement in Freight Rate Making 68
Navigation Improvements, Keystone of the LCA Mission 69
- Major Navigation Infrastructure Improvements 78
- Livingstone Channel 78
- Sault Ste. Marie, Davis Lock 80
- Sault Ste. Marie, Sabin Lock 82
- Private aids to navigation, lightships, patrol boats, water level gauges and dredging 84
- Lightships 84
- Dredging 86
- Patrol Boats and Water Gauges 88
- New Navigation Technology 89

Lighthouses, Reorganization of the Lighthouse Department 91
LCA Involvements with other Federal Agencies 92
- Lake Survey 92
- Support for Lifesaving Service 93
- Steamboat Inspection Service 94
- Weather Bureau Service 96

Labor Relations 97
- Grain Shoveling at Buffalo 98
- Labor Turmoil and the Views of the Labor Unions 99

Welfare Plan, another Keystone of the LCA Mission 102
- Safety First Campaign 104
- Sanitation Campaign 104
- Savings Plan 105
- Sobriety 105
- Schools 106
- Registration of Seamen, LCA Discharge Books, LCA Commissioners 108
- Assembly Halls or Shipping Offices 109
- Wage Setting 113
- Deaths of Seamen and Death and Permanent Disability Benefits 114
- Statistics on the Cause of Death for Seamen receiving Death Benefits under the Welfare Plan 1909-1925 116

End of the Livingstone Era, the Continuation of a Strong Association 121

Chapter 3 J. S. Ashley and Captain Joseph S. Wood, 1925-1937 .... **122**
    World and National Political/Economic Climate of the period 123
    Biographies of J.S. Ashley, A.F. Harvey, Joseph S. Wood 125
    LCA Organization 126
    The Economy and the impact on Tonnage Moved 129
    LCA Committees 131
    Legislative Matters 132
- National Industrial Recovery Act (NIRA), Great Lakes Shipping Code 132
- Chicago Drainage Canal 133
- The St. Lawrence Waterway 134
- Grain Trade Restrictions 134
- Regulation of Water Carriers 135

    Welfare Plan Committee 135
    Navigation and Shore Captains Committees 149
    Fleet Engineers Committee 156
    Vessel Losses 157
    Memorial to the Late William Livingstone 158
    Other Key Events of Period 159

Chapter 4 Alexander T. Wood, 1938-1946 .... **162**
    Economic/Political Climate during Pre-War and World War II Years 162
    Biography of Alexander T. Wood 164
    LCA Organization 164
    Economic and Government Actions before and During the War 167
    Great Lakes Protective Association 179
    LCA Committees 179
    Legislative Actions 180
    St. Lawrence Seaway 181
    Welfare Plan Committee 182
    Navigation and Shore Captains Committees 194
    Fleet Engineers Committee 202
    Education and Public Relations Committee 203
    Vessel Construction and Modernization 203
    Vessel Losses 205
    Other Key Events of Period 206

**Chapter 5 John T. Hutchinson and VADM Lyndon
Spencer, 1947-1962 .... 210**
Economic/Political Climate during Post World War II,
  Cold War, and Korean War Years......................................211
Biographies of John T. Hutchinson and Lyndon Spencer........211
LCA Organization...215
LCA Membership and Tonnage 217
Summary of Spencer Accomplishments and Disappointments ...217
War Clouds after World War II...220
Relations with the U.S. Coast Guard......................................226
St. Lawrence Seaway 228
LCA Committees 237
 • Legislative Committee...237
 • Welfare Committee..246
 • Shore Captains and Navigation Committees..............264
 • Electronics Committee...271
 • Fleet Engineers Committee..275
 • LCA Smoke Abatement Committee............................279
 • Public Relations Committee.......................................281
Vessel Losses...286
New Vessel Construction after World War II..........................286
Other Key Events of Period 289

Chapter 6 VADM James A. Hirshfield, 1962-1970 291
Economic/Political Climate 291
Biography of Admiral Hirshfield 292
LCA Organization...295
Summary of Objectives and Accomplishments 297
LCA Committees 298
 • Legislative Committee...298
 • Welfare Committee..301
 • Navigation Committee...314
 • Electronics Committee...316
 • Fleet Engineers Committee..319
 • Smoke Abatement Committee 321
 • Public Relations Committee.......................................323
Vessel Construction and Modernization 325
Other Key Events of Period 327

Chapter 7 VADM Paul Trimble, 1970-1982 337
    Economic/Political Climate in the World and in America 337
    Biography of Paul Trimble 340
    LCA Organization 340
    Traffic on the Great Lakes 343
    Major Accomplishments and Disappointments 345
    LCA Committees 347
        • Legislative and Government Affairs Committee 347
        • Welfare Committee; in 1980 the Vessel Personnel
          and Safety Committee 356
        • Great Lakes Maritime Academy 367
        • Shore Captains, Navigation and Ice Committee 372
        • Electronics Committee 379
        • Fleet Engineers Committee 381
        • Air and Water Conservation Committee 382
        • Public Relations Committee 384
    Shipbuilding, Modernizations and Ship Scraping 386
    Vessel Losses 388
    Other Key Events of the Period 389

Chapter 8 George J. Ryan, 1983-2002 392
    Political Climate in the World, Washington and State
        Governments 392
    Biography of George J. Ryan 394
    Personal Narrative on Background of Appointment as
        LCA President 395
    LCA Organization 398
    Lobbying Washington 410
    Economic Conditions Impacting Traffic 412
    Major Accomplishments and Disappointments in the
        1983-2002 Period 412
    LCA, George Ryan and the Maritime Unions 414
    American Iron Ore Association 418
    Coalition Building--Great Lakes Maritime Task Force 418
    LCA Committees 421
        • Vessel Security Committee 421
        • Public Relations and Publications 422
        • International Joint Conference 425
        • Legislative Committee 430
            • Taxes and Fees 430
            • Imported Steel and Iron Ore, Impact on Great

- Lakes Shipping 434
  - Cabotage Laws- the Jones Act 435
  - Another Coalition-- Maritime Cabotage Task Force (MCTF) 436
  - Environmental Issues 439
- Navigation and Electronics Committees 445
  - Establish Extended Navigation Season; from March 25 until January 15 445
  - Save the Old Mackinaw; Build a new large Icebreaker 449
  - New Poe-Sized Lock 454
- Captains Committee 465
- Fleet Engineers Committee 467
- Vessel Personnel and Safety Committee 469
- Great Lakes Job Referral Centers 478

Vessel Construction and Conversions 1983-2002 479

Chapter 9   James H. I. Weakley 2003-Present 480

Detailed Acknowledgements 489
Appendix 1 497
   Obituaries 497
Index 523

Introduction

When I retired in January 2003 after serving 20 years as President of the Lake Carriers' Association (LCA), I mulled over the need to document the work of the LCA through brief articles in *Inland Seas*, the Journal of the Great Lakes Historical Society, and those articles still will stem from this research. The last *Inland Seas* article on LCA was written by Bertram B. Lewis and Oliver Burnham in 1971 and it did not extensively cover the work done by LCA during the tenure of each President. It was my intention to start with the LCA Presidents who served since 1952, the four leaders, Admirals Spencer, Hirshfield and Trimble and myself who were selected by the shipowners to manage the Association, serving as the LCA Chairman of the Board and Chair of the Executive Committee. These four Presidents were a departure from the earlier period when one of the members, usually the President of his own shipping company, also served as President of the LCA. However, when I began looking into the historical records, a new perspective emerged. The LCA that the above four Presidents served would not have been the powerful and successful trade association it became if it were not for William Livingstone, who served a one-year term as President in 1895 and then served 23 more years as President after the reorganization of the LCA in 1903. LCA also would not have been successful if all the powerful members who served on the Board and many important committees did not give their well-considered advice and virtually unanimous support to their President and staff who carried out the LCA objectives. Thus this book is an attempt to tell the story of the LCA and its contributions to Great Lakes shipping since its founding days and through my tenure as President. The essential work of LCA continues, however, through the very capable leadership of my successor James Weakley.

As the book unfolded, I frequently asked myself who the readership might be and if my effort would become a valuable contribution for those seeking to know the history of the Great Lakes shipping industry. I hoped this book might be of interest to those men and women who follow the current Great Lakes shipping industry collectively and are affectionately known as 'Boatnerds'. I also hoped it might be of interest to those men and women working for the lake carriers on both sides of the U.S./Canadian border, to provide them with insights to help their industry by looking at some lessons and solutions from the past. I recognize that this piece of history is biased in that it draws the facts laid out in the book almost exclusively from LCA documents, primarily the LCA Annual Reports, the LCA *Bulletin* and other LCA files. I also recognize that it looks closely only at the contributions to the navigation system from the United States perspective. I hope a similar book someday will be published to recount the contributions of the Dominion Marine Association, now the Canadian Shipowners Association, to provide more inclusive documentation of our shared navigation system.

I learned a great deal about the work of the Association and, more importantly, I learned of the lifetime commitments so many leaders in the Great Lakes shipping industry gave and still give to the management of the Association. I had heard about many of the leaders through knowing there was ship on the Lakes that, at some time, carried his or her name. They earned their naming rights through leadership in their own company and their long-term commitment to the industry. It was not unusual for many of these men to serve on the LCA Board or to chair a committee for decades. As each annual report documented their contributions by including a brief obituary, I elected to include some abbreviated obituaries as an appendix in this book. Another book needs to be written honoring the men and women who served on the ships; it must include their struggle for improved wages and working conditions, their efforts to be represented by unions and the collective effort by management and the men on the ships to improve productivity and safety.

I chose to consider the founding of the Lake Carriers' Association to be 1880, the year the Cleveland Vessel Owners' Association, the predecessor organization of LCA, held its first meeting.

Personal Reflection

I had many role models in my professional and private life. Within the Great Lakes shipping industry since arriving in Cleveland, Ohio in 1975, there were several men in those early years who stand out, including VADM Paul Trimble, RADM Jim Gracey, James R. Barker, Rennie Thompson, Ward Fuller and Bill Buhrmann. However, once I was elected President of LCA, I had many predecessor leaders to study under. I knew Admiral Paul Trimble personally and I owe a great deal to his tutoring. Of those leaders I did not know in their lifetime, I realize I gravitated to studying the enormous contributions made by one man during his presidency. That man was William Livingstone who served a total of 24 years as President.

I knew William Livingstone only from his accomplishments in improving the Great Lakes shipping infrastructure that benefited the agricultural and the heavy industries on both sides of the border. I knew Livingstone was a man who was admired deeply by his comrades; upon his death they raised the funds to build a memorial lighthouse on Belle Isle in the Detroit River, named it the Livingstone Lighthouse and gave it to the city of Detroit. He is one of the less well recognized industrial leaders of America but was well known by the giants of his day, including Henry Ford who served as a pallbearer at his funeral. I thought of Livingstone whenever I was on a ship transiting the Livingstone Channel in the Detroit River and I knew he had to be a highly effective and respected leader to have such an important channel named after him during his lifetime.

However, I never really knew William Livingstone for the man he was and the passages he took in life to prepare himself for the collateral job as President of the Lake Carriers' Association. I never focused on the fact that he held several full time careers while serving as President of LCA. Details of those careers will be found later in this book.

I thought of a few comparisons between his life and my own since we both served the Great Lakes shipping industry with the same title as President, Lake Carriers' Association. Several clear differences struck me. Livingstone's parents came from Scotland, my mother and all my grandparents were born in Ireland. He served the industry at a time when the President was a LCA member holding a senior position in a ship owning company; the LCA presidency term usually lasted only a few years—yet after an initial one year term of service, he was later elected by his peers to serve them for 23 years until his death. In my tenure, the office was held by a professional manager, not a ship owner. I was subject to re-appointment annually based upon performance; a term that lasted 20 years.

As one might expect, Livingstone was a prominent Republican leader in Michigan and in the nation; he was elected to the Michigan State House for two years and was appointed to a federal position by U.S. President Chester Arthur. I was a registered Democrat, who previously served the U.S. government as a civil servant in Washington, D.C., London, England, and Cleveland for a number of years. Only after I retired from LCA did I publicly work for the election of Democratic Party candidates and served as a President of the Bay Village Democratic Club in Ohio.

Livingstone had hands-on ship board experience serving as Pilot on tugs and larger vessels in the Great Lakes; I served as a licensed officer including as Master on oceans and briefly on active duty as a U.S. Naval Officer. Livingstone and many other ship owners of his time were opposed to organized labor and fought hard to keep the open shop on all their vessels and fired strikers and union organizers. I had been a member of the Masters, Mates and Pilots Union and joined others in a strike, walking in a picket line outside the Grace Line pier in New York City where I was employed. There are many other curious disparities in our background that might have led me to discontinue honoring William Livingstone as my mentor. The more I studied his work for the industry and learned so much about his background, my admiration for Livingstone continued to grow. This book contains a little of what I have learned about my mentor William Livingstone and the Lake Carriers' Association that thrived in his wake.

Acknowledgements

I could not have completed this work without full access to all the files of the Lake Carriers' Association and the warm cooperation of my successor Jim Weakley, President LCA. I thank my wife Cornelia M. Ryan who encouraged me to continue working on my dream to complete and to publish the book no matter how many hundreds of hours it took me away from other aspects of life in my retirement. I also appreciate the support and encouragement of Christopher Gillcrist, Executive Director of the Great Lakes Historical Society, who allowed me access to the GLHS files in Vermilion, OH. I also thank the many who provided photographs to illustrate this history. Many of their names will be at the end of the book.

I am in debt to all those who helped me and the LCA during my tenure. Within the LCA membership at all levels and in the government agencies and trade associations there were many people who really cared about Great Lakes shipping. Many of them I considered my friends. LCA members worked closely with each other solving technical and operating problems even to the extent that they shared spare parts; they were very trustworthy. Their word was their bond. They negotiated and concluded with a handshake and a minimum of paperwork, trading cargos at times. I can never remember them all but at the end of the book I will mention many names of these people in no particular order. As I have prepared this history of LCA, their names surfaced and I was pleased to recall our interactions and friendships.

Chapter One

Lake Carriers' Association History 1880-1902

Political/Social Climate 1880-1902

The United States was growing as an industrial empire as well as a populous country welcoming shiploads of immigrants. The Civil War in America had required enhanced development of iron and steel and coal mining industries. They continued to grow as the increased population needed housing, food, heating and manufactured goods. Distribution systems using railroads, canals and major waterways were in great demand. The Great Lakes became a vital waterway for the iron ore, limestone, coal mining, and steel industries, as well as for the farmers and food processors they served.

Major cities grew exponentially along the American and Canadian Great Lakes shorelines. The 1880 census determined the resident population of the United States to be 50 million, an increase of 30 percent over the almost 40 million persons enumerated during the 1870 Census. By 1890 the population was nearly 63 million and in 1900, at the turn of the century, it was 76 million.

In 1880 Chicago was the 4th largest city in the United States, Cleveland eleventh, Pittsburgh twelfth, Buffalo thirteenth and Detroit eighteenth. In 1890 Chicago ranked second in largest urban places, moving up from fourth place in 1880 and Cleveland was tenth. In 1900 Chicago still ranked in second place while Cleveland moved up to 7th place and Buffalo hit the top ten, ranking in 8th place; Pittsburgh was 11th and Detroit was 13th and Milwaukee 14th. Great Lakes shipping concentrated in those major Great Lakes cities and the trade associations that supported them were formed in Buffalo and Cleveland.

Politically, on the national level, the Presidency was held primarily by Republicans: James A. Garfield, Chester A. Hayes, Benjamin Harrison, William McKinley and Theodore Roosevelt. Only Democrat Grover Cleveland held two non-consecutive terms. Unfortunately, during this period Garfield and McKinley were assassinated; the office then transferred to the incumbent Vice President. The Senate generally was led by the Republicans except in 1880, 1893 and 1894. During the entire period Senators were appointed by the Governors of each state. The House of Representatives was also Republican controlled except for 1880, 1883-1889, and 1891-1895.

The United States began to emerge as a world power during this period. The most significant event was the Spanish American War following the explosion of the USS <u>Maine</u> in Havana, Cuba. The victory of American naval forces led to the Treaty of Paris whereat Spain ceded indefinite colonial authority to the United States over Puerto Rico, Guam and the Philippine Islands. Then in 1900 the United States joined with European powers to put down the Boxer Rebellion in China.

Industrialization and innovation led to many improvements in living and working conditions. In 1880 Thomas Edison patented the electric incandescent bulb. Steel vessels began to replace the wooden schooners and the early iron and wood ships. In 1883 Congress authorized construction of the first steel vessel for the U.S. Navy.

Labor organizations were formed to challenge the tight control of management over workers' wages and working conditions. In 1886 the American Federation of Labor was founded in Ohio. Management fought back against the organization of workers and that led to many tragic conflicts. The Homestead Steel Strike took place in the Pittsburgh area when the Amalgamated Association of Iron and Steel Workers (formed in 1876) struck the Pittsburgh Bessemer Steel Works in 1882 in opposition to the enforcement of yellow-dog contracts on the workers. In 1889 there was another strike when the strikers took over the town of Homestead, and again in 1892 when the Pinkerton Detectives, a contingent of deputy sheriffs, and about 6,000 soldiers in the state militia were mobilized to put down the strike.

The economy had the usual cycles including the economic recession called the Panic of 1893; after which some industries such as the Pullman Company cut wages but not the rents for company housing in the company town of Pullman on the south side of Chicago. This action led in 1894 to the Pullman Strike and boycott that shut down much of the nation's freight and passenger traffic west of Detroit. There were many other strikes as American-born and immigrant workers unionized. Some of the steel companies attempted to thwart the unionization of workers by sending agents to European villages to offer the residents the jobs of the striking workers. The strategy was to have non-English speaking workers from different countries holding the jobs in different parts of the plants, thus making it very difficult for communications between workers speaking different languages as well as to the English speaking American union agents.

All of these political, international, social and economic issues were on the minds of the leaders of the steamship companies that formed the trade association that became the Lake Carriers' Association.

Cleveland Vessel Owners' Association and Lake Carriers' Association, Buffalo

Buffalo was a very important center of commerce for the Great Lakes maritime industry dating back to the construction of the Griffin at Black Rock in 1679, the first large sailing vessel built for the fur trade on the upper four Great Lakes. From research, I learned that the first important passenger ships under steam power, particularly for the immigrant trade, sailed from Buffalo in those early days but the ships seldom continued beyond Detroit. In 1836, the first shipment of grain came into Buffalo when the brig John Kenzie brought in 3,000 bushels of wheat, and the first grain elevator was built in Buffalo in 1842. It was the growing grain trade that was transshipped via the Erie Canal to New York and the world markets that made Buffalo a key center of commerce.

Buffalo shipping and grain elevators late 1800s

There was a great need for vessel owners to band together to further their navigation interests as well as to obtain crews. The association of vessel owners had its inception in Cleveland on September 1, 1880 when the nucleus was formed of the Cleveland Vessel Owners' Association (CVOA), which became stronger as the years passed and new tonnage was added. There was talk in other ports of a general association and local meetings being held from time to time. On December 18, 1880 the Cleveland vessel owners decided to meet with those of other cities on February 16, 1881 in Chicago. Articles of association in the form of resolutions were adopted, the most pertinent article setting forth that: "The object of this association shall be for the purpose of devising and discussing plans for the protection of the interests of lake tonnage (steam or sail), and for the better operation of local associations with each other." Another purpose was to establish shipping offices in Ohio ports to supply crews and to provide protection for the crews in port. Nevertheless, the CVOA was not formally organized until 1887 when Alva Bradley was elected President and H. M. Hanna was elected Vice President.

However, it was not Cleveland maritime leadership who led the way in the formation of the strongest association. Under the leadership of S. D. Caldwell, General Manager of Western Transit Co., Buffalo, with the support of other shipowners from Buffalo, Erie, Cleveland, Toledo, Detroit, Bay City, Chicago, Milwaukee and Duluth, the Lake Carriers' Association (LCA) was organized in May 1885. Franklin J. Firth, Philadelphia, had extensive interests in Great Lakes shipping and railroads (he was President of the Connecting Terminal and Railroad Company). He recounted that in route to a Chicago Conference, "I thought it advisable to unite the Buffalo, Erie and other rail and lake lines in an association to take in all competing lake lines." He drafted a constitution and by-laws on the train and secured their adoption in Chicago.

Franklin J. Firth, drafted 1st LCA constitution and bylaws

The purpose in the constitution stated in part "…to consider and take action upon all general questions relating to the navigation and carrying business of the great lakes, and the waters tributary thereto, with the intention to improve the character of the service rendered to the public, to protect the common interest of lake carriers, and promote their general welfare…" The first annual address of the LCA President Caldwell stated that the purpose was to concentrate influence in encouraging national legislation and appropriations in the interest of lake navigation. He noted that in 1884, 46,939 vessels representing 19,645,271 tons passed down the Detroit River. This was five times the combined tonnage of the Ohio and Mississippi Rivers for the same period. Yet, for the previous ten years, Congressional appropriations for navigation improvements in the Mississippi River system were $25 million; while the Great Lakes received $9 million.

In 1885, under the leadership of LCA President S. D. Caldwell, who served until 1891, the LCA dealt with Canadian wrecking laws, Sault Canal construction, the Treaty of Washington (a cabotage issue), uniform bills of lading, Buffalo grain shoveling charges, grain shortages, light and fog whistle signals, and a school for captains and mates.

- The Canadian Wrecking Laws issue was a matter of reciprocity to allow American vessels to tow another vessel, wrecked, stranded or in distress in Canadian waters back to the waters of the United States in exchange for the same rights that Canadian vessels would have in United States waters. Some of the issues related to the question as what waters were contiguous; Americans wanted the right to take salvage actions in the Welland Canal.
- The treaty of Washington issue would be a hallmark action in the LCA protection of the rights of American vessels to operate exclusively in the Cabotage trade, the port to port movement of cargo by ship between American ports. The Treaty had allowed Canadian vessels to carry American origin cargo to an American port, if part of the route was made by rail through Canada via Sarnia or Collingwood, but that exception was to terminate July 1, 1885. The Canadian lines worked hard to have this provision renewed. The LCA petitioned President Cleveland to deny that request. While the movement of grains from Chicago by Canadian vessels was stopped, from Duluth, Canadian ships moved cargo ultimately destined for an American port. The grain was being entered with U.S. Customs as freight, not destined for an American port, but for export to Canada. The Canadian line would then re-enter the freight in Sarnia, Canada as 'exported goods returned

to this country' consequently being free of duty. This subterfuge was vigorously protested by LCA to the U.S. Attorney General and the ruling was made in the favor of LCA since there were enough American vessels to carry the freight. This would be only the beginning of many actions taken by LCA to protect the few American cabotage laws prior to the strengthening of them under what became known as the Jones Act.

- Although the subject of training captains and mates is included in the President's address under 'other matters', it was a sign of more to follow by LCA members to provide for the proper training and certification of all seamen. In this case it was noted that it was desirable that captains and mates have some practical knowledge of navigation. Certainly this was an understatement; as some of the larger lines opened schools in Buffalo and Erie to instruct mates and captains in navigation and chart practice applicable to Great Lakes service. It must be noted that many of the officers gained their experience on the oceans and found Great Lakes navigation very different.

In 1886, in addition to some unresolved issues, LCA managers:

- Dealt with the vexing problem on how coal freight rates should be assessed, by gross or net tons (not a small matter since revenue was impacted by at least 10%);
- assessed and approved the proposal to build a bridge from Detroit to Belle Isle;
- assessed the plans to build the railroad bridge across the Sault Ste. Marie River and found it objectionable; however, recognizing the inevitability of construction, the LCA working with the Cleveland Vessel Owners' Association (CVOA), lobbied Congress to require the regulation of the bridge operation to be under the authority of the Secretary of War, and that the bridge shall remain open for vessel transits except when the bridge needs to be closed for the eminent passage of a train (despite this effort, the bill did not pass the Senate);

- discussed the possibility of establishing a National Board of Arbitration to deal with the maritime labor disputes that were arising, but stopped this effort since it was feared that the action would create more labor agitation;
- supported Harbors of Refuge by the acquisition of the U.S. Government of the Portage Lake Canals and the Sturgeon Bay and Lake Michigan Canal;
- recommended an LCA Board of Arbitration to decide disputes as to amounts paid for services rendered to vessels in distress; and,
- lobbied Congress to pass legislation prohibiting the establishment of private lights and buoys in public waters (there were enterprising individuals who installed private aids and then invoiced owners of passing vessels, a model used on land in the form of private toll roads).

In 1887:

- The Board of LCA in conjunction with the CVOA opposed the action of the U.S. Board of Supervising Inspectors of Steam Vessels who had ordered that all steamers on the lakes and on seaboard have wheel chains rove so as, when the wheel was put to port the vessel's head should go to starboard; and, when the wheel was put to starboard the vessel would go to port. LCA advocated straight chains. The Board finally rescinded the rule but left the mode of steering optional.
- The Board successfully opposed actions of City of Chicago to reduce bridge opening hours.
- A very unusual subject was addressed in response to the Secretary of the Navy request that certain U.S. commercial vessels be designated not as ships of war but as cruisers or transports. Provisions were outlined to allow the Navy to purchase or use the vessels in emergency and to train the crews in artillery and in the torpedo corps. Crews would be paid and drilled during the winter. The Board approved the general scheme but it does not appear that any action by the government took place.

- Due to the extensive representation needed in Washington and the cost of sending managers for long periods to Washington, the Board seriously considered hiring legal counsel to represent the LCA in Washington and this question was raised for many years and Counsel as needed was engaged.

In 1888, the Board continued to deal with many of the above subjects yet unresolved, and many new challenges.

- Most significant was the renewed effort of the railroad interests to obtain national legislation to build a bridge across the Detroit River. At this time, the proposal was to build a high level bridge that clears the tallest masts and to have only two piers in the river. LCA had always advocated that tunnels were the best solution and would maintain this position for decades to come.
- Another major issue was the need to dredge the St. Clair Flats ship canal and to place the canal under the Department of War regulatory authority. All too frequently, overloaded vessels would go aground and delay significant numbers of other up and down bound vessels. The LCA successfully obtained the legislation for a 16 foot deep canal, 200 feet wide and Army control. Regulations drafted by the Army were approved by LCA.
- As an indicator of the labor strife that existed at this time, LCA members were concerned that, unlike in the ocean trades, seamen operating in the Lakes or coastwise trade, could not be punished for breaches of discipline.
- The Board aggressively began to advocate the permanent lighting of the Detroit, St. Clair and St. Marys Rivers aids to navigation. Delays were costly as vessels often could not safely navigate at night.
- Opposed the unregulated rafting of timber on the public channels since the rafts would destroy the floating aids to navigation.
- A discussion was held on the desirability of reaching a mutual agreement that no boats would commence navigation before May 1 since there was so little cargo. The Board could not enforce this action and thus merely recommended the action to members.

- As a sign that the work of the Board was becoming extremely onerous without a larger Association staff, a committee of two members in Detroit was designated to deal with the government on navigation matters, in particular with General Poe. Also, the President noted in his annual report that the load of work was falling on too few members; he noted that when he asked for information, he had replies from only 17 of the 86 members.

General Orlando M. Poe, U.S. Army Corps of Engineers, was instrumental in design and construction of first major lock at Sault Ste. Marie

In 1889, the Association formally recognized the leadership of William Livingstone. He was a prominent Detroit ship owner, manager of the Michigan Navigation Company and had been the Detroit Collector of Customs. He was elected to the LCA Board of Managers to replace a Detroit member of the Board who severed his connections with LCA by publicly supporting a low railroad bridge across the Detroit River, a position that Livingstone vehemently opposed. Livingstone was recognized by the board as the primary spokesman for all ship-owners on all Detroit River concerns.

Harry Coulby, President of
Pittsburgh Steamship Company and
Interlake Steamship Company

William G. Mather, President
Cleveland Cliffs, (Michael
Schwartz Library, Cleveland
State University)

John W. Westcott, founder of
J.W. Westcott Company.

Alexander McDougall, President,
American Steel Barge Company,
(Superior Public Museum)

Some of the early leadership listed in the 1899 Report of the Board of Managers included: William C. Farrington, Buffalo, President, and 14 Vice Presidents. There were 88 on the Board of Managers including: Thomas Wilson, M. A. Bradley, H. M. Hanna, George McKay, J. C. Gilchrist, Harry Coulby, J. H. Sheadle, W. G. Mather, William Livingstone, J. W. Westcott, Alexander McDougall, G. A. Tomlinson, and A.B. Wolvin.

Livingstone's skills and knowledge were drawn upon on the railroad bridge issue and all the major issues tackled by LCA that year: private lights; arbitration for members relating to salvage assistance; uniform bills of lading; raft towing; a call for a new government survey of the lake navigation system; and the discriminatory U. S. Customs charges that gave free services to the railroads and charged fees for services on lake vessels.

In 1890, Livingstone remained on the Board of Managers with S. D. Caldwell, Buffalo as President. Many of the past navigation issues were still on the docket and the members recognized that representation in Washington was essential, not only with local legal counsel but also with high level owner representation at committee meetings. There were over 140 bills introduced in the 51st Congress that had an impact on lake shipping. Arguments were made that congressmen should be invited to tour the lakes on member's vessel to see the difficult navigation conditions in heavy weather, fog, day and night without adequate lighting, charts and channel dimensions. Some of the new legislative challenges included:

- Load Line bill that would interfere with carrying capacity and the value of some lake vessels. After vigorous ship owner testimony in Washington, the committee reported the bill adversely.
- Light-house legislation was sought in Washington and in Ottawa. Republican Senator F. B. Stockbridge, Michigan, and Representative T. E. Burton, Ohio, introduced extensive light house and lighted aids bills. Appropriations were difficult to obtain; however, ultimately relief was obtained including light and fog signal at Squaw Island, a light at old Mackinaw Point, 37 lights in the St. Marys River, many range lights and fog signals, government assumption of the operation of the private lights in the American side of the St. Clair and Detroit Rivers, and funds for the construction of three lightships. While the Canadian Government officials took

a 'friendly" view to the entreaty of the LCA delegation, thus far Canadians only initiated studies of the costs for aids to navigation in the Great Lakes connecting channels on the Canadian side.
- The River and Harbors bill requested $4 million for improvements on the Great Lakes; while the bill did not pass, administrative action lead to the preliminary action on government purchase of the Portage Lake Canals and on preliminary work, prior to appropriations, for work on the Sault lock and Hay Lake.
- The Line Throwing Projectile Law passed congress and would have gone into effect in spring 1890; but in collaboration with coastal shipowner associations, LCA was successful in getting a one year reprieve of the law that would have applied to all lake craft. There was some recognition of the value of the line-throwing guns for passenger vessels, but the requirement for all vessels was considered onerous.
- LCA was successful in opposition to the private use of Government pier property at the harbor entrances by large vessels loading and unloading thereby decreasing the channel width and thus the use of the channels.
- The LCA effort to extend criminal jurisdiction of the U.S Courts to offenses committed by seamen on the Great Lakes and connecting waters, similar to the jurisdiction over cases of offences committed on the high seas, became law. This passage reflects the continued difficult labor relations that existed in those days.
- LCA fought off what they considered as 'hostile legislation' that would have required minimum manning of four licensed engineers on steam vessels and would have regulated the hours of work of licensed officer to 12 hours out of 24 hours.
- Gave strong support for General Poe's report advocating a twenty-foot depth in the connecting waters of the Lakes at a cost of $3.3 million. The LCA managers drew up plans to advocate this action in the ensuing years.

In 1891, LCA managers continued to wrestle with the need for a permanent counsel in Washington; they tried in vain to enlist the financial aid of the shipping interests on the Atlantic coast and the western rivers, but to no avail. Members did not want to accept an additional subscription to pay for counsel. The LCA secretary spent more time in Washington, in part to hasten transfer of the Portage Lake canals to the government. The canal owners had ceased maintenance dredging as soon as the government authorization to purchase became law thus causing masters to severely reduce draft. He also continued to deal with the projectile law, the River and Harbors Bill containing authorization for the 20 foot channel, a bill authorizing construction of a large number of aids to navigation stretching from the St. Lawrence to Duluth and Chicago. Even more vexing, he had to deal with the resurrection of the bill requiring a minimum number of licensed engineers, and a system of examinations covering knowledge that would require engineering school attendance along with technical requirements for the main engine shafting for vessels carrying passengers. It was very clear that vigilance in Washington and the willingness to pay the expense of counsel was needed in addition to working closely with the CVOA and other maritime associations. Two other matters were of importance:

- The issue of discriminatory tolls in the Welland Canal as a violation of the Treaty of Washington came up again as the Canadian government rebated Welland Canal tolls on Canadian grain discharged at Montreal but not if the grain was transshipped at an American port. Also a full toll was collected on Canadian or American grain discharged at an American port.
- Significant LCA work went into the Congressional tour of the Lakes in July 1891. Senator James McMillan and Honorable Stevenson of Michigan, Senators P. Sawyer (WI), F.B. Stockbridge (MI) and C. H. Gibson (MD) and Representatives N. C. Blanchard (LA), T. J. Henderson (IL), G. H. Brickner (WI) and others made the inspection tours. The trip included the harbors of Buffalo, Cleveland, Ashtabula, Marquette, Duluth, Superior, Escanaba, Green Bay and the connecting channels and some canals. LCA expected much benefit to come from this 'ocular demonstration' of the vastness of the Lake commerce.

1891 Congressional tour of Great Lakes, (Library of Congress, Detroit Photographic Co.)

1892 Reorganization of Lake Carriers' Association

With all the significant work on the plate of the few officers and a few members of LCA, there was a call by President Caldwell for changes in the by-laws to establish committees to deal with Finance, Aids to Navigation, Rivers and Harbors and miscellaneous legislation. LCA was being considered by many shipowners as a 'Buffalo" organization. The Committee leadership needed to be drawn from other cities and in particular from Cleveland, since the preponderance of membership was drawn from Cleveland and Buffalo.

The Committee to draw up changes in the by-laws did that and much more to advance the Association. S. D. Caldwell, Buffalo, was an outstanding leader, serving seven years as President; but he was identified with Buffalo. The new re-organized LCA needed to have a broader Great Lakes identity. LCA recognized that the CVOA was formed primarily for the purpose of establishing shipping offices in Ohio ports to supply crews and to provide protection for the crews in port. While both Associations engaged in legislative work and collaborated on major bills, at times, they acted at cross-purposes thus jeopardizing congressional action. CVOA members wanted additional shipping offices and because of the increased activity of union organization, and occasional violence, members of both associations wanted improved protection for the crews while in port.

M.A. Bradley, LCA President 1892.

George P. McKay, LCA Treasurer 1892

Conferences between ship owners were held in Detroit, Chicago, Buffalo and Cleveland and, at a meeting in Detroit on April 28, 1892, the LCA was reorganized. M. A. Bradley, Cleveland, was elected President of LCA and Captain George P. McKay, Treasurer. The first meeting of the reorganized LCA was held in Cleveland on January 2, 1893. The members agreed to maintain and increase the number of shipping offices, to lobby in Washington acting as representatives of all Great Lakes ship owners, and to maintain the private lights until the government would operate them.

LCA would also continue to collect vital statistics on lake commerce and provide them to the government as well as to the public. It was noted in the Annual Report that this statistical work and distribution was one of the most useful Association tasks. This valuable task continues to the present time.

The shipping offices of the CVOA in Cleveland, Toledo and Ashtabula were maintained and new offices were opened in Buffalo and Chicago. Union organization troubles were much on the mind of the ship owners. Protection was needed for crews in Buffalo, Chicago, Escanaba and Ashland. In Buffalo, 90 police were dispatched at different times for vessel protection; whereas in Chicago the city provided no police protection. In Buffalo there was an incident referred to as the Mabel Wilson affair. This schooner was boarded by members of the Sailor's Union; they assaulted the Captain and some of the non-union crew and threatened to shoot the Captain with a pistol. LCA spent a great deal of time and money to prosecute the case against the guilty parties.

Legislative Action of the Lake Carriers' Association

In 1892 under the leadership of M. A. Bradley, LCA President, there was much for which to lobby congress:

- With the help of agricultural interests in the west and northwest who wanted lower cost transportation, the long sought 20-foot-deep channel was authorized. Efforts continued to obtain appropriations for re-survey of areas of the lakes and channels as well as publishing correct charts. Unfortunately, legislation drafted to regulate owners of log rafts did not pass.
- While an extensive Omnibus Lighthouse bill did not pass, through sundry civil appropriations, the lake interests received fog signals, range lights, and several lightships. This appropriation would reduce some of the private LCA lights.
- The reciprocity of wrecking issue was brought closer to a solution when LCA advised Congress, the President, and Secretary of State that the privilege of carrying on wrecking operations in the Welland Canal was not important.
- Again, the issue of discriminatory Welland Canal tolls was not resolved; thus Congress passed a law requiring the payment of a toll at the St. Marys River locks by all vessels carrying cargo to Canadian ports.

- Continued vigilance took place to defeat efforts to legislate restrictions on vessel owners with respect to manning, training and vessel equipment.

In 1893, Thomas Wilson was President of LCA and the new organization was successful in advancing objectives to make lakes shipping safer.

- There was more violence in the efforts to unionize the crews. There were assaults on Captain Lennon in Detroit and Shipping Master Feldt in Chicago but calm returned to the waterfront for a while. The sixth shipping office was opened in Escanaba.
- Major successes in legislation took place as the wrecking reciprocity was resolved, the Canadian Government abolished the discriminating tolls and the tolls on Canadian cargo was removed at the Sault; the Brickner Lighthouse Bill passed but without the appropriations; new rules for preventing collisions in narrow channels became regulation following LCA petitions; funds were appropriated to widen the channel at Collision Bend in the St. Marys River following many groundings; the coastwise trade was exempted from onerous liability sought by National Millers Association, a group headed by Mr. Pillsbury; a joint resolution of Congress called for an investigation of raft towing and the study was completed and the findings were as advocated by LCA; appropriations were passed to survey the lakes and channels.

Captain James Corrigan was the LCA President in 1894. The 1894 Annual Report of the Board of Managers is missing but some of 1894 activities are covered in the 1895 Report.

The President of LCA in 1895 was William Livingstone.

- LCA members in 1884 protested the actions of the coal shippers in Buffalo who demanded that the ship owner purchase bunker coal fuel from them at prices much higher than prevailing bunker rates and the coal was often of poor quality. LCA members banded together and mutually agreed that they would not bow to this extortion in order to carry the coal. There was much competition to carry the coal out of Buffalo since there were so many vessels in port that had discharged their grain and were returning light. J. J. H. Brown, LCA member in Buffalo on the Fueling Committee, monitored the operations in 1895 to assure solidarity. The coal shippers reduced their higher rates for bunker coal so as to end the boycott.

- LCA paid for the placement of additional private aids to navigation in the Detroit River because of very low water levels.
- LCA petitioned the Lighthouse Board in Washington for new aids to navigation and, when the Board did not place any of them in the appropriations request, LCA petitioned Congress directly. In the past year, Senator McMillan, friend of Livingstone, obtained the desired increase in appropriations.

Senator James McMillan, friend of Livingstone, former shipowner, (Wikipedia)

- LCA complained to the U.S. and Canadian authorities that aids to navigation were removed or extinguished long before navigation ended for the season. Lighthouses, such as Stannard Rock were extinguished two weeks before the end of navigation; it was suggested by LCA that timid light-keepers and lightship operators

desirous of ending their season's work were at fault. However, the authorities seemed to side with the local decisions.
- LCA supported the call for observations, surveys and estimates to determine the extent of lower lake levels caused by the planned diversion of water into the Chicago Drainage Canal.
- LCA supported the deepening of the Erie Canal by one foot by the State of New York.

In 1896, J. J. H. Brown, Buffalo, was President of LCA.

- Many of the same issues faced the members. The Michigan Central Railroad obtained support of the Michigan Governor, Detroit Mayor, Chamber of Commerce and others to testify in Washington in favor of the Railroad Bridge to Windsor. LCA Counsel and many Captains testified against the bridge. Private lights fees were increased in the Detroit River and LCA asked the underwriters to share in the cost.
- Congress passed a law authorizing the Treasury Department to establish rules and regulations governing vessel operation in the dangerous parts of the St. Marys River. LCA commented on the regulations and worked with the Department to improve them since the rules were of great assistance in preventing accidents.
- The Report comments on a 'gracious act not to be forgotten' in thanking the Canadian government for installing two gas buoys off Pelee Point in Lake Erie. LCA continued to seek appropriations for gas lighted buoys in the U.S. waters of Lake Erie and pressed Congressman Burton, OH, for help.
- The work on the 20 foot deep channels from Duluth to Buffalo were getting dredged but many areas that needed dredging were not specifically mentioned in the authorization; thus LCA appealed to the War Department to work on them.
- The coal fueling overcharges in Buffalo seemed to be settled and since that effort and the grain shoveling arrangements in Buffalo worked so well, a committee was formed to reduce the ore trimming costs at the ore loading ports.

- LCA was successful in having deputy collectors of customs appointed at the Mesabi dock in Duluth to issue clearances thus saving long delays in obtaining clearances from the Customs Office in downtown Duluth.
- LCA opened a new shipping office in Milwaukee; thus seven were in service.

In 1897, James W. Millen, Detroit, was the LCA President.

- Over the years LCA lost many of the small ship owners as it was not a profitable business for them. LCA continued to borrow money to continue to provide services until the annual dues came in. Expenses were cut as much as possible. The operation of the private lights in the U.S. waters was discontinued but LCA lights were still needed in Canadian waters.
- Through the efforts of Senator McMillan of Michigan, appropriations for gas buoys on the lakes were passed; and as others were needed LCA pressed for additional appropriations. LCA arranged for the Lighthouse Board Chairman and the naval secretary to make a tour of the Lakes to prove the need for more lights. LCA also thanked Senator Marcus Hanna, OH, for his help in all matters.
- In a report to the Secretary of War, LCA outlined the need for major channel improvements, in particular nearly doubling the width of the Lime Kiln Crossing, and Ballard's Reef; building another channel at St. Clair flats; removing major shoals by Port Huron in the St. Clair River; and, either doubling the width of the Middle Neebish channel or a major improvement of the West Neebish channel so as one channel would be used for up bound and the other for down bound vessels.

Senator Mark Hanna, OH, 'King Maker' for President McKinley, (Wikipedia, WJRoot 1896)

Congressman Theodore Burton, OH, Chairman of the Committee on Rivers and Harbors

In 1898, James S. Dunham, Chicago, was the LCA President.

- LCA maintained private lights in the Canadian waters. It was expected that the government would place needed lights in the St. Marys River; when this did not take place 'light speculators' installed private lights in the river in 1898 and previous years. These speculators would then invoice the owners of ships that passed by. LCA decided that it would determine which lights were necessary and to install LCA lights until the government took them over.
- Another shortage of gas lights vexed the LCA members as the Lighthouse Board objected to appropriation that specified where the gas buoys would be placed. The Board also claimed they did not have sufficient vessels or shore facilities to handle the gas buoys. LCA asked that the government consider using some of the

vessels the government acquired to pursue the war against Spain; the Board claimed none would suffice.
- LCA prepared a brief for the American Commissioners to the International Conference to be held at Quebec to consider outstanding U.S. and Canadian issues such as calling for the abolition of tolls on the Welland Canal. LCA believed that the end of tolls would permit many of the smaller U.S.-flag vessels to carry grain to Canada or American ports east of the Welland.
- The War Revenue Law, passed in 1898 to fund some of the expenses of the Spanish-American War, contained a provision that was onerous in its interpretation to the lake vessel owners. Treasury claimed that all chartered vessels must pay a tax. Had the provision been applicable only to written charters, the Great Lakes tax would have been about $50,000; however Treasury interpreted the law to mean that every charter, oral or in writing, must pay the tax, about $250,000. The LCA General Counsel pursued the case to Treasury and to the U.S. Attorney General arguing successfully that the law applied only to 'registered' tonnage not to the 'enrolled and licenses' tonnage in the Great Lakes and other coastal trades. LCA thus helped the entire coastwise trade dodge this burdensome tax.

LCA Ex-Presidents 1892-1899

In 1899, Frank J. Firth, Philadelphia, was President; he was also a principal of the Pennsylvania Steel Company of New Jersey. There were 14 Vice-Presidents, one of whom was William Livingstone. There were Committees on Aids to Navigation and a Committee on Legislation on which William Livingstone served.

- A major expense in 1899 was related to the grain shoveling strike, the extra expense born only by those owners carrying grain. (The LCA involvement with the Grain Shovelers is included in brief, in a separate paragraph later in this book.) At that time, since many of the International Longshoremen's Association (ILA) Buffalo Local #51 members were of Irish background, LCA and the ILA called upon Bishop James Quigley of Buffalo to mediate the dispute. After much negotiation between LCA, New York State Board of Mediation, and the ILA, an agreement was reached and was signed by Harvey Goulder for the LCA.

Archbishop James E. Quigley,
Buffalo, mediator during
1899 dock strike, (Wikipedia)

Harvey Goulder,
LCA General Counsel
(Maritime History of the Great Lakes)

- With respect to the maintenance of private lights by LCA in American and Canadian waters for the past five or so years, Senator McMillan, MI, gave a written opinion to the Lighthouse Board that the LCA should be reimbursed by the U.S. Government.
- LCA again supported the improvement of the Erie Canal from Buffalo to the Hudson River to allow movements of Great Lakes grains to the Atlantic coast.
- Senators Hanna, OH, and McMillan, MI, were both called upon again to support the acquisition of additional gas buoys and a lighthouse tender for lakes service.

In 1900, William C. Farrington, Buffalo, was President. Livingstone was on the Board of Managers and the Committees on Aids to Navigation and Legislation.

In 1900, the Board of Managers considered as the most important event of the year, the Congressional Tour of inspection through the Great Lakes made by the River and Harbor Committee of the House of Representatives. The tour was arranged by LCA and included 13 of the 17 members of the committee, as well as a Senator from Virginia, a member of the Commerce Committee, a senior staff member of the Appropriations Committee and many Corps of Engineers officers. Other congressmen joined the tour as the inspection ship went through their district. The inspection group, including LCA leadership, numbered 39 people. They traveled by Revenue Cutter <u>Fessenden</u> (placed at their disposal by the Secretary of the Treasury) to Cleveland via Erie, Conneaut, Ashtabula, Fairport, and Lorain. After 'magnificent entertainment' in Cleveland at the home of Chairman Burton they proceeded to Detroit to tour the river. The party transferred to the Steamer <u>North West</u> at the St. Clair Flats and proceeded to the St. Marys River; they had mine tours in Michigan and then on to Duluth and Superior for harbor tours. A special train took the party to tour the iron ore mines on the Mesabi and Vermillion ranges. The party embarked on the Steamer <u>North Land</u> to Mackinac to join a special train to the harbors of Sheboygan, Manitowoc and Milwaukee then onward to the Chicago River and drainage canal and the ports of South Chicago and Calumet. One can understand why the inspection trip was the most important event of the year. The officials were impressed by the extent of the lake traffic, and the immense business enterprises underway in the Great Lakes region. As a result of the trip, congressional legislation was introduced in 1900 to improve the Middle and West Neebish Channels, authorize a 20' deep channel from Duluth to Chicago and Buffalo, an additional canal at the St. Clair Flats, widening and deepening of portions of the Detroit River, and numerous special Lakes wide project improvements such as breakwaters and harbor improvements. While the River and Harbor Bill did not pass in 1900, it was reintroduced by Theodore E. Burton, Clevelander and Committee Chair. The bill, including most of the important Great Lakes improvement projects, was passed by both Houses in 1902 and it became law. The high level inspection trip through the Lakes was clearly the most important event of the year and would benefit lake shipping for decades to come.

Vessel used on Congressional Inspection Tour through Great Lakes by River and Harbor Committee, North Land

Revenue Cutter Fessenden

- The Secretary of War on May 8, 1899, granted the Chicago Sanitary District permission to operate the drainage canal making it a condition that the Sanitary District assumes all responsibility for damages to navigation interests. LCA was convinced that damages were taking place and that there was insufficient remedy; thus LCA requested a meeting with the Secretary of War Elihu Root. On May 16, 1900, the meeting was held and LCA asked for a temporary restraining order until a series of physical improvements would take place thereby making it possible to operate ships without damage by the diversion. The remedy was not granted and LCA raised the issue that this was an international matter with Canada because of the reduction of water levels on the Great Lakes.

- The matter of a suspended cable transfer across the entrance to the Duluth harbor was referred to a special LCA committee.
- The concept of a death or disability payment to Great Lakes seamen was discussed and referred to another special committee. Because of labor problems, the issue was tabled in the next year.

In 1901, A. B. Wolvin, Minnesota, was elected President and 14 Vice Presidents, including William Livingstone. The Board of Managers had 88 members; the Executive Committee had 28 members and there were committees on Aids to Navigation and on Legislation—William Livingstone served on the Board and the Committees.

- The Lighthouse Board began sending LCA reimbursement for operating some of the private lights. Thanks were given to Senators McMillan, MI, and Hanna, OH, and to Congressman Burton, OH.
- A Shipping Office was opened in Conneaut, OH; thus LCA operated 8 offices in 1901.
- When numerous accidents were occurring at Southeast Shoal, Lake Erie, LCA chartered the schooner Smith and Post and outfitted her as a lightship at Southeast Shoal; unfortunately after a short time the vessel was destroyed by fire. LCA then purchased the Kewaunee at a price of $10,000 (from the profits on operation of the grain shoveling) and fitted her out as a lightship for Southeast Shoal. Efforts were then made to recover these expenses from the government.

Southeast Shoal lightship Kewaunee, (Library and Archives Canada)

- Labor problems attended the opening of the season and the executive committee unanimously voted that LCA should not fix salaries of engineers on the Lakes in 1901.

1894 LCA Officers and Managers

Chapter Two

The Livingstone Presidency and the Reorganization of 1903

William Livingstone (1844-1925) Shipowner and President of the Lake Carriers' Association

I begin this section of the history of the Lake Carriers' Association by recognizing the life of William Livingstone before and during his direct involvement with the LCA and its predecessor organization.

William Livingstone was born in Dundas, Ontario, and when he was five years old, with his parents he moved to Detroit, MI, in 1849. He was an only child of William Livingstone, Sr., and Helen Stevenson Livingstone. His father, born in Lanark, Scotland, had been a ship's carpenter on the Clyde River and when he moved to Detroit he worked for the next 15 years in local shipyards. Young Livingstone did odd jobs in a dry goods store, wrapped and mailed out of town copies of a small local newspaper; at age 17 he worked as a machinist in the Michigan Central Railroad shops. Later, he became a partner in a grocery store and then at age 21, with his father, they established the firm of Livingstone and Company as a wholesale and retail grocer, dealing in flour, feed and country produce in Detroit on the corner of Woodward and Grand River streets. He gradually gave up selling groceries and became a forwarding and commission merchant specializing in feed and grain.

Detroit 1889 Bird's eye view, (Wikipedia, Calvert Lithographing Co.)

Livingstone was no stranger to the Detroit River and lake shipping; he knew every bark, brig and sloop that touched on the Detroit waterfront. However, it was the growing fleet of propellers and side wheelers with steam engines that fascinated him most. He obtained the Detroit agency for the Western Transportation Company, owners of the biggest fleet of steam vessels on the lakes. By the time he was 25, he owned six tugs and was elected secretary-treasurer for the Detroit Tugman's Association. He was a licensed river pilot and he ran his tugs and barges into the small rivers in Canada where he bought cordwood from farmers and the Indians; he became the most important cordwood dealer in Detroit. That experience led him into the lumber business; he controlled a tract of land on the Au Sable River, north of Saginaw Bay. He had the pine cut and formed into log rafts that were towed to Detroit mills. While his fortunes always seemed to move upward, he had his first major business loss in the Panic of 1873, when all his accumulated fortune was swept away. Like a Phoenix from the ashes, within three years Livingstone controlled the largest fleet of tugs in the waters around Detroit.

During the political and economic unrest of the times, the Republican party saw in him the leadership they needed and in 1875 they convinced him to run as a candidate for the Michigan House of Representatives; he won with the support of Democrats, many who had been the working men with whom he attended school and had dealings on the waterfront. Livingstone served for a short time and never ran for public office again. The experience however whetted his appetite for politics and he eventually became chairman of the Michigan Republican State Central Committee. He became friends with many wealthy and prominent business and political leaders, in particular Thomas W. Palmer, for whom Livingstone campaigned within the Michigan legislature to have Palmer appointed as a Michigan Senator in Washington in 1883. This was a time when Senators were not popularly elected. Palmer was appreciative and prevailed upon President Chester Arthur in 1884 to appoint Livingstone Collector of Customs for the Port of Detroit. President Arthur knew what political power that position could wield as Arthur had been appointed Collector of Custom for the Port of New York by President Grant. However, Livingstone held that office only until 1887.

President Chester Arthur, (Wikipedia)

Livingstone was primarily a business man whose knowledge of Great Lakes shipping was the loadstone that directed his efforts. He was agent for the Western Transportation Company and in 1880 he organized the Michigan Navigation Company. He was now a steamboat owner. In 1882, he served as President of the Detroit Board of Trade. While Collector of Customs he turned the management of the Michigan Navigation Company over to his cousin John Stevenson. The Customs job was not enough for Livingstone; reminiscent of his youthful newspaper endeavors, in 1885 he entered the newspaper business by purchasing the Detroit Evening Journal taking personal charge of the paper's business and editorial policies. He turned the failing paper around and sold it in 1887. This allowed Livingstone to return full steam to the Great Lakes shipping business. He was secretary-treasurer of the Michigan Navigation Company and became treasurer of Percheron Steam Navigation Company, organized with his old friend Senator Palmer. They soon acquired two of the largest bulk freighters on the Lakes, the T.W. Palmer and the Livingstone. He became general manager of both companies.

SS Thos. W. Palmer

Michigan Senator Thomas W. Palmer,
friend of Livingstone (Wikipedia)

Livingstone was called back to the newspaper business and to politics when the Detroit Journal was again on the brink of financial collapse. He and Senator Palmer bought the plant and good will at a Sheriff sale in 1892 and he set the policy to the staff; first they were a Republican newspaper and second he wanted the news regardless of likes or dislikes.

For nine years he was owner and publisher as he turned the paper into a powerful and profitable force in Michigan. He served as a member of the Advisory Committee of the Republican National Committee in the 1896 and 1900 Presidential campaigns, serving as the Chairman of the Michigan delegation to the 1900 National Convention in Philadelphia. In 1901, the newspaper was sold again and Livingstone returned to banking and improvements to the Great Lakes waterway system.

Livingstone had helped organize the Dime Savings Bank of Detroit in 1884. After being associated as a stockholder, director and vice-president, he was named President in 1900, a position he held until his death. In addition to local leadership in Michigan Banking associations, he served also as President of the American Bankers Association in 1911 and 1912.

One of Dime Bank's best customers was Henry Ford who was grateful that Livingstone was the first newspaper owner who published an account of Ford's car in the Detroit Journal. Over a course of years, they became fast friends, seeking each other's counsel on a number of matters from investments into the River Rouge plant to the Peace mission to Europe in 1915. William Livingstone died in 1925 and Henry Ford was one of the pall bearers at the funeral service.

Henry Ford was a longtime friend of Livingstone and was a pallbearer at his funeral

The Livingstone obituary in the LCA Bulletin included"...If the Livingstone Channel that represented years of his toil is a fitting monument, so also is the commerce of the Great Lakes..." John J. Boland said "The Livingstone Channel now stands and ever will remain a flowing memorial to him."

SS William Livingstone

NOTE: Much of the information on the accomplishments of William Livingstone prior to 1900 was drawn from a genealogy prepared in 1966 by David Sanders Clark, Notes on the Livingstone Family of Lanark Scotland and Detroit, Michigan and Related Families. What follows that period is drawn primarily from the Annual Reports of the LCA, other LCA publications and LCA archives.

Political and Social Conditions 1903-1925

The United States was a world power but still maintained the philosophy behind the Monroe Doctrine promulgated in 1823. The U.S. government would not accept that any of the territory of North and South America should be subject to new colonization by European powers. President Monroe stated that any attempts to colonize lands in the Americas would be considered an act of aggression requiring American intervention. At the same time American political leadership wanted not to be involved in European conflicts. Vice-President Roosevelt in 1901 articulated that in his foreign policy "to speak softly, and carry a big stick." Keeping with those policies, Roosevelt believed it was in the interests of the United States to gain control of the Panama Canal that was under construction by French interests in the territory controlled by Columbia. When the Columbian Government would not allow the US to purchase the canal, Roosevelt implied to rebels living in Panama that, if they revolted against Columbia, the U.S. Navy would assist their cause. The Panamanian rebels declared independence and in a show of 'gunboat diplomacy' the USS Nashville impeded interference from Columbia. In gratitude, in 1903, the new government of Panama allowed the U.S to control the Panama Canal Zone through a treaty that paid $10 million to Panama. The U.S took control over the French property in 1904 and proceeded to construct the Canal. U.S colonization brought about by the Spanish-American War caused the U.S. to continue to fight the Filipino struggle for independence from Spain that started in 1896; that war continued against the USA until the struggle ended in 1913 with an American victory. The removal of non-European colonies continued in 1917 when America purchased some of the Virgin Islands from Denmark.

America wanted to stay out of wars in Europe, and in 1914 when the Great War began, the U.S. stood aside from the carnage even when by 1917 the world was in the turmoil of war and revolution and the war in Europe had dragged on with major loss of life. America remained out of the war even though 128 American citizens were killed when the German submarine torpedoed the Lusitania. President Wilson was reelected to a second term with one of the campaign slogans "He kept us out of war." While much public sympathy was in favor of the British and French,

Americans favored neutrality. In 1917, the British intercepted a telegram sent by German diplomat Alfred Zimmerman to the German embassies in Mexico and United States and they publicly shared it with Americans. The Zimmerman telegram offered tactical support to Mexico in retrieving territories in the southwest states that had been Mexican in exchange for an alliance against America. There was outrage but no declaration of war. Then the Germans resumed unrestricted submarine warfare in February 1917 during which 500 ships were sunk in sixty days; that total included eight American ships. In 1917 the Russian Revolution began and Britain captured Palestine from the Ottoman Empire. The U.S. entered the Great War in April 1917 when President Wilson asked Congress for a declaration of war against Germany. American troops landed in France in June. On November 11, 1918 the war ended with the Treaty of Versailles.

In 1918 the misnamed Spanish flu, that was to be the deadliest natural disaster in the history of the world, came to the U.S. Revolution was feared in the U.S. as there were race and political riots and the Red Scare leading to the mass deportation of suspected Bolsheviks. In 1920 enlightened and fearful legislators finally granted women the right to vote and in the same year the experiment in the prohibition of alcohol began. The roaring 20s became significant years of economic growth and prosperity.

Politics on the national level began in this period with the Office of the President held by Theodore Roosevelt who took office after the assassination of President McKinley in 1901. Except for the eight years of President Wilson terms, the Presidency was held by Republicans. In 1908 the Secretary of War, William Howard Taft was elected President. In 1912 Woodrow Wilson was elected President and was reelected in 1916. The strong economy of the 1920s insured that the Republicans controlled the White House, Senate and House of Representatives. In 1920 Ohio Senator Warren G. Harding was elected President and he was succeeded by his Vice President Calvin Coolidge in 1923 when Harding died of heart attack. Coolidge was elected to the office in his own right in 1924. The Senate was controlled by the Republican Party except for the period 1913-1919; as was the House except for the period 1911-1917.

William Livingstone and President T. Roosevelt
on board Tashmoo in Detroit River

The battles between Management and the Unions continued throughout America in this period. The Industrial Workers of the World (IWW), also known as the Wobblies, was founded in Chicago in 1905 and was considered one of the more radical organized labor groups. By 1910, U.S. Steel had nearly succeeded in driving all unions out of its plants. Unions in other iron manufacturing companies also vanished. Violence became common place as employer's resisted unionization. This was the case in many regions of the U. S. One particularly violent struggle was in the bombing of the Los Angeles Times in 1910 when 21 persons were killed. The infamous Ludlow Massacre took place at the Rockefeller owned Colorado Fuel and Iron Company in 1914 when 25 people including children were killed by militia using machine guns. After World War One, there were many strikes; management and some in government considered the unions to be Communist front organizations. The Red Scare was prevalent after the Russian Revolution in 1917. Major strikes included the 1919 Steel strike and the Coal strike. The post-war recession was one reason for four million workers to be on strike in 1919.

Other significant events of the period included the formation in 1903 of the Ford Motor Company and the automobile industry became very big business in 1908 when Henry Ford, a friend of William Livingstone, mass produced the Model T Ford. The Sixteenth constitutional amendment establishing an income tax and the Seventeenth Amendment establishing direct election for Senators was ratified in 1913. The granting of statehood to New Mexico and Arizona in 1914 consolidated America geographically as a nation from sea to shining sea.

Issues on the Great Lakes in the years before William Livingstone became President of LCA included: concerns for maintenance of water levels particularly regarding the operation of the Power Canal at the Soo; reimbursements from the U.S. government for placement and maintenance of lights; (Livingstone called upon his friend Senator McMillan, Michigan, to assist in the introduction of legislation for repayment); ice blockades in the St. Marys River; improved night navigation in the St. Marys River; concerns for the diversion of grain cargoes from the lakes to Montreal via the Welland Canal thereby depriving Buffalo of grain shipped via the Erie Canal to New York City and thus an appeal was made to New York Governor T. Roosevelt to widen and deepen the Erie Canal; a call for the building of a new lock at the Soo (tonnage shipped through the Soo locks increased substantially in these early years: 1889-7.2 million tons; 1899-22 million); the operation of the Chicago drainage canal that reversed the flow of the Chicago River that caused damages to vessels and added costs for tugs and vessel delays. Many of these issues remained unresolved and many more issues would arise.

George J. Ryan

The Livingstone Presidency 1902-1925

William Livingstone, LCA President 1902-1925

In 1902, William Livingstone was elected President of LCA. The 1902 LCA Annual Report summed up the philosophy of Livingstone and the other leaders of LCA.

"The Lake Carriers' Association has accomplished much for the benefit of lake transportation interests, in procuring and maintaining the establishment of aids to navigation and the removal of obstructions, and its work has been very effective in the movement for deep waterways and harbor improvements. In these public affairs the association has not sought simply selfish ends, but has worked for and accomplished much for the country at large. The deepening of waterways, improvements in harbors and establishing aids to navigation, which tend to greater safety of life and property, have all had their share in lessening the cost of transportation… This has been of benefit not only to the commercial interests directly involved, but to every citizen of the land. It has had its full share in the development of the iron and steel industry…worked to the benefit of the farmers of the west and northwest… Stating the facts in general terms, we say that the waterway improvement has been of advantage to all, because it has provided transportation at low cost… One reason, therefore, why the work of the Lake Carriers' Association has been so effective in promoting

improvements of a general public nature is that the association has never been used for personal and selfish ends;...it has always been for the benefit of the public interests."

Livingstone recognized that LCA needed to reorganize from a voluntary association of members to a corporation. The LCA had entered into many contracts with the federal government to provide aids to navigation in Canadian waters, with labor in the handling of grain in Buffalo and in the operation of shipping offices to assist in the employment of seamen. It was foreseen that the LCA would engage in more extensive contractual obligations on behalf of members. A call to all members was made to attend a general meeting on December 13, 1902, for the purpose of considering plans for reorganization. A committee was formed consisting of Messrs. Harvey D. Goulder, General Counsel, F. J. Firth, William Livingstone, J. C. Gilchrist and Harry Coulby with direction to report to an adjourned meeting on December 20, 1902. At that time, the committee was directed to submit the plan for reorganization to the members at the annual meeting on January 22, 1903. The plan for incorporation under the laws of the state of West Virginia was unanimously adopted and this action was taken on January 26, 1903. Losing no time, the stockholders of LCA held a meeting in Detroit to adopt by-laws, elect directors, form an executive committee and elect officers. The architect of this reorganization, William Livingstone was again elected President, a tenure that would last until his death in 1925.

The vision for the future of the reorganized LCA was shared by other major leaders in the Great Lakes maritime industry. Particularly Harry Coulby, an emigrant from England, who traveled the world as a young man and, when in Cleveland, set his sights on the Great Lakes shipping industry. Ultimately Coulby directed two of the largest fleets, the Pittsburgh Steamship Company and Interlake Steamship Company; he managed over 100 ships. He was described as the "Czar of the Lakes," a tribute to his leadership qualities. Another leader was Joseph Clough (J. C.) Gilchrist, President, Gilchrist Transportation Company, Cleveland and Vermilion; he also had a major role to play in the reorganization of LCA. Together, Coulby and Gilchrist controlled 44% of the LCA enrolled tonnage in 1901.

SS James C. Gilchrist, (Al Hart Collection)

SS Harry Coulby, (Al Hart Collection)

LCA Organization and Offices

LCA leadership was a team; Livingstone did not direct the LCA by himself. Livingstone maintained his offices in Detroit in the Dime Building, as he was president of the Dime Savings Bank from 1900 until his death in his Dime Building office in 1925. The annual reports were published in Detroit, and for legal reasons, as stated in the 1903 Articles of Incorporation, the principal place of business was 125 Griswold Street, Detroit, a few blocks away from Livingstone's office. However, the main offices of the LCA and the Great Lakes Protective Association (GLPA) were in Suite 1504 Rockefeller Building, Cleveland, since this was the city where J. H. Sheadle, George McKay and Harvey Goulder had their principal officers. Over the next 100 years the Associations moved offices within the Rockefeller Building several times.

Livingstone was ably assisted by J. H. Sheadle, a principal officer of Cleveland-Cliffs Iron Company, who was LCA Vice President until his death in 1916; and then by an active Board member J. S. Ashley who became Vice President until Livingstone's death, whereby Ashley became President. Harvey D. Goulder, who had helped form the reorganized LCA in 1885, was General Counsel from 1903 through November 1925. The Treasurer George P. McKay also was a principal in forming the new LCA; he was a Master from 1861-1882 and General Manager of the Cleveland Transportation Company and was LCA Treasurer from 1903 through 1918. The Secretary was Harvey Brown from 1902-04 and was followed by George A. Marr in 1904 until 1918; Marr became Secretary Treasurer from 1918 through 1925 after the death of McKay. There were many others LCA leaders, particularly A. R. Rumsey, Chief Commissioner of the Assembly Rooms and Thomas W. Kennedy Grain Superintendent in Buffalo. Longevity in leadership was a strong characteristic of the LCA organization.

Cartoon showing LCA leadership arrayed on a ship: Rumsey, Morford, Richardson, Brown, Livingstone, Ashley, Marr, Tomlinson, Sheadle, Mitchell, Sullivan, Goulder, and Kennedy

Members of the LCA Executive Committee of longstanding included Harry Coulby -- the only person to serve during the entire Livingstone presidency -- G. A. Tomlinson, J. H. Sheadle, J. S. Ashley, J. C. Gilchrist, John Mitchell, C. L. Hutchinson, H. S. Wilkinson, and A. E. R. Schneider. These men also served on the Board of Directors along with the leadership of all the ship owners, such as George M. Steinbrenner who served from 1914 through the Livingstone era.

The officers and Executive Committee leadership were elected by the members of the Board of Directors. Over the years, the majority of the directors were from Cleveland; others were from Chicago, Detroit, Buffalo, Detroit, Bay City, Syracuse, Pittsburgh, Philadelphia and New York; and, in 1916, W. H. Smith was from Montreal.

Other committees were formed as needed. In the Livingstone period, the most important committees were the Aids to Navigation (later referred to as Navigation), Fleet Engineers, Welfare Plan, Safety, Industrial and Sanitary. In 1917, because of the U.S. entry into the European War, LCA formed the Mobilization Committee. In 1919 a Shore Captain's committee was authorized by the Board.

The Mobilization Committee was chaired by Harry Coulby. He quickly organized many committees including the Dispatching of Coal and Grain; Coal; Wages; Food Conservation; Ore movement and Distribution; Ore Operating; and Vessel Operating. While these committees were short lived, they became the prototype for the government to recognize that the LCA could be counted upon in any national emergency to organize the transportation of needed raw materials for defense and the civilian economy.

During the Livingstone leadership, he brought to the table a wealth of knowledge about State and Federal politics. He knew how legislation was drafted, introduced, debated, and passed into law. As a well-regarded Michigan Republican, he was to benefit from the Republican years in Washington that were to follow.

Senior members of the Senate and the House came from the Great Lakes states and some of them were very powerful; in particular, Senator Marcus (Mark) Hanna, Ohio, and brother of H. M. Hanna. In 1874, Marcus A. Hanna and H. M. Hanna organized the Cleveland Transportation Company in connection with the Cleveland Iron Mining Company. The

Hanna brothers, for nearly half a century, were closely identified with the development of the iron and coal business, the lake carrying trade, and railroads. Marcus Hanna was chairman of the Republican National Committee in 1896. There can be little doubt that Livingstone and Hanna worked closely together on the Republican National Committee in the 1896 and 1900 Presidential campaigns. H. M. Hanna was Vice President of the Cleveland Shipowners Association in 1887 until 1892 and would also have worked with Livingstone on shipping matters.

Rationale lobbying congress and the administration

American Modern Freighter as she would look in comparison with the Capitol at Washington in 1907 Annual Report

LCA always argued that improvement in infrastructure such as depth and width of channels and a reduction in ship groundings would be a major benefit to the nation, in particular to the farmers, the iron and steel industry and the citizen consumers, because larger vessels brought about reduced freight rates. There was also the valid regional equity argument that the navigation systems and infrastructure on the other coasts and the Mississippi River system obtained substantially more appropriations from the government. Additionally there was the case that these navigation improvements increased safety for the vessels and the crew members. Direct discussions with Great Lakes members of Congress were essential and were possible due to the connections that many of the LCA members had with the congressional leadership. Trips to Washington and tours of the Lakes similar to the 1900 tour helped get the messages across. The Chair and members of the House River and Harbors Committee and the Chief of Engineers made an inspection trip in 1904 on a lake vessel accompanied by LCA officials from Buffalo to Duluth to observe the continued need for channel and harbor improvements in the Great Lakes. Without doubt, the support of key senators from Ohio and Michigan such as Hanna and McMillan and representative Burton, Ohio, helped a great deal in achieving legislative support.

LCA Interaction with the Canadian Government and Ship Owners

The Welland Canal was and still is the most important link for the movement of American and Canadian grain to Eastern Canada and to the world. American ships participated in the Canadian trade and thus LCA was opposed to all customs taxes in the U.S./Canada trade and Welland Canal tolls. LCA joined in the discussions about enlargement of the Welland Canal as well as the possibility of building an all-Canadian canal. In 1909, there was serious review in Canada of a Fort William to Montreal route via a Georgian Bay Ship Canal that would have 27 locks and a potential savings of 282 miles over the Welland Canal route.

It was decided by the Canadian government that the Welland Canal should be improved in order to expedite the movement of grains to Montreal and the world. The work was started in 1913 before the Great War but was stopped at the end of 1916 for the duration of the war. The resumption of the construction in 1919 moved forward rapidly as part of the post-war expansion. The new canal would have seven locks, whereas the old canal had 25 locks. The locks would be 800 feet long, 80 feet wide and allow 30 feet of water over the sill. This 1913 dimension prevails nearly 100 years later.

William Livingstone and other LCA officials on November 29, 1924 attended the Centennial Celebration of the Welland Canal during which a cairn was unveiled.

William Livingstone, upper left, at the Welland Canal Cairn dedication November 29, 1924.

The Dominion Marine Association (DMA) was the Canadian counterpart to the LCA. The LCA Annual Reports occasionally mention the cooperation and interaction with the DMA. Grain issues frequently brought the two organizations together. In 1914, LCA and DMA met in Ottawa to discuss grain hauling contracts. Later, both associations met with the Association of Lake Lines (a railroad group) to take joint action on the perennial problem of grain shortages.

LCA Communications

The most significant document prepared for members, shippers, and government officials was the Annual Report. In 1907 the Annual Report was issued as a blue hard back pressed linen book that contained detailed information on all the activities of the association, relevant government agencies, cargo carried, worldwide technical maritime developments, freight rates, photographs, obituaries and much more. Clearly this document printed in Detroit bore the fine hand and direction of President Livingstone, who as a former legislator, political leader and newspaper publisher knew the value of communications. The Annual Report was the 'Bible' of the Great Lakes shipping industry for over 100 years. In 1909, the 'Circulars' were sent to members that included sailing directions, navigation information and newly discovered shoals or wrecks, the welfare plan and much more.

In July 1912, The Bulletin was co-produced by LCA and the Great Lakes Protective Association (GLPA), having both names on the covers until July 1944; it contained information on accidents provided by the GLPA. In the first edition of July 1912 it was stated that the objective was to publish the Bulletin monthly for the information of the members of LCA and the GLPA and for the guidance of the officers of the vessels under the management of those members. "In short, the object will be to disseminate information in the interest of safe navigation and to keep the membership and vessel officers advised of the activities of the Lake Carriers' and Great Lakes Protective Associations."

In 1914, LCA stated that the Bulletin was the house organ of both associations to communicate to Masters and Engineers; that it was to be published monthly or as needed, later bi-monthly during the navigation season in order to keep the widely scattered members of the family together. The Bulletin was to be supplemented by circulars dealing with matters of the immediate moment. Later the Bulletin added other objectives such as for the benefit and education of the sailors and officers to promote the five "S" policies of the Welfare Plan; Schools, Sanitation, Safety, Savings and Sobriety.

Recommendations for the Prevention of Accidents

LCA set wages for the entire crew since 1883

Many other publications of LCA assisted the sailors.

- The Distance Tables of the Great Lakes was published by LCA in 1919 since there were many non LCA publications of tables with erroneous information.
- Periodically booklets on the Separate Courses and Whistle Signals were republished. The LCA Distance Tables took into consideration the adherence to the course separation between upbound and downbound vessels each of which would be a different distance.
- As the LCA members set wages for every rank and rating in the crew since 1883, Wage Cards were published each year; thus the Master would know the prevailing scales for all crew members.
- The booklet 'Recommendations for the Prevention of Accidents' was periodically updated.
- The LCA booklet 'Welfare Plan for the Benefit of Employees of Vessels' was updated with the changes in the benefits for death or total dismemberment.

LCA and the Great Lakes Protective Association

The Great Lakes Protective Association (GLPA) was founded in 1909 following a series of meetings before the opening of the season. The founders were members of the LCA and their objective was to '... advance the safety of navigation...' There were far too many groundings and collisions and other accidents that were driving the insurance rates sky high, from 5-10% of the value of the vessel. The London and New York marine insurance underwriter markets were consulted to determine if there was any objection to the establishment of a protective association that would work to reduce all accidents while taking on a percentage of the insurance risk in order to reduce the overall premiums. The founders were strongly supported by the underwriters. In the first year the GLPA had enrolled $80 million worth of vessels in the membership.

The GLPA Advisory Committee and the Board was almost identical to the LCA, including General Counsel Harvey Goulder and Secretary George Marr. Leaders included Livingstone, Coulby, Ashley, Sheadle, Tomlinson, Mitchell, Richardson, Wilkinson and other LCA leaders. The membership was open to Canadian owners and thus there was to be a Canadian member on the Advisory Committee. Owners of passenger vessels, package freight boats and rail car ferries were not included in the membership.

LCA and GLPA publications and circulars recommended vessel drafts, advised masters of the specific locations of hazards including shoals and lost anchors in channels. They provided bulletin boards at many locations on the lakes to warn mariners of draft limitations. Personnel were stationed at the Soo to advise masters of dangers and to report back to the Association and to the owners about masters who overloaded their vessels. Both associations advocated the placement of amidships draft marks since many vessels sagged and thus grounded in channels and on the sill entering or leaving the locks.

This history will end on the GLPA by noting that LCA and GLPA had the same objectives—the safety of navigation on the Great Lakes. The history of the success of the GLPA deserves a separate lengthy treatise.

Vessel Losses and Crew casualties

The hazards of seafaring are no different on the Great Lakes than on the oceans of the world. Major storms come up quickly, the seas build up in shallow waters and short reaches. In the early days there was inadequate weather communications as well as placement of aids to navigation. Sail was giving way to steam; wood hulls were being phased out as steel hulls were built. The LCA members recognized these hazards and as emphasized in this book, the members petitioned the government for improvements in navigation aids, dredging of shoals and weather warnings. The LCA and the GLPA worked very hard to reduce the losses of life and vessels. Nevertheless, tragic losses took place. Equally unfortunate were the deaths and injuries due to accidents onboard ships and at the dock, often traceable to inexperienced and untrained seamen.

In the 22 years of the Livingstone presidency, Canadian and American ship owners lost 335 Great Lakes vessels including bulk freighters, barges, lumber carriers, schooners, tugs, passenger vessels, etc. In these losses, 980 crew members died, including 76 French navy personnel and two Canadian pilots who died when two mine sweepers built in Canada for the war effort sunk in Lake Superior in 1918. During that time frame, LCA members lost 93 vessels in which 438 crew members died.

From 1909 onward, during the period of the Welfare Plan, LCA Annual Reports recorded the name and cause of death or dismemberment of each man whose beneficiary received the payment. The causes of death included: drowned in collision, drowned in wreck, drowned from steamer, washed overboard, drowned attempting to board or leave a vessel, drowned while painting ship, fell off gangway, killed while landing steamer, killed by falling in hold or tank top, killed when caught in machinery, killed by locomotive at dock, killed by train, killed by explosion, killed handling cable, lost overboard, fell from dock, fell from spar, shot onboard vessel, shot by deck hand in Ashtabula, blood poisoning following operation caused by injury, knocked into hold by ore bucket, scalded when tube blew out of boiler, boiler explosion, accidental strangulation, fell from ladder, explosion of gas tank, hit by clam shell rig, and the sad list went on. There were many more accidents that did not lead to death. The Welfare Plan

Safety Committee had its work cut out for them to minimize deaths and injury to seamen.

During the Livingstone period there were three major storms in 1905, 1913 and 1916 that took down many ships: bulk freighters, barges, schooners, lumber carriers and a small passenger ship. In the early years of the century the majority of ships lost were of wood construction. In the 1905 storm, there were 38 American and Canadian ships lost, 30 wooden and 8 steel, and 95 crew members died. Of that total, LCA members lost 26 ships; 18 were wood and LCA crew loss was 74 men. In the 1913 storm, the 10 bulk freighters that sunk were of steel construction and seven were owned by LCA members. In 1913, 201 crew members died of which 150 were onboard LCA ships.

In 1916 there were major storms on May 3 in which the steamer S. R. Kirby was lost causing the death of fifteen seamen and on October 20 the loss of the Merida and the James B. Colgate causing the death of forty-six seamen. In 1916, a total of 73 crew members perished; 47 were onboard LCA ships. In the 1913 storm, 10 bulk freighters sunk were of steel construction.

1. Hydrus
2. John A. McGean
3. Argus
4. Isaac M. Scott

In the 1913 storm, 10 bulk freighters sunk were of steel construction.

1. TURRET CHIEF
2. H. M. HANNA JR.
3. MATOA
4. L. C. WALDO

1. CHAS. S. PRICE
2. WEXFORD
3. REGINA
4. HENRY B. SMITH

The Great War-The European War- Impact upon the growth of the Lake Carriers' Association

Viewing the text of the 1914 and 1915 LCA Annual Reports, it is clear that business interests acknowledged there was a European War that had a major impact in America. In 1915, Livingstone stated that the object of our nation was to restore peace. In regard to the devastation to European industry and the later impact on American industry, Livingstone made the comment "We shall need many thousands more immigrants than we have now in order to supply the demand for common labor." In 1916, the heavy industry of the United States increased production to the extent there were inadequate numbers of railcars and the Great Lakes shipping capacity was stretched to its limits. Livingstone noted in January 1917 "There will be a war for trade supremacy after the European struggle ends…the U.S. must play a large part, for this country is coming to be the world's workshop and its most powerful lender…To win out in the coming struggle, it will be necessary for the American people to develop intelligent teamwork between government and business."

In January 1917, LCA leadership did not anticipate that the U.S. would enter the European War as a combatant; but by March 1917 there was recognition that it was inevitable that the War would include the United States. In March, the Association pledged its support to the President of the United States. In the Annual Report, Livingstone stated "We seem to have been slow to realize the terrible significance of our entrance into the war and dilatory in rising to our full duty in connection with it…business has gradually been placed under martial law and had to adjust itself to the abnormal conditions produced in the financial affairs of the country." On April 6, President Wilson made a declaration that a state of war existed between America and Germany.

Needless to say, 1917 was not to be business as usual. In fact it would be the beginning of a more centralized operation of LCA on behalf of its members. On a positive side for the LCA members' balance sheets, there was a significant increase in the freight rates and water levels were high. However, the negatives more than offset the positives. There was a severe rail car shortage that impacted the mines, the steel mills, the farmers and the water carriers. The season was beset by long periods of bad weather starting with ice conditions that were the worst in a decade, lasting until mid-May. Ice blockades had to be contended with in eastern Lake Erie, the Straits, St. Marys River, Whitefish Bay, Fort William and Duluth. In addition to long delays, most ships suffered ice damage to hull plates and propellers. Cold weather and snow returned in October. Deliveries were significantly behind demand.

LCA set up a committee of members to work together so as ships would be made available where needed for the national welfare, not for corporate gain. The federal government Council for National Defense concerns for delivery of coal caused the Lake Erie Coal Exchange and the LCA committee to work closely together to expedite deliveries. Mandatory government orders were given to expedite coal delivery. The federal government gave specific orders for priority shipments. By the end of the year, the 1917 grain harvest delivery was essential to the nation and to the world; the government stepped in to assure delivery.

In the 1918 Annual Report, Livingstone recognized that "The war had been won and peace is assured...May their splendid triumphs be unmarred by vengeance and unsullied by injustice. May the new peace of the world be in truth that peace and humanity for which America had fought." Livingstone made many salutatory statements congratulating those who served in the industry and noted that the U.S. was now a world leader and involved in matters that in the past were entirely outside of our jurisdiction or interest.

Operation of ships carrying grain in the fall and winter of 1917

The government had already ordered that the handling and transportation of grains be pooled in 1917 and the LCA agreed to haul grain as long as weather permitted.

Because of the mild weather in November, the Department of Agriculture, Food Administration, proposed that the season be prolonged at least until December 20. The insurance underwriters and the GLPA granted insurance until December 22. Harry Coulby was authorized by the government to employ icebreakers to keep the channels free from ice and to direct the movement of icebreakers. December weather turned bitter with a vengeance; by December 4, Duluth was 4 degrees below zero and within a few days it was at 10 below. A cold wave settled in the northwest and gradually spread down to the lower rivers and lakes. Ice formed to a thickness between 8-12 inches and windrows of five feet in height were encountered. A total of 107 ships had to be assisted through the ice from December 11-21. Temperatures were never above 20 degrees F. and were often below zero.

In December 1917 while attempting to meet the demand for grain, many ships were stuck in the ice blockade at Whitefish Bay.

The plan to engage icebreakers was activated. LCA sent Captains to the Soo, and with the assistance of L.C. Sabin, Superintendent of the American Locks, they directed operation in the St. Marys River area. President Livingstone, with the assistance of other LCA Captains and COE staff directed ice operations in the lower rivers from Port Huron to Southeast Shoal. Coal fueling stations in the Detroit River were either depleted of coal or often, because of the ice, vessels could not get under the coal chutes. The lighter Rescue with clamshell equipment was requisitioned to take coal on to steamers in need of bunkers at an anchorage near Belle Isle. The freighter Thomas Barlum was stopped by the Fuel Administration and was directed to transfer 815 ton of coal to the lighter in order to fuel passing vessels. The self-unloading coal laden vessel Conneaut was held for two days at Amherstburg to supply bunkers to several vessels.

Over 19 vessels were pressed into service for icebreaking, including car and passenger ferries, whalebacks, freighters and tugs, many from

Great Lakes Towing Company. Cargos of coal, flour, grain, limestone, ore, and pulpwood made it to their discharge ports. There was ice damage to the assisting vessels and, unfortunately, the sinking of the Henry Cort in Lake Erie on December 17. While not all the expected movement of grain made it to Buffalo and other ports, the operation was a success since all but one vessel made it through the ice to a safe winter berth.

Historical Collections of the Great Lakes
Bowling Green State University

The whaleback Henry Cort sunk in Lake Erie...the ice to Midvale
(Historical Collection of the Great Lakes, Bowling Green State University)

Selective Service and LCA

The War brought other duties for LCA to perform with respect to assisting in the initial registration of over 2,000 seamen for the draft by the Selective Service. LCA, through the Bulletin and the Assembly Halls, kept the sailors informed of the requirements to register for the draft. In order to deliver the expanded movement of raw materials and grains to meet defense and food needs, the ships needed to be properly crewed. The first call was for all men between the ages of 21 and 30 years of age to register by June 5, 1917. On September 12, 1918, the age for registration was changed to require males between 18 and 45 to register. There were three selective service registrations in 1918; LCA helped the men register and responded to the questions of the local boards with respect to the government policy on exemptions for certain seamen.

LCA negotiated directly with the Provost Marshall General to arrange for the timely physical exam of seamen in any port when they were called to report by their local draft board rather than returning to their home address; to allow for the exemption of certain essential seamen; to authenticate that seamen who had exemptions when discharged from a vessel would retain that exemption if they were to return to the vessel in the spring; and, that all licensed pilots were exempted from the draft. The influence of LCA on the Provost General, who had the responsibility of raising an army through registration of over 10 million young men, showed the importance the nation placed on Great Lakes shipping. However, there were many cases where the local draft boards were unfamiliar with the status of seamen and many unfair decisions were made leading to the induction of seamen into the Army. In those cases brought to the attention of LCA, the LCA appeal to the local board saved the seamen to serve on the ships, thereby maintaining the efficiency of the mobilized fleets on the lakes.

First Class Pilots were considered so essential that they were placed last among deferment classifications; they had a 5-1 deferment. Other mariners were considered fourth class and had a 4-B classification. However, the exemptions were valid only when the men were actually constantly employed on the vessels and the men were required to notify the draft board when they changed ships. To not be employed under the deferment could lead to an immediate call up. This rule became a problem due to winter layup. LCA negotiated with the government to allow draft boards to accept an affidavit from the seaman that he was returning to his ship in spring; or, if the draft board required, then an affidavit from the shipping company was required. LCA also advised the sailors that they could do winter work on the ships for their employer or for the shipyards.

Since there were many Canadian citizens working on U.S. vessels, by treaty in June, 1918, Canadian or British citizens would also be subject to draft and eligible for deferments the same as American citizens—with the exception that Canadians had to register between the ages of 20 and 44 years of age. Similarly Americans working in Canada were to register for the draft in Canada. Of course, a citizen of any country could return to his own country to enter military service.

War Regulations at the Soo

The war also brought on extensive regulations regarding vessel transits of the Soo locks. In order to prevent sabotage by "disloyal crew members", ship owners were told to be selective in hiring of crew members; particularly that captains, mates, engineers, and quartermasters should be 'native born Americans', and the other crew members should be selected so as to eliminate all who would have "Teutonic sympathies as would cause them to be disloyal to the United States." These precautions may seem draconian and insensitive today but the fact is that many sailors in the American Merchant Marine were aliens. In 1917, 90% of the men signing on American ships in New York City were aliens; but by 1920, about 60% were American citizens. Most of the aliens at that time were in the fire hold. While no crew citizenship statistics are available for the Great Lakes, it is known that in the effort to eliminate union members, many aliens who were anxious for American wages were employed on LCA ships.

At the Soo, laundry bags from the ships had to be discharged and delivered by launch and only a few newsboys were allowed at the locks to sell newspapers. Deck hands landed to handle lines were to be inspected to assure they were not carrying packages of explosives. Many of the other regulations were practical, necessary and precautionary.

Wartime Mobilization Committee Activities in 1918-1919

On November 7, 1917, 85% of the shares held by the LCA Board agreed to mobilize the entire fleets of LCA members in 1918 and to "place the operation of our ships in the hands of an executive committee with the full authority to co-operate with the government and the allied industries to the desired end..." for the service of the nation in the most efficient manner possible. The Executive Committee, later to be referred to as the Mobilization Committee, unanimously elected Harry Coulby, J. S. Ashley, H. S. Wilkinson, C. D. Dyer and C. L. Hutchinson to this committee. The LCA placed all of its assets and leadership skills in the service of the nation for the duration of the war.

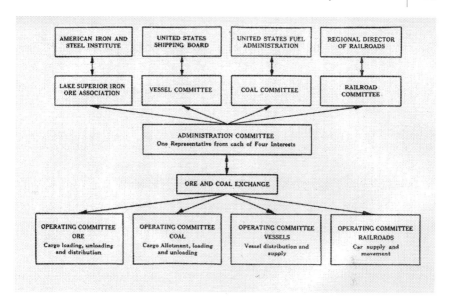

World War I lakes transportation organization chart

During the winter of 1917-18, the Mobilization Committee prepared for operation and in meetings with the Shipping Board in Washington in 1918, the plan was approved. **The LCA Mobilization Committee had absolute power and was to be in full control of the Great Lakes tonnage movements.** While each individual owner was to carry out the contract obligation to the shipper, the committee assumed the obligation for an equitable distribution of the available vessel tonnage. The Committee recognized that there was sufficient iron ore at the mill docks at the beginning of the 1918 season and decided that it was not necessary to begin the season until the dangers of ice damage and delays were over. The success of the Mobilization Committee and the Ore and Coal Exchange can be measured in the movement of over 88.8 million tons of iron and coal in six months of 1918. Clearly these LCA organizational instruments helped win the war in Europe. In order to stabilize the economy in the post war period, the federal government retained control of the railroads and other basic industries after the War ended. The LCA Mobilization Committee, with the approval of the Shipping Board, retained control of lake shipping and even recommended a freight rate structure that was also approved by the government.

Ore and Coal Exchange, born of the Great War

In order to coordinate the delivery of iron ore and coal from mines to steel mills and coal consumers, the Ore and Coal Exchange was organized in Cleveland on March 29, 1918. This was an action called for by the government agencies responsible for shipping, railroads and fuel coal. The federal government had nationalized the railroads, an action that helped reduce railcar shortages since all Great Lakes region railcar movements were now controllable by the Exchange. The LCA had already formed the Mobilization Committee and thus all vessel activity was controllable within one organization. LCA now felt it was necessary to coordinate the rail car availability at the docks. Uniquely, Harry Coulby, manager of two of the largest lake fleets, a member of the LCA Board, and the LCA Mobilization Committee was now elected to Chair the Ore and Coal Exchange.

The Ore and Coal Exchange is another subject that deserves much research and a long treatise written about its nearly 90 year history.

Maritime Union Grievances and Actions during the War

A significant negative aspect of the Great War for LCA members was the resurgence of union pressure to gain representation of lake sailors, to dismantle the LCA Assembly Halls and to oppose the LCA Continuous Discharge Book. Labor and management on the Atlantic coast had agreed to significant wage increases in order to assure a greater supply of seamen and to avoid labor disruptions. The LCA Open Shop policy and the Welfare plan were under attack. Pressure was placed upon the LCA by the Departments of Commerce and Labor to negotiate with the unions. LCA President and General Counsel met with the Secretaries of Commerce and Labor in Washington and reaffirmed that the Association would not resume relations with the unions. LCA agreed to pay any wages scale set by the Shipping Board and to modify the Discharge Book, if investigation by the Shipping Board showed such need. While the Shipping Board commended many aspects of the Welfare Plan, including safety, education, sanitation, death benefits and more, they recommended that LCA cease use of the Discharge Book and to issue Discharge Certificates that would be the property of the seaman. In the opening of the 1918 Season, LCA issued new Discharge books to be held in the possession of the seaman, without the space for notations on character and performance by the Captain.

LCA member continuous discharge book

Union leadership continued to oppose the LCA Welfare Plan and threatened a strike effective July 29, 1918. The Shipping Board stepped in and directed LCA to issue individual certificates of discharge, not in a book form and without notations by the Captain that could constitute a black ball. These certificates would be the property of the seaman. Further, LCA was to agree to hire men regardless if they were members of the Welfare Plan and that seamen would not be required to register in shipping offices or assembly halls. The Shipping Board had already ruled that there would be no overtime payments on lake vessels and then ruled that a strike was not justified.

After the War ended, by 1919 labor discontent was worldwide. Because of the Russian Revolution there was palpable fear within industry of a worldwide Bolshevik takeover. In the U.S. there were many strikes that impacted lake shipping, strikes in the steel industry, longshoremen on the Atlantic Coast, ore and coal handlers, and segments of the railroad industry. Lake seamen did not strike even while LCA maintained its policy of an open shop, the right to work without union membership. The dock strikes in Great Britain and the U.S. caused grain stocks to be backed up in Buffalo and eventually all the way to Duluth. The same labor discontent continued into 1920 although there were no significant attempts at work stoppage on lake vessels. An indicator of the importance of the assembly halls is in the number of referrals made; in the period 1915-1919 there were an annual average of 58,368 referrals made and in the 1920's the annual average was 41,542 referrals.

Other Wartime Actions Impacting Lake Shipping

As expected, when the declaration of war went into effect on April 6, 1917, the direction of the Coast Guard, including lighthouses, lifesaving and cutter services passed from the Treasury Department to the Navy Department. The Naval Auxiliary Reserve received permission from LCA to place two men or more on many ships for training in seamanship and to determine their fitness to become officers. During 1917-18, 2,925 reservists were trained aboard LCA bulk freighters. The Navy transferred some of the Coast Guard cutters to the Atlantic coast during the war. On August 28, 1919, the Coast Guard was returned to the Treasury Department.

The demand for U.S. flag Atlantic coastal and foreign going vessels caused the transfer of some lakers out of the Great Lakes. Many of the lakers moved to the coasts were manned by sailors hired by the Emergency Fleet Corporation out of the LCA assembly halls.

One major loss to the Lakes was caused by the Navy Department requisition of the wrecker vessel Favorite in 1917 and subsequent transfer to the Atlantic coast. This action left the lakes without a single wrecker capable of handling serious disasters to over 500 freight vessels. Fortunately in 1919, the Great Lakes Towing Company built a new wrecker steamer and named it Favorite.

SS Favorite, Wrecker, requisitioned by Navy 1917.

The new SS Favorite, built in 1919 by the Great Lakes Towing Company

Water Pollution by Ships

The newly formed International Joint Commission (IJC), created by the 1909 Boundary Waters Treaty, began looking into a myriad of issues impacting the Great Lakes; and, in 1914 one of those issues was the pollution of the waters by riparian communities and by ships. In 1914, LCA and Dominion Marine Association appeared before the IJC and testified that the pollution caused by ships was insignificant compared to the amount of raw sewage pumped into the rivers and lakes by the cities. LCA argued that there should be no requirements for ships to sterilize their sewage before an effective remedy was applied to the cities, the much greater source of water pollution.

The IJC conducted studies for several years ranging over 2,000 miles of boundary waters from St. John in the St. Lawrence to the Lake of the Woods. The good news of the bacteriological studies was that much of the system was still pure, in spite of the reality that 8-10 million people lived in communities that dumped raw sewage into these waters. At times, typhoid epidemics had been a result of this misuse of the water system. The IJC recommended that all sewage from ashore and from ships should receive some purification and that vessel black water should be disinfected before being discharged into the boundary waters. The IJC did not have jurisdiction to enforce the recommendations and the two governments asked the IJC to develop specific recommendations for the governments to follow.

LCA Involvement in Freight Rate Making

It appears that from the records in the Annual Report that there was no established committee structure to impact on rate making. The association members were drawn from the shippers, who controlled the movement of iron ore, coal, stone and other cargos and moved them on their own ships, and the independent ship owners, who depended upon the shippers for their tonnage commitments and thus income. However, in the Annual Reports there is frequent reference to freight rates paid in the past year.

In any case, some of the independent members clearly recognized the need for a fair profit on their investment. In the 1893 Annual Report, under the title of 'Improving the Earnings of Vessels in 1894', there is a section dealing with the problem of excessive competition on the part of 'producers' that was leading to the inability for the independent shipowner to make a fair profit. The report noted that several members had been discussing the possibility of some form of agreement to bring the excessive competition under control in 1894; it noted that the LCA could take no action that did not command universal support and which could be successfully carried out. The report ended with the view that the Association had a field of usefulness entirely outside this subject of freight rate making, and its members could not afford to endanger its prestige or impair its effectiveness in the field it has hitherto occupied by leading it into doubtful paths.

It was noted that in 1910, due to low freight rates and lack of tonnage offered to Independents, the independent members met in June and agreed among themselves to lay up 20% of the tonnage for 30 days, causing 40 ships to go into ordinary (layup); as business conditions were still bad, the agreement extended into August.

As it still is today, the shippers controlling the float adjusted the percentage of cargo carried by their own ships based upon tonnage requirements, referred to as the float; they also set the freight rates for the independent shipowner. In 1911, the rates were so low that shippers used the independents with larger vessels rather than the shipper's smaller ships. Then in the 1912 Annual Report, it was noted that for 1913, "the freight rate by common agreement was marked up five cents." In 1916, because of the tremendous demand for tonnage of iron ore and grain to be shipped and not enough vessel capacity, freight rates were increased. The war years covered elsewhere show the involvement of the Mobilization Committee in establishing freight rates approved by the government.

The 1921 Annual Report stressed the impact of a serious national recession that caused many ships not to operate; whole fleets didn't have a single ship turn a wheel until later in the season. The Report indicates that freight rates were drastically dropped in order to encourage some orders. In many of the Annual Reports there are tables of tonnages carried, cost of iron ore, rail rates and the freight rates from 1855 to the time of Annual Report publication.

Navigation Improvements, Keystone of the LCA Mission

As indicated in the first annual report of William Livingstone, the work of the LCA was "…in procuring and maintaining the establishment of aids to navigation and the removal of obstructions, and its work has been very effective in the movement for deep waterways and harbor improvements…" This objective was an important part of the reason for the establishment of the Cleveland Vessel Owners Association and the Buffalo based LCA.

Much of the later work of the LCA was as an outstanding success in the improvement of the safe and efficient navigation of ships on the Great Lakes. The following sections included some of these achievements, not necessarily in order of importance or timeframe and many achievements are not described.

Separate Courses

One of the most important navigation safety measures initiated by LCA in 1907 was the requirement for its members to use the recommended east and west bound sailing courses, not just in thick and foggy weather but at all times. These recommended courses were to keep the up and down bound vessels separated by several miles. In 1915, the Dominion Marine Association agreed to accept these recommended courses on Lake Huron and requested LCA members to observe the separated course line on Lake Superior. The Shore Captains Committee would periodically review the separate courses, and as needed would recommend changes to the Executive Committee for approval.

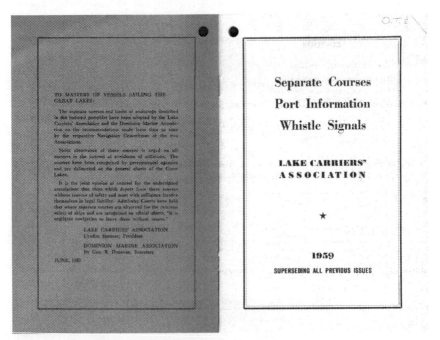

Separate Courses booklet

Bridges over Navigable Rivers

One of the most significant and long lasting achievements of the LCA during the Livingstone period was the determined and successful opposition against the railroads who since 1867 were determined to build railroad bridges across the Detroit River. The vessel interests advocated the construction of tunnels; the full report on the Detroit River Tunnel is in the 1909 Annual Report. That report stated, "The building and completion of the Detroit River Tunnel closes one of the most historic struggles in the history of the Lake Carriers' Association." The water carrier interests battled the railroad interests in Washington, Lansing and Ottawa. The COE Board of Engineers studied the issue and recommended a bridge was possible but vessel interests continued to oppose the plan.

When the St. Clair River tunnel was completed in 1890 at Port Huron, the Board of Engineers began to realize a tunnel under the Detroit River was feasible. About 1904 in New York City, the New York Central Railroad demonstrated that electric locomotives could be built and used in tunnels; a major technical obstacle was overcome. The Detroit River Tunnel Company was organized in 1905. The U.S. and Canadian governments granted charters for the construction of what was to become the first railroad tunnel under the Detroit River. LCA participated in the discussions on how these tunnels would be built in order to assure the continuance of safe navigation during construction. The Michigan Central Railroad Tunnel construction began in 1907 and the last section was put in place in 1909 with the expectation of operation in 1910.

Detroit River Tunnel Entrance 1909.

Sinking last tubular section of tunnel.

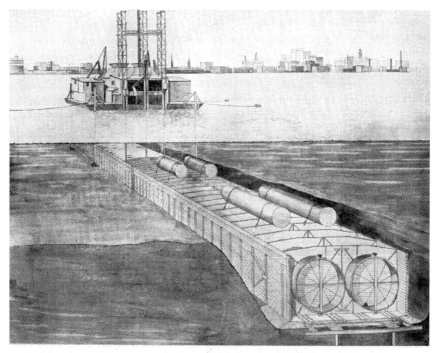

DETROIT RIVER TUNNEL
PHOTO FROM SKETCH SHOWING METHOD OF CONSTRUCTION.

Sketch of tunnel construction

The railroad bridges at Sault Ste. Marie also demanded LCA attention so they would not hazard navigation through the locks. At one time when the railroad bridge did not lower properly, the opening for ships was narrowed significantly. Until the bridge failure was repaired, the railroad provided tugs to assist the vessels through. On another bridge matter, LCA successfully petitioned the War Department to condemn the Canadian railroad bridge between Grosse Ile and Stony Island, MI.

In 1921, the Canadian and U.S. governments authorized the construction of an international bridge over the Detroit River. The initial projection was for a 1,800 foot span with a vertical clearance of 110 feet; LCA reviewed the plans when they were submitted to the War Department for approval.

Water Levels and Flows-The Chicago River
Water Diversion and Other Diversions

LCA voiced strong opposition to the lowering of lake levels through the Chicago Diversion of Lake Michigan water into the South Branch of the Chicago River, thus reversing its flow so as to pass the Chicago contaminated water down to the Mississippi River. The Secretary of War on May 8, 1899, granted the Chicago Sanitary District permission to operate the drainage canal making it a condition that the Sanitary District assumes all responsibility for damages to navigation interests. In 1901, a conditional permit was granted by the War Department allowing the diversion of 4,167 cubic feet/second (cfs); however, despite the opposition of the navigation interests and the Secretary of War, the Sanitary District continued to withdraw a larger amount of water. Many ships were damaged by the increased flow of water as Captains found navigation in those close quarters very difficult.

In 1907, the International Waterways Commission recommended that the U. S. Government prohibit a diversion of no more than 10,000 cfs through the Chicago Drainage Canal since that was considered ample for sanitary purposes. LCA claimed that 10,000 cfs lowered the lake level 4 ½ to 6 ¼ inches. The Chicago authorities wanted a flow of 14,000 cfs. LCA countered that this would lower lake levels by 6-8 ½ inches. It was stated that the vessels had a tons per inch immersion of 85; thus there would be a great deal of tonnage delivery lost to industry with increased diversion flows. In 1913, the Secretary of War ruled in favor of 10,000 cfs; LCA, Canadian interests and others in industry protested in Washington but were overruled. The Issue would need to go to the International Joint Commission and ultimately to the Supreme Court of the United States.

In 1913, a law suit was filed in the U.S. Court in Chicago against the Sanitary District and; in 1924 the court sustained the government and ruled that the Sanitary District conform to the 4,167 cfs within 6 months. While the Chicago political representatives in Washington submitted legislation to authorize an increased withdrawal from Lake Michigan, none of these bills passed. Meanwhile the Sanitary District appealed to the Supreme Court to overrule the lower court decision. On December 8,

1924 the Supreme Court heard the case; Harvey Goulder, LCA General Counsel, filed a brief and made oral arguments favoring the lower court decision. On January 5, 1925, Chief Justice Holmes delivered the opinion of the court in favor of the lower court. However, the court allowed the Corps of Engineers to modify permits. The Supreme Court was clear that the waters of the Great Lakes were not to be drained in large quantities by Chicago for purposes of sanitation.

Chicago did not give up; the City applied to the Supreme Court for a rehearing that was denied. Chicago then applied for a Corps permit to discharge 10,000 cfs. The Secretary of War permitted 8,500 cfs for five years subject to congressional action and ruled that the city must construct a $54 million modern sewage disposal program approved by the War Department. Chicago continued to press Congress for permission to divert more water. Several of the Great Lakes States attorney generals joined Wisconsin's petition to the Supreme Court stating that the Secretary of War had no authority to permit permanent diversion of water from one watershed to another. This litigation continued for decades until in 1967 the Great Lakes States entered into a consent decree stating that Illinois could not divert more than 3,200 cfs for navigation, domestic or sanitary uses.

In other water level matters, LCA was consistent and vigilant. Livingstone personally petitioned the International Commission on Lake Levels against the diversion of water that would be caused by construction of power canals in the St. Marys River and the Niagara River. This was necessary in order to preserve water levels for navigation.

Connecting Channels, Harbors of Refuge, Ports

Each LCA annual report went into great detail describing the need for and the efforts to obtain authorization and appropriations for each navigation project, followed by the government actions in completing the projects. Navigation improvements in virtually every commercial port were authorized and completed; they are too numerous to itemize. They included the step by step improvement in channel depths, harbor entrance piers, breakwaters, and lighthouses as well as the LCA and local authority efforts in Washington to achieve the navigation improvement.

While the authorized depth of water in the connecting channels was 20 feet at the beginning of the Livingstone period, it was necessary to obtain the appropriations to reach that goal. Needless to say, the amount of tonnage moved on the Great Lakes increased substantially. In 1905 LCA began the effort to obtain authorization to deepen the system to 25 feet throughout the entire Great Lakes. While this goal was not attained during the Livingstone administration, it remained the goal.

Through consistent LCA lobbying efforts, gradually the channel system was deepened to 21 feet (one foot was over depth for safety) in the St. Marys River, in conformance to the depth of the Soo Locks and other locations such as Hay Lake, Neebish, and Vidal Shoals. The West Neebish Channel, started in 1904, would have a minimum depth of 22 feet including over depth; this was the biggest project on the Great Lakes since the building of the first Poe Lock, costing $4.5 million. It was completed on August 16, 1908. New channels at Lime Kiln Crossing were appropriated in 1907. The deepening of the St. Clair Flats Canal was later approved. The Buffalo Ship Canal and the Black Rock Canal received appropriations and opened for traffic August 17, 1914, a very essential project to move grain to the U.S. Atlantic coast

To achieve the maintenance of the channels, LCA supported obtaining the dredge Burton in Cleveland in 1904; and in 1907 supported the Corps of Engineers obtaining suction dredges on the Lakes similar to those used on other coasts.

Harbors of Refuge were essential along the shores of the Great Lakes, where there were very few natural protected anchorages for a vessel to find a lee in a storm. The Captains believed that Harbors of Refuge were the answer and LCA petitioned the government to build many of them.

One of the ways that LCA maximized the carriage of cargo with fewer delays was by LCA recommending drafts for every lock, major channel and major port. In 1910, LCA went so far as to advise members transiting the Sault Locks to load one third of their vessels for Poe Lock downbound rather than the Canadian Lock that had four extra inches clearance. In this manner, long and expensive delays waiting transit at the Canadian Lock could be avoided.

Ice Operations and Icebreakers

The beginning and the end of each season had the usual problems of heavy ice preventing the transit of the St. Marys River, the Soo Locks, the Straits of Mackinaw, the lower rivers and Lake Erie, particularly at the eastern end to Buffalo. In the early part of the 20th century, April 15 was the official opening of navigation on the lakes since that is when hull insurance was effective. The Canadian and U.S. locks at the Soo opened generally after the 15th; and often the Canadian lock opened first because of the demand for grain from Fort William (now Thunder Bay). Of course, everything depended upon getting the ice cleared from the rivers and straits. The season usually ended when normal insurance coverage expired on November 30. Some large shippers and independents operated without insurance. In 1910, the Annual Report noted that Captain John Mitchell's fleet operated without the insurance date constraints.

Since there were few government icebreaking vessels, LCA charted commercial vessels to break the ice. In 1916, because of unusually high demand for iron ore and other cargos and the persistent cold weather and ice, it was necessary for LCA to force the opening of the season in the upper rivers, Whitefish Bay, the Straits of Mackinac, Escanaba and Green Bay. Ships chartered included the Nevada from South Chicago and the Canadian ferry Algomah sent out by the Canadian government; they worked together to open the tracks. As was described previously in ice operations, in 1917 at government expense LCA chartered the necessary icebreakers to keep the ships moving in December in order to get the grain moved from Lake Superior ports.

Major Navigation Infrastructure Improvements

Livingstone Channel

Panoramic view of excavation of Livingstone channel 1909

The Livingstone Channel opened for navigation on October 19, 1912. It was 12 miles long (six miles of which were dug out of limestone), had a depth of 22-23 feet, and a width of 450-800 feet. At that time it was the most expensive, $7 million, and extensive undertakings of the United States within its borders. Starting on July 20, 1907, working day and night every day except Sunday, the builders removed 9.5 million cubic yards of material; 2.1 million tons were hard rock.

Opening of Livingstone Channel, SS William Livingstone was first vessel to use channel October 19, 1912

Opening of Livingstone Channel, SS William E. Corey was first vessel to carry cargo down the channel October 19, 1912

With a 21 gun salute from the revenue cutter Morrill, the steamer William Livingstone, piloted by William Livingstone himself, was the first vessel to pass through the channel. She was followed by the passenger steamer Britannia carrying over 1,500 members of the Detroit Board of Commerce and their ladies. A number of other vessels followed in the inaugural parade. At a celebratory dinner that night, the LCA Vice President J. H. Sheadle presided as toastmaster praising Livingstone for his vision and the government officials for completing the project. This major construction project necessary for the safe navigation of the Detroit River, from its inception, was titled the Livingstone Channel by LCA. The November 1912 Bulletin reported that the Livingstone Channel was thrown open to navigation on October 19, 1912. The government also had begun calling it by that name during construction and so it is called today; a fitting tribute to the Detroit President of LCA. Over the years ahead there were many more improvements in depth and width to this key channel.

Sault Ste. Marie, Davis Lock

Since 1903, LCA had been petitioning the Congress and the Secretary of War to build a new lock at the Soo. President Livingstone personally met several times with General William L. Marshall, Chief of Engineers, Department of War, to press the petition; and, in 1907 the appropriations were passed for the third lock, to be later known as the Davis Lock. The government had to acquire land above the locks owned by an electric power company so as approach channels could be widened; there were prolonged negotiations and lawsuits before that land was acquired. In 1907, the power company docks along the river from the Canal Park to the power house were vacated by the power company and these government docks at the Sault became available for mooring of lakers awaiting transit.

The new lock was open to commerce on October 21, 1914. As the 1914 Annual Report stated, 'Chorus of Whistles greets successful opening of New Third Lock at Soo.' This lock with a length of 1,350 feet was the longest lock in the world. Over 5,000 visitors and residents of both cities at the Soo were on hand to observe the procession of ships. The flotilla of ships upbound was led by the inspection ship Gladwin carrying District Engineers from Buffalo and Detroit and Louis C. Sabin, Superintendent of the St. Marys Falls Canal. The Gladwin was followed by a revenue cutter, several Great Lakes tugs and a Great Lakes Dredge and Dock tug. Bringing up the rear was the Pittsburgh Steamship Company freighter Alva C. Dinkey. In nine minutes the vessels were raised to the level of Lake Superior and as the gates opened a chorus of horns and whistles sounded for over ten minutes.

The first downbound ship was the James A. Farrell, flagship of the Pittsburgh Steamship Company, loaded to nearly 20 feet with 11,745 tons of cargo. She was followed in the same chamber by the Richard Trimble carrying 11,711 tons. Both vessels had a combined length of 1,200 feet. In one lockage, the 23,456 gross tons of iron ore was a record breaker for a single lockage.

Harry Coulby, President of the Pittsburgh Steamship Company, LCA officials William Livingstone, Harvey D. Goulder, George A. Marr, and other members of the LCA Board were onboard the James A. Farrell. This was an occasion to celebrate the efficiency in which the rapidly growing lake commerce could be moved to the industrial heartland of America.

SS <u>James A. Farrell</u> passing through new Bascule bridge approaching third lock 1914.

Opening of Third Lock. First Vessels to Lock Up, October 21, 1914.

Representatives of Lake Carriers' Association at the Opening of the Third Lock, October 21, 1914.

Sault Ste. Marie, Sabin Lock

In 1909, while construction was underway for the third lock LCA began petitioning for a fourth lock because of the estimated seven years it would take from initial authorizations for study until a completed lock would be open to navigation. In the same year, LCA, recognizing there was a growth in American and Canadian tonnage through the Soo, began working with the Canadian vessel operators and the Canadian government to build a new Canadian lock.

In April 1913, construction of the fourth lock began. The total cost of the lock was $2.5 million and it took 6 ½ years to complete. The grand opening of the fourth lock, known informally as the Sabin Lock, was on September 18, 1919. It was attended by a large number of LCA officers and members including William Livingstone, Harvey D. Goulder, and George A. Marr, and many other LCA Board members as well as government officials.

Ship transits new Sabin Lock September 18, 1919

Livingstone with other vessel-men on board ship
transiting new Sabin Lock September 18, 1919

The attendees arrived by train at the Soo and proceeded to board the W. C. Richardson Company vessel, <u>William Livingstone</u>, the same vessel that inaugurated the opening of the Livingstone Channel. The party boarded the vessel for a luncheon on the <u>William Livingstone</u> during which

Livingstone was the toastmaster who recited the historical significance of this important twin lock. Speeches followed by several Department of War officials including Louis Sabin.

At 5 PM that day, the <u>William Livingstone</u> accompanied by several government boats and tugs proceeded to enter the Fourth Lock. It was noted that without prearrangement, a vessel was locking up in the Poe, three vessels were locking down the Davis and a vessel was in the Canadian lock. Whistles, sirens and a general din welcomed this historic occasion.

While in the lock, during the toasts and festivities, the LCA General Counsel Goulder proposed that the lock be christened the Sabin Lock recognizing the many achievements of L. C. Sabin, superintendent of the American locks, for efficient service to the country. This was the unofficial naming ceremony of the Sabin Lock. Congress officially named the fourth lock the Sabin Lock at the time the MacArthur Lock was dedicated in 1943.

Private aids to navigation, lightships, patrol boats, water level gauges and dredging

Shipowners could not depend upon the government for the necessary aids to navigation along the lake shores, in the connecting channels, or at the entrances to important harbors. The surveys of the lakes and channels were also inadequate and many a ship grounded or foundered on unknown shoals. LCA not only petitioned the government of the U.S. and Canada for help; but in the interim, expended the members' money for the aids to navigation including lightships, buoys, water level gauges and patrol boats in the channels. This was essential in the newly established channels until the government lights were installed.

Lightships

Early in the Livingstone presidency, the LCA lightship <u>Kewaunee</u> was maintained at Southeast Shoal, and range lights and float lights were installed and maintained by LCA at Amherstburg, Lime Kiln Crossing and Bar Point channels. LCA petitioned the Canadian government to build lightships for use at Southeast Shoal to replace the Kewaunee. Later, the Kewaunee was used in Lake Erie in the U.S. waters near the Canadian boundary, near Point Abino, Ontario, in order to aid vessels approaching Buffalo. The Kewaunee in 1911, with lights and fog whistles, was maintained near the wreck of the steamer Joliet that sunk near Sarnia at the entrance to Lake Huron. When navigation opened in 1912, the Kewaunee returned until the wreck was removed. During the salvage, LCA maintained lights and stakes to guide the ship past the salvage operation. Earlier efforts to have the federal government repay LCA for private lights was successful, however in 1911, the government paid for no private lights. In later years, some of these private aid services were paid for by the Lighthouse Board.

The LCA lightships also served at the end of the season to take government lighthouse keepers from Bar Point Light and, with an agreement from the Canadian government, from the Colchester lighthouse.

In May 1913, LCA negotiated with the Canadian government to 'borrow' the Ballard's Reef South lightship in order to station it on the west side of the Livingstone Channel so as to mark the turn into the rock cut of the Livingstone Channel. It was maintained there by LCA until the end of the season.

The LCA also installed and maintained at members' expense other floating aids at Lime Kiln Crossing, Bois Blanc Island, Elliott's Bay, and Ballards Reef and operated the LCA owned Bar Point lightship, and the Martin Reef lightship. In many locations at loading ports, LCA and GLPA maintained bulletin boards advising masters of the maximum depth for vessels transiting channels and locks throughout the system from Duluth to the St. Lawrence Canals. LCA also maintained telephone connections at Lime Kiln and Fort Gratiot Lighthouse in order to advise Captains of the fluctuating water levels. As needed, LCA placed lights to mark wrecks.

In the tragic aftermath of the November 1913 storm LCA engaged a tug to stand by in Lake Huron by the wreck of the Charles S. Price that 'turned turtle' in the storm.

SS Charles S. Price upside down before salvaged (Wikipedia)

Dredging

In 1917, it was recognized that Vidal Shoals above the Soo locks was a controlling point for vessel draft between Lake Superior and the lower lakes. Frequently vessels reported touching bottom in this area. LCA sent a Pittsburgh Steamship captain to survey the area and found that boulders were sticking up in a length of about fifteen feet on the bottom of the channel. LCA petitioned the COE to remove the boulders but since there were no appropriations for the work, the government could not do the work. LCA quickly received a permit from the COE to conduct the dredging and removed 210 yards of rock thereby providing an average depth of 22 feet over Vidal Shoals. In order to advise Captains of the water depth, LCA then installed a gauge station and staffed it with three keepers. The gauge recorded the water depth every 15 minutes 24/7 and displayed the depth using illumination at night so as passing vessels would know the water depth. The expense of both of these aids to navigation was borne fully by LCA.

Boulders removed at Vidal Shoals at LCA expense

Water gauge station near Saulte built at LCA expense

Patrol Boats and Water Gauges

Before there was a U.S. Coast Guard organization, the Revenue Service cutters assisted in navigation matters, boarded and examined vessels, assisted vessels in distress, saved lives and property, controlled regatta courses, aided local authorities in celebrations of public character and extinguished fires. Unfortunately the service had too few boats to cover all the channels. At the urging of LCA, the Revenue Service established the St. Marys River Patrol in 1897 to prevent collisions and other accidents in the river where increased traffic was creating hazards. In 1914, the Patrol Service operated the tug Mackinac and launches Vigilant and No. 21-D and six lookout stations with 36 enlisted men. In October 1914, LCA officials evaluated this valuable service, congratulated the leadership and the men and made a number of recommendations for improvements that would require appropriations.

LCA procured and operated their own patrol boats for service in other important channels in order to report on extinguished lights, to light those floating aids when possible, to advise captains of navigation concerns ahead, and to report back to LCA when some captains were overloaded or were not displaying proper navigation lights. In general the LCA patrol boats were in the channels to promote safety. Every ship owner would be jeopardized when collisions and groundings clogged the channels and halted navigation. In 1913, there was a LCA patrol boat in the Livingstone Channel. In 1914-17, the patrol boat Despatch transferred from Buffalo patrolled the Livingstone Channel; this was particularly important in 1917 and 1918 due to the vastly increased traffic in the Livingstone and Amherstburg Channels.

When the 1918 season ended, the Despatch was transferred back to Buffalo to aid in the mooring and the safe guarding of the large fleet of vessels anchored there with winter storage grain. In 1919 and for many years to follow, the Despatch returned to the Detroit River. In 1925 the Despatch became unserviceable and was replaced by LCA with a steel gas launch rechristened Despatch II that patrolled the Livingstone and Amherstburg Channels. A bulletin board at Mullen Coal Dock, Sandwich, Ontario, was supplemented by erection of a large illuminated arrow to give advice of the Lime Kiln Crossing stage of water- rising, falling or stationary.

The automatic water gauge at the Detroit River Light was enhanced by installing a continuous light on the board showing available depth in the Amherstburg Channel.

Another LCA patrol boat, the Minnemac was stationed at the Sault near Brush Point in 1918 in order to facilitate the rapid movement of vessels by advising Captains of water levels and which lock to use. In 1919 and after, a government vessel replaced the Minnemac but was assisted by an LCA representative onboard to give advice to the masters. When the government moved the dispatch boat from Big Point in 1923, LCA hired two tug boats to perform the navigation information service. Also in 1923, in order to maximize cargo carried during the low water period that year, the allowable draft was increased to 20 feet. LCA stationed captains at the Soo to inform masters of the channel conditions and speeds allowed. The extreme low water period continued into 1925 and that necessitated additional private aids.

New Navigation Technology

LCA and the individual members attempted to keep up with new technology, installing this new equipment on older ships and the many new larger ships being built to maximize the use of the deeper and wider locks and channels. Some examples follow.

Submarine Signals. In order to improve navigation safety, LCA agreed to the installation of submarine signals transmitters on the LCA lightship Kewaunee that would allow vessels equipped with receivers to ascertain their proximity to the transmitter in fog or reduced visibility. Many LCA ships were equipped with receivers. The Lighthouse Board installed the signals on all the Great Lakes lightships. Consideration was given to installation at other points near lighthouses on the Lakes.

Wireless stations. LCA in 1909 advocated that the principle lifesaving stations on the Great Lakes be equipped with wireless telegraph. In 1919, congress authorized the construction of automatic wireless stations to reduce the danger of navigation. Ships approaching dangerous shoals or reefs would be warned by high pitch signals that could be picked up by wireless apparatus on a ship.

Radio Compass Stations and Radio Direction Finders. LCA supported the installation of Radio Compass Stations by the U.S. Navy so as ship's radio detection finders could use them for navigation. In 1920, the Bureau of Navigation planned to build ten direction finding stations on the Great Lakes. By 1924, there were four stations at Detour Point, Grand Marais, Whitefish Point and Eagle Harbor. Ten more were contemplated to be installed by the end of 1925.

New Construction and Diesel Engines. LCA shipowners were always attempting to install state of the art technology. The Henry Ford II, launched at American Shipbuilding Company yard in Lorain on March 1, 1924, and the Benson Ford from Great Lakes Engineering Works, Ecorse on April 26, 1924, were the first ships on the Great Lakes equipped with diesel engines. These 3,000 horse power ships also had the latest navigation equipment: deep sea sounding machines, patent recording logs, master Gyro compass, submarine signal device, radio detection finder and draft indicators.

STEAMER HENRY FORD II, FIRST LARGE BULK FREIGHTER ON GREAT LAKES WITH DIESEL ENGINE

First ships on the Great Lakes equipped with diesel engines

MV Benson Ford equipped with diesel engines (Al Hart Collection, A.E. Young photo)

Lighthouses, Reorganization of the Lighthouse Department

Navigation on the Great Lakes was very hazardous as Great Lakes commerce increased since there were inadequate aids to navigation. LCA petitioned for appropriations for many lighthouses in the U.S. such as at Middle Island, Split Rock, Rock of Ages, Sand Hills, and White Shoals, as well for virtually every harbor entrance in the Lakes. In the interim, before the lighthouses were built, lightships were a timelier, and often a less expensive remedy. It took a great deal of effort to obtain the appropriations for aids in Canadian waters; the aids were particularly needed in the connecting channels where all vessels navigated in the waters of both nations. After many years of LCA providing private aids in key areas, in 1910 the Canadian government placed a lightship at South East Shoal and took over management of the Detroit River aids to navigation on the Canadian side.

LCA leadership was a major supporter of improved aids to navigation and they had their firm opinions about the management of lighthouses. In 1909, LCA was opposed to the idea that the management of lighthouses would be turned over to civilian manning for fear that appointments would be made for political purposes. The LCA view in 1910 was rejected by Congress; and by 1913 the Lighthouse Service was reorganized and under the management of civilians. LCA officials worked with them to continue to improve the system.

LCA Involvements with other Federal Agencies

Lake Survey

The over 6,000 ship wrecks on the Great Lakes attest to hidden shoals and unreported wrecks. As noted in the History of the Detroit District of the U.S. Army Corps of Engineers, the Lake Survey begun in Buffalo continued its work until 1882 when it considered its field work complete. Navigation charts were engraved, printed and distributed. The charts were adequate for 12 foot draft navigation. Congress provided funds for additional limited surveys and updates of charts after a ship struck a 14 foot shoal in 1897 in a location that on the chart indicated there was 22 feet of water.

In 1901 the Lake Survey was reestablished as a separate Corps function but was still not adequately funded. Since many navigation charts on the Great Lakes were often inaccurate because of inadequate lake surveys, in 1907 LCA called for the completion of the surveying and charting of the Great Lakes and the connecting channels. In all the years that followed, LCA continually petitioned for permanent annual funding for the Lake Survey just as Congress did for the Coast and Geodetic Survey on the other coasts.

As a parenthetical observation, one must note that the boundary line between the U.S. and Canada on the Great Lakes and the connecting channels was not definitively established and placed on the navigation charts until 1915.

Support for Lifesaving Service

Lifesaving medal courtesy National Museum of the Great Lakes

The employment of qualified life savers at the 61 lifesaving stations in 1909 on the Great Lakes was very important to the shipping industry. From 1905 and onward Livingstone appealed to Congress to improve wages for these men and to provide a pension for disabled and retired life savers. LCA continued to call for improved appropriations for more life boats, including powered life boats in 1907, and for books and writing materials for the stations. In 1912, a bill was introduced to provide pensions but it failed passage.

LCA over the years maintained that the government did little to recognize acts of bravery and heroism that take place on the Great Lakes every year particularly performed by the Lifesaving Service. In 1909, LCA took steps to cast gold medals and arranged to have them made at the U.S. Mint.

Steamboat Inspection Service

The LCA frequently was opposed to legislation regulating the certification and qualifications of crew members and opposed government regulations on standards for ship construction, equipment required onboard and engineering machinery. LCA opposed Steamboat Inspection rules in 1904 and 1905 because the government proposed to require freight vessels to have crew sizes and equipment similar to that required on passenger vessels. An example of what was considered an impractical regulation by LCA was a regulation in 1914 requiring ships, not equipped with wireless radio to have onboard a floatable message case to permit the person in charge of a ship in imminent damage of sinking to place a report in the document case outlining the reasons causing the event. There is no record available to LCA indicating how often these message cases were used by the person in charge who was trying to save the ship and his life. While the preceding example is cited by LCA leadership as an unnecessary regulation, most of the proposed regulations were opposed because in the opinion of the leadership, they unnecessarily added to costs of operation.

Eventually federal legislation was passed to regulate Great Lakes ship operations, but not without much lobbying pro and con. The 1913 Annual Report notes that the Wilson Seaman's Bill (Seaman's Bill of Rights) was vetoed by President Taft, practically as the last act of his presidency. LCA commended President Taft for his wisdom since it would have increased crew size by at least 33%. However, in the next session of congress the Wilson-LaFollette Seamen's Bill was introduced, largely inspired by Andrew Furuseth, International Seamen's Union. In 1915 the Seaman's bill passed and came into effect November 4, 1914. After much deliberation the LCA Board had earlier voted to accept it. One of the requirements was to have all able bodied (AB) seamen pass physicals given by the U.S. Public Health Service (USPHS). A lifeboatman had to be an AB and had to show qualifications to obtain a lifeboatman certificate. Prior to this regulation, LCA decided who was qualified to be an AB and which crewmember, regardless of department, would be assigned to man the lifeboat. The report indicated that some seamen failed the physical or declined to take one and left the industry causing crew shortages on the ships.

In the 1915 Annual Report, there is a note of high level government concern about the safety of vessel operations on the Great Lakes. The European War caused the United States to become the major supplier of food stuffs and manufactured goods to many European countries. It was to be a record year for vessel passages and lockages through the Sault locks. Late fall navigation was anticipated and in fact the last transit of the American locks was December 20. In October 1917, Secretary of Commerce Redfield addressed a letter to President Livingstone stressing the need for safety in carriage through the rest of the season. Redfield noted that many vessels sailed in an overloaded condition and not properly trimmed; there were no load line laws in place and the Secretary felt that many Captains would take risks as the owners pressed them for time and cargo delivery. He asked President Livingstone to use his influence on the members in the interest of safety. Livingstone promptly replied providing a copy of the circular letter prepared by Harry Coulby, President of the Pittsburgh Steamship Company, and operator of over 100 ships at that time. Livingstone said that Coulby's view reflected the Secretary's and that of the LCA. Coulby reinforced the need to trim cargos and not to overload; he also noted that at least 70 percent of the ships in the LCA were modern vessels. As fate would have it, no ships in LCA foundered later that year; although perhaps the Secretary had in mind the sinking of the iron hull steamer <u>Onoko</u> in mid-September 1915.

As the years went on, LCA continued to express concern for the inadequate staffing of the steamboat inspection service on the Great Lakes at vessel fit out time. Many ships were delayed awaiting inspectors. In 1916-17, the Secretary of Commerce successfully petitioned Congress for more appropriations for staff, thus permitting the hire of fourteen additional permanent inspectors and some temporary assignments in the spring from other coasts.

Some decisions and recommendations of the Steamboat Inspection Service were supported by LCA including the ruling that the licenses as Master to command an American ship could not be issued to Canadian citizens; and, in 1917, the recommendation that regulations be passed to prevent the overloading of freight steamers. LCA had long been against overloading vessels; frequently these overloaded vessels grounded in channels thus blocking or delaying other vessel transit.

In the 1922 Annual Report it was noted that the USPHS assisted the Steamboat Inspection Service by examining applicants for license as master, mate and pilot for color sense and acuity and in the examination of applicants in the principles of first aid.

Weather Bureau Service

The genesis of the storm signal service was in 1870 when President Grant ordered the establishment of storm signals following the request of Great Lakes shipping interests. In 1869 there was an unusually stormy season during which hundreds of vessels were wrecked or damaged. The vessel owners asked for a cautionary service to be displayed in many parts of the Great Lakes. The storm warnings for the lakes were issued from Washington. In 1922 the responsibility was transferred to Chicago as there was excellent telegraph service to the lake stations and display points for storm signals from Chicago.

In that same year the Navy Radio Station at Great Lakes, IL, improved twice daily broadcasts of weather information.

At the turn of the 20th century, the Weather Bureau was a part of the Department of Agriculture. LCA petitioned the Secretary to build a Storm Warning and Vessel Reporting Station at Devil's Island, Lake Superior and for underwater cable connections to Beaver Island to improve storm warning reports. There was a continuous dialog between LCA and the Weather Bureau on ways to improve communications, particularly after dangerous storms such as in 1913 that sunk many ships.

By the end of 1922, the Naval Radio Stations at Buffalo, Cleveland, Alpena and Duluth were closed, thus terminating distribution of weather forecasts and warnings. Vessels with radio phones could obtain weather information from many commercial stations but the void in broadcasts in the Lake Huron area made the loss of the Alpena station apparent. Michigan Limestone in Rogers City stepped in to make available their radio station for weather rebroadcasts obtained from the Weather Bureau in Detroit.

Labor Relations

In 1901 the LCA developed a coordinated plan to not negotiate with maritime unions. While many members, particularly the fleets owned by the steel companies, advocated the plan it did not have the unanimity needed to carry out the plan. Individual members negotiated with the unlicensed seamen's unions and the licensed engineer's union. They all agreed that there would be no negotiation with the unions claiming to represent the deck officers, and in particular the Captain who was considered by management to be the vice-principal of the owner. The Marine Engineers' Beneficial Association (MEBA) was able to negotiate with the owners in 1901 and did so up through 1908. LCA in 1904, acting for its members, negotiated contracts with various unions: Lake Seamen's Union; Marine Firemen, Oilers and Watertender's Union; Marine Cooks and Steward's Union; and Grain Scoopers. In 1906, there was an effort to organize the mates into a union. This effort was backed by the Longshoremen's Association who provided labor for the docks and tug boats; LCA vehemently opposed the effort and a strike occurred in May 1906. While the brief strike was settled without recognition of a Mates union, severe strains between management and labor was prevalent.

In 1905, there was a major initiative to improve relations between LCA and the Masters who were part of the Shipmasters' Association, a professional beneficial association that did not act as a collective bargaining agent. All ship masters, shareholders and managers were granted honorary membership in the Association, thereby permitting these honorary members to participate in discussions, but without a vote. Within a few months, the Masters attempted to seek contractual relations through their union, the Masters, Mates and Pilots; the request was irrevocably rejected since management firmly believed that the Master represents the management and thus cannot be represented by a union that tells management what to do. The mates were considered to be the persons acting on behalf of the master in his absence and the persons who would eventually become masters. In 1907, the LCA members removed the overtime payment provision in the union contracts to reduce frustration of the officers and the employees.

In 1903, LCA operated Shipping Offices, later known as Assembly Halls at Cleveland, Ashtabula, Conneaut, Toledo, Chicago and South Chicago from which the LCA Shipping Master, also called Shipping Commissioners or Custodians by LCA, dispatched mates, wheelsmen, watchmen, firemen, cooks, seamen, deck hands and oilers. In 1904 these offices shipped 9,470 men. Later, in 1907, offices were opened in Erie, Fairport, Lorain and Duluth. In 1906, 12,490 men were shipped; in 1907-15, 181 were shipped. In 1908, LCA set up the Assembly Halls under the Open Shop policy and this will be covered in brief later.

Grain Shoveling at Buffalo

LCA began its assistance to the members to bring about more efficient grain shoveling in Buffalo in 1893 by forming the Grain Handling Corporation of Buffalo that terminated in 1921. In the early years the corporation contracted with James Kennedy, Buffalo, to provide men for all the shoveling on all the Association vessels at a uniform rate irrespective of the kind and condition of the grain and of its situation on the vessel with no distinction between steam and sail vessels. Many other operational improvements were made by Kennedy such as assuring that once a ship was started in its discharge it would be finished without stoppage; hitherto if only a small portion was onboard at midnight on Saturday, work would stop until Monday morning, thus delaying the vessel departure. In 1898 the Grain Shoveling contract was given to William J. Connors. There was a great deal of contention in fixing the price for handling the grain and it took much negotiation between LCA members, the elevator owners and the contractor to fix a price before the season started. It was noted that the money saved for owners of the vessels, $45,000, was more than double the amount of the membership dues paid by all of the members in 1898.

Because of labor turmoil in 1900 between the grain shovelers union and the contractor who performed the service of discharging grain vessels in Buffalo, many vessels were delayed. As an emergency short term measure, LCA contracted with the Grain Shovelers' Union for unloading lakers and for loading canal boats. The service was provided to LCA members and non-members. Buffalo labor peace was achieved, much to the credit of the

LCA Superintendent Thomas W. Kennedy. Since the system was working, the unique LCA service continued until March 31, 1921. LCA considered this a 'special service' for grain carrying members; the employees were not considered LCA staff.

In 1920, the LCA Executive Committee decided that LCA ships would only accept grain if the bill of lading, the contract of carriage, stated "free in and out" to the vessel. This action was opposed by the elevator and grain interests and while negotiations were held with these interests, they refused to accept the terms of a new bill of lading. The LCA held firm and discontinued the grain shoveling operation. The LCA decision was made also with the recognition that many of the members had the core of their business in serving the iron and steel industries and did not haul grains. Also, the Association was responsible for and had the liability for all accidents even though the tools and equipment for unloading was provided by the elevator operators who took no responsibility for their condition. A new organization took over the grain shoveling and engaged Mr. Kennedy who had managed the operations for LCA since the beginning. In all the LCA Annual Reports through 1920, there was a Grain Shoveling Report including all income and expenses should anyone wish further details on this unusual LCA mission. Undoubtedly, there is another side to the story about labor problems in Buffalo that should be told by union historians. I am certain it will be interesting reading.

Labor Turmoil and the Views of the Labor Unions

It would take extensive research, and become the subject of a separate book, to report upon the conditions surrounding the operation of the ships and its impact on the men working on the ships at the turn of the twentieth century that lead to the formation of maritime labor unions and associations. It would be equally difficult to enter into the mindset of the owners of ships that led them to an unbridled and vehement opposition to dealing with union officials representing Masters and other personnel on the ships.

Suffice it to say that severe tension existed between management and union officials on the Great Lakes. Masters and owners bridled at the

Union Red Book that laid out what work was to be done by crew members and what constituted overtime. LCA members developed a policy of no negotiation with unions and the support of what was called an 'open shop' employment policy. In 1907, the LCA members, particularly the steel companies, recognized that 1908 would be a recession year and therefore ran the boats very late in the 1907 season to build up stockpiles of iron ore, stone and coal. Management knew that this was the time to eliminate negotiations with the unions. There was enough material in stockpiles to accept a strike through the summer if needed. On April 9, 1908, the LCA members unanimously approved the open shop policy. The genesis of the plan was previously outlined in the 1901 Annual Report calling the plan "Lake Carriers' Beneficial Federation." It was not approved at that time, thus from 1902-1907, many members had union closed shop contracts governing labor employment conditions. All those management and labor negotiations ended in 1908.

LCA management created joint procedures and facilities that assured the ship owner of the services of all shipboard personnel, from master to ordinary seaman from chief engineer to coal passer. Members immediately demanded that if anyone wanted to work, they had to sign the infamous 'yellow dog contract', an agreement not to join a union.

LCA leadership was well aware of the demands of labor for improved working conditions, wages and hours of employment. In those days the maritime trade unions on other coasts were seeking legislative relief for the plight of seamen. There were few standards for qualifications of the officers and seamen. LCA members alone decided who qualified as able-bodied seamen or other ratings. Frequently the LCA argument was that, while changes may be needed elsewhere, they were not needed on the Great Lakes.

In the 1908 Annual Report it is stated that ship owners advised Captains to give their men fair treatment including no unnecessary work such as scraping and painting on Sundays or working over the side of the vessel when underway. In a further effort to improve the conditions and treatment of seamen, LCA published guidelines. In a circular letter of July 17, 1909, President Livingstone stated:

- There shall be no Sunday or legal holiday work such as painting, scrubbing of paint or cleaning brass, and unnecessary cleaning of decks.
- Crews shall be given time off during working hours to keep their quarters clean and sanitary.
- In case a vessel goes out of commission before the completion of a trip for which the crew had been engaged, the crew shall receive railroad transportation to the port where the trip commenced.
- No man shall work more than ten hours per day for one day's pay without a watch below, unless he is given watch and watch, the Captain however to be the sole judge as to the necessity of when he requires the services of the entire crew.
- All vessels shall provide well lighted, well ventilated, clean sleeping quarters, properly heated in the winter, the beds shall have good mattresses, springs and pillows, and clean linen at least once each trip.
- All vessels shall carry a full equipment of life saving apparatus.

In 1913, the Bulletin advised that "By an action of the Board of Directors it is required on all vessels of the Association the firemen shall be divided into three watches"; and for vessels over 4,500 ton to employ a Boatswain in order to relieve the Chief Mate of those duties. The Masters were considered Associate Members of LCA. In 1914, it was noted by the LCA Industrial Committee that on only half of the member vessels, the wheelsman stood three hours watch on the wheel and three hours lookout. It was the Committee consensus that a six hour wheel watch was excessive and that all vessels should have the wheelsman stand only a three hour wheel watch followed by three hours on lookout. Later that year LCA stressed sanitation, cleanliness, allowing the men time to wash up before meals and to serve all of them plain food, the same food for officers and crew. Instructions were given to run the dynamo from 4 pm until 6 am so as the crew would have light in their quarters.

The years following the Great War were periods of labor unrest; LCA stated that at that time there were more than 60,000 strikes and labor unrest in the U.S. and that there were none in the Great Lakes shipping industry. There was an effort by organized labor to call a strike in the fall of

1922 as characterized by LCA "on the frivolous demand for a three watch system in the forward end." The strike failed to stop shipping as only a few men left the boats.

In the remainder of this book I will comment only upon the positive aspects of the Open Shop Policy that lead to the Welfare Plan, Registration of Employees and the Assembly Halls. For a complete history of maritime Labor-Management relations at the turn of the 20th century, I recommend H. E. Hoagland, Ph.D., Wage Bargaining on the Vessels of the Great Lakes, University of Illinois Studies in the Social Sciences, Urbana, IL, September 1917; Charles P. Larose, Maritime Labor Relations on the Great Lakes, Michigan State University, 1959; and District 2 MEBA-AMO, AFL-CIO, Coulby to Potts to Beukema, U.S. Steel Pulls the Strings at Lake Carriers' Association, 1973.

Welfare Plan, another Keystone of the LCA Mission

The Welfare plan went into effect during the fit-out in 1909. As the years moved along, the plan changed with the times; some of the positive aspects are outlined below.

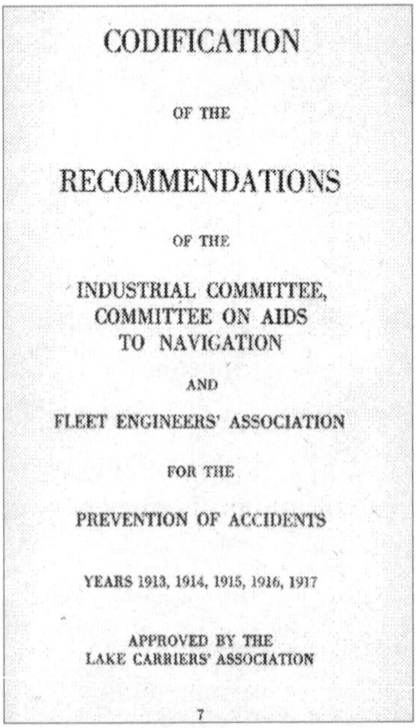

CODIFICATION

OF THE

RECOMMENDATIONS

OF THE

INDUSTRIAL COMMITTEE,
COMMITTEE ON AIDS
TO NAVIGATION

AND

FLEET ENGINEERS' ASSOCIATION

FOR THE

PREVENTION OF ACCIDENTS

YEARS 1913, 1914, 1915, 1916, 1917

APPROVED BY THE
LAKE CARRIERS' ASSOCIATION

GET THAT RAISE OF GRADE!!

DECKHANDS

12 months service qualifies you for Able Seamen's examination

COAL PASSERS

6 months service qualifies you for Oiler and Fireman's examination

We have study material in this office and will be glad to assist you

Safety First Campaign In order to reduce accidents, in 1914 the LCA took on a long term Safety campaign using signs onboard ship, Bulletin messages to crew and safety training. In 1917, Ship Safety Committees were organized on each LCA vessel whereby six members of the crew held meetings with other crew members to find ways to reduce accidents and to pass along information from LCA on safety procedures. In 1918, there were a reduced number of accidents reported as 137 steamers actively participated in the Safety First Campaign and in 1919 there were 250 steamers organized with committees. As the program progressed, some progressive companies paid a stipend of $10 to the members of the Safety Committee. Earlier in this book there was a section that enumerated the vessel losses and crew casualties. These reported accidents and fatalities spurred the Safety First program to improve safety training and awareness.

Sanitation Campaign. After recognizing that the crew was often sick from water they drank onboard, a major initiative in 1914 by the USPHS was to identify the locations within the Great Lakes where it was safe to pump in drinking water. Altogether 17,784 samples were taken in 1,477 points on the Great Lakes. Many locations such as in the Detroit River and the St. Marys River were so polluted that no purification system known at that time could make it fit for drinking. The Bulletin indicated that the pollution in the Detroit River at Fighting Island was 63 times greater than that of Lake St. Clair. Even 15-18 miles out into the Lake, the water was too polluted to purify. The LCA Sanitation Committee immediately notified the Masters of the areas to avoid and the areas of unquestioned purity in the lake supply. This became a continuous effort.

At the same time there was greater recognition of the illnesses caused from consuming food that was not cared for properly by the chandler supplying the food and by the cook while it was stored on the ships. Particular emphasis was given to protecting meat from being contaminated by flies. All suppliers were put on notice and the cooks were instructed in this regard. Efforts were made to assure that the crews on LCA ships had pure drinking water, milk, ice and foodstuffs. In order to reduce cases of typhoid, the crew was encouraged to go to the USPHS hospitals to receive a vaccination and to practice personal sanitation.

In September 1918, the Spanish influenza (as it was called since only the Spanish newspapers reported on Flu in Europe because of wartime censorship), which had spread throughout America as soldiers returned from Europe, began to show up on Great Lakes ships. This pandemic killed 50-100 million people worldwide, and may have killed more people than the Black Death in the 14th century. LCA sent the best information on this disease to the ships. Fortunately, as sailors were away from major cities for long stretches and were living in a more fresh air environment, it did not impact the crews as much as the population as a whole. The Annual Report noted that about 25 sailors died from the influenza while about 500,000 other Americans died.

Savings Plan In 1911, LCA set up an administrative arrangement to allow seamen to direct deposit a portion of their wages into a bank account and to make withdrawals without leaving the ship. In the past some crew members would ask ship's officers to take custody of the money until they would sign off for the last voyage. Other sailors lost their money through theft, carelessness, or shore side excesses. The object was to promote sobriety, efficiency, industry and self-reliance.

The Captains, who paid out advances on wages and final voyage payments, were encouraged to promote this saving plan in order to promote thrift, reduce incidents of sailors using the wages for booze and other port temptations. Competitions were encouraged between and within the fleets to find out which company and ship adhered to this policy of savings. The first bank to be enrolled in the Lake Marine Savings Program was the Cleveland Trust Company, Cleveland, OH. In 1911, deposits were less than $100,000. During the War years and up until the recession of 1921, the crews authorized savings deduction in excess of $1 million each year. When the recession ended in 1923 and 1924, deposits again exceeded $1 million. In 1923, the Guardian Savings and Trust Company of Cleveland offered a similar savings plan for mariners; and, in 1924 the Marine National Bank of Ashtabula joined in the Savings Program. To encourage savings, the Cleveland Trust, starting in 1916, awarded cash prizes to seamen who had the largest proportional increase in savings and offered other incentives for saving. Prizes were also offered to Masters for encouraging the program

Sobriety The campaign against intemperance began in 1914 when LCA directed the placement of signs indicating No Liquor Allowed onboard ships. Temperance pledges were advocated and temperance buttons issued.

In many issues of the Bulletin, the crews were reminded of the personal dangers of consuming alcohol. When the Prohibition movement advanced throughout the nation, there was no stronger supporter of prohibition than the LCA members who too often found crew members missed the ship due to boozing and many accidents were booze related. In the May 1918 Bulletin it was stated '…in one year it will be impossible legally to obtain an intoxicating drink anywhere in the United States.'

Schools In 1912 and 1913 the LCA Assembly Hall in Duluth provided for seaman an instructor who taught spelling, reading, writing and arithmetic. The Duluth Board of Education was a partner in this endeavor. At the same time the Assembly Hall in Marine City taught the same basic courses and added some navigation and engineering training. In 1914, 20 of the students in Marine City studied for and sat for their license exam and 15 passed. The Annual Report indicated the intention to spread the teaching mission to Buffalo, Cleveland and Detroit. In 1915 the first school of seamanship and safety opened using stereopticon slides to show the right and wrong way to perform tasks. They also taught resuscitation to assist drowned men.

In 1915, LCA opened a School of Navigation and Marine Engineering in the Perry-Payne Building in Cleveland, OH. In 1917, a 14 week course at the Cleveland school was held at the Beckman Building, 409 Superior Avenue. The other schools in the LCA system were doing equally well in preparing men for original licenses and in learning basic seamanship.

Navigation School, Lake Carriers' Association, Class of 1917.

Marine Engineering School, Lake Carriers' Association, Class of 1917.

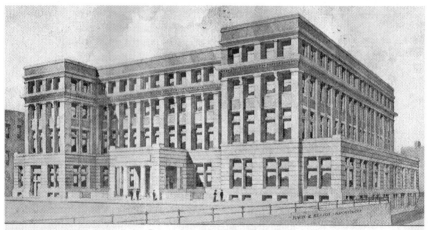
Proposed Sailors' Institute at Cleveland.

In 1918, the educational program continued unabated as navigation and engineering schools prepared men for the licenses needed to operate the increased number of ships. As in Duluth, the LCA was working with the Cleveland Board of Education on this technical extension training. By 1920 the LCA schools were in full swing employing at least 11 instructors teaching general education, seamanship and license preparation. In 1920, LCA began to pay a stipend of $12 a week for 10 weeks to defray costs of living expenses for students working on their original license.

While shipping was depressed in 1921, a number of men undertook courses of study. In 1923, a Student Aid Fund was established to help students studying for a license who were in financial straits and in need of a loan to help them complete the courses. The instructors made recommendations to the Welfare Committee for these loans; the approved loans were all paid back shortly after the men returned to the ship.

The schools had been very successful during the Livingstone era. Many men enrolled in the correspondence courses and used the material while on the ships during the sailing season. LCA also provided technical books through the Soo Library when it opened. In the ten years of operation, since 1916, 360 men received the original third engineer license; 79 raised licenses to First Assistant and 90 raised to Chief Engineer. In the Deck Department there were 260 original licenses as Pilot and 41 Master's license. In 1922 LCA added a course in First Aid and Hygiene since the Steamboat Inspection Service required those taking new license exams to pass a course on that subject.

Registration of Seamen, LCA Discharge Books, LCA Commissioners

LCA operated Assembly Halls or Rooms where any worker could register for employment. The Open Shop policy required applicant seamen to sign certificates saying they were not union members. LCA issued Continuous Record Discharge books that contained the infamous and controversial notations on the workers conduct to be inserted by the Master, good or fair, after each period of employment. The Discharge Book was given to the Captain or Chief Engineer when the seaman signed articles on the vessel and was held by these officers until the seaman signed off. If a seaman deserted the vessel before the articles stipulated, or if the seaman failed to serve properly and thus didn't warrant a good or fair assessment, the book was returned to the Secretary of the LCA. These books were labeled 'Fink Books' by many union leaders.

By the end of 1909, 90% of the seamen and officers were registered. Over the years the LCA encouraged all Captains to hire only seamen registered in the Assembly Rooms and to not hire a man who just showed up at the dock. Hiring of LCA registered seamen was never 100 percent but often was in the mid-90 percentile. LCA, following the direction of the Shipping Board in 1918, discontinued the solicitation of registration although seamen continued to register to obtain some of the benefits of the welfare plan.

In 1922, no longer bound by the Shipping Board, the LCA Discharge book was reinstated ostensibly because the seamen wanted a return of the book as it was proof of their employment, useful in obtaining citizenship and a general reference to their reliability.

Assembly Halls or Shipping Offices

Alfred R. Rumsey, LCA Chief Commissioner since its inception served forty years as a commissioner starting with the Cleveland Vessel Owners Association in 1881. Rumsey directed the establishment, maintenance and staffing of the Assembly Rooms throughout the Great Lakes until his death in 1921. Although the shipping office directors were not government employees, they were given the title of Commissioner and many of them wore uniforms. The official sounding title and the uniform helped them impress upon the seamen the need to register with the LCA.

A. R. Rumsey
Chief Commissioner

The Assembly Halls were clearly a success during the Livingstone presidency. The shipping offices had been in place long before as a function of the Cleveland Shipowners Association. The initiation of the Welfare Plan and the LCA Open Shop policy caused the registration to grow significantly, despite the temporary halt by the Shipping Board during the Great War. The registration of seamen continued after the war; in the first year of enrollment in 1909 there were 9,752 sailors enrolled, by 1920 there were 13,094, 1921 had 14,002, 1922 jumped to 19,097, 1923 leaped to 26,305 (the highest number of sailors registered in that period) and in 1925 there were 24,645 seamen registered.

The Chair of the Welfare Plan Committee changed periodically after the death in 1916 of Jasper H. Sheadle, Cleveland. He had been chair since the inception of the Welfare Plan in 1909. In 1917-19 the Chair was E. C. Collins, Cleveland, and from 1922 through 1941, George M. Steinbrenner, Cleveland, chaired the monthly meeting of the Welfare Plan Committee.

George M. Steinbrenner,
Chair Welfare Plan Committee

Much of the work and expenditures of the LCA in 1899-1902 was for operation of Shipping Offices in seven cities: Cleveland, Chicago, South Chicago, Buffalo, Ashtabula, Toledo and Milwaukee. At that time, this function was 42-44% of the LCA expenses. The cost of shipping each man was 64 cents each in 1899. Statistics from 1896 indicate 11,838 shipped; 1897-13,139; 1898-16,508; 1899-16,681; 1900-14,987; 1901-16,766; 1902-11,523. These statistics were for men shipped, some of whom had multiple assignments. There is no information on the number of men registered as there was later under the Assembly Hall/Welfare Plan system.

The Assembly Halls were usually in the building where seamen registered and from where they shipped out. Initially the halls were for both officers and seamen but in short order, there were separate halls for officers.

The Officer Halls, over a period of time, were improved with the objective of making them 'well-appointed club houses'. There were billiard tables, a library, reading room, current magazine subscriptions, some had pianos and many had the Victor talking machine with a rotating set of classical and popular music. Many of the halls were kept open in the winter in order for the men in port to have a place to rendezvous. Most had shower rooms and/or bathtubs, coat rooms and luggage storage. During the winters, many ports encouraged Pool Tournaments between the deck and engine officers in an effort to bring both ends of the ship together.

Assembly Hall, Erie, PA

Officer's Hall, Duluth, MN

The Assembly Halls were staffed by experienced Commissioners who knew the trades of the ships calling upon their port. They knew and anticipated the impact of a loss of seamen as many of the crews returned to farms for harvests in midsummer and to logging camps in the early fall. Round the clock they had to know how to get hold of the men needed to staff the ships.

When due to the 1921 recession, only half of the normal number of seamen and officers were employed, the open assembly halls provided a welcome place to congregate with other seamen. Due to the recession, LCA encouraged members to obtain all men through the sixteen Assembly Halls giving precedence to those who have worked on the lakes for a long time. This certainly helped retain the officers who gladly took jobs of much lower ranks in order to have some income that year. In 1925 there were fifteen Assembly Halls: Buffalo, Erie, Conneaut, Ashtabula, Fairport, Cleveland, Lorain, Toledo, Detroit, Gary, South Chicago, Chicago, Milwaukee, Ashland and Duluth.

Wage Setting

LCA Wage Card

The joint setting of wages by laker vessel owners started in 1883, before the LCA was re-organized. LCA set the wages each year for all officer and seamen ratings by size of vessel and issued wage cards each year to the Captains. It is noted that when there was a bad business year, LCA would stress that they were not reducing wages but were maintaining the high wages of the previous years. It was noted that in good business years, wages were often frozen, although certain ratings that were in demand, such as oilers in 1913, might get an increased wage. From 1910-1914 there was virtually no increase in wages. LCA officials knew what each class of seaman earned on the other coasts and usually paid a higher wage so as to keep the men from seeking union help to increase wages.

When the 1916 season brought about an unprecedented demand for vessel capacity, the LCA Board voted to increase wages three times during the year with bonuses paid to officers to stay on until the end of the season. Wages continued to improve as demand for all seamen increased, particularly just prior to and during the Great War. Due to inflation after the war, wage increases continued; although in recession years there were small reductions, or at times no increase despite the inflation that existed. At all times, the LCA annual reports stated that their members were paying higher wages than other industrial sectors and other American maritime employment.

Deaths of Seamen and Death and Permanent Disability Benefits

LCA leadership studied marine management practices of the British Shipping Federation, and practices among the railroads in the United States with respect to assisting the families of workers who were seriously disabled or killed by accident on the job. The Welfare Plan provided for death benefits or permanent disability payments to designated beneficiaries of crew members who were registered with the LCA Welfare Plan. These payments were made out of the funds of LCA and were made without any impairment of the sailor's rights in future litigation. These payments were not made to each person who died or was disabled but only to those seamen who were registered in the Assembly Rooms and who had designated a beneficiary. The payments were relatively small; they were primarily to assist with burial expenses and a source of ready cash for the beneficiary at the time of death. In 1908 the benefit payments varied by position of the crew member from $500 for a Master down to $75 for an ordinary seaman. In later years these benefits were increased a little. The Plan also provided a small payment to help pay for the burial expenses of indigent seamen who were registered in the Assembly Rooms who died ashore when they were not employed.

There was also a stipend paid to registered seamen onboard shipwrecked vessels to defray costs of their lost clothing and other effects; these seamen were also paid travel expenses back to the port of engagement. The payment in 1908 was $50 for licensed officers and $30 for other members of the crew. These payments did not impair the legal rights of the seamen to petition for a larger sum.

The documents of registration in the Welfare plan contained a complete description of each person. In the unfortunate circumstances of loss of life in major storms such as in 1913, these descriptions allowed the authorities along the shorelines to properly identify the bodies and to arrange for the next of kin to be notified and payment of the death benefits to be made.

Summary of Statistics that follow: From 1909-1925 during the Livingstone presidency, the LCA Annual Report recorded the name and cause of death or dismemberment of each man whose beneficiary received the payment established under the Welfare Plan. The causes of death included: drowned in collision, drowned in wreck, drowned from steamer, washed overboard, drowned attempting to board or leaving vessel, drowned while painting ship, fell off gangway, killed while landing steamer, killed by falling in hold or tanktop, killed when caught in machinery, killed by locomotive at dock, killed by train, killed by explosion, killed handling cable, lost overboard, fell from dock, fell from spar, shot onboard vessel, shot by deck hand in Ashtabula, blood poisoning following operation caused by injury, knocked into hold by ore bucket, scalded when tube blew out of boiler, boiler explosion, accidental strangulation, fell from ladder, explosion of gas tank, hit by clam shell rig, and the sad list went on. A narrative on the causes of death by year is contained at the end of the chapter. Not recorded were the many accidents that did not lead to death. As one considers the large number of seamen registered in the Assembly Rooms each year (see statistics at the end of the book), despite the gravity of the accidents that killed so many seamen, it was a relatively small number of seamen who died each year.

The Welfare Plan Safety Committee had its work cut out for them to minimize deaths and injury to seamen. In 1913 the Committee required each ship to send in to LCA the personal injury reports in order to take steps to prevent future accidents. Communications went out to the ships' officers recommending operational changes and training to prevent accidents; articles were regularly placed in the Bulletin so as the crew could read and see these recommendations. Signage was placed on the ships near where accidents often occurred. Eventually it was realized that the ownership of Safety belonged as well with the crews of the ship thus a new Safety First campaign was conceived in 1917 that included a Ship Safety Committee. The Committee went into full force in 1918 with membership of six crew members. In 1918 there were Ship Safety Committees on 137 steamers. The reports from these Committees went back to LCA who communicated recommendations to all the ships. There was a major downturn in fatal accidents and in personal injuries.

Ship Safety Committee pin

Statistics on the Cause of Death for Seamen receiving Death Benefits under the Welfare Plan 1909-1925

In 1909 there were 20 deaths and one permanent disability recorded where benefits where paid. The deaths were caused by: 10 drowned off of steamer, in collision, boarding vessel, in a wreck, falling from dock, washed over board; 5 fell into cargo hold; two were caught into machinery; one was struck by a locomotive on dock; one was crushed between the lock wall and ship; and one was mortally injured while docking. The disability payment was to the Chief Engineer whose right hand was severed at the wrist.

In 1910 there were 36 deaths eligible for payment of death benefits, five at that time, were unpaid for lack of proper address of beneficiary. The deaths were caused by: 15 drowned in wrecks, 12 drowned from falling off ladder while boarding or leaving vessel, falling from dock or from the vessel, six fell into cargo holds; one man was fatally burned, another man died in an explosion and one man was shot while on the vessel.

In 1911 there were 19 deaths where benefits were paid. The deaths were caused by: five drowned in wrecks, five drowned after falling while boarding or going ashore or falling overboard from ship, three fell into cargo hold, three fell from the dock, one fell between ship and dock, one was shot by a deckhand, and one died of blood poisoning after a foot injury.

In 1912 there were 21 deaths where benefits were paid. The deaths were caused by: 12 drowning of which five fell off dock, four fell overboard and three drowning were unspecified, two fell into cargo holds, one fell from a mast, one fell from a gangway, one cook died from blood poisoning after a cut, one man was scalded, one man died handling cables, one died from an accidental strangulation, and one from an unspecified hatch opening accident.

In the 1913 storm, 10 bulk freighters of steel construction were sunk and seven were owned by LCA members. In this storm that lasted from November 7 through November 10, 1913, Great Lakes Storm Wikipedia states that it killed more than 250 people and destroyed 19 ships, and stranded 19 others. It was called the deadliest and most destructive natural disaster ever to hit the Great Lakes. The LCA Annual Report states that 201 crew members died, of which 150 were onboard LCA ships. According to Wikipedia, the number of men who died on the LCA ships was: Argus, 28; Hydrus, 25; J. A. McGean, 28; C. S. Price, 28; I. M. Scott, 28; and on the H. B. Smith, 25. Three men were swept over the side from the Nottingham. This number totals 165 deceased; the LCA Report may not have been complete.

Not all of the men who died in this storm were eligible for any death benefit payment as several men were not registered with the Assembly Halls and therefore had not designated a beneficiary. The 1913 Report stated that 132 death benefits were payable; that 96 payments were made and that 36 others who were eligible had incorrect address or the beneficiaries had to be found as they lived in foreign countries. Payments were made to 17 beneficiaries in 1914.

In 1913 there were 27 other deaths where benefits were paid. The primary causes again were falls, engine room accidents and drowning. There were eight who drowned; five fell into cargo holds; one engineer fell onto the tanktop; five men died in boiler explosions; one died from scalding; one was struck by machinery; five men fell to their death onto the dock, from the boarding ladder and off the dock into the water and drown; and one was struck by a cargo unloader.

In 1914 there were 16 payments made for deaths or disability; seven fell to their death- six were in the cargo hold; eight drown and one was struck by a train on the dock.

In 1915 there were 16 payments for death. Eight men fell overboard and drown and one other was listed as an accidental drowning. Four died from falls: two into a cargo hold, one from a spar and another into a drydock. One died from an injury from a cable and another from an exploding gas tank. The most significant cause of deaths on a ship in 1915 was from the Eastland disaster where 831 died; however the Eastland was not an LCA vessel.

In 1916 there were two major storms that sunk ships on the Great Lakes. Among the LCA member ships, the May storm caused the foundering of the S.R. Kirby and the Black Friday Storm of October 20 sunk the Merida and the James B. Colgate. Forty-five payments were made to beneficiaries of sailors who died on these and other ships that foundered.

In 1916 additional death payment was made to 22 beneficiaries and two permanent disability payments were made. Drowning and falls took the majority of lives. Thirteen men drowned from unstated accidents, falling overboard, while painting the side of the ship and falling from a ladder. Three others drowned after falling from the dock. Four men fell into cargo holds and two fell from a ladder or other cause. One man was hit by a clamshell during cargo operations. The disability payments went to a Master disabled in a fall and to a watchman whose arm was severed by a cable.

In 1917 there were 20 death benefits and one disability payment made. Four death payments were made due to vessel wrecks, one of which occurred the previous year and three from the wreck of the Athens. Eight drowned, seven fell overboard and the other was washed overboard in a storm; five fell into cargo holds; one was crushed by a rig; one was killed by a train on the docks and a Chief Engineer died from exposure, not otherwise clarified. The permanent disability payment was given to an ordinary seaman whose limb was injured by a cable.

In 1918 there were only five accidents causing death. This is in marked contrast to the previous year and is in part attributed to the establishment of the Safety First Committees onboard ship. While eight death payments were made, three were due to accidents of the previous year. The payments for accidents occurring in 1917 were due to a fall into a cargo hold, struck by a cable and washed overboard. The five accidents in 1918 were two falls into a cargo hold, two died of an explosion of a lantern and another was washed overboard. While the 1918 influenza pandemic, the so called Spanish influenza, impacted many seamen there is no note of flu deaths.

In 1919 there were 19 death benefit payments, in large part due to payments to eight beneficiaries of men who died in the wreck of the John Owen. Another payment was to beneficiary of the man who died in wreck of Manola in 1918. The other accidents were caused primarily by falls. Seven men fell to their death, three fell overboard and drowned, two into cargo holds, one from a ladder and drowned, and one off the dock. A man was struck by a cable and another was struck by a grain elevator leg. One man died of natural causes.

In 1920 payments were made for 19 deaths from drowning, 12 of whom served on the Superior City, wrecked on August 20, 1920, and another on the wreck of the John Owen in 1919. A total of 35 payments were made of which 4 events had occurred in 1919, two of natural causes, one drown, and one was burned. The other 1920 deaths were caused by: six men drown; four died of natural causes; four were scalded; two fell into cargo holds; one was asphyxiated; and a fireman was killed ashore. A permanent disability payment was made to a coal passer; the reason was not stated.

In 1921 there were 12 death benefit payments, only four of which were classified as industrial accidents onboard ship, a noted success of the Safety Programs. Four men downed; three died of natural causes; 2 fell into cargo holds; one fell onto boiler room floor, one was struck by a cable; and one was killed on the rail road.

In 1922 business picked up, more men were registered, there were no ship wreck deaths, only eight deaths were attributed to fatal injury sustained onboard ship, payments were made to families for burial expenses of four men registered but not employed (it was the LCA policy that no registered seaman who died ashore of causes not connected to ship board employment would be buried in a Potters Field). Falls claimed six lives; three fell into cargo holds, two from masts and one fell off the dock and drown. Three others drown, circumstances not stated. A Master was struck by a train, a wheelsman was hit by a boom, a man died from an infection and another from pneumonia following injuries.

In 1923 there were 18 payments made of which 10 were to provide money to bury unemployed indigent seamen and one was to finalize payment to a father whose son died in the wreck of the Kirby in 1916 (his father was in Germany at the time of The Great War and payment could not be made). The other seven death payments were primarily caused by falls, one each: to a cargo hold, off the dock and drowns, down a stairway, off a stage and drown, and from the boat to the dock. A Chief Engineer died when a pipe exploded and a fireman was scalded in an explosion.

In 1924 the majority of casualties eligible for payment under the Welfare Plan was due to the sinking of the whaleback Clifton (formerly Samuel Mather) in the September 22 Lake Huron gale. The crew of 24 died and 19 were eligible for death payments. A payment was also made to a family in the Netherlands due to an accident that had occurred in 1917. As far as accidents onboard ship, it was a remarkably good year in that there were no deaths from falls into the cargo hold or due to machinery accidents. There were four fatal falls: two fell off dock and drown, one fell from ladder and another was crushed between ships. A First Assistant Engineer was killed when gas and flames from a furnace door burst out on him. A Chief Engineer was struck by an inter-urban train and an oiler was struck by a railroad car.

In 1925 14 death payments were made for accidents during the year, two payments for deaths in previous years and three payments for burial of indigent seamen. Four men including a Master fell overboard, two others were washed overboard, two fell off the dock and drown, one fell off a stage, one off a ladder, and one into the crank pit. One ordinary seaman was struck by a clam shell during cargo operations and a lookout while performing ship's duty on the dock was assaulted, thrown into the water and drowned.

End of the Livingstone Era, the Continuation of a Strong Association

When William Livingstone died on Saturday October 17, 1925 in the Dime Bank Building, Detroit, in his LCA office overlooking the Livingstone Channel in the Detroit River, he left a strong association with leadership that would continue his legacy.

LCA Membership and tonnage in 1904 was 608 vessels of 1,390,027 gross tons and in 1925 membership was 423 vessels with 2,223,143 gross tons.

The Board elected J. S. Ashley, Vice President since 1917, as President, and L. C. Sabin, Superintendent of the American canals at the Soo, as Vice President. When Harvey D. Goulder resigned as General Counsel, shortly after Livingstone's death, Newton D. Baker, former Mayor of Cleveland and former Secretary of War, was elected General Counsel. The strength of the association was in the solidarity of its members and in the Association leadership and staff.

Chapter Three

J. S. Ashley
Vice-President 1917-1925
President 1926-1930
Captain Joseph S. Wood
President 1931-1937

J. S. Ashley, President

J. S. Wood, Vice President

World and National Political/ Economic Climate of the period

After a weak beginning, the roaring 20s were great years of economic growth and prosperity. The strong economy insured that the Republicans controlled the White House, Senate and House of Representatives. Republican President Calvin Coolidge easily won his 2nd term in 1924. Commerce Secretary and Republican candidate Herbert Hoover won the 1928 elections by a 58% popular vote landslide. There was a belief that good times would last forever.

In his acceptance speech a week after the convention ended, Secretary Hoover said: "We in America today are nearer to the final triumph over poverty than ever before in the history of this land... We shall soon with the help of God be in sight of the day when poverty will be banished from this land." Al Smith, the Democratic candidate in 1928, was plagued by his anti-prohibition stance, the anti-Catholic sentiment and the corrupt Tammany Hall New York connection.

Republicans controlled the Senate until 1932. The House was also Republican in this period, usually by strong majorities except in 1930. During the 1930 election cycle, the nation was entering its second year of the Great Depression. Hoover was perceived as doing little to solve the crisis, and his personal popularity was extremely low. The Republican Party was initially applauded for instituting protectionist economic policies that were intended to limit foreign imports and to stimulate the domestic market. However, after the passage of the heavily damaging Smoot Hawley Tariff, a policy that was bitterly opposed by the Democratic Party, Republican business-oriented policies began to fall out of favor. Democrats gained a total of 52 House seats in the 1930 election. Although the Republicans retained a narrow majority after the polls closed, they lost a number of special elections following the deaths of 19 representatives and representatives-elect prior to the reconvening of Congress.

In 1932 the elections took place as the impact of the 1929 Wall Street crash and the worldwide Great Depression was being felt deeply across the USA. The Democratic candidate Franklin D. Roosevelt took 42 states, losing only Pennsylvania, Maine, New Hampshire, Vermont, Connecticut, and Delaware. He won electoral votes 472 to 59 and the popular vote by

57%. In this Democratic landslide they had a majority in the Senate and House; in the House it was 72% Democratic.

The 1934 elections in the House and Senate were a referendum on New Deal policies. In the Senate the Democrats took nine more Republican seats. While conservatives and people among the middle class who did not bear the brunt of the depression saw New Deal programs as radical, ordinary people overwhelmingly voted in this election cycle to continue implementation of Roosevelt's agenda. The Republicans were reduced below one-fourth of the House chamber for the first time since the creation of the party.

The presidential election of 1936, in terms of electoral votes was the most lopsided presidential election in the history of the United States. The election took place as the Great Depression entered its eighth year. Incumbent President Franklin D. Roosevelt was still working to push the provisions of his New Deal economic policy through Congress and the courts. However, the New Deal policies he had already enacted, such as Social Security and unemployment benefits, had proven to be highly popular with most Americans. Roosevelt's Republican opponent was Kansas Governor Alf Landon, a political moderate. Roosevelt went on to win the greatest electoral landslide since the beginning of the current two-party system in the 1850s, carrying all but 8 electoral votes. Roosevelt carried every state except Maine and Vermont.

By winning 523 electoral votes, Roosevelt received 98.49% of the electoral vote, the highest percentage since 1820. Roosevelt also won the largest number of electoral votes ever recorded at that time. Roosevelt won 60.8% of the national popular vote, the second highest popular-vote percentage won by a U.S. presidential candidate since 1820.

This 1936 Democratic landslide increased the Democratic control of the Senate and House. In the Senate the Republicans were reduced to 17 seats. In the House the Democrats held about a 75% majority. The 1936 elections showed the continuing trust of the American people who believed that Roosevelt would guide the nation from depression. Despite setbacks, the people had faith in the New Deal and elected leaders who supported its measures.

This political summary, much of which was drawn from Wikipedia, is extensive since there is a need to recognize that the LCA leadership was strongly Republican and strongly anti-Union. After the depression hit the country, LCA had to battle Congress and the Administration as LCA opposed aspects of the National Economic Recovery Act, Social Security, union rights and changes in the seamen laws.

Brief Biography of J. S. Ashley

John Stanley Ashley was born in Pardeeville, WI, in 1856 and was drawn to a career in Great Lakes shipping; in 1900 and in the following years he was an outstanding leader in vessel operations and lake navigation. As marine manager for the M. A. Hanna Company during the Great War he directed the third largest fleet of 32 vessels. He was Chairman of the Great Lakes Protective Association from its inception in 1909 until February 1, 1939. In 1909 he was asked to serve on the LCA Board, the Executive Committee, and in 1917 he served as LCA Vice President. Upon the death of William Livingstone in 1925, Ashley became the President of LCA until 1930 when he was succeeded by Joseph S. Wood. Ashley died on July 29, 1941.

Brief Biography of A. F. Harvey

In 1930 Allyn Fitch Harvey became Chairman of the LCA Board in a short period of need during the Ashley presidency. He had served on the LCA Executive Committee for seventeen years. Mr. Harvey began his business life with Pickands, Mather, and upon the formation of the Pittsburgh Steamship Company in 1901 he was appointed as assistant to the president; and in 1924 he was elevated to president, succeeding the late Harry Coulby. He died in Cleveland on October 22, 1941.

Brief Biography of Joseph S. Wood

Joseph S. Wood was the nephew of Thomas Wilson, founder of the company that became the Wilson Marine Transit Company. Born in 1874, his career encompassed the transition from wooden vessels to steel and from sail to steam. He worked his way up the hawsepipe from seaman; he was given his first command at age 24 in 1898 and served as Captain for 14 years. He came ashore to become the marine superintendent in the Wilson Transit Company. He served as President of the Wilson Martine Transit Company from 1928 until early 1948. At the time of his death he served as LCA Chairman of the Board. Wood served within the LCA on the Shore Captains Committee from its inception in 1919 and as a member of the Board of Directors from 1926 until his death. In 1931 he was elected President of LCA until 1938 when he was succeeded by his son Alexander T. Wood.

LCA Organization

LCA President and Officers

During the J. S. Ashley and Joseph Wood periods the officers were L. C. Sabin, Vice President; Newton D. Baker, General Counsel; George A. Marr, Vice President and Treasurer. In 1936 Gilbert R. Johnson was appointed Secretary and in 1929 George Marr was elected to Vice President and Treasurer. On December 25, 1937 Newton Baker passed away.

L. C. Sabin, Vice President

Newton D. Baker, General Counsel, (Wikipedia, George Grantham Bain)

George Marr, Vice President and Treasurer

Gil Johnson, Secretary

Board of Directors

In 1926 there were 40 persons serving on the Board including all of the LCA officers and others, the majority drawn from among the leadership of the major member companies. Cleveland was the headquarters of many of the major members thus the Cleveland members of the Board numbered 32 while the remaining eight were from Buffalo, Pittsburgh and New York. In 1937 there were 42 Board members, of which eleven were not from Cleveland; these members had offices in Bethlehem, Buffalo, Chicago, Detroit, Pittsburgh, Rogers City and Sheboygan.

The Executive Committee

The most senior members of the major companies guided the policy developments and actions of LCA. Membership was usually long term. The LCA President chaired this committee with few exceptions, notably in 1930 when A. F. Harvey, Pittsburgh Steamship Company, became Chairman of the LCA Board during the Ashley presidency in a brief period of need, which goes unexplained. During the Ashley presidency, the Executive Committee consisted of eleven men, of whom eight served during his tenure. They were A. F. Harvey, J. S. Ashley, J. J. Boland, C. L. Hutchison, H. K. Oakes, A. E. R. Schneider, G. A. Tomlinson and H. S. Wilkinson. In 1926, seven of the eleven members were from Cleveland.

During the entire Ashley and J. S. Wood period the following leaders served on the Executive Committee: J. J. Boland, Harry Coulby (until his death in 1929), J. C. Evans, A. F. Harvey, C. L. Hutchinson, H. K. Oakes, A. E. R. Wilkinson, and H. S. Wilkinson. Joseph S. Wood joined the Committee in 1928. During the Joseph S. Wood period in 1934 the Executive Committee was enlarged from 11 members to 13 members and later to 25-27 members. Captain Wood had the experienced advice of many leaders in the industry.

Throughout the J. S. Wood period, Adam E. Cornelius, A. F. Harvey, A. E. R. Schneider and G. A. Tomlinson served. Others joining the Committee in 1934 that remained during the Wood tenure were John M. Gross, Elton Hoyt II, George M. Humphrey, John T. Kelly, W. W. Newcomet, and G. A. Tomlinson. Those who joined the Committee in 1935 who stayed on were

R. W. England, A. H. Ferbert, E. B. Greene, John T. Hutchinson, Warren C. Jones, F. I. Kennedy, Walton H. McGean, Frank C. Oakes, Crispin Oglebay, A. C. Sullivan, and George H. Warner. In 1937, twenty of the twenty-five members of the executive Committee were from Cleveland as were all the Officers.

The Economy and the impact on Tonnage Moved

Apart from the brief recession of 1921-22, the economic boom of the roaring 20s continued until 1929 when the LCA fleet carried more cargo in that year than at any time in history, 138.6 million tons. In 1929, the LCA membership carried more cargo than in the previous year with the same number of vessels due to an early thaw and opening of the season coupled with higher water levels that allowed vessels to load on average an additional eight inches over 1928 and a foot over 1925 when the water level was very low. The iron ore trade, which made up 52.7% of the bulk trades, had a new record for average loading of iron ore at 9,494 gross tons. As the grain trade fell off at the end of the season there was not the usual congestion at the Soo as ice didn't begin to form a blockade until November 29, 1928.

Although the nationwide depression started in late 1929, it began to be felt very severely in 1930 when the annual tonnage carried fell to 112.5 million net tons. Only the largest ships were generally in service; many small vessels never turned a wheel. In 1931 there was optimism expressed in the 1930 Annual Report when it was stated that 1929 was not as bad as the depression of 1921-22 when LCA vessels were idle much more of the time. The statement also noted that the last ten year average, including 1929, was 110.5 million tons. In 1930, the soft coal movement was brisk, moving 37 million tons upbound. Despite declining water levels, the average load of iron ore reached a new high of 9,594 gross tons/trip and iron loading dispatch had improved for the fifth straight year.

Nevertheless, the 1931 Annual Report, in a strangely worded comment, recognized that the depression was upon the nation. "The Industrial prostration that drastically reduced remunerative vessel operations in 1930 was even more acute throughout the navigation season of 1931, and brought about an average rate of fleet operations so low as to result in heavy absorption in the margin of profit." Only a few ships began operation before June first and only a few operated after October 15. Midsummer had only 66% of the fleet operating and 98 ore carriers in 1930 did not raise steam. The only bright spot in the year was the fact that not a single life or vessel was lost through stress of weather.

As with many others in the country, there was hope that the depression would end. It worsened in 1932. An annual tonnage figure of 42 million net tons had not been seen during the life of LCA. The Annual Report stated "The persistence with which the economic disturbance has held iron and steel making in its grip and has wielded adversely such direct influence upon trade in general that maximum requirements from the membership of the Association for the movement of iron ore, coal, grain, and limestone scarcely exceeded 140 ships... from a revenue earning point of view, 1932 was the most disastrous year encountered in the last quarter of a century." Coupled with that economic disaster, water levels were at the lowest point in 21 years. With the virtually drying up of the iron ore float, the independent fleets were hit very hard as the consuming fleets carried essentially all the iron ore. The self-unloaders carried the limestone and the Canadian fleets took almost all of the grain movement.

A ray of hope for coming out of the depression came in 1933 when the iron ore trade picked up from the previous year yet it was still down more than 50% from the highs of 8-10 years before and only reached 37% of the 1929 high. A summer rush of orders brought out 148 additional ships. The grain trade in U. S. bottoms continued in decline as the Canadian ships benefited from the preferential rate given to ships carrying grain to Canadian ports for shipment to the United Kingdom.

The 1934 navigation season began with a hope of significant recovery in the iron ore trade but the order books stalled mid-season. A drought spread across the Canadian and American wheat farms. Iron ore was moved from May through November; no ore moved in April and December. LCA members lamented that increased crew sizes, higher wages, the draught, low water levels and the static low demand in the float requirements conspired to make 1934 another bad year economically. In 1934 only 286 of the 399 LCA ships operated, fewer than in 1933.

The 1935 Annual Report stated "...under the influence of great artificial stimulation in 1933 and 1934 the business barometer changed so swiftly and irregularly that it was difficult to ascertain what economic gain, if any, accrued, but the fairly steady upward progression in 1935...has been the best since the depression began and affords a basis for tempered optimism..." While iron ore and stone increased, much of it being moved on consumer industry owned vessels, the independents suffered as the grain and coal trades were almost static. Of the 306 LCA vessels, the maximum number in service at one time was 186 and the maximum number carrying ore was 160.

In 1936 iron ore and bituminous coal shipments came back and the total float made it the best year since 1930. In 1937, tonnage moved increased to a level only 2.8% under the high of 1929. The greatest gain was an increase in nearly 20 million net tons of iron ore, a sign that industrial production in the nation had returned. Unfortunately grain trade continued in the doldrums: despite a bumper crop, lake shipments were the lowest since 1910 and receipts of grain in Buffalo were the lowest since 1888.

LCA Committees

The most important Committees were the Navigation/Shore Captains and the Welfare Plan Committees. There was no group identified as the Legislative Committee; it appears that the Executive Committee and the LCA Officers handled all legislative matters.

There does not seem to have been a formal committee on Public Relations. The person most directly responsible for many of the speeches and publications, such as the Bulletin and the Annual Report, was George A. Marr, LCA Secretary and Treasurer. The Annual Report continued to be printed in Detroit by the P. N. Bland Printing Company just as was done in the Livingstone period; the economic impact of the depression apparently called for a reduction in the publishing costs of the book by printing fewer pages, fewer photographs and a lower quality paper. In 1935, the Annual Report printing contract was given to the S.P. Mount Company, Cleveland. The Bulletin and other safety related publications was a communications function of the Welfare Plan Committee and the Officers.

There was no committee designated to be an environmental committee. During this period the major environmental issue seemed to deal with making certain that the dumping of coal ashes from the ships did not take place in the improved channels.

Legislative Matters

National Industrial Recovery Act (NIRA), Great Lakes Shipping Code

The NIRA in 1933 required the shipping industry to formulate a code of fair practices and competition. A tentative code was prepared by LCA General Counsel that was reviewed by members, modified and ultimately approved for submission to the NIRA Administrator on October 25, 1933. The statutory provision for this code called for collective bargaining; the LCA plan was to enable only the men employed on the operating ships to elect representatives. No right of representation was given to the unemployed seamen. It must be kept in mind that since 1909, LCA members maintained their operations without any labor contracts with any union.

In the meantime, coastal interests advocated a General Shipping Code under a General Code Authority made up of 14 members of which the Lakes would have one member. LCA demanded at public meetings that the Great Lakes, because of segregation and specialization of lake shipping, have a code independent of other geographical divisions. After many public meetings in 1933 and 1934 there was a failure to reach agreement with the deep sea interests; the Code was never adopted. George Marr, LCA Vice-President, prepared a comprehensive statement that outlined the relations with employees of vessels in the LCA membership. The comprehensive document supported Assembly Halls and the open shop principles that guided the LCA Welfare Plan. Emphasis was placed on the registration of seamen, referral of seamen, living condition on the vessels, safety programs to prevent injury, schools, ship's libraries, wages and savings plans, club rooms and death benefits.

Chicago Drainage Canal

In the 1920s and 30s, LCA was concerned with the need to increase tonnage moved through the channels; despite improved depths in some channels and ports the maximum draft was frequently restrained by low water levels. LCA supported the actions of various states to appeal to the Supreme Court to restrict the flow of water out of Lake Michigan by the Chicago Sanitary District.

This dispute reached the Supreme Court of the United States and was settled by a series of judicial decrees. In its 1925 decree, the high court stated that the diversion be limited to 8,500 cubic feet per second.

In 1926, the States of Wisconsin, Michigan, Minnesota, Indiana, Ohio, Pennsylvania and New York allied themselves in an injunction proceeding before the Supreme Court of the U.S. to restrain the State of Illinois and the Chicago Sanitary District in the diversion of water from Lake Michigan. The Court appointed the Honorable Charles Evans Hughes as a special master in chancery to take testimony and make a finding of fact and law and to report to the court with his recommendations.

On November 23, 1927, the Honorable Charles Evans Hughes made his report and conclusions to the Supreme Court as follows:

1. Complainants present a justifiable controversy.
2. That the State of Illinois and the Sanitary District of Chicago have no authority to make or to continue to make the diversion in question without the consent of the United States.
3. The Congress has the power to regulate the diversion; that is, to determine whether and to what extent it should be maintained.
4. That Congress has not directly authorized the diversion in question.
5. That Congress has conferred authority upon the Secretary of War to regulate the diversion, provided he acts in reasonable relation to the purpose of the delegated authority and not arbitrarily.
6. That the permit of March 3, 1925 is valid and effective according to its terms, the entire control of the diversion remaining with Congress.

On January 3, 1928 the states formally presented to the Supreme Court bills of exception to the findings and recommendations. Full details were reported in the 1929 LCA Annual Report.

A second decree in 1930 called for a three-step reduction of the diversion. The first reduction was to 6,500 cubic feet per second in 1930, followed by another reduction to 5,000 cubic feet per second by the end of 1935. The final reduction to 1,500 cubic feet per second was required by the end of 1938.

The St. Lawrence Waterway

On July 18, 1932 the U.S. and Canada signed a treaty to complete the St. Lawrence waterway to a depth of 27 feet. The treaty was referred to the Senate Committee on Foreign Relations. LCA strongly expressed disapproval and voiced that opposition at a hearing on November 16, 1932.

Grain Trade Restrictions

In 1932 the Welland canal was opened to vessels of 600 feet drawing 22 feet. At the same time the British Economic Conference Treaty provided for a six cent-per-bushel preference on Canadian wheat; this preference only would be granted if the wheat was carried on Canadian vessels. No transfer at American ports such as Buffalo was permitted in order to make sure that there was no mixing of American and Canadian grains; thus grain was no longer transferred to barges via the Erie Canal to New York City. These two factors caused the wheat cargoes to be shipped to Kingston, Toronto and Montreal to the detriment of Buffalo and Port Colborne. In 1934, a delegation of transship interests in New York went to London to appeal the rule to the Customs authorities. An agreement was reached that as long as the U.S. Customs provided a certificate of non-manipulation and exportation so as to preserve the Canadian source identity of the grain, the transshipments could take place in a U.S. port.

Regulation of Water Carriers

In 1934, following the completion of transportation studies called for by the Roosevelt Administration, bills providing for the regulation of water and motor carriers were introduced to both houses of Congress. The regulations would extend to common carriers, contract carriers and private carriers to varying degrees.

Welfare Plan Committee

This Committee was probably the most important of all the committees in the breadth and depth and long term nature of its work. The Chairman was George M. Steinbrenner during these periods. This Committee was responsible for:

1. Operation of the Assembly Rooms
2. Registration of seamen
3. Recommending scale of wages to be followed by all member companies
4. Training of unlicensed crew and officers in LCA schools
5. Maintenance of the Library at the Soo
6. Safety program
7. Bulletin publication
8. Payment of death and dismemberment benefits
9. Savings Plan promotion
10. Sanitation and health promotion on the ships
11. Continuation of a policy since 1909 that no member would sign contracts with labor unions.

Industrial Committee

This Committee was established in 1913 and consisted of six Masters and six Chief Engineers employed on the vessels. They met to review the work and recommendations of the ship board Safety Committees and to take actions that would reduce personal injuries and deaths aboard ships. In 1935 the Chairman was Chief Engineer George H. Emrey.

Assembly Rooms

Crew members seeking employment registered with the LCA Shipping Commissioners at the Assembly Halls. When the Master needed additional crew he made a phone call to the nearest Assembly Hall. LCA was proud to proclaim that the 15 Assembly Halls, managed by the LCA Commissioners, were open during the periods of ice delays at the beginning and end of the season to afford a comfortable place for seamen to enjoy each other's company in warm and clean surroundings. Victrola music and literature was available and the men could stow their gear in the baggage rooms. In the winter, many of the halls were open. The officers had special halls in several ports, including Cleveland, Buffalo and Detroit where dancing and other entertainment could take place.

When the depression hit hardest in 1931, jobs were scarce afloat and ashore. Men who had a job stayed on. In an effort to keep the experienced men in jobs, the hiring of inexperienced men was discouraged, registrations in the Assembly halls plummeted, officers were willing to take unlicensed positions and the wheelsmen and oilers took lesser positions. In 1932, considering the reduced demand for seamen, the Rooms at Erie, Conneaut, Fairport, Lorain, Gary and Milwaukee were closed. Only seven Assembly Rooms were maintained open with reduced staff and reduced salaries: Buffalo, Ashtabula, Cleveland, Toledo, Detroit, South Chicago and Duluth. These Assembly Rooms were kept open in the winter of 1932-33, as was the Assembly Room at Marine City. The Officer rooms at Buffalo, Conneaut, Cleveland, Marine City and Port Huron also were open in the winter. In July 1933, due to the increased number of vessels in operation, Assembly Rooms in Conneaut, Lorain and Erie were reopened. For the entire year of 1934, 1935 and 1936 the rooms at Buffalo, Conneaut, Ashtabula, Cleveland, Lorain, Toledo, Detroit, South Chicago and Duluth were kept open. During the shipping season the rooms at Erie and Gary were opened. Winter club rooms were available at Algonac, Marine City and Port Huron.

Registrations at the Assembly Rooms were the 2nd highest in LCA history in 1926 with 25,844 men registered, the lowest during this period was 6,433 in 1932 as the depression caused so many ships to be laid up. In 1934, there were 11,068 men registered and this number approximated the number of men employed since the LCA policy was to discourage registration of those not actually employed. In the 1930s the average annual number of men referred was only 7,704.

In 1937, despite major improvements in tonnage moved and jobs available, many men did not register as the new Seaman Laws were in effect. There may have been a misunderstanding that sailors no longer needed to register in order to obtain a continuous discharge book, a book previously issued by LCA and at that time was issued by the government.

The 1936 Bulletin noted that W. M. Ford, LCA Shipping Commissioner at Conneaut died on September 21. He was the dean of the Commissioners having been appointed Commissioner on September 27, 1904; he served nearly 32 years. He was succeeded by his assistant Carl O. Kresin.

Impact of the Seaman's Act of 1936

In 1936 the amended Seamen's Act of 1920 brought many new requirements for the Lakes trade. Government issued Certificates of Service were required for deck, engine and galley crew; on all vessels of 100 gross tons and upward a three watch system was required; and government inspectors were to inspect crew quarters to ascertain they were of approved size, were properly ventilated and were equipped with proper plumbing and mechanical appliances.

Concerning Certificates of Service, one of the functions of the Assembly Rooms was to register seamen into the LCA Welfare Plan and to issue documents such as a Certificate of Membership in the Welfare Plan and Discharges, known as continuous discharge books, to show to the captain when signing on the ship. As these books also allowed the captain to make permanent notations into the book as to the quality of service of the seamen, they were often considered by some seamen as black list books and, in union parlance, were called 'fink books'. On the national level the unions petitioned Congress to modify many of the seamen laws and on December 25, 1936, a law came into effect on the Lakes that only allowed the government to issue a continuous discharge book or certificate of service; and, it prohibited other parties from issuing these books, thus ending the 25 year history of the LCA book that helped men maintain a record of employment for purposes of upgrade. A significant decrease in registrations in the Welfare plan took place in 1937, perhaps since seamen may have believed that other elements of the Welfare Plan had terminated. The Bulletin in 1937 encouraged the men to register with the Welfare Plan in order to obtain the Plan benefits.

Continuous Discharge Book, Able Seaman

Continuous Discharge Book, Able Seaman

Wages and Working Conditions

Throughout this period of time the Welfare Plan activities continued and, in the view of LCA, maintained labor peace through payment of wages better than seamen received on other coasts, provided assembly halls for the men in 15 ports, stressed safe working conditions, a Saving Plan and provided opportunities for education and assistance in getting licenses, naturalization papers and hospital services. From 1926 through 1931, LCA continued recommending a wage scale that was set in 1923 despite reduced freight rates for members that had prevailed in 1923. Of course one must recognize that on average the vessels were larger and with improved water levels many vessels carried more cargo and thus earned a higher gross return per voyage. However with the depression hurting the balance sheet of members the LCA recommended a reduction in wages of 20% for those below the grade of licensed officer. LCA contended that this wage was still better than wages paid to seamen elsewhere in the U.S. In 1933 the wage rate was maintained until business picked up substantially in midsummer; effective September 1, 1933, a 10% increase in wages was given to all crew including officers.

In 1934 the Executive Committee called for an increased crew on all the vessels in the A, B, and C classes. These ships required the added employment of a third mate, a third assistant engineer, a wheelsman, a watchman, a deckhand and where necessary a porter. In essence this was the acceptance of a three watch system on all but the smaller LCA vessels. The Executive Committee also recommended another 10% increase in wages for all crew members including officers, even though the economy did not warrant such an increase, they did so "...in harmony with the announced advance in wages of the steel industry and also out of a desire on the part of the lake carriers to co-operate fully with the policy of the administration at Washington to increase both the pay and the number of employees in the interest of recovery."

The 1934 Annual Report notes that due to the large number of unemployed men who came to the lake ports seeking jobs, there was labor unrest; it was fomented, according to the LCA directors, by outsiders from other coasts who had never sailed on the Lakes. The report continued "... whatever success they had in the disturbance of unemployed men, it did not in great degree infect the regular unemployed seamen nor did it reach the men aboard the vessels."

The next wage increase came with the increased demand for tonnage to be moved in 1937, an approximate 20% increase for the unlicensed personnel and a 10-15% increase for the officers. Wages were then at the highest level since 1921.

Winter Schools and Training

Classes in navigation and marine engineering were held in Cleveland under the direction of David Gaehr (since 1916) assisted by James E. Gatons, George W. Heckel and Alan Mason; and in later years by Charles R. Dennis and Arthur E. Urdal for engineering and for the mates it was Captains John C. Murray, Clayton A. Martin and Lloyd W. Smith. In Marine City navigation was taught by Captain N. M. Hetherington and engineering by Ralph Britz. In 1937 there were several changes in instructors at the schools. William A. Fearer joined the navigation school in Cleveland. The Port Huron navigation school was under the direction of Captain George R. Manuel and he was assisted by Captain George Gay. The Cleveland Engineering School had assistance from Hubert F. Parker and James J. Nolan. The Marine City Marine Engineering School was assisted by Arthur A. Baker.

LCA Engineering class 1917

A student aid fund, established in 1923, was available to provide loans to students who otherwise might have to drop out of class to help families. The Welfare Plan sold all marine engineering and navigation books to the men during the year at cost in order that they would be prepared for the winter schools. Books on English, composition, grammar, spelling and First Aid were also available. Despite the depression and the dim prospects of gaining advanced employment, there was a demand by the seamen for upgrading and the schools were open in 1931 and 1932. However in the winter of 1932-33 the schools were closed until the winter of 1933-34.

A special need for education came about by a legislative change that required all able bodied seamen to obtain certificates as lifeboatman. LCA published nearly five thousand booklets titled *Lifeboat Knowledge* for the use of the men in studying for the certificate exam. The men purchased them at a nominal price of 25 cents postage paid, far less than the 60 cents cost of production.

Lifeboat training Cleveland Harbor

Library at Sault Ste. Marie

The library was considered a function of the Welfare Plan. Since 1920, LCA helped finance the service of the free library operated by the American Merchant Marine Library Association at the Soo. Books and Victrola records were provided to all merchant ships of U.S. registry, to Coast Guard ships, stations, lightships, and lighthouses, to U. S. Corps of Engineers ships, and to workers at the Pittsburgh Coal Company fueling dock. The library was usually open from May 1 to November 30 on a 16 hour service six days/week unless economic conditions reduced traffic significantly. Each ship received a box of 30 books and special book orders were available. In 1927, the men on the ships were asked to show their appreciation for the library services by making voluntary library contributions through the master. In that year the seamen contributed $3,315. Even in the depression year of 1930, crews donated $4,160 and in 1932 they contributed $3,432. LCA suspended its payment of support in 1932 due to the depression but continued a contribution in later years.

Seaman Library at Sault

Savings Plan

Records were maintained by LCA of the deposits seamen authorized to be deposited in the Cleveland Trust Company (since 1911), the Guardian Trust Company (since 1923), the Marine National Bank of Ashtabula (since 1924), and the Central National Bank of Cleveland (since 1927) and the Buffalo Savings Bank (reported in the 1929 annual report). These banks had established a lake marine savings department for seamen as requested by the Welfare Plan. In 1928 Security National Bank of Sheboygan, WI, offered banking services to lake sailors but did not report the deposit activity to LCA. Some of the banks offered cash prizes to the ships that increased savings.

J.W. Westcott Co. Mail Delivery Service

The Westcott service began as a marine reporting service at Detroit in 1875 with subsequent branch offices at Amherstburg and Port Huron. The delivery of mail to passing vessels was organized in Detroit in 1895 under contract with the U.S. Post Office, significant additional delivery of vessel supplies and personnel developed over time. LCA began providing a subsidy for this service in 1927 through 1936. In 1937, Westcott resumed operations as an independent contractor and was financed by the U.S. Post Office and the LCA. LCA payments ranged from a low of $16,200 in 1937 to a high of $50,000 in 1957, 1959 and 1960. In 1969, the contract payment was $29,000.

Ship Safety

The Welfare Plan administered safety committees since 1918 that were made up of six members of the crew on participating ships. In 1926, there were 204 committees on different steamers. The committees recommended improvements in safety and made reports to LCA. The objective was to reduce the number of accidents, injuries and fatalities that occurred on the ships; there were high instances of falling into cargo holds, falling overboard, falling from a mast to the deck or the deck to a dock, or being caught in cables or machinery. Small bonuses were paid to committees where there were no accidents that caused a seaman to leave the vessel during the season.

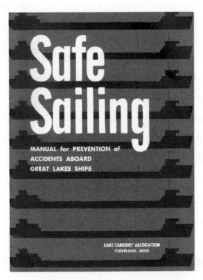

Safe Sailing Pamphlet

The Welfare Committee in 1926 worked with the Industrial, Navigation and Shore Captains Committees to publish a revised book of *Recommendations for the Prevention of Accidents* that was approved by the Executive Committee.

In 1934 the ship safety committees concentrated on efforts to reduce the personal injury and death caused by the most common accidents: drowning as a result of falling off the ladder or dock.

Use ladder with both hands free;
use bag for hauling up luggage

Health

Health issues, disease prevention and sanitation were part of the responsibilities of the Welfare Plan Committee. Over the years the Committee worked to improve the drinking water by determining safe lake locations for pumping it in and for treating water to prevent typhoid fever. The proper care of milk, ice, meat and other food stuffs from the vendor to the storeroom was vastly improved. Working with the USPHS, LCA through the Bulletin and shipboard notices advised crews of the availability of prophylactic tubes, a term for condoms that is not commonly used today.

Death Benefits

Since the Welfare plan started in 1909, burial benefits or long term disability payments were made to the beneficiaries of men who were registered with the plan and who at the time of death or dismemberment were employed on the ships. Payments were also made to beneficiaries to allow Christian burial for deceased indigent seamen who, while unemployed at the time, had been registered with LCA.

Summary of Statistics that follow In the period 1926 through 1937, despite the efforts of the Safety Committees onboard ships, the Welfare Plan education efforts on the ships using Bulletins and posters, and the work of the Industrial Committee, seamen continued to die at alarming rates while working on the ships, primarily from falls and from drowning. A review of over 120 fatalities in this 12 year period onboard LCA member ships shows that sinkings and standings were not the deaths to be feared. About 50 men fell from the ship, staging, dock or ladder and drowned; 23 fell to death in cargo holds; 27 died from a variety of other accidents in the engine room or with cargo gear; nine fell or were washed overboard and drowned; five died in train, trolley or car accidents while ashore; and two were murdered. A rundown of this unfortunate aspect of life while working in a dangerous environment follows.

In 1926 death benefits were paid to 16 beneficiaries, including families of four fatalities that occurred in 1925, and five payments were made to provide Christian burial for seamen that died of natural causes. Fatality causes in 1926 were: gas asphyxiation, scalded, three fell into cargo hold, one fractured skull and one washed overboard.

In 1927, a number of payments were made, many for past years accidents. In 1927 two were killed by trains; three fell off the dock and drowned; three fell off stage planks or ladder and drowned; two fell into the cargo hold; one died of heat prostration; one died of a fractured skull (cause not stated); and one was assassinated (this was the term used for nature of accident with no further details).

In 1928 payments in order to provide a Christian burial, payments were made to families of eight indigent seamen who died of natural causes or injury while unemployed. Falls from the deck, scaffold or dock to the water, from ladders took the lives of eight seamen again in 1928; falls into cargo holds took the lives of three; engine room deaths from scalding and turbine explosion took two; one was lost overboard and two bodies were found in rivers; and one seaman was killed ashore by a streetcar.

In 1929, in addition to payment for burial of indigent seamen, payments for fatalities and dismemberments were still at very high levels. Falls from the deck, scaffold or dock to the water and from ladders took the lives of seven seamen again in 1929; there were no falls into cargo holds; two died from fractured skulls; engine room deaths from various causes took four; two were lost overboard; three died as a result of a vessel stranding; and one seaman was killed ashore by a train.

In 1930 many of the same causes of accident took the lives of 14 seamen while on ship duty and four others died ashore. In 11 cases a fall of one kind or another took place; five fell overboard and drown; two fell from ladders and drowned; one fell off a dock and drowned; two fell into cargo holds; two were hit by a train; a 2nd mate was crushed by a magnet and another man was caught in an unloading rig; one was burned in a fire and another fell into a dry dock.

In 1931 falls contributed to the majority of deaths, three fell into the cargo hold; two fell overboard and one fell down a stairway; and a 2nd mate died of a fractured skull (cause was not stated). The most heinous death was the murder of Ole Haroldsen, First Mate, who was serving as shipkeeper on the Charles S. Hebard in Duluth harbor. He was robbed and murdered; while the LCA offered a reward of $1,000, no one assisted in finding the murderer.

In 1932 due to reduced operations only one fatality was reported during the season when an ordinary seaman fell off the dock and drowned. Earlier in the year a shipkeeper fell from the boarding ladder and drowned. The Plan paid for the burial of seven unemployed indigent seamen and other active crew members who died of natural causes.

In 1933 falls continued to be the primary cause of death for seamen. Five men fell overboard or from a ladder and drowned; and one fell into a cargo hold.

In 1934 there continued to be deaths caused by the same accidents as in the past. Three seamen fell into cargo hold, two fell from staging or a ladder and drown, one fell overboard at sea and drowned, and one died of gas asphyxiation.

In 1935 death came to seamen from the same types of accidents: three drowned, including a Captain and Chief Engineer; two fell into a cargo holds; three fell off ship, mast or ladder; one was caught in machinery and one was killed ashore by an auto.

1936 was not a better year for fatalities from the same causes; five men fell off the ship ladder or dock and drowned; two fell into the cargo hold; one was lost at sea and another died in an auto/train collision.

In 1937 the report states that despite improved training and the safety committee efforts "…through mental lapses fatal injuries were sustained in 1937 by four men who fell either off the ladder or into the cargo hold." Two other seamen drowned, one falling overboard at sea, and another died of burns.

The Bulletin

The Bulletin of the Lake Carriers' Association and the Great Lakes Protective Association, known simply as the Bulletin was first published in 1911 by the Welfare Plan for the purpose of providing masters and engineers with the workings of the LCA and GLPA and to promote safe vessel operations. Within a few years the Bulletin developed into a vehicle to influence all the men working on the LCA ships in matters of safety and the other objectives of the Welfare Plan. Copies were sent to the officers and the safety committee and they were encouraged to read them, pass them around and at the end of the year to return them to LCA Secretary

George Marr for binding so as they could be returned to the ship for use as a reference library.

During the Ashley tenure the Bulletin was a black and white glossy paper pamphlet issued seven times from May through November unless the economic recessions caused vessels to come out late or lay up early. By today's standards the Bulletin was a drab corporate communication only occasionally interspersed with poems, wit, humor and sea lore. There were no color images. The topics of most interest to LCA and GLPA were safety, safety committees, navigation and engineering schools, Sault Library, sobriety, savings plans, sanitation, vessel and personnel accident information and the locations of the Assembly Halls and the USPHS hospitals. Some editions also contained brief obituaries of captains, engineers or LCA leadership, medical and first aid advice, navigation related information and instruction on new equipment such as Radio Direction Finders, and pen and ink drawings of deck or engine department safety features.

LCA political positions such as opposition to the La Follette seaman protection bill were also included. There was information directed at the alien crew members in order to help them obtain citizenship.

Cartoons teaching about elements of the Welfare Plan began to appear in 1929. Cartoons offered by crew members such as Ray H. Knight, Second Mate, William G. Mather and Russ Taylor, William Edenborn were printed in the Bulletin. Cross word puzzles also were started in 1929 using puzzles submitted by crew members such as Fred Hoyt, Second Mate. Black and white photos appeared more frequently in the 1930s showing how to build safety devices, such as how to make and use a device to prevent the chain type hatch cover from tipping into the cargo hold, nick-named "the grief saver."

In 1932 due to the depression and the need to cut costs, the Bulletin was not published in that year.

In the July 1933 Bulletin, LCA published an explanation about the intent of the National Industrial Recovery Act in order to counter an attempt by labor unions to organize the Great Lakes sailors. A letter from General Hugh S. Johnson was quoted as follows: "It is not the function or the purpose of the Administration to organize either industry or labor." It was noted that this statement was made in order to refute statements made by labor agents that it was the intention of the Government to support general unionization of labor. General Johnson declared such statements to be without foundation; and that any statements that newly formed company unions will be favored was also untrue. He went on to say that it was the intention of the government to see that all labor, organized and unorganized, got a square deal. Johnson continued "Labor in any industry has the right to organize and bargain collectively. The law also recognizes the right of individual workers to bargain for their own conditions of employment."

LCA President J. S. Wood noted "... that there was a satisfactory relationship between employers and employees on the Great Lakes... which need not be disturbed...no employee need feel obligated to join any union."

In 1934 the Bulletin published a series of articles to educate the men on the ships about the LCA explaining the leadership roles; and J. S. Wood emphasized the fact that there were 396 ships enrolled by 63 companies in the LCA.

Navigation and Shore Captains Committees

Although it was not described as such in the Annual Reports, in the July 1935 Bulletin, the Navigation Committee was described as the Aids to Navigation Committee having been organized 23 years ago in 1912. This committee consisted of twelve active masters who met in the LCA Offices with the Shore Captains committee at the end of the season to act upon matters which pertained to the general good of the lake trade. In 1935 the Chairman was Captain Herman Wendorf, Cleveland Cliffs Iron Company. The Shore Captains Committee was established in 1919 to deal with any safe navigation issue that could not be deferred until the Navigation Committee met at the end of the season. The Chair in 1935 was Captain R. W. England, Interstate Steamship Company.

Separate Courses

After recognizing that there was a complete absence of collisions in 1925 when the separate courses were adhered to on Lakes Huron and Superior, LCA approved separate courses for Lake Michigan. The committee investigated cases where collisions took place when masters did not adhere to these separate courses where ever they were established.

Radio Telegraph (Wireless) and Radio Telephone

According to J. D. Cain, President of Lorain Electronics, while wireless was not required on Great Lakes vessels, by 1908 three merchant ships were equipped and by 1913 the number of equipped ships was 40. By 1935, the peaks of wireless activity on the lakes, 195 ships were equipped. In the mid-30s Lorain Telephone Co. was awarded an experimental license for a ship to shore radio telephone station that became WMI, a public service coastal harbor station. In 1934 the Wilson Marine Transit William C. Atwater was equipped with a radio telephone; and, as that proved very successful, the entire fleet was so equipped. There was a need for a structured and orderly development for the other fleets, so in 1936 LCA engaged C. M. Jansky, consulting Radio and Electronic Engineer to promote and assist in development of a safety distress maritime radio telephone system.

Captain George Rapp calling from Lake Superior

Radio Beacons were first installed in June 1925 and in the months that followed six others were in service. This navigation improvement was to become extensively used on the Great Lakes. At the close of 1927 there were 19 radiobeacons in operation on the Great Lakes, 18 of which were installed by the U.S. Government from Duluth to Buffalo and one by the Canadian government at Southeast Shoal. In 1927 there were 262 vessels equipped with radio direction finders (RDF) and during the winter it was expected that 100 more vessels would be so equipped with RDF. The Bulletins issued in 1927 had extensive instruction as to the use of this navigation aid.

Weather broadcasting of storm warnings was transmitted in 1926 on radiotelegraph and radiophone was carried out by many stations around the Great Lakes but the principal telegraphic stations were the naval station at Great Lakes, IL, and the Radio Corporation of America (RCA) at Chicago. At the same time there were 91 stations along the Great Lakes coast lines that displayed storm warning signal flags by day and lanterns by night. While it may sound unlikely today, there was also a U.S. Coast Guard service provided at lookout stations 4 and 5 in the St. Marys River where by megaphone the downbound ships could ask for weather forecasts between 8 and 11 am.

U. S. Navy radio stations were equipped to furnish radio bearings upon request and in 1926, commercial ships made over 6,000 requests, an increase of 44% over 1925. Of interest in the 1926 LCA annual report it was noted that "The studies of the Navy department indicate that in order to exercise proper strategic control of lake shipping, ten U. S. Navy radio stations are needed on the Great Lakes."

The Committees also concerned themselves with other important matters such as:

- Improvements to dimensions of connecting channels and ports in the Great Lakes.
- Prohibition of the use of flood lights while navigating in the rivers in order not to blind the oncoming traffic.
- Establishment of new aids to navigation and improving old aids.
- Loading Drafts.
- Rules for navigation of St. Marys River effective June 1, 1932 during the improvement of the West Neebish Channel, and special

- rules for the Amherstburg Channel when the Livingstone Channel was improved and closed as well as after the channel reopened.
- Straightening and deepening the Cuyahoga River.
- Revision of the station bills for lifeboat and fire drills to meet the requirements of the Steamboat Inspection Service
- Opposed many of the proposed regulations for Great Lakes vessels that stemmed from the disasters on the Atlantic coast such as the Morro Castle and the Mohawk.
- Promotion of the installation of Gyro Compasses. In 1936 Sperry Gyroscope Company stated that nearly 300 or nearly 25% of all the merchant marine gyro compasses were in operation on the Great Lakes.
- Recommendations for the length of tow lines between towing steamers and barges when in the channels

Ice Operations

This section on ice operations is included with the Navigation/Shore Captains work since it was a vital part of their work. LCA recognized that with member resources alone, they could not keep the shipping channels open at the beginning and end of the navigation seasons to move the traffic so essential to the economy of America; LCA developed a consistent policy to ask for USCG and COE vessel assistance when needed.

In 1926 the opening of the season was hampered by heavy ice formations. The Sault Ste. Marie, Michigan, locks opened on April 29. The Harvester was again the first ship to clear, leaving Chicago on April 24, she encountered solid ice in the Straits and 24" thick ice at Round Island, finally making it to Detour on April 28. Whitefish Bay was also thick with ice and thus she did not make it to open water on Lake Superior until 1 pm on May 1st. In order to keep the channels open the whaleback steamers Henry Cort and J. B. Neilson made trips between the Sault and Whitefish Point from May 5 until May 10. On the lower lakes, eastern end of Lake Erie was clogged solid with ice from Westfield to Buffalo, NY. This caused the worst ice blockade of Buffalo and Port Colborne in fifty years. Normal sailing conditions into Buffalo did not start until May 25.

The end of the 1926 season was the most threatening that LCA ever had to deal with; it involved 247 vessels. Despite the engagement of the tugs L.C. Sabin, Illinois, Alabama and Iowa, ships were still stuck in the St. Marys River. LCA engaged the car ferry Sainte Marie on December 4 at which time there were 60 downbound and 25 upbound vessels ice bound in the St. Marys River with the thermometer reading 12 below zero. LCA directed Captain F. A. Bailey to take sole charge of the icebreaking operation. Several ships in succession were caught in the Rock Cut and swung across the channel. On the morning of December 9, over 100 vessels were moving. To alleviate fuel shortages LCA ordered the J. J. Turner to discharge part of her coal cargo at Kemps Dock. By December 10 another blockage occurred in the West Neebish holding up 80 vessels. Three additional tugs came to assist—the General from Detour and the Canadian tugs Strathbogie and Murray Stewart. The weather continued to deteriorate and many vessels returned to the Canadian head of the lakes and to the Sault to winter over there. On the lower lakes the situation was also dire. The car ferry Marquette and Bessemer No. 2 was engaged to assist many vessels. Many vessels were ice bound also in the New York State Barge Canal and the St. Lawrence River.

In 1927, an almost identical ice blockade occurred at the close of the navigation season. Twenty-five vessels cleared Fort William on November 30 before the expiration of regular insurance; on December 5, 26 more vessels departed Fort William and another big fleet departed on December 9 when the temperature was twenty degrees below zero. Lake Superior gales and extremely low temperatures delayed the fleets; on December 9, the Middle Neebish was clogged, not permitting any further use of that channel; two tugs were engaged to move traffic through the West Neebish Channel; on December 11 with tugs at work, LCA again engaged Captain F. A. Bailey to take charge. The wrecker Favorite was engaged and the whaleback steamer James B. Eads was leading small convoys down but became ice bound. Despite prodigious effort by all the tugs and the Favorite, on December 14 through 17 it proved impossible to open either channel. Captain Bailey called for all operations to cease. Twenty two grain steamers were laid up at the Soo for the winter.

Tug Favorite

Tug General

In 1928 the opening of the season was just as bad as the St. Marys River had 18-24 inches of ice. The Eads with a full load of grain was still ice bound at the lower end of the West Neebish channel. The wrecking vessel Favorite and the tug General began working up the river on April 11 and finally broke the Eads free on April 25. Some vessels began to work their way up this down bound channel and by April 30 some of the wintered over grain ships began to steam downbound. The locks opened on May 3. Lake Erie fared no better as the eastern end was clogged with heavy ice until May 7. The end of the sailing season was just the opposite of the previous two years as summer sailing seemed to prevail with temperatures in the high 30s at the Soo and in many Lake Superior ports.

In 1929 the opening of the season was met with milder weather and the locks opened on April 14. The closing days were as severe as in past years but LCA, learning from the past years, was prepared. On November 28 the temperature in Duluth was 16 below zero; and at the Sault the temperature was 8 below zero. On November 29 LCA dispatched Captain C. O. Rydholm to take charge of operations at the Soo. Four tugs were procured to provide convoy escort in the river. The effort was a success and with improving temperatures the icebreaking operation in the St. Marys River was discontinued. The cold weather and ice blockades moved to the St. Clair River where it was necessary to engage tugs to move the ice bound ships. Fortunately, as the grain trade fell off at the end of the season, there was not the large number of grain ships transiting in December as there were in the previous two years.

The 1935 Annual Report noted that the opening of the season was well executed and successful thus establishing a new milestone in procedures. At the request of the oil tanker and paper carrier interests, the USCG cutter Escanaba departed Grand Haven on March 27 with the objective of opening Lake Michigan, the Straits and to the open water in Lake Huron. She worked until April 11 until navigation could be two way in the Straits. In the meantime, tankers began running April 4 while paper carriers and colliers passed through on April 11.

USCG cutter Escanaba assists traffic

In 1936 the Escanaba attempted to perform the same service battling 14 inches of hard blue ice. Within two days of operation she broke a propeller blade; she went to Manitowoc for repairs, returned to the ice and broke a second blade. At the end of the season winter came early. On October 23 Duluth recorded 10 degrees above zero and 4 degrees at Port Arthur. Ice formed in the St. Marys and vessels were assisted by the tugs Iowa and Sabin until the Escanaba came to assist.

In 1937 despite balmy weather conditions in the Lake Erie range that allowed vessels to operate in February and March in limited trades, the grip of winter returned to the northern parts of the lakes just as the floats of iron ore and coal were needed to be in full swing. In addition to the cutters Escanaba and Tahoma that were deployed in various ports and the Straits, several other icebreaking assets were engaged by LCA. The wrecking tug Favorite and the smaller tug Iowa worked the St. Marys River; the Chief Wawatam worked the Straits and elsewhere as needed. While the locks opened on April 8 and the Straits were open to navigation on April 10, icebreaking assistance was needed through April 17. The close of the season had the greatest difficulty in the Detroit River and western Lake Erie; this was the first time blockades occurred there since December 1918. The USCG cutters Tahoma and Frederick E. Lee were dispatched to assist the vessels.

Fleet Engineers Committee

This Committee, also known as the Fleet Engineers Association in the 1935 Bulletin, was made up of 15 former chief engineers and they met to discuss the mechanical operation of the ships and ship construction. They met periodically with the officials of the Marine Inspection and Navigation for the Great Lakes District to discuss boilers, valves, tubes and welding as the government issued new regulations on the inspection of boilers.

Vessel Construction and Modernization Because of the depression, there were no new ships ordered until the winter of 1936-37 when construction began in three shipyards on the lakes. Three ships were completed that winter and three others were launched. The use of electric arc welding on the hulls began to predominate on many vessels.

Vessel Losses

- In 1926 for the ninth year none of the LCA vessels were lost in a gale. No lives were lost in the bulk freight trade; however 15 other vessels, some of Canadian registry and mostly of wood or composite construction, nine vessels under 1,000 gross tons, were lost in the Lakes or the Gulf of St. Lawrence.
- In 1927 there were a number of vessel losses, many of which were Canadian. The only vessel enrolled with LCA that was lost was the E. W. Oglebay when she went aground in a gale on December 8 ten miles east of Marquette. The crew of 24 was rescued by the Coast Guard and the tug Columbia.
- In 1929 the only vessels lost were through stranding.
- In 1930 only three small vessels were lost; however in one case 20 seamen and a passenger woman and child died. In a storm on September 26, the last sailing vessel, Our Son, was sunk off Big Sable Point in Lake Michigan,

Schooner Our Son, Last Sailing Vessel to Ride the Upper Lakes, Foundered on Lake Michigan, September 26, 1930.

- In 1932 there were five complete vessel losses, four of which were old and destroyed by fire. The John J. Boland, Jr. was lost in a gale in Lake Erie ten miles off of Barcelona; four lives were lost.

- In 1935 a Norwegian flag ship Viator suffered in a T-bone collision with the Ormidale due to fog and conflicting whistle signals between Great Lakes Pilot Rules and the International Rules. Fortunately there was no loss of life, as the master of the Ormidale, whose vessel's prow struck the Viator amidship, tearing a deep hole in her, kept the vessels joined until all the crew of Viator was taken aboard; at which time he backed off and the Viator sunk in deep water south of Thunder Bay Island.
- In 1936, 12 vessels and 54 lives were lost; of these, two sand carriers shipped water into their loaded holds and 34 lives were lost.

Livingstone Monument, Belle Isle, Detroit

Memorial to the Late William Livingstone

The Board of LCA in 1927 planned for a memorial to the late William Livingstone who had served the LCA as President for over 25 years. The members agreed to provide approximately $50,000, half of the cost over the period of the work that was estimated to take three years. The monument was to be erected in Belle Isle Park and the other half of the cost was to be paid by the citizens of Detroit. The initial plan was to provide for a stone lighthouse to serve as a range light and a life sized bronze statue of Livingstone.

The work was completed in time to permit the commissioning of the light at the opening of the 1930 navigation season but the formal dedication took place on October 17, 1930 on the fifth anniversary of Livingstone's death. The lighthouse is built of Georgia marble, ornamental, yet dignified in design and is surmounted by a gilt bronze lantern, 58 feet above lake level; the lighthouse is of 11,500 candlepower and is visible for 15 miles. The lower elevation has a bronze bas relief portrait of Livingstone and a bronze tablet honoring him.

A large gathering of Detroit city officials, the steamship community, members of the Livingstone family and many of his personal friends were in attendance. A detachment of marines was present and a squadron of airplanes from Selfridge Field executed a series of maneuvers over the monument. The structure was presented by the chairman of the committee to the city of Detroit with pledges of proper maintenance and the Bureau of Lighthouses agreed that the light would be operated by the federal government for the benefit of navigation.

Other Key Events of Period

The 1926 annual report stated that 1926 was another banner year for grain shipments but it was the stone trade of 12.6 million net tons that exceeded expectation by surpassing the 12.1 million net tons grain trade.

The 1930 Annual Report noted that the Welland Ship Canal improvements were completed by November 19 when vessels drawing 18 feet were admitted for up and downbound traffic. Passage from Port Colborne to Port Weller took 7.5 hours. The first of the lake freighters now could pass through with grain to Toronto.

The 1932 Annual Report noted that the USCG Cutter Escanaba was launched on September 7, 1932 at Defoe in Bay City and the 1934 Annual Report noted the USCG Cutter Tahoma was commissioned on October 22, 1934 and stationed in Cleveland for rendering assistance to marine commerce and for enforcement of federal laws and regulations. The Tahoma was also built at Defoe and was generally similar to the Escanaba.

USCG cutter Escanaba

USCG cutter Tahoma

The July 1933 Bulletin indicated that the USCG patrol service below Sailors Encampment was discontinued so far as stopping the upbound vessels in times of obscurity of vision. The Bulletin in 1934 also indicated that three USCG patrol boats were transferred from the Coast and assigned to the Lower Lakes for permanent station; they were built at Bay City in 1926, were 110 feet long and 23 feet wide. The Eagle was stationed at Charlotte, NY, the Petrel at Erie PA, and the Patriot at Cleveland.

The May 1936 Bulletin noted that the Grays Reef Lightship was to be decommissioned from service on Lake Michigan when the Grays Reef Light Station was completed. This would be the last lightship on Lake Michigan.

Chapter Four

Alexander T. Wood
President 1938-1946

Alexander Wood, LCA President

Economic/Political Climate during Pre-War and World War II Years

The period of A.T. Wood's leadership encompassed almost a decade when America came out of the deep economic depression of the 1930s and began to produce manufactured goods on a post-recession and pre-wartime level. This growing economy was followed by the World War II years when record tonnages were shipped to meet the military demands of the world. This period included a short time of reconstruction after the World War but that was to be only a brief period of relative peace before the Cold War and Korean War.

The depression seemed to be over in 1937, even though vessel traffic in 1938 was substantially down from 1937. In 1938, there were only 239 member vessels in operation out of a membership of 374. The 1938 tonnage of 75 million net tons was the lowest moved since 1934. World War II in Europe was said to begin in September 1939, but the war began in 1935 when Italy invaded Ethiopia and the war was in full progress in 1938 when Germany unilaterally annexed Austria on March 12, 1938. Then within a few months, Hitler demanded the autonomy of the Sudetenland in Czechoslovakia as well as other demands; unfortunately the European countries of Great Britain and France chose not to seriously challenge Hitler. On September 21, 1938, Czechoslovakia capitulated and then was required to adhere to territorial claims of Poland and Hungary.

The beginnings of the World War in the Pacific may be said to have begun when Japan invaded Manchuria in 1931 and then clashed with the Chinese military in 1937. In that year the Japanese attacked and destroyed an American naval vessel Panay and American merchant ships in the Yangtze River. The United States was not in any mood to participate in the wars in Europe or Asia, thus in America and in the Great Lakes, business was as usual until the pace of industrial activity picked up in support of the Lend Lease Programs and National Defense production.

These war years saw the Great Lakes maritime industry expand significantly to deliver the cargo required. This was possible since the government recognized that industry executives could be trusted to decide the optimum way to deliver the goods for the war machine as well as the civilian economy. The government built additional ships when needed and when the war was over, and cargo delivered in 1946 fell precipitously, the government assisted the industry in scrapping the surplus vessel tonnage.

Biography of Alexander T. Wood

Alexander T. Wood was Vice President of Wilson Marine Transit Company when he was elected President of LCA from 1938-1947. He relieved his father Captain Joseph S. Wood as LCA President; he had been a Director since 1934 and he served on the Legislative and Advisory Committees. From June 1940 until December 1941 he was a consultant to Ralph Budd, Transportation Commissioner of the Advisory Commission of the Council of National Defense. He served as President of LCA all during the World War II years, although on a leave of absence while he served as the Director, Great Lakes Division Office of Defense Transportation. During this time frame, Gilbert R. Johnson, General Counsel, acted as Chairman of the LCA Board. When Wood left the position as LCA President in 1946, he returned to his family company and assumed the Presidency of Wilson Marine Transit Company in 1948, again succeeding his father Captain Joseph S. Wood. He was honored for his vast contributions to the Great Lakes shipping industry by being selected as the 1958 Great Lakes Man of the Year. Alexander T. Wood, age 57, and his wife died of drowning caused by sudden water turbulence while on vacation in the Bahamas on December 8, 1960.

LCA Organization

LCA President and Officers

During the Alexander T. Wood term of office, he was assisted by long term, experienced LCA staff Louis C. Sabin, Vice President, George A. Marr, Vice President, Secretary and Treasurer and Oliver T. Burnham, a long term employee who was promoted to Assistant Secretary. The Board elected Gilbert R. Johnson, Counsel in 1938, to assume the position vacated by the death of Newton Baker who passed away on December 25, 1937. In 1939 Oliver T. Burnham was elected Secretary and George Marr resigned as Vice President but retained the position as Treasurer. On May 15, 1942, Alexander T. Wood took a leave of absence as President in order to direct the Great Lakes Carriers Division of the Office of Defense Transportation; Gilbert R. Johnson was appointed Chairman of the Executive Committee and the Board during Wood's absence. L.C. Sabin, Vice President, was in charge of day to day LCA operations during the Wood leave that ended in December 1945. In 1943, F. J. Hollman joined the officers as Treasurer upon the death of George A. Marr.

L.C. Sabin, A.T. Wood and Lyndon Spencer

In August 1946, Alexander T. Wood engaged Vice Admiral Lyndon Spencer, USCG, Retired, to serve as LCA Vice-President serving along with Colonel Louis C. Sabin, Vice-President. Alexander Wood was very aware that it took a fulltime staff to run the LCA while he was on leave during much of the World War II years; it was recognition that in future years a professional full time leadership team was needed to manage the LCA. Alexander Wood was relieved as President by John T. Hutchinson who added a third Vice President, Gerald. S. Wellman.

Board of Directors

In 1938 there were 42 Directors, including the officers Gilbert Johnson, George Marr and L. C. Sabin. Only eleven were from outside Cleveland; these members were based in Bethlehem, Buffalo, Chicago,

Detroit, Pittsburgh, Rogers City and Sheboygan. In 1946 there were 46 Directors, including officers Gilbert Johnson and L. C. Sabin. Again only eleven were from outside Cleveland.

Executive Committee

In 1938 the Executive Committee was made up of 26 leaders from the member companies; and in 1946 there were 27 members. Uniquely there were two members from two of the same family companies serving in 1946; A. T. Wood and J. S. Wood from Wilson Marine and Gene C. Hutchinson and John T. Hutchinson of the Hutchinson & Co. and Pioneer Steamship Companies. Consistent long term leadership from industry characterized the Executive Committee. During the period of the Alexander T. Wood tenure from 1938-1946 the following ship owners advised him: J. Burton Ayers, John J. Boland, Adam E. Cornelius, W. C. Dressler, A. H. Ferbert. E. B. Greene, John M. Gross, Elton Hoyt II, John T. Hutchinson, Warren C. Jones, W. W. Newcomet, Frank C. Oakes, A. C. Sullivan, Baird Tewksbury, and Joseph S. Wood. In addition during the war years from 1944-45, the following men also served: George M. Humphrey, Gene C. Hutchinson, and A. E. R. Schneider.

LCA Membership, tonnage carried and carrying capacity

When Alexander Wood became President in 1938, LCA members had 374 vessels with 2.1 million gross tons capacity; in 1946, the year of his departure there were 318 vessels with 2.0 million tons capacity. In 1938 the fleet carried only 75.1 million net tons, the lowest since 1934. The depression was not yet over; in 1938 there were only 239 member vessels out of a membership of 374 in operation. However the pace of demand for steel for the war that began in 1939 increased significantly each year from 1939 through 1944 when the fleet carried 184.2 million net tons. After the war ended in 1945, the government laid up 26 of the overage vessels it received in exchange for 16 new vessels, thereby reducing the trip capacity by 160,000 tons. This was necessary as the iron ore demand was drastically reduced. The only improvement in cargo movement was in grain that was needed to ship to hungry nations in Europe.

Economic and Government Actions before and During the War

In the first half of the 1939 navigation season, only about 60% of the fleet was occupied. There was a continued decrease in the demand for iron ore, and bituminous coal was down due to the strike in April and May. On September 1st 1939, Germany invaded Poland and within a few days the British Commonwealth, including Canada, and France were at war with Germany. Inventories of finished steel were low in the U.S. Demand for iron ore, coal and grain surged to a level not previously attained. Delivery of that float was made possible by good weather and summer sailing until the vessels were laid up.

The 1940 Annual Report noted the quickening of industrial activity with inauguration of a definite program for national defense. Congress had appropriated billions of dollars for the construction of airplanes, tanks and other military equipment, some of which was being shipped to England and France for their defense. Monthly totals of traffic surpassed all records. The Great Lakes shipping industry was able to respond to the American defense program as a response to the war in Europe.

The government of the Dominion of Canada on June 17, 1940 promulgated rules for Great Lakes shipping to protect ships and ports due to the "present international crisis". On July 12, 1940 a meeting was called for by the LCA president to be held in Cleveland in order to have common rules for shipping throughout the Great Lakes. Shipowners, government representatives of the U. S. Coast Guard, the U.S. Army Corps of Engineers, and the Royal Canadian Mounted Police attended. They agreed to develop rules and precautions relating to the selection of crews, protective measures in port, supervision of loading, and navigation in the St. Marys Falls Canals and locks and the Welland Canal.

Canadian military patrol locks

On August 1, 1940 LCA published a booklet "Special Rules for the Protection of Great Lakes Commerce." Following consultation with the FBI, additional rules were published on January 14, 1942. The purpose was to provide the lake industry, particularly vessel officers, with measures to prevent sabotage. LCA gave full cooperation to the government, taking precautions to prevent sabotage to essential industry and the locks, stricter surveillance of aliens and assisting with the Selective Service. All men between ages 21 and 36 had to register on October 16, 1940 and LCA helped in order not to delay the ships carrying essential raw materials and grains. LCA President Wood stated "…needless to say that every member of the association will join in the common cause to make our country more secure than ever before." Registration of aliens started on September 1, 1940 and the Assembly Rooms assisted alien crew members to register.

In 1940 the Coast Guard assigned the cutter <u>Tahoma</u> to the Soo to replace the cutter <u>Ossipee</u> that was then transferred to Cleveland. In July 1940, the Shore Captains Committee met with U.S. and Canadian officials to formulate rules for the protection of vessels and to prevent sabotage in the locks and channels. The Coast Guard maintained a patrol of the St. Marys River to protect the locks and to safeguard navigational interests. The patrol was augmented in 1941.

In August 1941 the Military Guard at the Soo announced the discontinuance of concessions and other service at the locks; but that it would not affect the concessions and services required for the operation of vessels or welfare of the crew. Library, newspapers and laundry were continued under strict military supervision and control.

Barrage Balloon, Sault, WWII, Photo by Walter Materna,
Courtesy of Chippewa County Historical Society

U.S. Army guards at the Sault, Photo by Walter Materna, Courtesy of Chippewa County Historical Societ

The 1941 Annual Report was written after the Japanese bombed Pearl Harbor on December 7, 1941 and after the United States declared that a state of war existed with the Axis Powers of Germany, Italy and Japan. It should be remembered that America's merchant marine was already at war when the Japanese destroyed American ships in 1937 in China and more recently when a German submarine sunk the Robin Moor in May 1941 in the South Atlantic.

The iron ore float was completed for the 1941 season when the last cargo was loaded on the Bethlehem at Duluth on December 8, 1941. This was a record year for the movement of 89 million net tons of iron ore largely due to the demand created by government preparation for national defense. Blast furnaces using Great Lakes iron ore consumed a record seven million tons/month by December. Loading time per vessel and port time per vessel decreased significantly. It was a record year for all tonnage carried in 250 days of navigation; lake vessels carried 169 million net tons, 18.3% more than ever before. The Annual Report noted that "... kind Providence provided a minimum of prolonged fogs and violent storms, and an entire absence of frozen over channels in the fall."

In 1941 the Canadian Government issued regulations to prevent sabotage at the Canadian locks and canals. A licensed officer or other person designated by the master was required to be stationed on the deck during the whole time of the passage to guard against unwarranted boarding of or interference with the vessel. That person was required to wear an armlet of bright red bearing the word "GUARD" in letters two inches high. LCA provided a supply of these arm bands to the vessels that might pass through the Canadian canals.

In 1941 because of the European war emergency, Congress authorized Canadian vessels to carry iron ore cargo between American ports; in that year thirty Canadian steamers and two barges carried 712,500 tons in 90 cargoes. In 1942 thirty-five Canadian ships carried 2.7 million gross tons of iron ore, less than three percent of the total moved. Canadian ships continued to haul iron ore during the following years of war.

Upon entry of the U.S. into a state of war in December 1941, the USCG direction and control was turned over to the U.S. Navy. On July 1, 1942 the Bureau of Marine Inspection ceased to exist and their duties were taken over by the Merchant Marine Inspection branch of the USCG.

In June 1942 the Bulletin advised vessel officers that the U.S. Lake Survey has restricted the sale of maps, charts and other publications relative to river and harbors that may be of potential value to the enemy. Releases were confined only to those of unquestionable loyalty to the United States. Orders were to be place through the company office; however, a Master or Mate passing through the locks could ask for charts at the Canal office. The publication of vessel passages in the daily newspapers was discontinued.

During the war years, the Bulletin encouraged support for the war effort in many ways such as to save grease, scrap metal and rubber, scrap paper, to waste nothing, and to buy War Bonds. Ships that attested that 90% of the crew purchased War Bonds were allowed to fly the blue with white silhouette representation of the statue 'Embattled Farmer'.

In 1942 the Great Lakes Regional Office of War Shipping Administration (WSA) was established in the Terminal Tower, Cleveland with Herman C. Strom, Vice President Pittsburgh Steamship, as manager. Under the guidance of this office the WSA was provided with lake vessels tonnage suitable for coastal service. In 1942 the WSA took over 47 lake cargo carriers and a fleet of 14 package freighters and virtually the entire fleet of Ford Motor Company steel barges for coastal service. The Maritime Commission also took over the passenger steamers Seeandbee, Greater Buffalo and Octorara.

Seeandbee and Greater Buffalo converted to aircraft carriers

In 1942 about 3,000 American officers of the various lake fleets were enrolled as temporary members of the Coast Guard Reserve. Armed guards of Coast Guard enlisted men were placed onboard vessels to assure vessel passage safety as the ships passed the Soo Locks and other narrow channels and restricted waters. In 1943 it was possible to gradually remove the armed guards from the vessels, relying on the officers who were Coast Guard Reservists to maintain security.

Captain A.C. Drouillard, SS E.G. Grace, in USCG Reserve uniform

USCG activities on the Lakes were extensive during the war. In 1942 three ferry boats were acquired and turned into icebreaking cutters. Fireboats were purchased and private yachts were taken over to be used as patrol boats, some of which were transferred to the salt water ports where they were needed in port patrol. An elaborate Port Security Program was set up with a Captain of the Port at important harbors in order to afford protection to shore installations and the ships while in port; harbor patrols were set up on land and water and small vessels were denied unwarranted approaches to vessels. Controls were set up to deny access on land to persons not authorized to be at harbor facilities; crew members had to obtain ID cards that allowed the FBI to check their background. Of major importance to safety was the extension of radiotelephone service to many critical areas that allowed the USCG to maintain a 24/7 listening watch on the distress frequency; this was in connection with the lifesaving activities in many shore stations.

The Coast Guard mission included extending the navigation season to assure the transport of essential raw materials; this required the chartering and use of icebreaking steamers and tugs to supplement the regular USCG cutters. In 1943 three requisitioned ferry boats were converted, adding hoisting equipment to allow their use in servicing aids to navigation.

On January 1, 1944 the Coast Guard consolidated the Chicago District with the Cleveland District thus placing the entire Great Lakes in to one District office in Cleveland.

Ninth Coast Guard District Logo

By the end of 1945 there was a return to peacetime operation for the Coast Guard on the Great Lakes. Port Security operations were discontinued; demobilization of the Reserve and Temporary Reserve caused a sharp reduction in personnel; the U.S. Navy transferred the Air Station in Traverse City to the Coast Guard; icebreaking operations continued as needed by the Mackinaw, Acacia, Almond, Arrowhead, Chaparral, Sundew and Woodrush; patrol of the seven firing ranges were terminated on December 1, except for the Erie Proving Ground; and, the more than 3,000 Great Lakes vessel officers who served in the Temporary Reserve terminated their service on November 30.

Because of the restrictions placed upon normal economic activity during the war, labor unions could not actively seek gains through strikes that would seriously impact lake traffic. However in 1946 there was reduced tonnage moved at the opening of the season due to the strikes at the iron ore mines and the coal mines; then again on August 15 when maritime labor unions called strikes on companies with whom they held contracts. Efforts by the maritime unions to extend the strike to other fleets failed and the union called off job action on August 30. There were still some war time holdover restrictions laid on by the Solid Fuels Administration that reduced the amount of coal for bunker fuel thus bringing vessel movement to almost a standstill until June 1946 when bunker coal was more readily available.

War Production Board, the Office of Defense, Transportation and LCA

Almost immediately after the declaration of war, the Office of Defense Transportation (ODT) directed by Joseph B. Eastman was created to mobilize all domestic transportation facilities for the War Production Board (WPB). Before official entry of the U.S. into war, Alexander T. Wood was a consultant to Ralph Budd, Transportation Commissioner of the Advisory Commission of the Council of National Defense, from June 1940 until December 1941. This advisory group was dissolved and Wood was appointed by Eastman to be Director, Great Lakes Carriers Division of ODT. Eastman urged vessel owners and operators to take such action they considered feasible on a voluntary basis during a transition period. In April 1942, Wood called a meeting of 32 owners/operators under a group called the Lake Vessel Committee; he was elected Chairman and they established offices in the Terminal Tower, Cleveland. Other members of the Committee were A. H. Ferbert, Pittsburgh Steamship, S. D. Foster; E. B. Green, Cleveland-Cliffs, Elton Hoyt II, Pickands Mather, G. M. Humphrey, M.A. Hanna, J. T. Hutchinson, Hutchinson Company, and W. M. Reiss, Reiss Coal.

Joseph B. Eastman, Director, Office of Defense Transportation

Ralph Budd, Transportation Commissioner

A. T. Wood, Director, Great Lakes Carriers Division of ODT

The office was supervised by K. H. Suder, Chief Traffic Officer of the Akron, Canton and Youngstown Railroad (AC&Y) on a leave of absence. The mission was to assist and cooperate with ODT in the movement of iron ore, limestone, coal and other essential commodities. Sub-committees were formed: Ore and Vessel Committee, Chairman D.C. Potts, Pittsburgh Steamship; Coal Committee Chairman W. K. Bromley, Pickands, Mather; Coal Working Committee Chairman V. H. Palmer, Reiss Coal; Coordinating Committee Chairman D. C. Potts, Pittsburgh Steamship; Limestone Committee Chairman R. L. Dickey, Kelly Island Lime and Transport; Grain Committee Chairman John T. Hutchinson, Hutchinson Company. All of the members of the Committee were appointed by Eastman as Advisors to Wood.

When the WPB increased the minimum requirement of iron ore to be transported in 1942 from 88 million tons to 91.5 million gross tons, Wood volunteered to devote all his time to ODT as director, Great Lake Carriers Division; on May 15, 1942, Wood resigned from the Lake Vessel Committee and took a leave of absence as President of LCA.

The lake shipping industry had the responsibility of moving all the iron ore, coal and limestone required for national defense and domestic consumption. The War Production Board (WPB) determined the amounts of essential commodities to be moved by lake and the responsibility for the movement devolved upon the ODT. The operation of all vessels remained with their owners. In order to move the iron ore, ODT needed 311 ore capably ships of U.S. registry pressed into service to exclusively carry iron ore; these ships were released for the east bound carriage of grain when it was anticipated that the iron ore float goal would be achieved. The WPB in 1942 recommended that the Maritime Commission undertake the construction of sixteen large Great Lakes carriers in order to increase the iron ore carrying capacity by over 5 million tons.

In 1943, there was an acute shortage of feed grains for the northeastern states and thus there was approval to extend the late grain quota movement while maintaining the requirement to deliver 84.5 million gross tons of iron ore.

In March 1944, because of the difficulty obtaining occupational deferments for Great Lakes seamen, the Lake Vessel Committee established a Subcommittee on Manpower with offices in Cleveland to be managed by John B. Guthery, assistant director. The work of this subcommittee is contained in a later section dealing with the Selective Service and deferment of seamen.

While the war in Europe ended with the surrender of the German forces on May 8, 1945 and the Japanese government capitulated on August 14, 1945, the movement into a peacetime economy did not take place immediately. To assure continued peak operating efficiency for the movement of essential commodities the ODT continued to act as the liaison between government agencies and industry. The Subcommittee on Manpower of Lake Vessel Committee that coordinated requests for occupational deferments discontinued operation on September 1, 1945. Rationing of food continued. On December 14, 1945, all of the members of ODT Great Lakes Region submitted their resignations to Colonel J. M. Johnson, Director of ODT. Karl H. Suder continued to exercise general supervision of the committee activities until December 31, 1945 when its activities terminated. Alexander T. Wood resumed his duties as President of the Lake Carriers' Association.

Rationing of Food on Great Lakes Ships

Ration books and coupons were a fact of life on Great Lakes ships during the war. Just as for the rest of the population, there was rationing of shoes, coffee, sugar, processed foods, meats and fats and other items. The men were to remove the ration stamps by the correct number and color and give them to the Steward. Men who lost their war ration books had to apply to the Office of Price Administration for another book.

When food rationing hit the fleets in 1943, it was accepted as the right thing to do to be sure that the fighting troops got the food they needed and that the rest was properly shared among the American population. As the war went on, the government realized that the men on the ships needed an allocation of more red points to be able to get more food on the ships. Unfortunately, the ship chandlers who supplied the boats were classified by the government as wholesalers, even though they were retailers to a limited marine clientele. The chandlers did not have the large purchasing power to buy from the meat packers and they could not buy from other wholesalers at a price where chandlers could cover costs and profit since the sale price was government controlled for the chandlers who were regulated as wholesalers. The bottom line was that although the government allowed the ships the ability to purchase more food, they could not get it from the chandlers. Cigarettes were cut to one-seventh of what was normal for seamen; fortunately in 1945 the Coast Guard released a carton a week to its reserve officers in the fleet and that allowed a few more cigarettes to divvy up. In the Bulletin in June 1945 it was stated that "We're getting less meat and dairy products than we had in November 1944. And it was in that month that we were shoved back to only 61% of what we got in 1942." The article in the June 1945 Bulletin made the point that "… Americans should not submit to collective economic plans…unless we want to blindly sign away our rights and take such inequities lying down." LCA appealed to the government for improvements in the supply chain with limited success. Rationing of processed food was withdrawn on August 15, 1945; but rationing of meats and fats remained until November 24, 1945. At the end of the navigation season only sugar was still rationed.

War ration book

Government Support of Merchant Seaman during the War

The men on the lake ships during the war were eligible to earn and wear merchant marine service emblems, war zone bars, combat bars and mariners' medals. The Merchant Marine Service emblem was described as a circular metal pin about one inch in diameter having as its base a gold colored compass card, in the center of which is mounted a representation of the Federal shield in silver, with a superimposed gold anchor.

Merchant Marine Service emblem

In order to encourage the Great Lakes seamen in their work of delivering raw materials, the Chief of Transport, Army Service Command addressed a letter to the men of the Great Lakes Cargo Fleet that was published in the July 1944 Bulletin. Major General Gross thanked and congratulated the men for the record movement of raw materials that allowed the Army to deliver supplies to the battlefields in Europe and the Pacific. Later in the year, the Commandant of the Coast Guard Vice Admiral Russell R. Waesche awarded the Lake Carriers' Association the Security Shield of Honor, the Coast Guard's highest award for the prodigious war effort.

In order to more effectively and efficiently deliver the raw materials for the war effort, many changes in government maritime regulations were made.

- Load line regulations were amended consistent with safety to allow vessels to carry more cargo in the coastwise trades after the summer marks ended.
- A person with only 12 months of service in the deck department could apply to take the tests for AB and Lifeboatman and receive an emergency certificate.

- Able bodied seamen who had served on deck for only twelve months could constitute half of the required ABs onboard a vessel.
- A coal passer with only two months of service could apply to take the test for an oiler or fireman certificate.
- Deck and Engine officer original and raise of grade license experience requirements were also reduced during the emergency.
- The minimum employment age was lowered in order to bring youths not eligible for the draft into the crews first to 17 years of age and then to 16.
- At the end of the war the emergency certificates had to be exchanged for permanent certificates if the sailor could show that by that time the sailor had served sufficient time to qualify under peacetime regulations.

Great Lakes Protective Association

From its founding in 1908 until 1939 the LCA and the GLPA shared offices and expenses. In 1939 a Committee appointed by R.W. England, Chairman, GLPA made the recommendation that GLPA, should have its own office and carry its own expenses independent of LCA. The only joint expense they recommended be maintained was the cost of the monthly Bulletin. The Committee membership was A. E. R. Schneider; G. H. Warner; and, G. M. Steinbrenner. All four were also on the LCA Board of Directors. The GLPA office remained in the Rockefeller Building until 1950 when they moved to the Park Building, Cleveland.

LCA Committees

The record of actions by some members of LCA who served on ad hoc committees was often not recorded in the Annual Report. One such committee was the War Committee whose function included conducting a series of studies of problems related to Great Lakes transportation caused by the war. In order to unify communications between the shipping industry and the government, LCA considered inviting all non-members carrying bulk cargoes to join the LCA. These companies included Nicholson

Universal Steamship Company and the two McCarthy Companies that had been carrying automobiles but due to the war effort were carrying bulk cargo. It was the intention of LCA to represent all bulk carriers. There is no record of membership change as a result of this invitation.

The major committees included in the Annual Reports were the Executive, Welfare, Shore Captain, Navigation and Fleet Engineers. The legislative actions appear to have been approved by the executive committee and carried out by the staff, particularly by the General Counsel.

Legislative Actions

Unemployment Insurance

The authority for the states to provide unemployment compensation to workers who were unemployed stemmed from the Social Security Act in 1935. At that time only one state had unemployment compensation. As an inducement for states to set up more systems, the federal government provided that employers could deduct 90% of payments to state plans from the total federal tax. Seamen were excluded at that time because of the doubtful constitutionality of state taxes on maritime enterprises involved only in interstate and foreign commerce. This legal aspect was tested up to the Supreme Court in 1943 and the court sustained the power of the state to levy a state unemployment tax upon all employers of seamen.

LCA was very involved with opposition to state plans in the Great Lakes; Minnesota already had a plan but the state with the largest number of seamen employed by owner/operators of Great Lakes ships was Ohio. In 1945 the Ohio legislature introduced legislation to extend the unemployment tax to seamen and thus started a long period of negotiation as LCA lobbied on behalf of its members. Ohio tax law was very important to LCA since 85% of the operating offices of the vessel companies were located in the Cleveland area. The Ohio law went into effect on September 5, 1945 and it included language desired by LCA. It defined the season of employment as the 40 week period beginning the 4th Sunday of March in any calendar year. Seamen who worked a total of not less than 16 weeks for any time during that 40 week period were eligible to receive benefits for any time during that 40 week sailing season that they unavoidably were out of employment. No payments were made during the 12 week winter layup season.

The September-October 1945 Bulletin reported on a meeting in the LCA offices where tax officials from all the eight Great Lakes states assembled to map out a uniform method of paying unemployment compensation to seamen in the lakes fleet. At that time all Great Lakes states but Indiana, Michigan and Illinois included seamen under their compensation laws. The October 1946 Bulletin announced that a reciprocal agreement was signed between the states following a meeting in LCA offices that allowed a seaman to claim for unemployment in the state of his residence and that he would be paid under terms of the state in which the operating office of the steamship line where he was employed.

Cabotage

In 1941 because of the European war emergency, Congress authorized Canadian vessels to carry iron ore cargo between American ports. In 1941, thirty Canadian steamers and two barges carried 712,500 tons in 90 cargoes. In 1942 Canadian ships carried 2.2 million tons of iron ore between American ports. The waiver continued in effect through 1945.

St. Lawrence Seaway

In November 1943, in an article contained in the Annals of the American Academy of Political and Social Science, Transportation War and Postwar, Alexander T. Wood stated "In bridging the transition from war to peace, the federal Government may undertake vast public works. The St. Lawrence Navigation and Power Project perhaps will be one of the first to be put forward for action. The lake industry has consistently opposed the Great Lakes St. Lawrence Waterway as not in the national interest. Preposterous claims have been asserted by many of the proponents and opponents in the controversy. Certainly a comprehensive analysis of the project should be undertaken by competent authority to determine the underlying facts."

Welfare Plan Committee

George M. Steinbrenner, Chair of the Welfare Committee since 1922 when he was appointed by William Livingstone, resigned from the position at the end of 1940. He had been a member of LCA since 1912. A. B. Kern, marine superintendent of M. A. Hanna Company was appointed chairman in 1941. Prior to Mr. Kern, the Welfare Committee had only four Chairmen; in 1909, J. H. Sheadle, Cleveland-Cliffs, organized the committee; upon the death of Sheadle in 1916, E. C. Collins, Pittsburgh Steamship, took over until he was relieved by George M. Steinbrenner in 1922.

The Welfare Committee maintained the long term responsibilities it carried out in the past years as outlined below; additionally in 1941, the committee took on the work of the Claims Committee and the many responsibilities brought about by government regulations and national defense preparations and war participation. Significant efforts were needed to keep the vessels manned through aiding the seamen in obtaining deferments from military service, helping seamen register with Social Security, the registration of aliens and in 1942-43 coping with the rationing of food.

The Welfare Committee lost the services of several men who entered into government work but who would return as leaders in the lakes industry and in LCA after the war. They included: John Horton, Cleveland Cliffs, Dave Buchanan, Pittsburgh Steamship, Michael Tewksbury, Midland Steamship, and G. S. Wellman, Columbia Transportation.

Claims Committee

In the spring of 1938, a Claims Committee was organized to consider problems related to personal injuries, claims and matters relating to safety on the vessels. During the year the Committee discussed workmen's compensation, revision of the ship's medicine chest, and physical examinations of seamen. In 1939, there was concern for the extension of the Longshoreman's and Harbor Workers Compensation Act to seamen and revisions in accounting procedures made necessary by the extension of the old age provisions of the Social Security Act to seamen. In 1940, the Committee joined with others to organize the Great Lakes District, Marine

Section National Safety Committee. In 1941 the Welfare Committee was reorganized and took within its scope the work of the Claims Committee.

Selective Service Registration and Deferments of Great Lakes Seamen

In 1940, all men between ages 21 and 36 had to register for the draft; LCA assisted the seamen in registering and in obtaining deferments in order not to delay the ships carrying essential raw materials and grains. Seamen who received notices from their local draft board and who wished to seek deferment were advised to notify the Master of the notice or questionnaire in order that the company be notified and thus officially attest that the man was necessary on the vessel.

The Selective Service registration rules effective on July 1, 1941 required men who had turned 21 since October 16, 1940 to register on July 1, 1941. There were special provisions for lake seamen so as they could register without long absence from the ship and could do so after that date if their vessel was not in port. In Duluth and Superior the seamen could register at night. LCA worked with the government to allow seamen to register at 20 principal ports in the Great Lakes area rather than in their home town.

In 1943 there was an acute shortage of qualified men seeking employment on Great Lakes vessels. Working on a Great Lakes ship usually appealed to unmarried young men who were at that time being drafted into the armed forces. The War Production Board recognized the importance that Lake seamen for the war effort. While deferments for essential jobs were obtained it was necessary to remain on the job or else the deferment was invalid. When a ship laid-up in November and didn't fit out until May, the seaman was to notify the draft board of his 'notice of availability' and could be drafted. LCA worked out an agreement with the War Manpower Commission whereby referral cards were issued by the U.S. Employment Services showing that the card holder was a seaman and when the next season commenced he would go back to the ships on the Lakes. Evidence of a defense industry employment, such as in a shipyard during the winter was usually acceptable to local Selective Service Boards. The Boards were autonomous but did have directives to consider from higher authority.

In 1944 every industry was asked to give up more men to be drafted into the armed services. The LCA examined their needs for the 1944 season and decided to reduce requests for deferments even further than in the past. The LCA asked that, instead of each individual company making the deferment request, all requests should be handled through a single office. In March 1944, the Subcommittee of Manpower was set up as a sub-committee of the Lake Vessel Committee, an organization of vessel operators formed at the beginning of the war to cooperate in order to fulfill government war requirements. The plan was approved by the Office of Defense Transportation, the War Production Board and the War Food Administration. The War Manpower Commission, in April 1944, decided that the U. S. Employment Service would stand ready as the principal government recruiting agency for making available new men to supplement recruitment methods of the lake industry. This mechanism was helpful. In May 1944, the Selective Service announced that rigid requirements for occupational deferment remained in place for men 18-25; but that men in age groups 26-29 and 30-37, who are 'necessary to and regularly engaged in' an activity in war production were qualified for a deferred 2-B rating.

On May 17, 1944 another step was taken by the War Shipping Administration to reduce the manpower shortage when they announced that the United States Maritime Service will enlist young men between the ages of 16 and 17 1/2 years for training for service in the Merchant Marine of the United States with their parents' consent. Six weeks training was required for service as messman and utility men in the stewards department, and 13 weeks training for service in the deck and engine departments. Upon completion of training, men were to be assigned to merchant vessels within a few weeks.

Selective Service in practically all cases had deferred masters, chief engineers and other officers regardless of age for the navigation season; and, deferred skilled seamen 26 years of age and older and beginners over 30 years of age. A greater number of youth less than 18 years of age and men of mature years not likely to be inducted into the military were hired to fill the gaps in employment. In 1944 regarding the 'notice of availability' to the draft board for Great Lakes seamen, none was required when moving from one lake vessel to another and none when returning to a ship after the winter lay-up.

Another action of a government agency helped keep the ships sailing even if undermanned. In April 1944 because of the critical shortage of trained personnel other changes were made. Following the advice of the Acting Director of the Office of Defense Transportation, the Coast Guard issued waivers of compliance for vessels engaged in the business directly connected with the conduct of war, with respect to navigation and inspection laws and regulations regarding crew size and ratings qualifications.

A review of the manpower requirements on the Lakes and the status of deferments was contained in the April 1945 Bulletin. Of the total number of seamen and officers, about 53.3% were over or under the age brackets of 18-37 years, and thus in their current occupations not subject to call up; 17.15% of the seamen were either discharged from the military or had been rejected by the draft. Continued deferment of the remaining 29.55% depended upon their present essential work as seamen. About one third of the latter group was in the critical 18-29 age bracket that was subject to immediate call-up if they left employment. At that time, all officers and skilled ratings such as ABs, firemen and oilers were granted certification of essentiality by the Office of Defense Transportation (ODT). In the July 1945 Bulletin it was noted that in 1945, ODT had certified 1,009 of the 1,098 seamen for whom the deferment was sought. Only one of the ODT certified men was inducted and this case was appealed to higher authority in Washington.

Assembly Rooms and Registration

In 1938 despite the reduced traffic and thus demand for crew members Assembly Rooms were kept open for the convenience of the sailors in thirteen ports. The Assembly Room staff was called Commissioners or Custodians; they assisted alien seamen to register with the government and for the seamen to register for social security. In 1941 the welfare plan activities of the Cleveland schools, officers' club rooms and assembly rooms were centralized in the Century Building, 414 Superior Avenue. A new Assembly Room was opened in 1944 at Two Harbors, MN, due to the increased traffic at that ore loading port.

LCA Custodians 1940

Effective January 1, 1939 the nominal fee that was paid by seamen to register with the Assembly Rooms was discontinued. All employees regardless of registration were to be given the rights to all the benefits of the Welfare Plan, in particular the death benefits, without cost to them as long as they registered and designated a beneficiary. In 1940 13,173 men designated beneficiaries under the Welfare Plan; this compared to 10,825 in 1939. In 1941, 13,173 registered; in 1942, 15,966 registered; in 1943, 15,003 registered; 1944, 15,106 registered; 1945, 16,334 registered; and in 1946, 13,354 men registered. These numbers fairly well approximated the number of officers and crew working on LCA ships.

Wages

Since 1883, LCA and its predecessor organizations published a recommended pay scale for each person onboard, from the Master to the porter, including the barge crews. While for a few years from 1903-08, there were labor negotiations for wages, from 1909 onwards it was the Welfare Committee that established the recommended pay scale for everyone onboard an LCA member ship. During 1938, two LCA members negotiated collective bargaining agreements with representatives of their employees. In 1940 some of the member companies paid a higher wage than the LCA recommended wage scale. Pay scales were published in all the war years.

Winter Schools and Training

In 1938-39, because of the large enrollments for the winter schools, six assistants were engaged to help the Navigation Schools in Cleveland and Port Huron and the Marine Engineering Schools in Cleveland and Marine City. In the winter of 1940-41, there were so many applicants for the schools that eight assistant instructors were employed. In that winter, the 25th year of LCA schools, the number of original licenses issued to engineers during the 25 year period beginning in 1916 exceeded 1,000. Both deck and engine licenses earned through attendance at LCA schools reached 1,850 original licenses and 874 received a raise in grade. In 1942, the largest number of seamen in history attended the LCA schools and this number increased as the war requirements for more officers accelerated. Near the end of the war, the 1945 Annual Report noted that 2,293 original licenses and 1,249 raise in grade licenses were earned at LCA Schools from 1916 through the spring of 1945. In the winter of 1945-46, because of the reduced demand for officers, the LCA schools in Marine City and Port Huron were not operated. In the 1946-47 winter sessions of the marine engineering school was reopened at Marine City.

PORT HURON NAVIGATION SCHOOL, 1937-38

CLEVELAND MARINE ENGINEERING SCHOOL, 1937-38

In 1941, in order to help the forward end seamen obtain the lifeboatman credentials and to help the after end men improve their work as firemen and oilers and to obtain USCG documents, LCA held classes at the Assembly Rooms in Buffalo, Cleveland, Port Huron, South Chicago and Duluth. These classes were held again in 1941. When ice conditions permitted, the men received actual lifeboat maneuvering in the water under USCG supervision. Wartime rules allowed men with only 12 months service in the deck department to apply for the AB certificate test. LCA provided to each ship loose leaf text books *Rudiments of Navigation and Seamanship for Men Seeking Government Certificates as Lifeboatmen or Able Seamen.* Since coal passers with six months service in the engine room could apply for the Oiler certificate test, LCA also provided material to the ships for them.

In 1941 the students were required to obtain a physical exam, particularly of eyesight, before entering the classroom in order to avoid loss of time and expense on training a person who would fail the physical exam later. They were also required to show a copy of their birth certificate to prove American citizenship.

Maritime training of Great Lakes seamen between the ages of 18 and 23 was also carried out in the U.S. Maritime Service Training School at Fort Trumbull, Connecticut, and at Hoffman Island, New York. Apprentice seamen's training was initially for seven months; they received transportation expenses, room, board and uniforms and were paid $21/month.

Savings Plan

In 1938-1946 the Savings Plans for Seamen promoted by the Welfare Committee continued with the Buffalo Savings Bank, the Cleveland Trust Company and the Central National Bank. The LCA Bulletin also encouraged seamen to purchase Defense Bonds and Postal Savings Defense Stamps for patriotic reasons. Sailors could purchase War Savings Bonds through the banks where they sent their savings.

Ship Safety Committees

These committees were established only on vessels whose owners authorized their operation. Their recommendations were reviewed by LCA leadership and several committees, and many reports and recommendations were published in the Bulletin for all sailors to read. In 1938, there were 92 vessels with operating safety committees, about 50% of the number when there was a normal freight movement. In 1940, there were safety committees on 265 LCA vessels in 15 fleets; in 1941 there were 283 committees in 16 member fleets; in 1942 there were 268 vessels in 14 companies with committees; in 1943 there were 283 committees in 14 companies; in 1944 there were 281 committees, and with the many new men brought in due to the war, they worked hard to point out the hazards of shipboard work. In 1945, there were more than 250 vessels with safety committees; and in 1946 there were 192 safety committees

In order to foster and to teach better safety practices in 1943, the Welfare Committee issued a new edition of the 1939 safety book *Recommendations for Prevention of Accidents Aboard Ship.*

Health

In order to help the seamen obtain medical treatment and to obtain physical examinations, the Bulletin periodically published the location of the U.S. Public Health Service Marine Hospitals and relief stations.

USPHS Cleveland Marine Hospital

Death Benefits

As in the past, the benefits to assist in burial of a deceased seaman in the 1940s were nominal, ranging from $500 for a Master down to $100 for all unlicensed men. Despite the safety programs, the publications, the painted warnings such as "Keep Off Hatches", instructions to hold onto railings, and instructions to use ropes to haul bags up the boarding ladders, seamen continued to die from falls from ladders, down stairways and into cargo holds. In the years when there were many new men hired, there were many more accidental deaths but sadly those accidental deaths happened to more experienced crew members as well.

In the nine year period of the Alexander T. Wood tenure, over 130 seamen working on LCA ships died from the following accidents: vessel sinking, 47; falls from masts, ladders, deck to dock and into rivers and slips, 33; falling overboard and drowning, 18; falling into the cargo hold, 13; scalding, 6; miscellaneous other accidents, 13.

In 1938 there was only one death payment made as a result of an accident, that of a man who died after a fall into a cargo hold.

In 1939, while only one death occurred due to an industrial accident when a timberhead parted and killed a third mate in its path, three other drowned, one falling from a dock and the other two fell into a river.

In 1940 the Welfare Plan paid a total of $4,950 to the beneficiaries of the 33 crew members who perished when the <u>William B. Davock</u> sunk on November 11, 1940. Addition payments were made to those who died in the following accidents: 2 fell into cargo holds; two were scalded; two fell into the river or overboard and drowned; one was crushed between ship and dock; and, one was struck by a cable.

In 1941 eleven of the 14 deaths were caused by falling to the deck, dock, off ladder or into the cargo hold. Three fell into the cargo hold; four fell off a ladder or stairway; four fell overboard at sea or in a river; one was washed overboard; one was crushed and another drowned (cause was unstated).

Again in 1942, deaths were primarily caused by falls: two fell overboard; two fell off the dock; one fell off a ladder and one fell into the cargo hold. Deaths also were caused by scalding and a lost life on the <u>Steelvendor</u> (cause was unstated).

In 1943 deaths caused by falls took the lives of many seamen. Three fell overboard; three fell off ladders; three fell into cargo holds; two fell off the dock; two fell ashore or into the slip; and one each died of scalding, in a ship collision and by gun shot.

In 1944 thirty men died; twelve were lost due to the sinking of the <u>James. H. Reed</u>. In the other accidents while only one died falling into a cargo hold, six died falling from ladders, three from scalding, two drowned, one electrocuted, one from falling ore, one fell off a dock, one into a slip, one in a machinery accident, and one with a fractured skull (cause not stated).

In 1945 deaths due to falls continued to occur. Two fell into cargo holds; two fell off a ladder; two fell into a slip; one fell from the ship to dock; one was suffocated in a grain cargo; one drowned; and one was fatally injured by an engine (unspecified).

In 1946 all five fatal injuries were caused by a fall; two fell overboard; one fell into the hold and one each fell from the mast or dock.

The Bulletin

Each Bulletin contained information from the Welfare Committee on its programs: safety, savings, schools, Soo Library, sobriety, Assembly rooms, USPHS locations, and general information about the industry. It also included several pages from the Great Lakes Protective Association (GLPA) about accidents that occurred or cautions for the officers to take to reduce vessel accidents.

Over the years the Bulletin began to add black and white photos to illustrate safety points. In May 1941, in the first publication after the U.S officially entered the World War, the front page was illustrated with a tri-color American flag. In May 1944 the Bulletin no longer carried the GLPA name on the cover. It was bound in harder paper and had the front covers illustrated in color and monotones inside and back cover with photos of the war effort and appeals to buy War Bonds. The Bulletin began to carry many stories and images of the war effort, Selective Service draft information and news of the war effort from Washington. In 1945 the Bulletin appeared in April, the earliest in history.

Library at the Soo

The dispatch office of the American Merchant Marine Library Association (AMMLA) at the Soo continued operation as normal from May 1 to November 30 in 1938. LCA continued its annual financial support as it had done since 1921. The crews also contributed as they had since 1927, albeit at a lower level in 1938 as fewer vessels were in operation. As years went on more crew members donated to the library. In later years the book dispatch office opened on April first. In 1946 the Welfare Committee decided that LCA should bear the full expense of the library operation; although the AMMLA conducted its own fund raiser with the crew.

Navigation and Shore Captains Committees

The Committee of Shore Captains was authorized in 1919 and consisted of three very experienced Captains who were working ashore for the company. In order to obtain a broader range of experience from men serving on a variety of ships and in different rates, the committee had 10 members in 1938. When possible they met monthly, often with government officials present to work out improvements in navigational safety and productivity.

The Navigation Committee consisted of active masters on vessels who met at the end of the season, usually in January, along with the Navigation Committee, other LCA officers as well as masters from Canadian companies and with U.S. and Canadian government officials, to go over recommendations for navigations safety.

The Committees also worked on projects particularly with respect to new communication systems and navigation aids such as Radar. The recommendations from both committees are contained in the LCA Annual reports in great detail. A representative list of the recommendations follows.

Recommendations:

- Recommended drafts in the rivers.
- Improvements in Separate Courses.

- Approved plans for the lock to replace the Weitzel Lock at the Soo and for a bridge at Huron; opposed plans for a cutoff channel at Southeast Bend, St. Clair River and opposed plans for a highway bridge over the Keweenaw Waterway.
- Low power radio beacons were at Erie, Toledo, Two Harbors, Chambers Point on Lake Michigan, Port Colborne, and on Gros Cap Lightship. High power radio beacons were requested for Welcome Island, off of Thunder Bay, Lake Superior.
- Replacement bridges over the Cuyahoga River; removal of bridges in the Cuyahoga River; and concerns for the obstructive nature of the railroad bridges in the Calumet River. Protested to USACOE certain railroad bridges in the Cuyahoga River that constitute unreasonable obstructions to navigation.
- Fenders at the Soo Locks and regulations preventing unauthorized entry of small boats into the chambers as well as the need for fendering at numerous bridges.
- Filling of locks at the Soo while vessels are attempting to land at northwest pier.
- The need to ease congestion by having more vessels use the Canadian locks.
- Requested a semaphore system at the northwest pier at the Soo Locks to indicate the assigned lock for downbound vessels.
- Many improvements to channel widths and depths; need for breakwalls and removal of shoals, location of aids to navigation, vertical clearances under bridges, the installation of a radio telephone with the Coast Guard at the Soo.
- Improved weather broadcasting and the request to allow bridge to bridge interchange of weather information during the war.
- Considered in 1944 the question on the need for Pilotage for ocean going vessels
- Improvements to the weapons firing ranges on Lakes Erie and Huron were requested.
- Studied the proposal for the Ohio River-Lake Erie Canal.

Electronics

LCA members were proud of the leadership position they established in maritime safety by the installation of the latest technology in communications and aids to navigation. The 1939 Annual Report noted that 527 U.S. and Canadian vessels were taking full advantage of the 46 radiobeacons in the U.S. and the seven in Canada. By the end of 1941 there were 51 U.S. radio beacon stations in the Great Lakes. Also noted in 1939 was the fact that 316 Canadian and U.S. lake vessels were equipped with gyro compasses, representing 28% of the world commercial fleets. LCA member vessels had 256 gyro compasses and that represented almost 23% of all gyro compasses in the world fleet.

Regarding the radiotelephone system introduced in 1932, there were 202 ships equipped with radio telephones in 1939, of which 147 were LCA member vessels.

In the Armistice Day Storm of 1940 the use of the radiotelephone helped relay data concerning the progress and severity of the storm.

Radar Operational Research Project

The revolutionary navigation aid that was in use by the military during the war was of great interest to LCA as an aid to safe navigation but wartime restrictions made it impossible to begin installation on the ships. In the June 1944 Bulletin, it was noted that the first step in systems engineering of radar for the Great Lakes began when the Shore Captains Committee began to survey all known radar systems. The Navigation Committee met with Dr. C. M. Jansky, Chairman Jansky & Bailey, to discuss all the improvements in electronic navigation and communications that were under development. On March 15, 1945, the LCA Board established a special committee to collaborate with government and industry to expedite the application of radar to lake conditions. As the war ended, and security restrictions were withdrawn, the operational research began in earnest during the winter of 1945-46. With the full cooperation of the Coast Guard, Federal Communications Commission and six of the radar manufacturers, the consulting engineer and the LCA Committee prepared a set of minimum specifications for radar use on the Great Lakes.

Partial View of one radar class, Cleveland, Ohio, with inset showing temporary radar

The June 1946 Bulletin highlighted the LCA experimental radar research program; noting that the first radar, a Western Electric set designed by Bell Telephone Laboratories, was installed on a Great Lake commercial vessel, the John T. Hutchinson on April 24, 1946. The Ernest T. Weir installed General Electric radar weeks later; to be followed by a Raytheon on the George B. Rand; later, sets from RCA, Westinghouse and Sperry Gyroscope were to be installed on other ships.

Ice Operations

In the opening of the 1938 navigation season the USCG cutters Ossipee from the Soo and the Escanaba from Grand Haven opened the St. Marys River.

In the opening of the 1939 season, while the upper lakes and channels required no Coast Guard assistance, by April 11 several ships were ice bound in Lake Erie where heavy ice was encountered from off of Dunkirk, NY, all the way to Buffalo. The Cutter Tahoma was dispatched from Cleveland on April 15 and worked the vessels through until April 21.

While some coal moved on Lake Erie in late February 1940, zero temperatures in early March stopped that traffic until early April. The USCG cutters Ossipee from the Soo and the Escanaba from Grand Haven opened the St. Marys River and the Straits, meeting in Lake Munuscong, having encountered 22 inches of blue ice in the lower river. Continued cold weather required the cutters to return to assist beset vessels. At the end of the season, when large quantities of cargo had to be moved, delays started in October and November with dense fog and heavy weather including the Armistice Day Storm of November 11. By late November and into December, zero and below temperatures prevailed until the last grain vessels ended the season.

Ferry Sainte Marie breaking ice

Because of the world war emergency, industry and the Coast Guard were concerned that there might be heavy ice hindering vessel movements in the St. Marys River, Whitefish Bay and the Straits of Mackinaw at the opening of the 1941 navigations season. In that year, it was the first time that there was a clearly expressed USCG policy to extend the navigation season by icebreaking as a national defense measure. The USCG employed an air detachment in the ice operation, and coordinated ice observations from lighthouses, lifeboat station and the air patrol. The Cleveland based Tahoma was dispatched to the Soo in the fall of 1940 and arrangements were made to charter the car ferry Sainte Marie. On March 10 the Tahoma left the Soo and began breaking blue ice of 16-20 inches; she did not reach Detour until March 25. The Escanaba in the meantime was breaking ice in the Straits. On April 1 two limestone carriers proceeded upbound and the two cutters worked the upper St. Marys and Whitefish Bay. A fleet of eleven Cleveland-Cliffs ships sailed from Lake Erie and Michigan ports bound for the Soo and they locked down on April 3 but because of heavy ice did not make it to Lake Superior until April 6. 1941. The first iron ore cargo from a Lake Superior port was taken by the William G. Mather that led the convoy through ice choked Lake Superior. The closing of navigation was relatively mild.

On December 17, 1941 an appropriation of $8 million was included in a Defense Appropriation for the construction of a Great Lakes icebreaker, later to be christened the Mackinaw. The vessel was launched on March 4, 1944 and officially commissioned on December 20, 1944. Trials for the icebreaker Mackinaw took place in Lake Huron in November.

In order to prepare for the opening of the 1942 season, that in fact turned out to be abnormally mild, the government engaged the icebreaking car ferry Sainte Marie. Operations began on March 18, the icebreaker cleared the Straits and the St. Marys River, and thus the locks were officially opened on March 23, the earliest date in history. Unfortunately the cold weather returned on April 3 in the rivers and the locks causing an ice blockade; at one point 120 steamers were ice bound, many locking through at one ship per hour. Normal sailing was not possible until April 20. The closing of the season was much worse with freezing conditions starting on September 2nd. Subzero temperatures, gales and low visibility plagued the fleet until the last ship was in port. At the closing, the Duluth-Superior Harbor had 14 inches of ice and Chicago had 8 inches. Despite these natural obstacles, the fleets recorded a record delivery of 92 million gross tons of iron ore by December 7.

The opening of the 1943 season proved a larger challenge to the combined forces of the USCG and industry. While the opening initially appeared to be completed, cold wind and thick ice required a 40 day effort using the car ferries, the wrecking tug Favorite, six USCG cutters and six tugs (and the four USCG cutters built at Duluth, later transferred to the East Coast). As late as April 17 the Sainte Marie and the tug Wyoming were smashing through 24 inches of ice in the St. Marys River. Work continued in the Straits to Whitefish Bay and in eastern Lake Erie until May 10. The closing days were no easier as cold weather came early and gales rolled in to the Lakes. On November 9, 65 ore carriers were anchored in Duluth-Superior awaiting abatement of the storms; by November 15 there were over 100 vessels waiting out storms at the Lake Superior ports. At the end on December 14, Duluth had temperatures of 21 below zero. The last vessels locked through the Soo on December 14 when the temperature was 18 degrees below zero. The last vessel passed through the Straits on December 15, 1943.

The opening of the 1944 season was as brutal a winter as the previous year. On March 20, Duluth registered 17 degrees below zero and the Soo was at 6 below. Two USCG icebreakers Sweetgum and Basswood and the chartered tug John Roen III worked in Lake Michigan to open Escanaba and Port Inland; two others USCG cutters Planetree and Acacia worked the Detroit River and western Lake Erie; while a fifth cutter began working down from the Soo. On March 22, the Coast Guard ordered the Sainte Marie to open the Straits and by March 28-29, some limestone vessels passed through. The Sainte Marie then cleared a path to the Canadian Soo and entered the upper St. Marys but was called back to the Straits as many vessels were beset in drift ice. Ice continued to build up in the St. Marys River and the Straits; at one point, on April 4 there were 45 vessels icebound in the Straits. By April 8 the car ferry had the traffic moving in the straits, but she was still needed until April 20 when the ferry was released from service. Six USCG vessels and the chartered tug Roen II worked for several more days in the Upper St. Marys and Whitefish Bay. The first downbound cargo transited the locks on April 11, two weeks earlier than the previous year. It was a prodigious effort utilizing a vast array of USCG and chartered icebreaking vessels. The closing of the season was tranquil with moderate temperatures. The last lake vessel cleared the Soo on December 14 and the last lake vessel cleared the Straits on December 16.

Post season traffic however made records as three cargo vessels constructed in Duluth and bound for the Coast via the Illinois-Mississippi departed Duluth on January 6, 1945. The transits were aided by several Coast Guard vessels in order to transit the Sabin Lock in January 1945. The Woodrush worked through 20 inches of ice in Duluth to allow access to Lake Superior. The convoy was met at Whitefish Bay by the Sundew and the Chaparral. On January 8 the newly commissioned Mackinaw took over to escort them to open water in Lake Michigan. On January 13, a fourth ship departed Duluth and with Coast Guard cutters assistance made it to Lake Michigan. Later in January, the Mackinaw escorted the 306 foot auxiliary destroyer USS Donald W. Wolf from the Bay City, Michigan, shipyard to Lockport, IL, where on January 31 she was placed on pontoons for the trip to New Orleans.

Navy ships built on Great Lakes were fitted with pontoons in order to navigate the shallow river systems to the Gulf of Mexico

The opening of the 1945 season was marked by summer weather. At the head of the lakes there was rotting ice and open water and the March

28 daytime temperature was 70 degrees while loading at Fort William! In one day the cutter Chaparral opened the lower St. Marys River on March 22. The Mackinaw proceeded on that day to open Escanaba and Port Inland. Winter gales returned and ended summer sailing on April 4 with recurring storms and cold temperatures; however the season had started. At the end of the season, closing out the upper lakes was difficult but not harsh. Lake Erie was a different story experiencing ice blockades not seen since 1918. The Mackinaw and several other cutters were needed to help the last of the vessels reach their discharging and lay-up ports. The Mackinaw worked in the Straits January, 1946 to assist the car ferries Sainte Marie and Chief Wawatam that normally were called upon to free lakers.

The 1946 season opened with summer sailing for the most part. Because of the eminent coal strike, the Canadians were anxious to get coal from Toledo to fuel the Algoma Steel plant at the Canadian Soo. With the assistance of the Mackinaw, the coal was delivered on several Canadian ships. The end of the season was normal--very cold. On November 17 there was a gale on Lake Superior and the temperature at Duluth was 8 above zero and at the Soo it was 21 degrees F. when the last vessels received Coast Guard assistance. The Mackinaw was called upon to assist the Adam E. Cornelius loaded with coal from Toledo to Detroit and was beset at the Detroit River Light.

Fleet Engineers Committee

J. F. Wood, Pittsburgh Steamship Co., Chair in 1940-44; M. E. Kingsbury, Wilson Transit Company, Chair 1945

The purpose of the committee was to review the new rules and proposed changes in government or classification society rules in order to ascertain if they were applicable to the Great Lakes. The Committee met during the navigation season with officials from the Bureau of Marine Inspection and Navigation. They also discussed problems they had in common in the operation of the ships, methods of repairing the mechanical equipment and to evaluate new equipment. In 1941 it was recommended that there be five luncheon meetings. In 1945 it was decided there should be monthly meetings with assistant fleet engineers invited. A major issue studied jointly with the Shore Captains was the proposed U.S. Public Health Service sanitary regulations. In 1946 the Committee began to address the issue of Smoke Abatement with the city of Cleveland.

Education and Public Relations Committee

In 1946 the Annual Report contained news of this Committee chaired by John Sherwin.

Gerald Wellman joined the LCA staff in 1946 after leaving military service; LCA terminated the independent Public Relations counsel that had been retained from March 1, 1944. This committee carried on the operation of the LCA schools and the preparation of all publications including the Bulletin and handled all media relations.

Vessel Construction and Modernization

In 1938 Pittsburgh Steamship brought into service four new super-ore carriers: John Hulst, Governor Miller, William A. Irvin, and Ralph H. Watson. While they were in the 600 foot class, they carried over 1,000 more tons each trip and had fewer hatches with one piece steel covers lifted by a gantry deck crane. The steam turbine vessels were state of the art efficiency, burned 18.4 tons of coal a day providing an efficiency of over 50% more that the older reciprocating power plants.

SS Governor Miller

In the early 1940s the government turned to the many small and large Great Lakes shipyards to build a variety of vessels capable of reaching the salt water via the St. Lawrence River Canals and the Illinois Waterway for the war effort. By December, 1941, there were 222 vessels on order; 161 for the government (10 of which were submarines at Manitowoc), 34 for commercial interests and 27 lend lease ships.

In 1941 the American Shipbuilding Company and the Great Lakes Engineering Works had orders for 21 ore boats from 600-640 feet in length. Early in 1941, Pittsburgh Steamship ordered five of the largest vessels ever to be built on the Great Lakes. These five vessels were all completed and in service in 1942.

In October 1941 the U.S. Maritime Commission ordered six vessels from American Shipbuilding and ten from Great Lakes Engineering Works; this was the largest order in the history of Great Lakes shipbuilding. Keels were not laid until the spring of 1942; within 96 days, seven of these ships were launched. Within one year, all 16 vessels were in commission and delivering larger iron ore cargoes, as much as 16,000 gross tons with the summer load lines extended. This was the first time in history that Great Lakes shipyards had ever turned out more than eight steamers of more than 600 feet in length in a single year.

Vessel Losses

It was noted in the 1938 Annual Report that there were no LCA membership vessel disasters involving loss of life since 1929. Again in 1939 there were no LCA vessels lost.

On November 11, 1940, a horrendous gale swept through Lake Michigan and to a lesser extent on Lakes Huron and Superior. It was one of the worst storms in the recorded history of Lake Michigan; the storm claimed 5 vessels and 66 lives and became known as the Armistice Day Storm of 1940. The LCA member vessel William B. Davock went down with a crew of 33. LCA sent representatives to Ludington to join with Interlake Steamship Company officials to recover and identify the bodies as they came ashore and to arrange for proper disposition of the remains.

On June 15, 1943, the George M. Humphrey and the D. M Clemson collided in the Straits of Mackinaw. The Humphrey was loaded with nearly 14,000 gross tons of iron ore, sinking in 74 feet of water. Fortunately all onboard were rescued. As the wreck was an obstruction to navigation, the Corps of Engineers ordered its removal. Captain John Roen began work immediately and salvaged 10,000 tons of iron ore. The ship was brought to the surface on September 10, 1944 after being submerged for 15 months. She was taken to Manitowoc for sight and survey and then to the Roen shipyard in Sturgeon Bay for repairs necessary to place her in service in 1945.

On April 27, 1944, in dense fog in Lake Erie there were two collisions that day causing the death of 12 men and the loss of two vessels. The James H. Reed, with a full load of iron ore, collided with the Canadian steamer Ashcroft 20 miles north of Conneaut. The Reed sank quickly, causing the death of 12 seamen; fortunately 24 seamen were rescued by the Ashcroft. One hundred miles to the west, in Pelee Passage, the Steamers Frank E. Vigor and the Philip Minch collided causing the sinking of the Vigor, but all 32 crewmembers were saved by the Philip Minch.

Other Key Events of Period

In 1938 the U.S. and Canada signed new trade agreements making many changes in tariffs in order to promote trade between the two large trading partners. One important resolution was the abandonment of the six cent preference on British Empire grown wheat. It was expected that this would help restore Buffalo and the U.S. North Atlantic ports in obtaining some share of the Canadian export grains.

In the report of Alexander T. Wood, LCA President, in his Annual Report of 1939 the following was stated concerning the Annual Reports: *"Persons employed in Great Lakes Commerce and a widespread public have benefited by the data. I believe these annual reports have been and will continue to be a careful historic treatment of this vital industry."*

August 10, 1940 the Coast Guard, while celebrating the 150th Anniversary of their establishment, dedicated the new Coast Guard Station built at a cost of $360,000 on the west pier of the mouth of the Cuyahoga River.

USCG Station Cleveland Cuyahoga River

On May 7, 1941 a near record in lockages was made at the Soo, when in a 24 hour period 79 vessels locked up and 73 vessels locked down. This 152 vessel record compares with the record number of 161 lockages in July 5, 1917 when vessels were smaller and carried less tonnage.

On October 7, 1941 the bascule section of the International Bridge crossing the St. Marys Falls Canal collapsed while a freight train was crossing it. Approaches to the third and fourth locks were affected; fortunately the Poe Lock and the Canadian lock were not affected. Prompt action by the Corps of Engineers and other agencies had the locks operating within four days from the accident.

In December 1941, there were efforts by Chicago interests to increase the flow out of Lake Michigan to the Chicago Drainage Canal under the pretense that 10,000 cfs would allow for electric power generation and thus reduce the demand for coal used in power generation. The War Department replied that the maintenance of water levels in ports was a greater national benefit than the possible increased power generated.

On July 11, 1943 the new MacArthur Lock at the Soo was formally opened to commerce. The Carl D. Bradley was the first vessel to lock upbound and the Leon Fraser was the first downbound vessel. Many LCA and government officials attended the ceremony, and at a luncheon following the opening, L.C. Sabin gave remarks that included a lengthy history of the locks at the Soo, and in particular the decisions surrounding the location and size of the MacArthur lock. The Bulletin in August 1943 reported on the event and the comments.

In November 1943, the Maritime Commission announced that a Liberty ship under construction at Oregon Shipbuilding, Portland, OR, was to be named the George P. McKay. McKay was a Great Lakes master mariner who also served in 1882 as secretary and treasurer of the Cleveland Vessel Owners Association, in 1893 as the treasurer of the original Lake Carriers' Association and he continued with the reorganized LCA until he passed away in 1918. The ship's keel was laid on October 25, 1943; was launched on November 13, 1943; and delivered November 24, 1943 within a month of the keel laying. She survived the war and was scrapped in 1969.

Liberty ships under construction; two were named after George P. McKay and George A. Marr

The July 1946 Bulletin reported on the scrapping of 29 of the 36 over age freighters traded into the War Shipping Administration as part payment on the 16 new ships delivered during the war. The 29 ships were laid up in Misery Bay, Erie, PA; and on January 1, 1946 were sold for scrap for $300,000, about $10,000 per vessel, to By-Products Iron and Steel Company, Cleveland, OH. Terms of sale were that the vessels must be completely scrapped, dismembered, dismantled or destroyed; they were never to be used for transportation again in order to return the lake fleet to the pre-war tonnage levels. Several of the ships were built in 1892-93 and the lot included the Alexander McDougall, the famous whaleback, the only one built with a steamboat bow.

SS Alexander McDougall among ships laid up in Erie. PA, for scrapping

The 1945 Annual Report noted that as a result of government requisition of many smaller ships on the Great Lakes that were sent to the coast, for the first time in the history of the Great Lakes, there were no package freight steamers in service.

Chapter Five

John T. Hutchinson
President 1947-1952
VADM Lyndon Spencer, USCG, (Ret), Vice-President 1946-1952
President 1952-1962

John T. Hutchinson, President

VADM Lyndon Spencer, USCG, (Ret)

Economic/Political Climate during Post World War II, Cold War, and Korean War Years

The Presidents during the Spencer period were Harry S. Truman, (D) 1945-1953, Dwight D. Eisenhower, (R) 1953-1961, and John F. Kennedy, (D) 1961-1963. The House and the Senate had Democrat majorities, except for 1947 when the Republicans, by a small majority, controlled the House and Senate in the 80th Congress and in 1953 when the Republicans controlled the Senate in the 83rd Congress. The Democrat Party plurality in the Senate was narrow in the period from 1945-1959, however the Democrats held over 60% of the seats from 1959-1963. When the Democrats had control of the House they held from 51-65% of the seats.

The peace treaties that ended the Second World War did not bring peace to the world. It wasn't long before there was a Cold War between the Capitalist and the Communist Economies. War broke out again when the North Koreans invaded South Korea in 1950. Thus, regardless of which political party was in power in Washington, there was general support from Congress in building the Great Lakes navigation infrastructure needed by the iron and steel industry as it was a major element of national defense. This included the authorizations and appropriations for the deepening and widening of channels and harbors as well as the construction of a new lock at the Soo and the construction of the St. Lawrence Seaway. The area where LCA and the other navigation interests had to lobby the hardest was in avoiding user fees and tolls on the navigation infrastructure. The attempt to charge user fees was not confined to either the Democrats or the Republicans.

Biographies

John T. Hutchinson

John T. Hutchinson joined the firm of Hutchinson and Company in 1908. He was also president of Pioneer Steamship Company and a partner in Hutchinson and Company. The Hutchinson and Company represented family Great Lakes shipping interests that dated back to circa 1861 when John T. Hutchinson became part-owner of a scow as payment of a butcher bill. As he acquired income and secured loans, he purchased more vessels. His son, Charles L., began his career on a Hutchinson sailing vessel as a cabin boy at the age of 16 and rose rapidly through the ranks becoming its captain at 20. After sailing several more years, Capt. Hutchinson came ashore to manage the scows, and in partnership with Walton McGean, organized Hutchinson & Co. in 1901 to operate the Pioneer and other Great Lakes fleets. During the early 1900s, under Capt. Hutchinson Pioneer Steamship was a large and active business, carrying cargos of iron ore, coal, stone, and grain. Beginning with 3 wooden steamships and 2 wooden scows, the company grew to 38 ships and became the largest independent fleet on the Great Lakes by the 1920s. Hutchinson & Co. also operated vessels for Inland Steel Co. and International Harvester.

In 1923, Capt. Charles Hutchinson's son, John T. Hutchinson, organized the Buckeye Steamship Co. and served as President. With its smaller vessels, he was able to accept cargos and enter ports the Pioneer boats were unable to service, carrying the usual cargos of iron ore, coal, and stone along with pulpwood, salt, sulfur, and an occasional deck load of autos. The firm's wide variety of vessels and John T. Hutchinson's aggressive business methods enabled the firm to grow steadily during the Depression. Following the death of Captain Charles L. Hutchinson in 1944, John T. became the senior partner of Hutchinson & Company. A vessel bearing his name was completed in 1943 as flagship of the Buckeye Fleet. He served as President of LCA 1947-52. He had been a member of the Board of Directors and Executive/Advisory Committee from 1935 until his death on June 6, 1958

Lyndon Spencer

Lyndon Spencer was one of the Coast Guard heroes of World War II; he was one of ten Coast Guardsmen to receive the Croix de Guerre with Silver Star from France. The LCA Bulletin in 1946 stated that the award was a gold star and that it was presented to him by General Charles de Gaulle. Spencer was the Coast Guard Captain of the USS Bayfield, the Flagship of Admiral Moon, USN, who was in charge of the Allied landing at Utah Beach, part of the Normandy Invasion Operation. Spencer later received the Legion of Merit for his skillful and courageous command of the USS Bayfield.

The keel of the USS Bayfield (APA 33) was laid down under a Maritime Commission contract (MC hull 275) on 14 November 1942 at San Francisco, Calif., by the Western Pipe & Steel Co. She was launched on 15 February, acquired by the Navy on 30 June and placed in reduced commission the same day. She got underway from San Francisco on 7 July and arrived in Brooklyn, N.Y., on 29 July; was decommissioned and converted by the Atlantic Basic Iron Works to an attack transport and commissioned on 20 November 1943. Capt. Lyndon Spencer, USCG, took command until he was relieved on September 5, 1944.

Following shakedown training in the Chesapeake Bay and repairs at Norfolk, she conducted amphibious training in January 1944. She received orders to New York to embark troops for service in Europe. On 11 February, the ship departed New York with a convoy bound for the British Isles and arrived at Glasgow, Scotland on 22 February. From there she moved south to Portland, England, to await orders. On 11 March, Bayfield made the short run to Plymouth and joined a group of amphibious ships that then set course for western Scotland. The ships reached the River Clyde on 14 March and carried out landing exercises there until the 21st in preparation for the European invasion at Normandy.

On 29 March, she broke the flag of Commander, Force "U," Rear Admiral Don Pardee Moon, USN and served as headquarters for planning the landings on "Utah" beach. She joined with other Normandy-bound ships in practicing a variety of maneuvers and tactical operations during short underway periods until 26 April, when a full-scale rehearsal took place. Bayfield anchored again at Plymouth on the 29th and, on 7 May, began embarking troops of the 8th Infantry Regiment and of the 87th Chemical Battalion. By 5 June, the invasion force completed all preparations and got underway for the Bay of the Seine.

Passing along a swept channel marked by lighted buoys, Bayfield and the other transports reached their designated positions early on the morning of June 6th and disembarked their troops. Once the troops left Bayfield, she began service as a supply and hospital ship in addition to continuing her duties as a flagship.

The task of the Assault Force U was to land elements of the VII Corps, U.S. Army, in the Adeline sector of the coast of Normandy, to support the landing and subsequent army operations. This was achieved by naval gunfire, by establishing and operating a ferry service to unload ships and craft of follow up convoys and by coordinating the siting and construction of a craft shelter off the beach. To accomplish this task, Commander Assault Force U, Rear Admiral Moon, had under his command approximately 865 ships and craft.

Those assignments kept her off the Norman coast while other transports rapidly unloaded troops and cargo and then returned to England. On the 7 June, she shifted to an anchorage five miles off the beach and made smoke that night to protect Utah anchorage from Luftwaffe attacks.

Finally, on 25 June, she headed back across the channel. On 5 July, after quick repairs, the attack transport joined Task Group (TG) 120.6 bound for Algeria. Upon its arrival at Oran on 10 July the group was dissolved; and Bayfield continued on to Italy. At Naples, Rear Admiral Moon, still embarked, assumed command of Task Force (TF) 8 or "Camel" Force, for the invasion of southern France. Plans and procedures were refined, and full-scale rehearsals were held off beaches near Salerno between 31 July and 6 August. Following the suicide death of Rear Admiral Moon, a tragic victim of what would become known as "battle fatigue" on 5 August, Captain Spencer took command of TF 87 on 13 August, and Bayfield sailed for the southern coast of France. Early on the 15th, she put troops of the 36th Division ashore east of Saint-Raphael in the Golfe de Frejus. As its target, "Camel" Force drew the best defended section of the coast, the area where the Argens River flows into the Mediterranean, and the hard fighting there kept Bayfield in the vicinity of the Golfe de Frejus for almost a month.

Captain Lyndon Spencer was relieved as commanding officer on 5 September 1944 by Commander Gordon A. Littlefield, USCG. Spencer was assigned to the Office of Operations and as Chief, Office of Merchant Marine Safety. He served in that capacity for two years and was promoted to Vice Admiral at his retirement in 1946.

LCA Organization

In August 1946, Alexander T. Wood, Vice-President of Wilson Transit Company, who had served as LCA President since 1938, engaged Lyndon Spencer to serve as LCA Vice-President serving along with Colonel Louis C. Sabin, Vice-President who had served LCA since 1926; Sabin retired in March 1948 ending 23 years as Vice-President. Spencer was needed at LCA to take over the growing burden of government reports and liaison with the government agencies. In 1951, Spencer was elected Executive Vice-President; and, in March 1952 he was elected President, the first fulltime executive to hold the post. He succeeded John T. Hutchinson, partner in Hutchinson & Company, the largest independent Lakes fleet, who was LCA President from 1947-1952.

Others who served during the Spencer period included Gerald S. Wellman who was also elected a Vice-President in 1947 and served until 1952. Wellman was relieved by B. B. Lewis who served until 1967 and then by J. A. Packard; neither Lewis nor Packard served as Vice President as the Public Relations function was restructured to non-officer status. In 1953, after serving as LCA Secretary for 14 years, Oliver Burnham was elected Vice-President while retaining his post as Secretary.

Gerald S. Wellman was appointed in 1947 by John T. Hutchinson to the newly created full time office of Vice-President in charge of Public Relations. Wellman held a publicity director position with the Cleveland Chamber of Commerce until he joined Oglebay-Norton Company where he was editor of Columbia *Shipmate* and personnel director. He ended that career when he served as an officer in the Army Air Force; when he was released he held the rank of Lt. Colonel. After leaving the Lake Carriers' he became Vice-President of Case Institute of Technology.

In 1948 the Executive Committee became the Advisory Committee. There is not much data on the size of the LCA staff; however, in a 1951 Bulletin it was noted that LCA had 46 employees and that enrolled membership included 27 managements representing 48 fleets with 316 vessels. This was about 95% of the dry bulk tonnage on the lakes. In 1955 there was a LCA staff of 40 employees.

The Advisory Committee made all the major policy decisions that were later approved by the Board. One of the major recommendations was the amount of the assessment required to fund the LCA. It was always a matter of contention, particularly among the larger fleets such as U. S. Steel. In 1955 in a letter to Admiral Spencer, D. C. Potts, President of Pittsburgh Steamship, on behalf of Pittsburgh Steamship, Bradley Transportation and American Steel and Wire, strongly opposed the final assessment for 1955 as too large. Accommodations always had to be made to the larger fleets.

Assessments were not the only contentious matters, there was always the old guard and the bigger companies who resisted some new leadership from unknowns. In 1956 Hutchinson & Company, operators of the Pioneer, Buckeye and Inland fleets, appointed Captain Ed Jacobsen to succeed Captain Rutledge on the Shore Captains' Committee. Apparently some members of that committee opposed the appointment and requested that the company appoint a retired captain. In 1957, J. T. Hutchinson appealed to Admiral Spencer to reject the action of the committee that had exceeded its authority and to forthwith appoint Captain Ed Jacobsen who had the full support of Hutchinson & Company. Captain Ed was appointed and went on to serve in a commendable fashion for years to come.

LCA Staff Christmas Party, Louis Sabin, VP right of center and Captain Murray on far right; other staff unknown. LCA had a large staff at that time.

LCA Membership and Tonnage

The size of the LCA membership in terms of gross registered tonnage enrolled remained about the same during the Spencer tenure. The total enrolled tonnage was two million gross tons, slipping below 2 million in 1947, the fourth time since 1908 that tonnage was less than 2 million. The number of vessels was 318 vessels in 1946 and reached a high of 328 vessels in 1952, during the height of the Korean War. In all the years that followed there was a general decline in the number of ships enrolled as the newer ships increased in size and carrying capacity and the older smaller ships were scrapped.

In 1953 six small bulk carriers owned by Marad and chartered to ship owners since 1944 were withdrawn from service and sold for scrap. In 1956, the last of the bulk freight barges, a part of lake shipping since 1890, were withdrawn from membership. For a brief period in 1958, the number of ships enrolled peaked to 319 when the fleets of Browning Lines, Cleveland Tankers, T. J. McCarthy Steamship, Michigan Tankers, and Penn-Dixie joined LCA. In 1959, enrolled tonnage hit the mark of 2,244,000 tons, a historic maximum enrolled, when Ford Motor Co and National Marine Services enrolled. It wasn't long however before more vessels were scrapped, sold off the lakes or members withdrew. In 1960, the number of ships enrolled was reduced to 293, the lowest level since LCA was organized in 1882 when 615 vessels were enrolled, including 255 schooners. In 1961, the decrease to 264 continued with the withdrawal of 8 ships of the Browning and Midland fleets and other scrapings.

Summary of Spencer Accomplishments and Disappointments

Admiral Spencer served the LCA for 16 years. In the 1961 Annual Report, he summarized some of his accomplishments; there were many more that needed to be added to the list and they will be found at the end of this section. He described his tenure as a period of expansion by the building of larger and more efficient vessels, while fewer in number, the fleet had a larger gross tonnage and annual carrying capacity. Large scale taconite processing began and the start and completion of much needed deepening of the connecting channels and improvement of many harbors took place. In 1953, during the Korean War, the highest volume of bulk cargoes in history were moved on U.S. and Canadian vessels—216.5 million tons.

He reflected on sobering developments in the years since 1957; aside from the recession of 1958 and 1960, there was the steel industry strike of 1959. Also in 1959, the St. Lawrence Seaway began operations, thus opening the Great Lakes to ships of all the nations in the world, Spencer wrote "...the Seaway has been no boon to the U.S. Lake fleet although it helped the growth of the Canadian fleet, aided by the financial aid policy of the Canadian government." He ended his statement by saying that LCA has recommended policies to the U. S. government that will help the U.S. lake fleet if vigorously pursued.

His successor Admiral Hirshfield confirmed those successes in his first annual report of 1962, a year he shared leadership with Spencer; "A major program for which the Association has been a principal proponent came to substantial fruition during the year...on June 22nd when the Detroit and St. Marys River sections were made usable....the Association transmitted to its members advice that an additional 2 feet 2 inches in the St. Marys River and 6 inches in the lower rivers could be utilized." Also Hirshfield stated that the new dimensions of the new Poe lock were now set; since on October 30, 1962 the COE accepted the LCA recommendations for a larger lock to accommodate vessels of 900-1000 feet. While the dimension was increased, the essential groundwork for the authorizations was made during the Spencer tenure.

Other Major Accomplishments

1. LCA maintained the integrity of the Cabotage laws, in particular the Jones Act, despite the long period of waivers granted by Congress to allow Canadian vessels to carry essential cargo during the wars.
2. Successfully opposed maritime user fees and tolls.
3. Aggressively pursued the installation of state of the art safe navigation systems such as Radar through the Radar Operational Research Project, and communication systems such as VHF when LCA and DMA spearheaded the US/Canada Treaty requiring that all ships be equipped with radiotelephones for safety and navigation.

4. Continued the long standing effort to prevent water diversion from the Great Lakes system.
5. While not taking a stand against the St. Lawrence Seaway Project, LCA still forcefully demanded safe navigation requirements for the ocean going ships entering the Seaway.
6. LCA continued to oppose unnecessary regulation of Great Lakes transportation by vigorously working to retain the status quo on laws relating to seamen and the regulation of bulk commodity transportation on the Great Lakes.
7. Developed a long lasting rapport built upon mutual professional respect with the USCG, the regulatory government agencies responsible for safe vessel construction and operation. In small measure, this began with establishing a cooperative training program with the USCG to help Coast Guard Officers understand Great Lakes shipping. This professional level of cooperation helped bring about changes in the Load Line regulations, the licensing of engineers as vessel horsepower and the change from coal to oil took place, the assignment of Coast Guard icebreakers and LCA chartered icebreakers at the opening and closing of each navigation season, the need for compulsory Pilotage as the Seaway opened, and much more.
8. Recognizing the reality that the fleets of ships on the Great Lakes were built with coal fired plants at a time when there was no major concern for smoke pollution, LCA was forced to recognize that times had changed and through the Great Lakes Air Pollution Abatement Program worked with government agencies to reduce smoke emissions.
9. Developed a targeted media campaign directed at legislators and the public that helped bring about major legislation benefiting Great Lakes commerce.
10. Maintained enlightened programs for members' employees through the Welfare Plan despite the major initiative by labor unions during that period to unionize the sailors, this included training programs to qualify engineers to operate the new engine room systems and for navigators to learn the new communications and navigation systems such as VHF and Radar and later to obtain licenses for the Seaway transits, Operation X-Ray for TB detection, and functioning Ship Safety Committees.

The disappointments

A tragedy was the loss of life when two LCA member ships foundered, the Henry Steinbrenner in 1953 and the Carl D. Bradley in 1958.

The major disappointment for members was the opening of the Seaway that negatively impacted the U.S. fleet ability to carry grains destined to overseas markets and for the American lake fleet to exclusively depend on Lake Superior iron ore cargo tonnage.

War Clouds after World War II

Korean War June 25, 1950-July 27, 1953

Because of the 'Police Action' in Korea, the Soo was again protected by military sentries and gun emplacements were on the grounds of the locks. LCA published a pamphlet *Special Rules for the Protection of Great Lakes Commerce* to aid in the prevention of sabotage to Great Lakes vessels and the dock and terminal facilities. LCA also proposed that there be equipment placed at the Soo for transfer of cargo around the Canal in the event of an emergency that closed the locks.

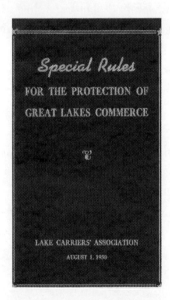

National Defense Planning

LCA formed a group in 1949 consisting of D. C. Potts, U.S. Steel, G. W. Callahan and H. L. Gobeille, Cleveland-Cliffs, to advise the National Security Resources Board and to prepare a report with respect to Great Lakes Transportation. Essentially the report drew upon the experiences of WWII concerning policy, orders and report forms. The Group advised on the current situation in the industry, probable wartime demands upon industry, the requirements of industry for manpower, improvements, facilities, equipment and the type of emergency organization, in case of national emergency, to administer temporary wartime controls—and the availability of personnel to fill key positions. Ultimately the Advisory Committee recommended to the National Security Resources Board that a central authority be established for all phases of water transportation of all vessels including manpower.

Selective Service, maintaining qualified officers and unlicensed men despite the Draft

In 1948 after passage of the Selective Service Act of 1948, LCA Advisory Committee tasked the Welfare Committee to be the liaison with the Selective Service officials and to establish a centralized agency for handling deferments for lake seamen similar to that which took place in WWII. In 1949, there were no inductions.

In 1950, Selective Service began to send out notices to men between the ages of 19-25 to report for pre-induction physical exams. Because of the eminent drafting of these men in the 19-25 year old groups, the Welfare Committee conducted a study to determine the number of licensed officers and skilled ratings in that group, the number of those with prior military service, and the number who were single and eligible for the draft if deferment action was not taken. The Committee recommended the reestablishment of the Manpower Subcommittee, as had acted in WWII to provide a uniform approach to the deferment requests. Later the Committee invited ship operators that were not LCA members to join the Subcommittee on Manpower and to share in the expense of the operation that included leasing space at the Frederick Building, East Fourth Street, Cleveland. Initial billing of members of the Subcommittee was $100/vessel.

At what was called transfer boards, LCA worked out an arrangement that allowed seamen who lived in distant cities to have their physicals in Detroit. Sailors were told not to sign off the vessel but rather to get off the ship downbound at Detroit, get the physical and return on the upbound trip. If the seaman was not on a ship passing Detroit, LCA was able to work it out that the seaman would visit a Great Lakes port selective service board and request a form to be send to their local board for permission to have the physical at that port location. This procedure was to avoid the loss of seamen when they were needed on the ships. Men were requested to advise their local boards that they will be returning to their ships in the spring and that they would seek employment during the winter months in defense industries such as shipyards. The Bureau of Employment Security, through offices of the U.S. Employment service in lakes states, made special provisions to place seamen in defense industries during the winter.

The Lake, Ore, Coal and Vessel Committee (LOCVC) was formed in 1950 to advise the Defense Transport Administration and to expedite on a voluntary basis the production and transportation of bulk commodities on the Great Lakes and to cooperate with the government entities to that end. Several committees such as the Lake Vessel Committee and the Subcommittee on Manpower were set up along the lines of what worked during WWII.

In July 1950 LCA set up the Subcommittee on Manpower; effective October 1, 1950 the committee was re-established as the Vessel Manpower Subcommittee of the LOCVC. Its function was to process claims for deferment, compiled statistics on manpower requirements and in all ways possible minimized the impact of Selective Service on the Lake vessel industry. LOCVC Executive Director was C. L. Wyman. The Subcommittee on Manpower leadership was: A. B. Kern, Chair, Oliver T. Burnham, Director, J. C. O'Donnell, Asst. Director, other members included David Buchanan, U.S. Steel, J. A. Collins, and L.C. Matia.

The Subcommittee advised each Local Selective Service Board that they would be seeking deferments only for skilled ratings including officers, able seamen, oilers, firemen, and chief cooks. These requests would be for employees constituting about 30% of the crews of the 345 bulk cargo vessels.

It was not contemplated to seek deferments for deckhands, coal passers or porters. They pointed out that Great Lakes vessels transported 85% of the iron ore used in the steel industry and 10% of the coal mined in the USA.

April 25, 1951, Colonel Lewis Kosch, Chief Manpower Division, Selective Service System, Washington, addressed a letter to all the Selective Service Directors in the Great Lakes states advising them of the importance to the nation that the maximum tonnage of iron ore, coal, limestone and grains be moved during the navigation system. He stated that it was the opinion of Headquarters that local boards give serious consideration to the occupational deferment of licensed and certificated seamen in the lake shipping industry. The letter had been sent following an appeal from the LOCVC Subcommittee on Manpower.

In 1951 the Subcommittee on Manpower considered but took no action on a recommendation that members hire 17 years old men instead of the current 18 year old minimum age.

Following LCA communications to the Secretary of Labor, on May 7, 1951, the Department of Labor issued a revised list of Critical Occupations and Essential Industries that included licensed officers on the Great Lakes; but the list did not include skilled unlicensed ratings. The LCA Office of Manpower Director reported that as of May 23, 1951 a total of 1,418 cases were processed; of this number 269 were given 2A status, 192 were inducted or all avenues of deferment exhausted, 173 requests were withdrawn, 332 persons were placed in other deferred classifications, and 452 cases were in process.

In 1953 there was serious concern expressed that the revised "List of Currently Essential Activities and Critical Occupations" omitted reference to licensed vessel officers and water transportation. In 1953 the Selective Service Boards were not granting deferments to younger men who had indicated they were eligible to study for their officer's license but had not yet entered school. Members discussed cooperation with the draft boards and perhaps not seeking deferments for younger men, particularly if they had been deferred several times.

The LOCVC Subcommittee on Manpower functions relating to obtaining occupational deferment for vessel crews in 1953 was transferred back to the LCA Welfare Committee; this arrangement continued throughout 1953. In 1954 the Welfare Committee recommended that this function be placed on standby as of May 1, 1954; thus LCA discontinued making requests for occupational deferments as of that date. It was noted that at that time there were deferments in place for 16 individuals; and on May 1, 1954 when the operations of the subcommittee was discontinued, there were 313 current occupational deferments. These deferments were to expire in time: 36% in December 1954 or later while 31% were to expire in April-July of 1954. There was to be a reduced number of vessels in service during 1954 and thus it was recognized there would be less favorable action from the Selective Service Boards.

During the active sponsorship of requests for occupational deferment, a total of 2,052 cases were processed with a maximum of 431 occupational deferments having been in effect. The LOCVC also concluded its operations on May 1, 1954; the office was closed and staff disbanded.

On April 12, 1955 the LCA Subcommittee on Manpower met to determine if the present manpower situation required reinstatement of the occupational deferment procedures. It was noted that the Coast Guard had withdrawn the waivers given to non-able bodied seamen to be used in the AB classification for the certificate of inspection manning.

Other Emergency Planning Actions

LCA requested an extension of the load line rules in March 1951 and was advised in September 1951 that the Coast Guard was granting an extension of the Summer Emergency Load Line through September 30.

In December 1953 a Defense Mobilization Order indicted concern for the nation's transportation system in event of atomic warfare. LCA in November 1953 drafted a "Proposal for a Great Lakes Treaty Between the United States and Canada in Furtherance of their Mutual Defense" in order to make provisions for adequate vessel capacity for the transportation of raw materials between the two countries on the Great Lakes. It is not known how the governments acted on the proposal that was based upon LCA experience in previous wars. In 1954 the government requested industry to prepare a defense manual for Great Lakes shipping. In 1955 LCA formed the Committee of Defense Planning with Fred R. White as Chair. In 1957 LCA published a defense planning manual to help Great Lakes shipping in the event of a nuclear attack; it was distributed to industry in 1957 and 1958.

Fred R. White, Chair LCA Committee of Defense Planning

In August 1961, during the Berlin Crisis period, the LCA Subcommittee on Manpower directed an industry survey to determine what impact the draft would have on the vessel operation. Results of the surveys indicated that there were 663 single men and 154 married men in the 18-25 age groups; and that only three were licensed officers. LCA contacted all the Selective Service offices in the Great Lakes to receive assurance of cooperation should the Berlin Crisis deteriorate further.

Ground Observer Corps (GOC)

In February 1950, Continental Air Defense Command (ADC) Commander General Ennis C. Whitehead proposed the formation of a 160,000 civilian volunteer GOC to operate 8,000 observation posts scattered in gaps between the proposed radar network sites. There was a concern that the Korean War served as a precursor to a possible Soviet attack; ADC had little difficulty recruiting volunteers. Eventually over 800,000 volunteers stood alternating shifts at 16,000 observation posts and seventy-three filter centers. The GOC traced its roots to WWII when 1.5 million civilian volunteers were enrolled by the Army Air Forces to man 14,000 observation posts positioned along the nation's coasts. With limited radar detection capability, the GOC's mission was to visually search the skies for enemy aircraft attempting to penetrate American airspace. With the declining threat to America from German and Japanese air forces, the Army Air Forces disestablished the GOC in 1944.

In 1958 the U. S. Air Force Chief of Staff awarded LCA members an Appreciation Award and commendation for participation in the GOC activities in recent years. The Air Force canceled the Ground Observer Corps program in 1959.

Labor unrest

In 1945 when the WWII ended, the pent up demand for wage increases and improvements in working conditions led to a long period of labor unrest and strikes. In 1946 the bituminous coal miners went on strike and there was a protracted labor dispute among iron ore miners. In August there was a short strike called by a maritime union.

In 1949 strikes in iron ore mining and steel industries coupled with labor disturbances in the coal fields severely reduced tonnage moved on the lakes. In 1952 there was a steel industry strike that lasted for 55 days. In July 1956 the steel workers strike caused layup of many ships; as that strike was settled, the licensed officers union called for a strike that was not settled until mid-September, at which time the entire fleet could be mobilized.

Relations with the U.S. Coast Guard

The USCG, as of July 1, 1946, took over the permanent responsibility for Merchant Marine Inspection; this had been a temporary wartime assignment. Fortunately for LCA, Admiral Spencer had experience in that office as one of his wartime assignments.

In 1952 Commander Willard J. Smith was appointed Commanding Officer of Mackinaw. Willard Smith a native of Michigan became very knowledgeable about the needs of the Great Lakes shipping industry and a good friend of the industry. He went on to become the Commandant of the Coast Guard and during his retirement he became a founder and Superintendent at the Great Lakes Maritime Academy, Traverse City, MI.

Admiral Willard Smith, Commandant USCG

Cdr. Willard Smith, CO, Mackinaw 1952

In 1956 Congress passed legislation supported by the LCA whereby USCG was authorized to require a biennial inspection of vessels rather than an annual inspection. The law also permitted a change in a method of admeasurement of vessels to allow a more liberal allowance for propelling machinery in computing the net tonnage of vessels with relatively small engine rooms; and the law prohibited vessels rebuilt abroad from engaging in the coastwise trades.

LCA/USCG Cooperative Industry Training Program

LCA and the USCG started a cooperative training program in March 1950 that allowed officers who would be assigned to a Coast Guard office in the Lakes or another part of the maritime industry to participate in a one year program that was later reduced to six months. RADM H. C. Shepheard, Chief, Office of Merchant Marine Safety, initiated the program. The objective of the training was to encourage cooperation between industry and the Coast Guard, to broaden the understanding of merchant vessel problems from a commercial point of view, and, thereby facilitate a balanced administration and supervision of marine inspection activities by qualified Coast Guard personnel. The first trainee was LCDR Robert F. Barber. Several of the officers were assigned to the Ninth District offices. The 24th trainee in 1978, LCDR James Comerford, became marine manager for the Ford Motor Company after retiring from the Coast Guard. The 35th trainee in 1990 was LT. James H. I. Weakley; in 2003 he became President of the Lake Carriers' Association.

Lt. James Weakley

LCDR James R. Comerford

The Coast Guard officers visited the member offices, made trips on as many different types of lake ships as possible, toured mines and port terminals, and met with other maritime related government and non-government agencies. These officers documented their assignments and many of them wrote extensive thought provoking essays on the maritime, iron ore and steel industries as well as on matters of value to the USCG for marine inspection purposes.

ST. LAWRENCE SEAWAY

A review of the traffic by foreign flag vessels in the Great Lakes trade was contained in the 1946 Annual Report. In pre-depression days there were as many as 40 foreign vessels trading in a single season; but in the Great Depression there were few and virtually none during the war. Shortly after the war ended a Norwegian ship came in to pick up a load of steel.

In 1946, three ocean trade shipping companies with 12 ships made 21 voyages to the Great Lakes and traffic slowly increased after that time.

In 1949 the LCA Board reversed its long held policy opposed to the St. Lawrence Seaway Project since there was no longer unanimity among LCA members to maintain the opposition. Some important LCA members had a vested interest in the iron ore developments in Labrador that needed an expanded Seaway to import iron ore to the American steel mills. The LCA could not be for or against the project; thus the LCA position was to:

1. Maintain surveillance to assure that the project was suitable and safe for U.S. Great Lakes vessels.
2. Assure that there would be no unreasonable burdens or impediments to U.S. Great Lakes vessels in the use of the project with respect to imposition of tolls, Pilotage fees, harbor charges, taxes or other means; and that the wages and living conditions of U.S. Great Lakes seamen, the safety of navigation on the Great Lakes and the general interests of the U.S. shipping on the Great Lakes would be adequately protected.
3. Take such action as necessary and appropriate for the protection of U.S. Great Lakes shipping.

On October 2, 1953 off of Port Huron, the German registered MV Wallschiff collided with the SS Pioneer causing the German vessel to sink, with the loss of one life. The sunken vessel obstructed navigation until it was removed from the channel. The Advisory Committee recommended that a licensed Great Lakes pilot be available at all times while the foreign vessels are underway. In 1953 the Shore Captains Committee expressed grave concern about the larger number of salt water vessels entering the lakes, in that the foreign officers onboard were not familiar with the Great Lakes Rules of the Road and other procedures thereby causing near collisions.

In 1953 LCA and the DMA met several times to discuss the possibility of a bi-national treaty to restrict international commerce solely to vessels of Canadian or U.S. registry; after extensive study, a draft treaty was prepared with the hope that the Senate would introduce the measure in

1954. However there was strong opposition to the initiative. In 1954 LCA made new demands for greater control of foreign vessels when another salt water vessel sank off of Milwaukee light. The Dutch MV <u>Prins Willem V</u> collided with the Tug <u>Sinclair-Chicago</u> and a tanker barge that sunk with no loss of life.

On May 13, 1954 President Eisenhower signed the legislation into law approving the St. Lawrence Seaway and Power Project. The size of the locks would be the same at those of the Welland Canal that was opened in the 1930s; 800'x 80'x 30'.

Given that reality, on September 10, 1954, the Association retained Robert Heller & Associates to make a survey and to prepare an objective report to determine the effect of the completion of the St. Lawrence Seaway upon the operation of vessels enrolled in LCA and the resultant effect on the national economy and national defense. Early in 1955 the report was delivered to the LCA and was distributed to members for careful and extensive consideration; no further distribution beyond the Association was contemplated. The Annual Report for 1955 was silent as to the contents of the Heller report; needless to say, many of the members of the Association were strong advocates of the Seaway construction in order to move iron ore into the Lakes from Canada and Venezuela.

Because of the influx of foreign vessels and the safety concerns their poor navigation caused, in 1954 LCA made representations to the Department of State and the USCG concerning the desirability of a Pilotage agreement with Canada requiring employment of qualified pilots and the licensing of vessel officers proven to have familiarity with the Great Lakes rules of the road and courses. In 1955, the Navigation Committee met with the USCG in Cleveland to urge the establishment of regulatory requirements for competent navigating personnel onboard foreign vessels trading into the Great Lakes. The Navigation Committee recommended that U.S. personnel authorized to serve as Pilots on foreign vessels should have sailed as Master of a Great Lakes vessel or have sailed under a Great Lakes pilot's license for at least five years and have good recommendations from those they had served.

The construction of the Seaway commenced in 1955 with a schedule for completion in 1959. LCA continued to give advice as to the engineering aspects that would affect the safe navigation of vessels. In 1955, LCA Vice

President Oliver Burnham was assigned to serve with a group called the Great Lakes-St. Lawrence Association to advise SLSDC on the users view of canal toll rates and to the equitable basis for the measurement of vessels for toll assessment.

In 1956 in preparation for the opening of the Seaway, the Corps of Engineers held a series of hearings to consider improvements to all the main harbors of the Great Lakes in time for the completion of the Seaway construction. LCA recommended that all the harbors on the Great Lakes be improved but specified that there were 28 harbors that had economic justification to be dredged to 28 feet in order to allow a new standard of 25.5 feet safe draft. Also in preparation for the Seaway opening, LCA recommended that the vertical clearance under all new bridges across the Detroit and St. Clair Rivers and the Straits of Mackinaw have a vertical clearance of not less than 120 feet and that all other bridges have a clearance of at least 100 feet. In that year LCA was given a collateral benefit to the domestic trade as the Corps of Engineers agreed to allow Seaway maximum vessels (730' x 75') to transit the MacArthur lock.

In 1956 the Electronics Committee recognized that since the Seaway would open soon and there would be many international ships in the Great Lakes, there would be a serious safety problem without a worldwide, international radiotelephone system. This was a matter of great importance since, at that time, the radio operators on international ships used radiotelegraph for safety-distress communications and the U.S. and Canadian vessels used a radio telephone system operated by the deck officers; there were no radio operators on the lake vessels.

In 1957 Admiral Spencer acquiesced to tolls on the new Seaway in order to have it built. LCA continues opposition to all other tolls but without the Seaway tolls to repay the Government of Canada. They would not proceed with the project. However, in 1958, Spencer called for the State Department to oppose the tolls on the Welland Canal imposed upon American ships as it violates a 50 year policy whereby Canadians were not charged for the use of navigation infrastructure in U.S. waters. He called for no toll to be charged on vessels hauling cargo to or from Lake Ontario ports and using the Welland Canal.

In 1957 the Legislative Committee continued to have an active interest in all matters relating to the Seaway including a law that would require certified competent navigators on the foreign ships and application of the Great Lakes Rules of the Road for the foreign ships. In 1957 the Shore Captains Committee discussed with the USCG the service requirements for extension of the Pilot's license to cover Lake Ontario and the Seaway since several LCA members planned to send vessels down the Seaway.

In 1958 the Navigation Committee heard from many masters stating that the foreign vessels failed to use or answer passing signals and they were unable to establish telephone communications. The Committee recommended that LCA prepare a booklet describing the Separate Courses on the Great Lakes and the differences in Great Lakes Rules of the Road from the International Rules; and that the booklet be given to foreign vessels before coming into the Great Lakes. The Shore Captains Committee prepared a course guide for the St. Lawrence River to help officers secure an extension of their pilot's license.

In 1958 Congress amended the Great Lakes Navigation Rules to clarify that these rules applied to the foreign vessels operating in the Great Lakes. However, Congress failed to pass a law that would require foreign vessels to have a pilot onboard while navigating in the Great Lakes; while the measure passed in the House, strong opposition raised by the foreign flag operators caused the Senate to table the measure.

In 1958 the first segments of the Seaway were placed in operation with the completion of the Iroquois Lock in Canada and the Eisenhower and Snell locks in the USA. There were no benefits to American shipping in 1958; however benefits were expected in 1959 following the formal opening of the system. Efforts continued by LCA and the DMA to have the Welland Canal free of tolls arguing that the use of the Welland was and would remain primarily an avenue of inter lake navigation.

Also in 1958 the Fleet Engineers Committee gave consideration to proposed regulations concerning dry docking of vessels that traverse the Seaway for a short period of time each year, whereas the majority of time the vessel was in fresh water. LCA believed such a regulation for shorter intervals between dry docking was a penalty on the lake vessel owners.

Opening Seaway 1959 Royal Yacht Britannia (Wikimedia, MIKAN)

The St. Lawrence Seaway opened to deep draft navigation on April 25, 1959; the first ship to enter the system at Montréal was foreign; the first American ship was the Grace Line steamer Santa Regina on April 26. In June and July, 'Operation Inland Seas", a force of 28 ships of the U.S. Navy, led by the heavy cruiser USS Macon cruised the lakes as far west as Duluth; all had Great Lakes masters onboard serving as pilots. During this period the British Royal Yacht Britannia inaugurated the system. On the voyage from Chicago to Sault Ste. Marie, Captain John C. Murray, director of the LCA Navigation School, provided pilotage assistance.

The 1959 Annual Report opened the Report of the President with a dismal note. Spencer stated that..."the year 1959 was fraught with adversities and problems...the season was doomed by commencement of the seventeen week strike in the steel industry. The influx of foreign vessels through the St. Lawrence Seaway...brought with it serious collisions and many reports of disregard of Great Lakes navigation rules...continued low water levels limited the carrying capacity... for the first time in over a half century, tolls were levied against the vessels using the waterways of the Great Lakes when Canada inaugurated such charges on vessels using the Welland Canal, as well as the St. Lawrence Seaway. Finally, foreign competition reduced the amount of grain available for movement by lake ships...with all these hindrances, the 1959 season must go into the record as one of the most frustrating periods in the recent annals of lake history." Despite this gloom, the tonnage carried by U.S. and Canadian vessels was 3% above the recession year of 1958.

In 1959, the Liberian steamer Monrovia sank on June 26 in Lake Superior following a collision with the Canadian steamer Royalton. On June 13 in the upper Detroit River there were a series of collisions involving ocean going vessels: the C. S. Robinson collided with the British steamer Roonagh Head while the Arcturus collided with the Wang Cavalier, an ocean vessel of U.S. registry.

The opening of the Seaway permitted the movement of iron ore from the St. Lawrence to the Great Lakes area in large vessels. There were 297 cargos of iron ore shipped into the lake ports; 35 were on ocean vessels, 239 were in Canadian Lake vessels and 23 in U.S. lake vessels. The first U.S. vessel loading at Sept Isle was the E. G. Grace.

SS E.G. Grace (Historical Collection of the Great Lakes, Bowling Green State University)

The other cargo movement that was permanently changed by the opening of the Seaway was the grains trade. In past years substantially all the grain was carried on U.S. and Canadian vessels. In 1959, 467 cargoes of grain in the export trade were carried by foreign vessels; this was approximately 24% of the trade by volume and number of cargoes. Canadian vessels loaded 59% of the volume compared with 75% in 1958 and the U.S. fleet share dropped from 24% to 17%. The Canadian and

U.S fleets lost 78 million bushels of grains to the foreign ships using the Seaway.

In 1960, Admiral Spencer opened the Annual Report with the statement that "Compounding problems were encountered by the United States Fleet as a renewed and larger influx of foreign ocean ships which entered the lakes in search of grain cargoes. The success of this foreign commercial invasion is best indicated by statistics which show that ocean ships loaded 463 grain cargoes…for direct shipment abroad. This compared with only 313 cargoes…taken by U.S. lake ships for delivery to American or Canadian lake and Seaway ports."

He also reported that Congress enacted provisions for the regulation of Pilotage for ocean vessels entering the Great Lakes through the St. Lawrence Seaway. He noted that while Congress did not enact all the safeguards that LCA sought to protect lake vessel operations, he hoped that implementing regulations would eliminate some of the hazards present during the past several years. The Regulations for the Great Lakes Pilotage Administration went into effect on May 1, 1961, requiring a certificated pilot onboard vessels in the Upper St. Lawrence River, the connecting channels between Lakes Erie and Huron and between Lakes Huron and Superior. In other waters of the lakes, such vessels were required to have a certified pilot unless an officer onboard had been found qualified by the U.S. or Canadian government. LCA recommended that compulsory Pilotage was also necessary in the Straits of Mackinac. The primary concern was that the legislation did not state as to where compulsory Pilotage would be in effect; that was left up to the Administration through the regulatory process.

Spencer notes in the 1961 Annual Report that a ray of encouragement was the fact that in 1961, for the first time since the Seaway opened, U.S. lake vessels carried more grains than the ocean vessels of foreign registry. The largest amount since 1958. He expressed hope that if there were more rigid adherence to the requirements of the P.L. 480, a law requiring that a major portion of the American food aid programs be carried on U.S. flag vessels, more cargo would be shipped on American bottoms.

Congresswoman Marcy Kaptur in 1980s onboard US Flag laker in Toledo loading export grain

Other Actions of the Legislative Committee

- In 1950 the Committee reviewed current legislation including matters relating to the waiver of navigation vessel inspection laws and the contemplated US/CN Great Lakes Radio Treaty.
- In 1951 the Committee worked on the revision of the Transportation Act 1940 and ship warrant legislation measures to restrict the transfer of vessels to a foreign registry.
- In 1952 the committee opposed proposals to establish a Safety Division in the Department of Labor and a proposal to have the Interstate Commerce Commission review reports of the Corps of Engineers where improvements to harbors and channels were concerned.
- In 1955 and for several years that followed, the Ohio legislature considered proposals to charge an ad valorem tonnage tax on vessels trading in and out of Ohio ports; the measure was not adopted.
- In 1957 LCA supported authorization for Ohio to become a member of the Great Lakes Compact.
- In 1959 LCA provided a representative to the U.S. Delegation to the Safety of Life at Sea Conference in London.

LCA Committees

Legislative Committee

Harrie S. Taylor was Chair from the inception in 1944 and served until his retirement in 1961; he was relieved by Herbert C. Jackson, another charter member of the committee, who served as Chair for the remainder of the Spencer period and beyond. There was no report of legislative committee work in the Annual reports until 1950.

The Legislative Committee was the group who worked most closely with the Executive Committee. They were very ably assisted by Counsel Gilbert R. Johnson and Assistant Counsel Scott Elder, who helped prepare legislative proposals and often testified before congressional committees on behalf of LCA. While much of the work of the other committees could be conducted independently from the Legislative Committee, if there were a need for government action such as regulatory or legislative change, the Legislative Committee was called upon to assist.

Cabotage Laws, the Jones Act

As Congress had done in every year since 1941, except 1946, exemptions to the Jones Act allowed Canadian vessels to carry certain cargo between U.S. ports on the Great Lakes. Congress in 1949, upon hearing requests from the shippers of iron ore, again permitted Canadian registry vessels to carry iron ore between U.S. ports. In 1949, Canadian ships carried a little over 1 million tons of iron ore between U.S. ports. In 1950, Canadians carried 1.2 million tons of iron ore; Congress also permitted Canadian vessels to carry coal from U.S. ports to Ogdensburg, NY. In 1951, Canadian vessels carried 568,359 gross tons of iron ore. Because of the concern of some grain shippers, on October 10, 1951, Congress authorized Canadian ships to carry grain for the remainder of 1951. LCA expressed concern for the waiver of the Cabotage laws to allow Canadian ships to engage in the grain trade between American ports and opposed this waiver; however no grain was carried on the waiver basis. In 1952 Congress again was petitioned by the iron ore shippers to allow

Canadian vessels to carry iron ore between U.S. ports. However, Canadian government action made it impractical for many ships to carry iron ore since there was a need to haul Canadian grain; as a result, the Canadians only carried 102,121 gross tons of iron ore. In the 12 years of waivers, Canadian vessels carried 5,357,950 gross tons of iron ore. In 1953, for the first time since 1940, due to increased U.S. fleet capacity and the end of the Korean War, no request for a Jones Act waiver was made.

In 1956 Congress again authorized Canadian vessels until June 30, 1957 to transport coal to Ogdensburg, NY from other U.S. ports in the Great Lakes. In 1957 the Legislative Committee was concerned over a bill authorizing a waiver of coastwise laws to permit Canadian vessels to transport coal between certain U.S. ports; while hearings were held, the bill was tabled in 1957.

In 1960, LCA supported a change in the Cabotage laws so as to prohibit a rebuilt vessel of more than 500 gross tons to engage in the coastwise trade if any major components of its hull or superstructure were built outside of the United States. Ultimately as the definition of major components was defined in regulation, the term substantial was interpreted to mean the percentage of weight of the new components compared to the existing structure. Vessels rebuilt for the domestic Great Lakes trades still could utilize major components of the hull that were constructed in foreign shipyards.

User Fees

In 1952 the issue of maritime user fees was raised to a high level in Washington as land based transportation interests supported a proposal that all users of the waterways be charged a toll to defray the government costs of the programs. In 1955 the Hoover Commission recommended the implementation of waterway user fees to President Eisenhower. In 1957 LCA opposed the user charges under study by the Department of Commerce. In 1958 the Legislative Committee along with many other organizations successfully lobbied for the removal of a 3% federal excise tax on the transportation of property and the $0.04 per ton tax on the movement of coal and against other measures that would have levied fees for Customs and Coast Guard services.

In 1959 LCA believed that since the Seaway opening caused the imposition of Seaway tolls, the Legislative Committee needed to gear up to oppose the demands for the imposition of user charges on various navigable waterways throughout the USA. LCA joined with a group called the Committee of Domestic Water Carriers to permit a coordinated approach with respect to problems affecting the water carrier industry.

In 1960 LCA was concerned with the attempt by the Illinois Central Railroad and Southern Pacific Railroad to acquire a common carrier barge line in order to engage in waterway transportation. The ICC hearing examiner found that this action would not be in the public interest. Railroad interests failed to obtain new legislation lifting the prohibition on railroad ownership of water carriers. In 1960 there was also accelerated activity relating to the initiation of user charges or tolls on domestic waterways through establishment of Inland Navigation Commission and by giving the ICC jurisdiction over proposed waterway improvements.

The Senate authorized a study of transportation policies that culminated in a report called the Doyle Report that contained highly controversial recommendations for user charges, repeal of the bulk commodity exemptions, restrictions on the right of private carriers to engage in for-hire transportation and the establishment of a Department of Transportation. Fortunately none of these legislative changes were enacted.

Water Diversion at Chicago

During every period in the LCA history there was concern for decreased water levels caused by water diversion from the Great Lakes system. The most elaborate and extensive diversion was the sanitary canal diversion at Chicago. In 1954, there was a strong effort by the City of Chicago to obtain the diversion of not more than 2,500 cubic feet per second from Lake Michigan into the Illinois waterways. Despite the strenuous lobbying to prevent passage of this legislation, the measure passed both the House and Senate. Fortunately, President Eisenhower vetoed the bill.

In 1957, the Legislative Committee followed actively the efforts of Illinois to increase the diversion of Lake Michigan water at Chicago; the House approved such legislation but the other Great Lakes states except Indiana petitioned the Supreme Court for a modification of its April 21,

1930 decree governing the diversion of water. In 1958, the Senate nearly passed a measure to allow greater diversion of water at Chicago but the measure was defeated. In 1960, the Supreme Court litigation over diversion of Lake Michigan waters at Chicago progressed slowly as the Special Master investigated the injury to navigation that would be caused by the diversion.

Unemployment Compensation for Great Lakes Seamen

As unemployment compensation became a part of the laws of each state and the improvement of these payments to laid-off seamen during the winter layup period was a legislative objective of many of the labor unions, there was continued tension between Great Lakes ship owners and the unions on this issue. Ohio was a critical state in this debate. Many of the corporate offices of the LCA members were in Ohio and thus the seamen who were not working in the winter were subject to the workers unemployment compensation laws of Ohio. These men were out of work from late November until April or May and needed money and the unions were there to help them. The companies would be assessed a higher premium if the sailors were eligible to receive unemployment payments in the winter. The issue had been on the table long before the Spencer term of office. The following, drawn from the LCA Annual Reports, mentions the activities of the Legislative Committee in fighting to keep the status quo.

In 1951, the committee worked on matters relating to unemployment compensation on the national and state levels. In 1954, the Committee addressed many state issues the foremost of which, in Ohio, was to retain the seasonal principle relating to payment of unemployment compensation to Great Lakes seamen. In 1955, a matter of concern raised by the Ohio legislature was the elimination of the seasonal provision relating to unemployment compensation for Great Lakes seamen; the measure was not adopted. In 1957, measures relating to repeal of restrictions on paying unemployment compensation to seamen during the closed season was raised again in Ohio but no action was taken. In 1959 LCA lobbied the Ohio legislature again opposed to a change that would eliminate the seasonal provision for seamen.

In order to understand the magnitude of the payments that the ship owners were attempting to avoid the following information is cited. In 1960 from January 1 to October 1, lake seamen received payments of $256,663; this compares to $651,009 during the same interval in 1959 when many vessels were laid up due to the steel industry labor disputes. In 1958 seamen received $1,083,885; this was the second highest payment on record. In 1950 benefits paid were $418,747. One small LCA victory was achieved when the Bureau of Unemployment Compensation was sustained in a ruling that benefits would not be paid out during a period of vacation pay at the termination of employment. LCA continued to seek a review by the Ohio legislature of the continued season benefits for lake seamen.

In 1961 the committee was successful again in opposing changes in the Ohio unemployment benefits laws. Efforts were also made by the unions to change this Ohio law through federal legislation. LCA formed an Unemployment Compensation Study Group to oppose these measures in Columbus and Washington.

Retention of the Status Quo on Laws relating to Seamen

In 1951, the Committee was concerned with and opposed a bill to permit promulgation of safety rules and regulations for longshoremen and proposals for approval of International Labor Organization (ILO) conventions relating to the marine industry. In 1958 Congress amended the Longshoremen's and Harbor Workers' Compensation Act to permit the promulgation of regulations governing the safe working conditions aboard vessels. The Committee was active in successfully opposing proposed laws that would bring seamen under the Fair Labor Standards Act.

USPHS Marine Hospitals face possible closure

In 1955 the Second Hoover Commission established by President Eisenhower to streamline government services recommended waterway user charges and the closing of the USPHS services to seamen.

USPS Hospital near Detroit

Regulation of bulk commodity transportation on the Great Lakes

In 1955 the committee lobbied against a proposal in the Report of the Presidential Advisory Committee on Transportation Policy and Legislation that called for the regulation of bulk commodity transportation on the Great Lakes.

In 1957 the railroads and some congressional interests began efforts to repeal the Interstate Commerce Act general bulk exemption for the Great Lakes. In 1958 LCA and member companies successfully lobbied against the Interstate Commerce Committee action seeking to repeal the bulk cargo exemption requiring the filing of freight rates for Great Lakes vessels; this repeal was supported by many railroads and common carrier barge lines.

Efforts to Obtain Government Assistance in Rebuilding the Great Lakes Fleets

In 1950 the Association became involved with a federal program called the Long Range Shipping Program and began a long term effort to obtain federal government assistance to rebuild the fleets of ships on the Great Lakes. In 1952 the Committee continued to work with Congress on the Long Range Shipping Program; however, only a few of the provisions sought by LCA were included. The legislation did allow the proceeds from the sale of vessels and total loss insurance revenues to be placed in a construction reserve fund to be used for modernization or new construction.

In 1955, Spencer responded to a request from Honorable Clarence G. Morse, Maritime Administrator, requesting views that the government could pursue to bring about the construction of Great Lakes vessels. Shortly after, the legislative committee drafted legislation that would authorize the Administrator to acquire obsolete vessels in exchange for an allowance of credit to be applied to the construction of new vessels. The draft proposed that the government would place these obsolete vessels into government reserve fleet to be utilized in a national emergency. D. C. Potts, President, Pittsburgh Steamship, advised Spencer in 1955 that his company would not take part in the LCA plan dealing with the replacement of Great Lakes vessels but would not offer opposition to the plans.

In 1956 LCA lobbied for a bill that included terms outlined to the Maritime Administrator in 1955 that would facilitate the construction of lakers; while the legislation passed in the Senate, the bill died. The Administration did not want to enact legislation for the Great Lakes industry, preferring legislation that would benefit all coastal trades. The Administrator was supportive of the industry proposal to deposit tax free earning into a capital reserve fund.

Congress did enact legislation amending the federal ship mortgage insurance provisions of the Merchant Marine Act to allow the Secretary of Commerce to insure the entire amount of the interest and unpaid principal of all vessel loans and mortgages covering construction and conversion of Great Lakes vessels.

In 1957 the Legislative Committee continued lobbying congress for legislation to permit use of earnings to be deposited tax free into a capital reserve fund. In 1959, President Eisenhower, in his budget message to Congress called for a review of National Maritime Policy in order to preserve and update the merchant marine. LCA followed the various government transportation studies and appointed a member to serve on the Advisory Council to the Senate Committee on Interstate and Foreign Commerce.

In 1960 efforts were made by LCA to convince the U. S. Treasury of the need for more adequate depreciation allowances for lake vessels as a means of effecting fleet modernization; hopes were expressed that the new Kennedy Administration would bring these changes about.

In 1961 the Canadian government provided a competitive advantage to Canadian vessel owners by announcing that within the next two years, there would be a construction subsidy of 40% of vessel cost, plus a very favorable depreciation rate. After 1963 the subsidy would be reduced to 35%.

On August 25, 1961, in response to a request from Secretary of Commerce Luther Hodges to submit recommendations that would allow American vessels to compete with lower cost foreign-flag ships, Spencer recommended the following:

1. Encourage fleet improvements by:
   - Relaxed depreciation requirements on the basis of a useful vessel life of not more than 25 years.
   - Permission for Great Lakes vessel owners to deposit earnings before taxes in a special construction and rehabilitation reserve fund.
   - Authority to trade in obsolete ships to the U. S. in exchange for credit on the cost of building new vessels.
   - Provision of funds for new vessel construction under authority of the mortgage aid provisions of the Merchant Marine Act of 1936.
2. Amend Merchant Marine Act of 1936 to remove the exclusion from participating in subsidies by Great Lakes vessels.
3. Continuation of the exemptions for transportation of bulk commodities provided in Part III of the Interstate Commerce Act.
4. Preservation of the government's historic toll-free policy with respect to the use of the Great Lakes for commerce and navigation.

5. Retention of the Panama Canal Act provisions which prohibit a railroad from owning an interest in a freight or passenger vessel with which it might compete for traffic.
6. Continuation of the Cargo Preference Act and institution of such administrative measures as are necessary to increase shipments of government sponsored grain cargoes from Great Lakes ports.

All of the above were to attempt to counter the loss of U.S.-flag ship participation in the U.S. / Canada trade that had declined from a carriage of 38% in 1930 to 15% in 1961 and to compete with the other foreign-flag vessels entering the Great Lakes through the St. Lawrence Seaway. Spencer pointed out that of the 500 cargoes of Labrador ore that came into the Lakes in 1959 and 1960, only 38 were moved on U.S. Flag vessels. Canadian vessels were granted construction subsidy and depreciation advantages. Unfortunately, by year end there was no response from the Administration. Two congressmen from Ohio and Wisconsin introduced a bill to extend construction and operating subsidy to vessels in the domestic and international trade on the Great Lakes but congress took no action.

By the end of 1961, in order to provide the federal government with data to support a government program of assistance to lake vessel owners, LCA prepared a study outlining comparative statistics relating to construction and operation of U.S. and Canadian lake vessels. LCA also spent considerable time in providing the Treasury Department with recommendations for a more realistic depreciation allowance on vessel property.

Admiral Spencer worked right up until his retirement. In March 1962 he addressed the Detroit Propeller Club of the United States. He outlined five steps needed to improve the competitive position of the Great Lakes fleets. He urged:

1. Legislative relief in terms of depreciation.
2. Permission for operators to create a construction reserve fund before taxes.
3. Authority to trade in obsolete vessels to the government for credit toward the building of new vessels.

4. Provision of funds for new vessel construction under Mortgage Aid Provisions of the Merchant Marine Act.
5. Deletion from the Merchant Marine Act the provision excluding Great Lakes vessels from eligibility for subsidies.

Welfare Committee

The Chair was A. B. Kern, M. A. Hanna Company, 1946-1955, who served on the committee since 1934. In 1955, John Horton was appointed Chair of the Welfare Committee. Captain Horton served on the committee since 1941, except for his time during World War II when he served as a deck officer on U.S. Army hospital and troop ships. He held unlimited master, oceans, and first class pilot Great Lakes licenses.

John Horton, Chair, Welfare Committee

Ever since 1908 this Committee was one of the most important and active committees of the Association. The mission was to provide personnel for the hundreds of ships of the association, to train them in needed skills and in safety, and to encourage these men to improve their engineering and navigation skills so as to obtain the necessary USCG licenses in order to keep the ships running. It continued to be one of the objectives of the members to keep the employees as company men and not union men. The Assembly Room system provided a seaman with a consistent point of contact for getting a job, finding out how to improve oneself by attending winter schools or correspondence courses, in taking advantage of a free beneficiary insurance in the event of death, and in believing that he was a part of the whole system of lake shipping. The Committee also managed other programs such as the Ship Safety Committees, the Marine Savings Plan, support for the AMMLA library at the Soo and health related programs such as X Rays for tuberculosis and flu vaccinations.

Puerto Rico offers to help alleviate Manpower Shortage

In July 1950, the office of the Government of Puerto Rico contacted Oliver Burnham, LCA, to advise the industry of the availability of 100,000 Puerto Rican workers, 26,000 of whom were veterans, who could assist in the manpower shortage on Great Lakes vessels. The Puerto Rican Economic Development Administration sent this message to many industries on the mainland. The EDA had many stipulations; e.g. they would contract to send 25 or more men to a given area of employment, would provide transportation (that would be paid back through payroll deductions); and the plan was only available to "...plants which do not practice formal segregation because in Puerto Rico neither white nor colored are used to such a custom." There was no indication of any response in the files from LCA to the Puerto Rican authorities on this offer.

Assembly Room System

In 1951 the shortage of seaman was acute and a special recruitment campaign was carried out in 19 cities from Minneapolis and Omaha to Rochester and as far as Altoona and Chattanooga. At a cost of $5,834 over 1,340 men were recruited. As of August 1951 the Assembly Rooms shipped 13,947 persons, an increase of 153% over the 5,519 persons shipped in 1950.

In 1952 there were eleven Assembly Rooms in operation employing 28 men. The Rooms were in Buffalo, Erie, Conneaut, Ashtabula, Cleveland, Lorain, Toledo, Detroit, Chicago, Milwaukee, and Duluth.

In 1957 approximately 400 former U.S. Navy men were recruited by LCA. In 1957 through December 5th, 8,956 men were shipped from the assembly halls including 73 mates and 149 assistant engineers. This compared to 12,232 shipped in 1956. The annual average of men shipped in the 1950s was 12,491. In 1960 the following men worked at the Assembly Halls: Buffalo- A. J. Zimmer and R. H. Plumb, Ashtabula-J. J. Gunn, Cleveland- A. E. Kurtz, Toledo-R. L. Hogle, Detroit-J. W. Krill: Chicago- M. L. Landro, Milwaukee- O. R. Buttlar, and Duluth- M. A. Ross.

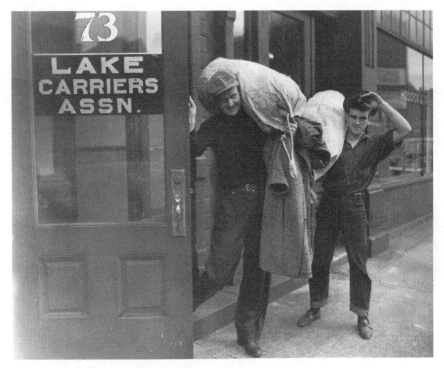

Men shipped from Buffalo Hall including a Navy man

In 1960, a committee was formed to review the operations of the Assembly Rooms in order to reduce expenses. Ashtabula and Milwaukee were placed on a one commissioner status and all other facilities except Cleveland were on a two man basis effective with the opening of the 1961 season. The 24 hour service was maintained through use of telephone connections.

In 1961 the committee centralized the Assembly Room system by providing facilities in Buffalo, Cleveland, Toledo, Chicago and Duluth and on May 20 the rooms in Ashtabula, Detroit and Milwaukee were discontinued. Following the extensive study of the Assembly Room operation chaired by John Horton, this major cut back took place whereas the program that employed 22 people on August 1, 1960 was reduced to six people in August 1961. Members were directed to provide a minimum of a four hour notice to seek a referral of a replacement crew member. In 1962 the cost of the Assembly Rooms operation was $84,073 compared to $215,618 in 1960. The budget for 1963 was projected at $76,986

Mr. A. E. Poole who was in charge of the Assembly Rooms since 1939 and an employee of LCA since 1922 retired on August 1, 1961; Russell H. Plumb who had served as supervisor of the Buffalo Assembly Room succeeded him. The average number of men referred through the assembly halls in the 1960s fell to 3,600.

Russell H. Plumb

Vacation Benefits for Crew

In 1951 Jones and Laughlin Steel Corp. provided unlicensed seamen with one week paid vacation after two seasons of employment, two weeks after five seasons, and three weeks after 25 seasons. A season was defined as employment commencing before August 1 through layup.

The Advisory Committee in 1953 received a recommendation from the Welfare Committee that the basis for vacation allowances be changed to provide for three weeks paid vacation after 15 years of service instead of after 25 years of service.

Winter Schools and Correspondence Courses

For a brief period in 1946 the schools were managed by the Education and Public Relations Committee. While attendance in 1946 was low, through promotion of the need for education, the winter schools that opened on January 2, 1947 had a large increase in student enrollment. There was a plan to reopen the Marine Engineering School at Marine City but an insufficient number of students registered. Navigation and Engineering schools in Cleveland were at 2994 West 25th Street where they had an increased number of students; including 32 former service men who received government subsistence allowances during the school term.

Navigation Class of 1948

CLASS FOR MARINE ENGINEERS SPONSORED BY THE ASSOCIATION AND GENERAL ELECTRIC COMPANY FEBRUARY, 1948

Winter Schools

Winter school responsibilities were returned to the Welfare Committee in 1947; they prepared for the 1948 schools and in all future years. Schools were held for new and upgrade deck and engine officer licenses as needed in Cleveland, Duluth and Marine City.

For the 2nd winter, in 1949, Engineers attended a two week class of the LCA Advanced School of Marine Engineering in cooperation with General Electric Company. In 1950 the course was managed by LCA with assistance from several equipment manufactures. In the 1951-52 winter, the Marine City School was reopened. In 1951-52 new revised course in Modern Marine Engineering was held to prepare men for the new ships and the new equipment they would operate. Manufacturer's reps assisted with the courses. In 1953, the three week Modern Marine Engineering course was held at John Marshall Law School, a location frequently used by LCA for training programs. 1953 was the 7th year for this engineering program.

In 1950 an extension training program for engineers on the ships was recommended by the Fleet Engineers Committee. A series of 40 lessons entitled *Know your Volts and Amps* were provided in four monthly sets. Costs were shared by the 18 participating fleets that requisitioned 2,086 sets; in the next year 1,867 instruction sets were sent to engine room personnel on 16 participating fleets. In 1952, at the recommendation of the Fleet Engineers Committee the program was enhanced to include

Feed Water Treatment; crewmembers from 14 fleets subscribed and 1,810 seamen received training.

In 1951, the cost of the winter schools was $13,511; revision of the Engineering Data Book was $7,500; renewal of Advanced School of Engineering material was $7,886; and printing of the summer technical bulletin for a two year period was $7,387.

In 1953 engineers classes were again held in Marine City. In 1954 discussions were held with the Duluth Board of Education seeking cooperation in holding classes there for deck and engine officers. Arrangements were made for instructors and the classes were set for January, 1955 at the LCA Duluth Assembly Rooms. As a result, in the deck classes 20 men were prepared for a raise of grade or an original license; and, in the engine classes, 24 men obtained an original license or a raise in grade.

In 1956 Correspondence Courses were arranged in six lessons each to be studied during the navigation season by 260 prospective deck and engine officers to prepare for the winter classes; and in 1957, 369 individuals were provided with instructional material.

In 1956 a course of instruction concerning turbine operation and electricity was arranged for a maximum of 30 individuals, February 3-28, 1957 at the U.S. Merchant Marine Academy. This program continued for many years.

In 1958 George Rector was appointed principal instructor at the LCA Cleveland Engineering School.

George Rector (Northwestern Michigan College Archives)

In 1958, a new program of a series of six lectures on Professional Topics were held in Cleveland in January and February for about 50 office personnel of member companies. A new Safety Discussion group affiliated with the National Safety Council was also established in Cleveland to meet monthly to review fleet safety matters. Duluth classes continued and new training was instituted for the St. Lawrence River and Seaway. Because of the new Coast Guard license exam requirements, a new course on radar was added for the 1959 schools to help men pass the license exams on radar operation. In 1960 the Welfare Plan held Cleveland navigation and engineering schools with a special radar course and a course for extension of license for the St. Lawrence River. The Duluth Engineering School was open but the Duluth navigation school was discontinued due to instructional difficulties.

Captain John C. Murray was not active as an instructor in Cleveland as he retired in 1960 but he was available as a consultant. He was succeeded by Captain William J. McSweeney who had been teaching along with Murray for the previous twenty years. George B. Rector continued as the principal instructor in the engineering section.

Capt. William J. McSweeney, Jr.

Marine Savings Plan

In 1946, the LCA Marine Saving Plan was still very popular with 217 crews who deposited over $1.3 million in the Buffalo Savings Bank, the Central National Bank and the Cleveland Trust Company. In 1947 and 1948 the deposits were over $2 million; in 1949, it was reduced to $1.8 million due to strikes and vessel layups. By 1950, in the 40 years of the savings plan, crews had deposited over $40 million in the banks; by December 31, 1951 over $50.9 million was deposited.

In 1954, there was a marked decline in participation in the marine savings plan. Nevertheless, crews still deposited in excess of $1 million/year; this was the 16th year that deposits exceeded $1 million/year. The contributions to the three banks declined except for the crews on the Boland and Cornelius ships. A peak of deposits had occurred in 1948; the Welfare Committee concluded that there was an increased tendency for crew members to send earnings for deposit in hometown community banks. In 1958, the amount saved in the Marine Savings Plan plummeted to $637,457 due to the reduced employment in that year; this was the lowest level since the depression year of 1933. In 1959 savings continued to decline in part due to the long strike at the beginning of the year, only $577,152 was deposited in the three banks. In 1960 there was an increase in savings by 7%; however in 1961 there was a decrease of 25%. Clearly the crew members no longer found it necessary to avail themselves of the LCA savings plan.

Ship Safety Committees and Safety Education

Because of the continued rapid turnover of crews on the Great Lakes vessels, there was a constant influx of new men, many were young and inexperienced in any industrial environment; among the older men many were new to shipboard work conditions. The training of these men was primarily up to the ship's officers and lead seamen. Helping members prevent accidents was a continuous effort of the LCA. In virtually every issue of the Bulletin there were safety posters and information from the safety committees.

Safety poster-Use hard hat and Gloves

Safety poster-Pulling ashes wear
leather gloves and shoes

All vessels were asked to form Ship Safety Committees comprised of officers and crews to evaluate accidents, make recommendations for improvement and to report their actions to the Welfare Committee. Many good ideas for improved procedures came from the ship's committees. In 1984 there were 186 active committees.

Safety Posters designed for Great Lakes vessels became a regular program in 1949 and were sent to subscribing vessels. Safety calendars with monthly slogans were placed onboard 305 member vessels in 1953. In that year, the Welfare Committee undertook a complete revision of the manual *Recommendations for Prevention of Accidents Aboard Ship* to include improved methods of presentation and more adequate pictorial treatment.

Health-Operation X-Ray

LCA Welfare Committee was concerned about the spread of Tuberculosis (TB) among crew members who lived in close proximity to each other. Tuberculosis usually attacks the lungs but can also affect other parts of the body. It is spread through the air, when people who have the disease cough, sneeze, or spit. It was recognized that if infections progressed to an active disease and left untreated, it killed more than 50% of its victims.

XRAY Mobile unit heading for the Soo

Because of this concern, in July 1950 the LCA Welfare Committee commenced 'Operation X-Ray' seeking to give chest X-ray to all Great Lakes seamen. The program started with X-Rays of the 35 officers and crew of the John P. Reiss at the Soo. LCA received the cooperation of the USPHS, the Michigan State Health Department and the Corps of Engineers to X-ray seamen passing through the Soo Locks, using portable x-ray equipment. The Corps built a shelter for the equipment, the crew members presented a card filled out by a ship's officer to the technician and brought the stub back to the ship. If no request for a re-check came back within six weeks, the sailor assumed his chest was OK. Because of the new security in place due to the Korean War, only four crew members could leave the ship at any one time and always accompanied by an officer. By September 1950 nearly 4,300 seamen were x-rayed during an eight week period, of which 79 tested positive, the preponderance of those being in the 45-70 year range.

In 1951 the cost of the program was estimated to be $1,000.

In 1952 LCA asked for and received permission for Canadian seamen to debark at the Soo for X-Rays but Dominion Marine Association rejected the offer. The cost for LCA in 1952 was estimated to be $1,500 for one month.

In 1956, 2,831 men were x-rayed at the Soo; and in order to X-ray the sailors who did not transit the locks, arrangements were made to place a mobile unit at the Toledo Lakefront Dock, where 96 seamen and 180 dock and railroad workers were X-rayed; and at the South Chicago Rail to Water dock on the Calumet River where 80 seamen and 124 dock personnel were X-rayed. Of the 2,831 sailors who had their chests X-rayed at the Soo, 44 were abnormal, and 25 indicated 'suspect reinfection tuberculosis'.

In 1950, 4,102 sailors were X-rayed, 141 of whom were referred for further diagnosis. In 1951, 3,750 sailors were x-rayed; only 56 were referred for further diagnosis. In 1952, the X-Ray program was organized and ready to operate but was cancelled because of the severely reduced traffic as a result of the steel strike. In 1953, 5,895 men from 23 fleets were x-rayed at the Soo and a unit was set up at the Toledo Lakefront Dock; but only 170 men were x-rayed in the 5 day period.

In the 1954 Annual Report there is no report of this program. In 1955, 5,454 men were X-rayed from 20 fleets and 152 were found to have abnormalities of whom 72 were labeled 'suspect reinfection tuberculosis'; this compared to 5,865 tested in 1953. In 1956, x-rays were made at the Soo, Toledo and South Chicago. Even with the labor disputes in that year, the Soo technicians x-rayed 2,830 seamen; at Toledo during a two day period, 96 men were processed; and, in South Chicago in two days, 83 men were x-rayed. In 1957, 6,084 men from 20 fleets received x-rays; 123 showed abnormalities of which 78 were 'suspected reinfection tuberculosis'.

At the same time in 1957 due to a worldwide concern for the Asian influenza (H2N2) outbreak, LCA authorized a flu vaccination program at the Soo whereat 3,134 crew members on 110 vessels from 12 fleets were given the Asian flu vaccination. The vaccine was provided by the USPHS and administered by five doctors and thirteen nurses. Doctors and nurses boarded the ships at the Soo around the clock including weekends assured that the maximum number of sailors was vaccinated. In addition, Pittsburgh Steamship arranged for crew member vaccination on each of their 57 vessels.

In 1959 the X-Ray program took place at Rogers City from September 1-7 in order to reach the crews of the self-unloaders; a total of 373 seamen and a large number of plant employees at the Calcite quarry were examined.

In 1960 the report states that the X-Ray program was re-established when 4,102 persons on 162 vessels in 19 days were X-rayed; there is no record of those testing positive. Due to the inability to obtain equipment the program was suspended in 1961 and 1962.

The Welfare Committee looked into the possibility of administering the Sabin anti-polio vaccine but was advised that there were technical difficulties with such a program.

Death Benefits for Seamen Registered at the Assembly Hall

In order to receive death payments to the next of kin or permanent disability payments a seaman or officer had to be registered with the LCA through the Assembly Halls. Years before at the beginning of the registration system, a seaman had to vouch that he was not a member of the union but over time that requirement was dropped. Other benefits such as the winter schools were available to registered seamen. The vast majority of seamen registered each year with the LCA Assembly Halls. In 1946, there were 13,354 seamen registered and that reached a high of 18,304 seamen in 1951. By 1958 and 1959 due to a diminished shipment of freight and a strike in 1959 the average in those two years was 8,282 seamen.

The payments to beneficiaries due to death of a family member or to a seaman due to permanent disability continued each year. The payments were small based on today's standards. In 1908 the payments were set by the Board of Directors for Master at $500; Chief Engineer $400; Steward, Mates and Engineers from $150-250; and other unlicensed seamen from $75-100.

The Welfare Committee tailored the Safety Program to reduce the accidents that caused these deaths. The record of payments and the cause of deaths follow.

1946- Payments were made to relatives of five sailors who died; two fell overboard; one fell off dock; one fell into hold and one died from unspecified injuries.

1947- There were nine fatalities or disabilities; six fatal falls from ladder, stairway, to dock, off staging, into cargo hold, off vessel and drowned; one struck by cable; one injured in machinery; one fractured skull and one disability.

1948-There were 15 fatalities. Two highly unusual deaths occurred to Masters killed on separate occasions while driving in automobiles on ship's business. Seven were from falls from vessel and drown, from ship between dock and vessel and drown, into cargo hold, and on to dock. Three others were the aftermath of vessel collisions.

1949- Seven payments were made for fatalities; four from falling, two from drowning and one struck by a railroad car when sailor was returning to the ship.

1950- Seven payments for fatalities two fell into cargo holds; and five fell into the water and drowned, two while boarding the ship.

1951- Ten cases were approved for payment. Four fatal falls into cargo hold, off ladder and off staging; three drowned off the vessel; one disappeared and one was crushed between ship and dock, the tenth was for funeral expenses, cause of death not stated.

1952- Thirteen payments due to fatalities were paid to beneficiaries. Eight men died from drowning after falls from staging, shoreside cat walk, boarding ladders, handling mooring lines and over the side while underway; five others died, one from a fall from a ladder fracturing his skull, two men fall into cargo hold, one fell from a boom, and one was crushed by the swing of a crane.

1953- Twenty six payments were made; seventeen of which were for casualties as a result of the sinking of the <u>Henry Steinbrenner</u>. Of the other nine deaths, two fell into the cargo hold, one drown while handling mooring lines and the others all drown after falls from ladders, catwalk, while returning to ship or over the ship's rail.

1954-Seven payments were made; three drowned, a Master died off the vessel; a fireman returning to the vessel and a deck watch fell off a ladder into the water. A 2nd Mate was crushed by a deck crane, a man fell into the cargo hold and another man fell from a ladder. This was the 5th consecutive year that one or more seamen died falling into the cargo hold.

1955- Six payments were made; two were due to deaths in auto accidents of a Master and a Chief Engineer going to or returning to a ship; two fell into the cargo hold; and, two drowned off the vessel.

1956- Six payments were made. Unfortunately this was the 7th year that a man died falling into a cargo hold; three men died of drowning returning to the vessel; one sailor fell off a ladder and a Chief Engineer fell from a hatch ladder.

In 1957 the Advisory Committee approved a change in the Death Benefit to become effective January 1, 1957; payments ranged from $200 for unlicensed personnel to $600 for Masters. They approved that the Death Benefits be increased by $100 for each benefit and that the Steward's rate be classed with the 3rd mate and 3rd assistant engineer. The benefits had been in place since 1909, and except for minor revisions, had not been increased.

1957-Six payments were made; four from drowning-three of which were while returning to vessel; one fell off a ladder; and one deckhand was crushed between the ship and the dock while handling mooring lines.

1958-The steamer <u>Carl D. Bradley</u> foundered off Gull Island in Lake Michigan on November 18, 1958 during a period of strong gale winds and heavy seas. Of the 35 crew members only two survived. Death payments were made to the families of 33 crew members. Additionally, six other crew members from other vessels died; one fell into the cargo hold; three drowned, two of whom were returning to the vessel; one disappeared from the vessel and one fell off a ladder.

1959- Five payments were made; two died falling from a ladder; one died from falling off the dock and two drowned off the vessel.

1960- Five payments were made, and except for 1959 when there were five, this was the lowest number of payments since 1939. Mention is made in the Annual Report that this improvement may be due to the success of the safety first program and the reality that due to the reduced number of men employed there were fewer inexperienced men onboard the ships. Three men drowned and two fell off the dock.

1961- This was a very good year for safety in that only one man died from drowning while boarding the vessel.

Reviewing the preceding one can conclude that with the exception of the 50 payment to families of crew members who perished when the Steamers Henry S. Steinbrenner and Carl D. Bradley foundered, the causes of death were primarily from falls and drowning.

SS Carl D. Bradley (Al Hart Collection)

SS Henry Steinbrenner Soo locks (Wikipedia, Detroit Publishing Co.)

At least 30 men died from drowning after falling over board from various known or unknown reasons; another 15 fell from boarding ladders, catwalks and docks or where struck by a railroad car while returning to the ships, some of whom drown; the largest single cause of death by falls were the 17 men who fell into cargo holds and another 17 who fell from ladders, staging and stairs; other men fell from the dock into the water while handling mooring lines; were struck by cables or deck cranes.

During the tenure of Admiral Spencer over 80 men died from industrial accidents, not related to ship sinking. The Welfare Committee Safety Education program was committed to reduce this carnage through training and new equipment.

Safety poster boarding the ship ladder

Shore Captains and Navigation Committees

Chairmen of the Shore Captains were: Captain C. O. Rydholm 1946-1953, Captain H. F. Wiersch June 1953-58, and Captain P. J. Healy from 1958 onward. The Navigation Committee Chairs were rotated frequently as they were the working captains on the lake freighters. 1961 was the first year that it was recognized that there were an insufficient number of shore captains employed as shore management within the member companies thus they recommended asking recently retired captains to be assigned to the committee.

While the Navigation Committee was extremely important from the standpoint of bringing to the management table at the end of each navigation season the pressing needs for improvements in the system, I have chosen to consider their work as a part of the Shore Captains Committee since that committee approved actions recommended by the Navigation Committee. The Shore Captains were in a position to meet frequently during the year and to make recommendations to the Advisory and Legislative Committees.

Major issues with which the members dealt included: expansion of the Navigation infrastructure; working closely with the USCG to open and close the ice clogged navigation channels at the beginning and end of the season, including the chartering of car ferries and tugs to assist the USCG; changing the Load Line regulations; monitoring and modifying the separate courses designated on each of the Lakes; the navigation dangers caused by the opening of the St. Lawrence Seaway (outlined with the legislative committee work); and the installation of Radar on lake vessels.

Expansion of the Navigation Infrastructure

One of the major efforts of the LCA in the Spencer period was to improve the navigation channels and ports by deepening and widening them in order to accommodate larger vessels that would lower the cost of the transportation of raw materials for the iron and steel industry and the agricultural interests. The Shore Captains and the Legislative Committees worked jointly on these projects.

From 1948-50 the Shore Captains Committee continued working with the Corps on harbor and channel improvements, in particular the need for deepening of the connecting channels in preparation for the new ships under construction. They continued over the years advising the Corps on various river improvements and enlargement of harbors.

In 1953, Congress approved funds for the Corps to study improvements to the channels after the Legislative Committee testified in favor of appropriations and for the Corps to study the need to increase the depth to 27 feet in the connecting channels. In 1954, the North Central Division completed the report and recommended the depth be increased to provide a safe draft of 25.5 feet at low water datum. The cost of the project was estimated to be $109 million.

In 1957, the legislative committee gave support for improvements in harbors and channels to allow the larger vessels to carry a maximum draft. In that year the Shore Captains Committee spent a great deal of time with the Coast Guard and the Corps regarding deepening the connecting channels. There was significant concern about the Corps plan to deepen the eastern half of the upbound channel to the 25.5 feet safe draft and then to use those channels for both up and down bound vessels while the downbound channels were being deepened. The principle concerns were for potential collisions and for long delays unless there were some restrictions placed on deeply laden vessels until all the deepening work was completed. Committee members traveled to the Corps facility at Vicksburg, MS, to observe models of various harbors and also made many recommendations regarding improvement in other harbors and entrances.

In 1958, Congress provided $25.5 million appropriations for the deepening of the connecting channels.

In 1960, Spencer reported on the excellent progress on deepening the connecting channels and on a series of twenty harbor studies for improvement to be recommended to congress; and he reported that preliminary work was initiated on the new lock at the Soo.

New Lock at the Soo

The Committee in 1956 recommended that any new lock to replace the Poe Lock have a minimum length of 1,000 feet and a width of 100 feet. In 1959 the Shore Captains reviewed the plans for a new lock to replace the current Poe Lock with a new lock of 1000 x 100 x 32 feet over the sill.

In 1960, Spencer speculated that with adequate appropriations the new lock would be completed in 1965, 22 years after the completion of the MacArthur Lock.

Charter of and Expenses for Commercial Icebreakers

Unlike in the World War II years when the USCG chartered icebreaking vessels, in 1947-52, the LCA chartered the carferry Sainte Marie to work in conjunction with the Mackinaw in the Mackinac Straits, St. Marys River and Whitefish Bay. In 1951, invoices for icebreaking aggregated over $139,912 which was paid for by collaborating interests at a rate per gross registered ton for a separate fee based upon the date of service and the area traversed. Fees were Straits of Mackinac, April 2-5 inclusive $.0781536 per GRT; St. Marys Fall Canal, April 6-9, inclusive $.0928474 per GRT and Head of the Lakes April 10-23 $.0445444 per GRT.

In March 1953 the Mackinac Transportation Company advised LCA that the charter hire for an initial 14 day period would be increased to $99,200 from the $91,700 paid in 1951. An optional charter was offered if LCA would assume the cost of repairs in excess of the $5,000 deductible average and not exceeding $10,000. Fortunately as the season opened in 1953 the weather seemed good for an early start and thus the Sainte Marie was not chartered; however due to a rapid wind shift in the upper St. Marys River, an ice jam quickly developed in the channel leading to the locks for the period April 3-10.

LCA chartered a number of tugs to assist the vessels through the ice; at one time as many as 80 vessels were awaiting lockage with the rate of passage slowed to one vessel/hour. In the period April 3-10, 1953, the cost of icebreaking operations in the St. Marys River was $15,222 during which period 402 vessels locked through. The costs were apportioned to benefitting members.

In the following years, opening of the season were aided exclusively by USCG vessels. In 1956 and 1957, the Sainte Marie was again chartered for the LCA account to open the season.

Load Line

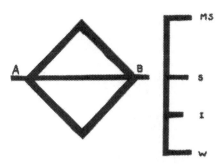

Plimsoll marks for the Great Lakes have four season indicators.

In 1947, 1948 and 1949, because of the excessive demand for cargo movement, LCA requested the USCG to give the operators an assignment of emergency load lines for the vessels during the summer load line season; this was the same authority granted during the War from 1941 through 1945. Summer load lines were extended from September 15 through midnight September 30. In 1948 the Canadian Department of Transportation authorized similar action on Canadian vessels. In 1949, following the recommendation of the Shore Captains Committee, the Board approved making a request to the Coast Guard to make a permanent change to the Load Line Act whereby the emergency load line would become permanent. The Commandant rejected that request and stated that there would be no further granting of an emergency summer load line. However in 1950 and 1951, due to the emergency conditions caused by demand created by the Korean War, summer load lines were allocated for approved Great Lakes vessels from May 16-September 15, and the regular summer load line was extended through September 30. In 1952 the extensions were granted again. Due to the steel strike in the summer, there was excessive demand and the summer load line was extended through October 15. During 1952, ABS had approved the LCA proposal to amend the load line regulations to allow to deeper loading of vessels that had a proven safety record during the past 12 years without a waiver process. At year's end the Coast Guard was considering this proposal. In 1953, new Load Line Rules for the Great Lakes were established: Winter (W) November 1-April 15; Intermediate

(I) April 16-30 and October 1-31; Summer (S) May 1-15 and September 16-30; and Midsummer (MS) May 16-September 15.

Separate Courses

During the Spencer leadership period, LCA continued to advocate improved navigation safety by reviewing, changing and adding new Separate Courses throughout the Great Lakes. In 1948 the committee called upon vessels with Radar to continue to follow the Separate Courses and obey all Pilot Rules. In 1950, Separate Courses were approved for Lake Ontario and the west end of Lake Erie for vessels of Canadian and U.S. registry. This completed the LCA Plan that started in 1911 calling for separate courses for each of the Great Lakes.

In 1951 and 1952, the Shore Captains and the Navigation Committees reviewed reports submitted by members on those vessels that did not adhere to the separate courses. This was a consistent concern particularly as the foreign vessels were entering the Great Lakes. In 1958, the Shore Captains Committee continued to review reports on vessels that did not adhere to the separate course lines and asked the companies to review these claims and to provide justification for the departure. In 1961 separate course line amendments were proposed and approved.

Radar Operational Research Project

Radar, the new almost revolutionary navigation device, was viewed as a valuable and necessary device on the lakes to prevent collisions and groundings in the close navigation waters and channels on the Great Lakes. As early as March 1945, the LCA Board formed a special committee to work with the government to expedite the application to vessels on the Great Lakes. LCA engaged Dr. C. M. Jansky, Jr., Chairman of Jansky & Bailey, as consulting radio engineer. The Navigation, Shore Captains, and Electronics Committees all supported this project.

In the winter of 1945-46 after many meetings with manufacturers, radar sets were placed on six vessels by six manufacturers. The objective was to help the manufacturers produce radars that were most suitable for the Great Lakes. A number of improvements were made and by the end of 1947, four passenger ships and 28 cargo vessels of U.S. registry had radars as well as 8 passenger ships and 10 cargo ships of Canadian registry. In 1948 American ships had radars on 4 passenger ships and 88 cargo vessels; the Canadians had radars on 8 passenger ships and 32 cargo vessels. By 1949, 177 radar sets were in service on U.S. vessels and 69 on Canadian; by end of 1950 there were 305 (93% of LCA membership) on American ships and 90 on Canadian ships; by end of 1951 there were 347 sets (96% of LCA members) on U.S. ships and 95 on Canadian. In 1952 there were 362 radars on U.S. vessels and 103 on Canadian.

In 1948 the FCC raised the question if the operators of radars should have a special license. The LCA and many others opposed this idea in that radar was navigation equipment in the same category as a radio direction finder. In 1948, the Navigation Committee called for radar charts of the St. Marys River.

In 1949, in conjunction with five radar manufacturers, six five day classes were held for deck officers in the use of radar. Approximately 350 masters and mates attended. In 1950, 213 officers attended. Hands on classes were held with radar equipment at the Nicholson Terminal. In 1951, radar class was attended by 149 officers.

Additional Work of the Shore Captains and Navigation Committees

In 1946, the Committees continued requests for improvements in the location of maritime aids, dredging of specific locations in the ports and connecting channels, fendering of bridges, removal of disused railroad bridges as well as published recommended drafts for connecting channels. In 1947 they made recommendations to widen and deepen the Black Rock Canal, the movement of buoys, on the need to broadcast current conditions in Duluth and Superior, the need for Barographs and Anemometers on ships and lighthouses, and published circulars on water levels and draft recommendations. The Navigation Committee called for the operation of aids where possible before the season started.

In 1948 the Committees continued to seek channel improvements in various ports, proper disposal of garbage and other waste material, improved bridge opening hours, and called for new lighthouse structures.

In 1949-50 the Committee met with the Coast Guard on simplification of the First Class Pilot license exam and with the Weather Bureau on reducing the number of broadcasts without losing necessary data. In 1951-2 the issues they dealt with included: speed in the St. Marys River, turning basin in the Saginaw River, recommended location for a new fuel dock in the St. Marys River, actions to reduce accidents in the vicinity of the Soo locks, vertical clearances for fixed bridges, the impact of 'squat' on draft and thus the need for reduced speed in confined water, a request for the removal of the Huron Light vessel and replacement with a fixed structure, construction of new private harbors, new rules for the St. Marys River, and improvements to the aids to navigation. In 1949 the Shore Captains requested that all vessels use Eastern Standard Time in all reports.

In 1953 the Corps responded to LCA concerns about water levels by looking at measures to minimize the fluctuation of lake levels. The Committee reviewed plans for the pipe lines across the Straits of Mackinaw, a bridge over the Saginaw River and new docks at various ports. In 1954 the Committee reviewed plans for construction of private docks in Detroit and Saginaw and new harbors in Silver Bay and Cedarville and the new bridge over the Mackinaw Straits. In that year the Committee worked out a plan with the U.S. Air Force for participation in the Ground Observation Corps program for reporting airplanes sighted over the open lakes.

In 1955 the Committee worked with the USCG to fashion regulations that were not onerous for navigating the Rouge River following a number of accidents there. The Committee also worked with the USCG to construct a new station bill for emergency drills. The Navigation Committee raised the issue that some officers on ships were not adhering to the Rules of the Road with respect to passing signals and that this matter should be brought up at spring meetings. The Committee recommended to the Corps to allow no permit for construction of bulkheads and piers along the connecting channels unless the structure was built at least four feet above high water; the Corps advised they did not have the authority to make that requirement but would so recommend to permit applicants. In 1956 the committee worked closely with the Corps to place reasonable restrictions on the operation of sand-suckers in the St. Clair River since many Masters reported difficulty in passing these vessels. They petitioned to remove a disused railroad bridge across the St. Marys River and the removal of Bridge Island in the St. Marys River.

In 1959, the Committee recommended that all vessels on the Lakes be equipped with VHF-FM telephones as rapidly as possible. In 1960 Spencer reported that LCA representation in London at the SOLAS Conference was to assure that adequate recognition was given to the special problems of Great Lakes navigation. The committee objected to the establishment of a floating breakwater in the Detroit River opposite the Detroit Civic Center as it would encroach upon the harbor line and create a navigation hazard.

In 1961 the committee had a busy year reviewing fifteen harbor improvement plans, two bridge replacements and three turning basins as well as new harbor lines. Changes proposed by the USCG in the Rules of the Road and Pilot Rules were reviewed and an LCA position was presented.

Electronics Committee

P.L. Tietjen, Chair 1947-1952; Joseph B. Ayers, Jr. Chair 1953-1858; A. S. Thaeler, 1958

After the war, in part because of the accelerated development of communications and navigation systems such as radar and other electronic systems, it was essential for LCA to take a leadership role in the development of the communications and navigation systems and to influence any regulatory regime surrounding the use of such equipment.

In 1947 the Electronics Committee was permanently established and the Radar Coordinating Committee was disbanded. In 1948 the Committee was authorized to consider all matters relating to radio, radar, direction finders and other electronic devices installed on a vessel. Recommendations included:

1. LCA take no position regarding installation of VHF offered by a commercial company as part of a land mobile service since individual members would decide on the worth of each system.
2. That assignment of VHF frequencies within the band of mobile maritime service should be requested for the Great Lakes.

3. That licensing of radar maintenance personnel by FCC should be opposed.

In 1949 the Committee held discussions concerning negotiation of the Great Lakes Radio Treaty and problems relating to use of VHF short range radiotelephone usage. There was recognition that there was a need to reduce vessel traffic on existing long range frequencies. All matters relating to improved radio communication equipment and frequency allocations were coordinated with the Dominion Marine Association.

In 1950 the Committee, in conjunction with DMA members, drafted a US/Canada Treaty requiring that all ships be equipped with radiotelephones for safety and navigation purposes with the objective that there would be a development of a supplemental VHF radiotelephone system for the Lakes. LCA wanted to preserve the current Great Lakes radiotelephone system. Committee opposed more stringent operator requirements for navigation personnel and supported the installation of Ramark beacons at critical navigation points.

In 1951 the Radio Treaty was completed and was approved by both countries in 1952, to become operative on November 13, 1954. All cargo vessels over 500 tons would be equipped with a radiotelephone capable of operating with at least two frequencies. Vessels would maintain a listening watch when navigating and there would be at least one qualified person onboard having a certificate to operate the radiotelephone.

In 1951 new rules for VHF were promulgated by the FCC, all in agreement with LCA recommendations. The Committee recommended the installation of VHF on vessels ASAP. Thirty two sets were available from manufacturers and 25 were installed on Great Lakes vessels in short order. In 1952 the committee was concerned with retaining the AM and FM channels allocated to the Lakes as the demand for channels for use in other areas were strong.

In 1953 the Committee published an instruction booklet on the use of VHF equipment. Committee recommending that nothing less than 8-channel VHF sets should be used in the system. Experiments were made on a vessel identification system called RADENT, developed by Sperry Corporation. Conferences were held with the FCC regarding criteria and procedures in connection with the examination of personnel and inspection of equipment required by the new Great Lakes Radiotelephone Agreement.

In 1954, the Committee spent a great deal of time working with the FCC in having the vessels adhere to the Radiotelephone Agreement with respect to inspection and certification of the new equipment and the licensing of personnel.

In 1955 an FCC inspector was temporarily assigned to inspect vessels in the Lake Erie area and was provided with temporary office space in the LCA offices; another temporary office was established in Duluth in order to facilitate the inspection of all vessels adhering to the Agreement. The Committee recommended that with respect to the construction of a VHF coastal network of stations, the FCC should institute a complete investigation of the system of communications employed on the Great Lakes for safety and navigation purposes. The FCC did not accept the LCA recommendation and preferred to hold hearings in 1956 on the applications for permits to construct VHF stations at several locations—LCA did not participate in the hearings.

In 1956 the Committee stressed to the members the importance of having an annual inspection of the Radiotelephone equipment by the FCC and to install the VHF equipment. By the end of 1956 at least 75 vessels in LCA membership had such equipment. The Electronics Committee recognized that the Seaway would open soon and thus there would be many international ships in the Great Lakes and there would be a serious safety problem without a world-wide, international radiotelephone system. This was a matter of great importance since, at that time, the international ships had radio operators onboard who used radiotelegraphy and radiotelegraph for safety-distress communications.

In 1957 Committee noted that the Great Lakes radiotelephone system had been in effect since 1932, for over 25 years, and that it must be maintained. LCA, through its consultant, continued to support the use of radio telephone for safety and navigation purposes in meetings of the International Telecommunications Union in Geneva. The consultant report noted that 161 lake vessels had VHF installations installed, of which 108 were enrolled in LCA; and that those using the VHF reported it was a valuable supplement to MF-HF systems. Committee noted that the new FCC regulations taking effect in 1963 were more severe than anticipated.

USCG proposed that effective in 1958 all applicants for an original or upgrade license pass a radar use exam.

In 1958 Committee was occupied with the communications issues caused by the opening of the Seaway; specifically the problem that the salties carried radio telegraph equipment and not radiophone. Committee also recommended that weather forecasts continue to be broadcast on MF-HF rather than VHF. LCA electronics consultant prepared a radar training manual to be used in the LCA schools.

In 1959 Dr. C. M. Jansky, Jr. was designated as the LCA representative in Geneva, Switzerland at the Administrative Radio Conference, International Telecommunications Union. It was fortunate for LCA that he was present as he authoritatively explained the radiotelephone system for safety and navigation on the Great Lakes and thus thwarted an effort that would have limited the effectiveness of the system. LCA nominated Dr. Jansky, Jr. to be LCA representative on the National Industry Advisory Committee which was organized to supervise CONELRAD plans that were effective as part of civilian defense in time of emergency.

***CONELRAD (Con**trol of **E**lectromagnetic [or **E**lectronic] **Rad**iation) was a method of emergency broadcasting to the public of the United States in the event of enemy attack during the Cold War. It was intended to serve two purposes: to prevent Soviet bombers from homing in on American cities by using radio or TV stations as beacons, and to provide essential civil defense information. President Truman established CONELRAD in 1951. After the development of intercontinental ballistic missiles reduced the likelihood of a bomber attack, CONELRAD was replaced by the Emergency Broadcast System on August 5, 1963, which was later replaced with the Emergency Alert System in 1997; all were administered by the Federal Communications Commission (FCC).*

In 1959 the Committee continued to express concern that the foreign vessels entering the Lakes did not adhere to the Great Lakes Radio Telephone Agreement thus it was impossible to contact those vessels; there was also concern that these vessels did not maintain a watch on the calling-distress frequency.

In 1960 it was noted that since LCA had representation in Geneva and London at international conferences; nothing inimical to the Great Lakes system took place.

The Committee reviewed a proposal from outside the Great Lakes for the use of an auto alarm with the radiotelephone in order that a continuous oral listening watch could be discontinued. The Committee asked the Advisory Board to oppose the adoption of an auto alarm. Committee advised members that the Seaway authorities were prepared to handle all communications with VHF and thus starting January 1, 1962 all vessels in the Seaway and Welland Canal must have VHF radio telephones.

In 1961 the use of VHF for communication to vessels from bridges started with the bridge at Houghton-Hancock, MI, that was authorized to use a VHF frequency. The committee continued to work with the FCC to bring the Great Lakes VHF system in accord with the Geneva Radio regulations. Jansky and Bailey continued as the LCA electronics consultant.

Fleet Engineers Committee

M. E. Kingsbury, Wilson Transit, Chair 1945-through the Spencer tenure.

Ships making smoke

Passenger Ship making smoke (Zenith City Press)

One of the biggest issues facing the Fleet Engineers was to find a way to reduce the smoke emissions from the large number of coal fired engine rooms on the Lakes. Municipal, State and Federal government agencies were committed to reducing the smoke pollution in the port cities and in the channels where the ships transited. In 1946 the Committee met to discuss smoke abatement issues in Cleveland; in 1947 there were smoke abatement issues raised in Milwaukee and Toledo; and in 1948 the IJC considered water and smoke pollution particularly relating to the St. Clair-Detroit area. It was absolutely necessary for LCA to take some positive action to reduce emissions. In 1949, the Committee worked on smoke abatement practices and equipment in conjunction with the International Joint Commission; they tested a number of pieces of equipment to reduce smoke emissions but noted that a dependable solution was still in the development stage. As the years went on the Fleet Engineers worked closely with others to try to minimize this problem.

Great Lakes Air Pollution Abatement Program

LCA organized this program in July 1950 to establish facilities and methods that would reduce smoke emissions and that would improve the efficiency of lake vessels using coal for fuel. They were aided by an Engineering Advisory Committee representing contributing sponsors and they included LCA, DMA, Ohio Coal Association, Bituminous Coal Researchers, Inc., Coal Producers Committee for Smoke Abatement, and Pittsburgh Consolidation Coal. The activities of the group were in three fields: 1. Standards for fuel. 2. Equipment and facilities onboard vessels. 3. Education of vessel personnel. The Technical Advisory Committee of the International Joint Commission took an active part in the program. The objective of the group was to achieve acceptable standards, utilizing to the maximum extent possible the existing shipboard equipment. Emphasizing the importance of this work, the Chair of the Advisory Committee was Lyndon Spencer.

In 1951 a marine type Scotch boiler was erected on shore in the yard of American Ship Building at Lorain, OH, to make extensive tests and experiments to seek solution to the smoke pollution problem. Despite the hard work on the problem and reported improvements onboard vessels, it was not solved in 1951. The Advisory Committee recommended that the Program be continued through 1952 at a cost of $10,000; and that DMA would be invited to contribute $5,000

In 1952 more progress was made in developing and installing smoke abatement equipment. Six vessels were equipped with over fire steam air jets that were developed during research by Battelle Memorial Institute on a Scotch marine boiler. Tests showed the installations brought the vessels into compliance with allowed emission limits. Other vessels were equipped with under feed stokers that brought emissions down to satisfactory limits. While all these efforts showed continued improvement, the desired goal was still a long way off.

In 1953 and 1954 IJC smoke observers used radiotelephone to advise the Captain when the smoke emission exceeded the IJC limits. IJC provided the owners with a record of these calls. LCA issued a bulletin to the fleets with instructions for applying over-fire jets for two furnaces, induced draft, hand fired Scotch marine boilers based on the research at Battelle and trial installations. In 1953, the IJC reported that since 1950 through 1953 there was an improvement of 57% of vessels emitting smoke at a certain standard and an improvement of 46% in the duration of objectionable smoke. In 1954 the IJC reported continued improvement, finding that after observing smoke on 515 vessels of the 2,476 passages in the Detroit River, there was an improvement of 72% over the base year 1950; and, the amount of time smoking was decreased to 11.8% of the time as opposed to 51 % of the time in 1950. However, the IJC stated that there were still a number of vessels that showed erratic performance and others that produced much more smoke than should be necessary. The IJC continued stating that management and vessel personnel must take a more active interest in the smoke abatement program.

In 1955 progress continued on smoke abatement as vessel personnel gave more attention to the proper burning of fuel and vessel operators supplied the vessels with better equipment. The IJC indicated they would be developing a code that would set one standard for emissions for all vessels regardless of the type of fuel and that a means of enforcing the code would be recommended to the governments of the U.S. and Canada.

In 1956 work continued by the IJC to monitor smoke from vessels in the Detroit River area. Immediate notification of Masters was instituted and member companies were informed. The group developed a clear standard for maximum permissible smoke emissions in any 30 minute period for each type of fuel burning propulsion plant—oil fired and under-feed stoker fired, spreader stoker fired, and hand fired.

In 1957 work continued as before but while some improvement was noted, it was only slightly above 1955. Committee concluded that not all Great Lakes vessels are able to meet the established voluntary objectives but that the number of those vessels had been sharply reduced. Those needing attention were those having hand fired Scotch boilers. These were the older vessels that the great expense of installing new boilers could not be economically justified.

In 1958 LCA continued cooperative relations with the IJC in this program that started in 1950. However, the partners decided that further funding was no longer necessary citing the continued work would be carried on by the newly established LCA Smoke Abatement Committee. The group noted they awaited the final report of the IJC Technical Advisory Board on the Detroit River study.

In 1959 the group met only once although there were continued efforts to control smoke in the Detroit River area. Unfortunately preliminary reports received early in the season indicated that vessel performance deteriorated in 1958; a slightly better performance seems to have been recorded in 1959. In the President's report, he indicated that a number of Canadian canalers and other older vessels were decommissioned in 1959 as these vessels were no longer needed as the Seaway opened; many of them were responsible for smoke emission violations.

LCA Smoke Abatement Committee

David L. Buchanan, Pittsburgh Steamship Company

In September 1958, a special Smoke Abatement Committee was formed by the Advisory Committee under the chairmanship of David L. Buchanan, Director, Industrial Relation, Pittsburg Steamship Company. LCA was galvanized to greater action and accelerated involvement in the smoke abatement project as Chicago, IL and Lorain, OH passed smoke ordinances and Detroit began issuing more citations for smoke emission violations. LCA took one case to the Supreme Court of Michigan but lost the case.

The new Committee worked with Detroit officials to prepare a model smoke abatement ordinance, keeping in mind the needs of ship operation.

In 1959 in collaboration with the Fleet Engineers the firing manual for coal fired boilers was prepared. The Committee met in Washington and Ottawa along with the International Joint Commission and with the Detroit Air Pollution Control Bureau in order to resolve smoke abatement issues.

In 1960 the committee met many times to help establish workable smoke emission limitations and to reduce those emissions from ships. The Committee was gratified when substantially all the complaints issued by the Detroit Air Pollution Control Board were withdrawn and the industry was congratulated for the cooperative attitude and efforts to reduce emissions.

In 1961 after working with the Trenton, MI, officials for two years to develop a practical smoke emission regulation, the Committee was disappointed that the officials were unable to recognize the practical difficulties involved in compliance by coal-fired vessels. By the end of the year the Committee was pleased to report that the federal government came to the conclusion that federal legislation was not necessary to control atmospheric pollution in the Detroit River unless local authorities could not cope.

Other issues dealt with by the Fleet Engineers

From 1946-1951, the Fleet Engineers held conferences with USPHS over proposed sanitary rules relating to cooking and sanitary facilities for Great Lakes vessels. Committee reviewed sewage equipment requirements on vessels with USCG but regretted that the USPHS could not recommend sewage disposal plants since the agency did not have authority to prescribe systems, yet new vessels were under construction that could install sewage disposal plants if there were standards.

In 1953 Committee met in Washington to brief the USCG on the Great Lakes viewpoint on the proposed revised rules and regulations relating to vessel modernization and new construction. Committee also met with the Coast Guard over the concern that existing practices for issuances of engineer's licenses was preventing industry efforts to qualify enough engineers to serve on the new higher horsepower vessels; the Coast Guard modified the requirements to help solve the problem.

In 1954 the Committee also worked with the USCG to avoid delays of vessels during reinspection of lifeboats and the conducting of lifeboat drills. In 1955 the Committee called for Advanced Marine Engineer training on turbines and electric installations either at the USMMA, Kings Point or the New York State Maritime College. A subcommittee was appointed to look into the availability of adequate fuel oil supplies for vessel bunkers.

In 1956 the Committee again expressed concerns to the USCG about the difficulty encountered by applicants for marine engineer's licenses; and, they worked with the Welfare Committee on preparation of a revised manual for prospective coalpassers, firemen and oilers. In 1957 they continued working with USCG on horsepower limitations on licenses since the new vessels being delivered were of higher horsepower and few engineers could have had experience on them to upgrade; they supported courses on turbines offered at the USMMA, Kings Point, NY, in 1958.

In 1958 the Committee began working on a firing manual for coal fired plants to distribute to engine department personnel in order to bring about compliance with the various smoke emission laws as far as it was possible. The Committee also gave consideration to proposed regulations concerning dry docking of vessels that traverse the Seaway for a short period of time each year, whereas the majority of time the vessel was in fresh water. LCA believed such a regulation for shorter intervals between dry docking was a penalty on the lake vessel owners.

Public Relations Committee

Chair John Sherwin 1944-1957; Loren F. Hammett 1958-until the end of the Spencer tenure. In 1946 the public relations work was carried on by the Education and Public Relations Committee. In addition to the operation of the LCA schools, they carried on the preparation of all publications including the Bulletin and handled all media relations. In 1947, the name was changed to the Public Relations Committee.

When Gerald Wellman joined LCA staff in 1946, LCA terminated the independent Public Relations counsel that had been retained from March 1, 1944. In 1947, LCA actively participated for the first time in the American Merchant Marine Conference in New York City.

In 1948 the PR Committee developed a broad and continuing relationship with newspapers and radio and was able to get feature articles in newspapers; produced a color film *Great Lakes Miracle* to be shown to transportation classes at colleges and circulated through libraries; published a 16 page picture booklet called *Great Lakes Miracle* and a four page handout to attract new seamen called *The Men who sail the Lakes*.

In 1949 the committee worked on getting full length stories to be carried in the *Saturday Evening Post* and the *Readers Digest* after allowing the writers to ride the Great Lakes vessels. Other actions were as in earlier years. By 1950 the efforts in gaining national attention paid off as articles on the importance of Great Lakes shipping appeared in *Holiday, Saturday Evening Post, Readers Digest, Colliers Magazine* and *National Geographic,* as well as numerous articles in trade publications and area newspapers.

The Bulletin was extensively used to promote the free X-Ray program, the Safety and Education Programs and information on the Selective Service. A new series on the history of various Great Lakes fleets was included in the Bulletin.

In 1951 the Korean War caused the national media to focus on the importance of Great Lakes shipping. LCA helped enhance this focus with news releases of the new vessel construction, movement of vessels up the Mississippi River, speed of the Cliffs Victory, the X-ray program and more. The Bulletin now had a circulation of 20,000—it was sent to crews, libraries, schools, government offices, and business offices related to shipping. Subjects continued on the histories of member companies, the development of taconite, radar and more.

SS Cliffs Victory

In 1952 much of the publicity was focused on the new freighters, in particular the journey of the longest freighter in the world, the Joseph H. Thompson, the impact of the steel strike and the need to move large quantities of iron ore in the fall. This was the year that Gerald S. Wellman retired and Bertram Lewis, Marine Editor of the *Plain Dealer*, joined LCA as Director of Public Relations. He edited the Bulletin and directed the winter schools.

In 1953 the articles written by LCA appeared in many newspapers; LCA provided information to the media for news articles on new construction, the proposed Senate legislation to reserve commerce on the Lakes to U.S. and Canadian vessels, and other matters. Exhibits on Great Lakes shipping were developed and provided to libraries and Universities for educational displays. LCA engaged Edward Howard Co. to assist in designing a new booklet on *Great Lakes Shipping*. In 1954, the distribution of the new booklet was extensive. The Committee began to prepare for the celebration of the centennial of Great Lakes shipping following the 1885 opening of the first lock at the Soo.

LCA booklet Great Lakes Shipping

In 1955 the Committee centered its Public Relations program on the 100th Anniversary of Great Lakes Shipping and the Soo Locks Centennial. In addition to major newspaper and maritime journals coverage of the events, there were articles in the *Saturday Evening Post* and *Fortune* magazines and on television stations. LCA wrote a special centennial section for the *Cleveland Plain Dealer Sunday Magazine*; printed several thousand copies of a poster with the fleet stack insignias; they also collaborated with the Soo Centennial Commission to have a commemorative U.S. postage stamp issued; a film *Story of the Soo Locks* was made by the University of Michigan and was shown throughout the nation; coordinated a program with members to have eleven open houses in seven lake ports where more than 50,000 people boarded the ships and received a new pamphlet *Freighters that Sail the Great Lakes;* centennial luncheons were held at the Soo, Duluth, Detroit and Cleveland. This was truly a year to celebrate the 100 year history of Great Lakes shipping.

Sault Sainte Marie Locks Aerial View

In 1956 the Committee assisted with the filming of *The Ohio Story*, a TV feature that described life on a Great Lakes freighter. LCA was one of the ten sponsors of the 1957 U.S. Post Office Truck Maritime Poster Contest. In this effort, in conjunction with *Scholastics Magazine*, thousands of children were introduced to Great Lakes shipping and received LCA brochures. The Committee began to prepare for the production of a new film to replace *Great Lakes Miracle;* gathered material for a permanent LCA exhibit for the Great Lakes Historical Society (GLHS) Museum in Vermilion, OH, and for another exhibit to be placed in the windows of the American Merchant Marine Library Association in New York City.

In 1957 LCA participated in the fourth year of a transportation program at John Carroll University, Cleveland; gave talks to several university transportation classes; continued with the annual American Merchant Marine Conference; assisted with Post Office Poster Contest; produced six issues of the Bulletin; and contracted with Frank Siedel to write the script for a new movie to be produced by Cinecraft Productions Inc., Cleveland.

In June 1958 the LCA Room at the GLHS Museum in Vermilion was dedicated. Work on the 28 minute film was temporarily halted to be resumed in 1959 with Storycraft, Inc. and Cinecraft, Inc. Six Bulletins were published with increased circulation. A post card survey of the Bulletin readership determined that there was an unusually large request to keep publishing the Bulletin and to maintain the responders on the mailing list.

In December 1959, the 30 minute color film *The Long Ships Passing* was completed and it was expected that the seven film prints would be in constant circulation. Because of the long strike in 1959 only two Bulletins were published. In 1960, the movie was shown 200 times to 25,000 viewers in 14 states and in Ontario. Four Bulletins were issued. Committee worked with the Cleveland Safety Council to distribute posters to the area Yacht clubs urging discontinuance of practices by small boat operators that were considered hazardous to navigation.

Vessel Losses

After almost nine years without the loss of a vessel in the LCA membership, on May 11, 1953, the Henry Steinbrenner, built in 1901, foundered 15 miles south of Isle Royale Light Station after battling heavy seas during the night. A radiotelephone distress call brought several ships to assist in the rescue of crew but 17 men including seven officers perished. This was the first U.S. flag Great Lakes freighter to be lost since 1944.

Another loss occurred on November 18, 1958 when the Steamer Carl D. Bradley sunk in a storm on Lake Michigan with the loss of 33 officers and crew.

New Vessel Construction after World War II

There was new vessel construction and major vessel conversion period following the return to a post-world war economy when the United States was the source of capital, consumer goods and agricultural products for the rest of the world that was rebuilding cities after the devastation of war. The demands for tonnage increased with the Cold War rearmament and the Korean War.

In 1949 the Wilfred Sykes, 678' x 70'x 37', became the largest vessel ever built on the Great Lakes. In 1951 the Cliffs Victory and Tom M. Girdler were delivered and there were 16 more U.S. vessels under construction. This was the largest single expansion of tonnage in the history of lake shipping. The Notre Dame Victory rebuilt as Cliffs Victory was delivered to the Lakes via the Mississippi River. In 1952 nine new bulk freight vessels and three converted C-4 freighters were commissioned. In 1953 five new bulk freighters and one new self-unloader were commissioned along with two converted ocean vessels. In addition the conversion of coal fired vessels to oil fired and improved coal fired plants continued. In 1954 the last of the new bulk freighters George M. Humphrey was delivered; she was the vessel with the largest cargo carrying capacity on the lakes. On her first voyage she set a record for loading of iron ore and on her second voyage she carried more than 22,000 gross tons.

Wilfred Sykes

Tom M. Girdler

George M. Humphrey

In 1957 new vessels were ordered and the Joseph S. Young was commissioned. On May 3rd 1958 the steamer John Sherwin, flagship of the Interlake Steamship Company, was commissioned. In September the steamer Edmund Fitzgerald, longest vessel on the Great Lakes was completed; she was constructed for the account of Northwestern Mutual Life Insurance Company and placed on long term charter to Oglebay Norton Company to be operated as part of the Columbia Transportation Division. In 1959 the Herbert C. Jackson, Shenango II, and Adam E. Cornelius (largest self-unloader built on the lakes and deepest vessel) were commissioned.

In 1960 Arthur B. Homer, the first vessel built to Seaway dimensions and the same size vessel Edward L. Ryerson were commissioned. In 1961 four ocean tankers were converted: Pioneer Challenger, Walter A. Sterling, Leon Falk, Jr., and Paul H. Carnahan. In three instances the mid-sections were built in Germany and one in Holland and towed across the Atlantic. The Pioneer Challenger and the Falk, converted in Baltimore entered the lakes via the St. Lawrence River taking their first ore cargo at Seven Islands.

Other Key Events of Period

The May 1948 Bulletin announced the success of the LCA delegation that went to Washington in April to urge continuation of the marine post office in Detroit. The facility was slated to be closed on June 30, 1948 at the expiration of the current contract. The delegation included Don Potts, Pittsburgh Steamship; A. B. Kern, M. A. Hanna; George W. Callahan, Interlake Steamship; and Oliver Burnham, Secretary, LCA.

Detroit Mail Boat J. W. Westcott

In 1953 the Lake Head Pipe Line from Superior, WI to refineries in Sarnia, Ontario was completed thus causing a long term reduction in Canadian flag tanker traffic.

In 1954 the first cargo of the year from Lake Superior was a full cargo of taconite pellets from the Reserve plant at Babbitt, MN; it was loaded on the <u>Reserve</u> at Two Harbors, MN. This was the largest single consignment of taconite to be shipped—certainly this was a portent of things to come.

In 1955 LCA celebrated its Diamond Jubilee, tracing the LCA origin to September 1, 1880 when the Cleveland Vessel Owners Association was formed.

The new <u>Aquarama,</u> a passenger ship, converted from the former C-4 ocean vessel <u>Marine Star,</u> was completed in 1954 at Muskegon. The vessel, owned by Sand Products Corp, Detroit, was not placed in operation but was towed to Chicago to operate for exhibitions and as a night club. She represented the first new passenger ship for open lake operation since the construction of the <u>Greater Detroit</u> in 1924.

In 1956 the new taconite loading port of Silver Bay, MN, was opened and shipped 3.6 million tons, ranking the port as the sixth largest of nine iron ore loading ports.

The 1958 Annual Report noted that the International Joint Conference, formerly known as Canadian Joint Conference began in 1938 and all of the conferences were held in Canada until 1960 when the venue was Washington; Fred R. White was the Chairman. LCA and DMA considered alternating the venue in future years.

In 1960 the Dagwell Marine Reporting Station closed its operation. Ever since 1898, when Charles T. Dagwell established a reporting station at his home in Mackinaw City, freighters sounded the ship's whistle using their code signals to inform the agency of their identity. Dagwell would wire a report of the vessel passage to the owners and to newspapers for the marine section. He used a large telescope in the daylight hours and listening for whistle signals in bad weather. When a ship was ice bound the company could rely on the Dagwells to keep in touch with the crew and to report progress. The service stemmed from the old *Lake Marine News*, founded by Forrest Stimpson at Mackinaw City in 1890, with Charles T. Dagwell as chief reporter. The task continued with members of the family until Elton Dagwell decided it was time to close an operation no longer needed since radio telecommunications performed the task.

Chapter Six

VADM James A. Hirshfield, USCG, (Ret), President 1962-1970

VADM James A. Hirshfield, USCG and LCA

Economic/Political Climate

During the Hirshfield period of leadership there was turmoil in the U. S. and in the world including assassination of political and social leaders, civil unrest in the U.S caused by opposition to the Vietnam

War and a call for end of racial discrimination, the Cuban Missile Crisis, Middle East and internal political unrest in China.

Again the history of the LCA was influenced by the reality of the volatile world in which the United States took commanding leadership of the free market or capitalist economies of the world. The Cuban missile crisis, the failed CIA backed Bay of Pigs invasion of Cuba, the accelerated warfare in Vietnam following the Gulf of Tonkin resolution, the assassination of President Abdel Nasser in Egypt, the Six Day War in Israel, the formation of the Palestinian Liberation Organization, the disruptive Cultural Revolution in China and other world events required the government to continue to support a strong merchant marine and national defense industries.

Within the United States, the assassinations of President John F. Kennedy, Attorney General Robert Kennedy and civil rights leader Martin Luther King all combined to make this decade a most difficult period in American history. There were major race riots throughout the United States. Perhaps the one crowning memory of the period might be the reality of Astronaut Neil Armstrong walking on the moon.

As a result of grass roots pressure to improve air and water quality, including in the Great Lakes region, there was continued pressure for environmental legislation. The Federal Water Pollution Control Act of 1962 became federal law and it was followed by the Clean Air Act of 1963.

The U.S. presidents during the Hirshfield tenure included John F. Kennedy (D) until his death on November 22, 1963, Lyndon B. Johnson (D) until January 29, 1970, and Richard M. Nixon (R). Democrats were in the majority in both houses of Congress.

Biography of Admiral Hirshfield

James Albert Hirshfield was born in Cincinnati, Ohio, on 30 July 1902. He was appointed a cadet in the U. S. Coast Guard in July 1922 and graduated from Coast Guard Academy on 17 October 1924. Out of the Academy, he served nearly nine years of sea duty before being assigned to a shore station. He served on many Coast Guard cutters and rose through the ranks. Later, upon transfer to Headquarters at Washington, D.C., he attended George Washington University Law School. He received a Bachelor of Law Degree in 1939 and was admitted to the District of Columbia Bar in 1940. LCDR Hirshfield served as commanding officer of the cutter *Onondaga* at Astoria, the Maritime Training Ship *City of Chattanooga*, and then the cutter *Campbell*.

USCG cutter Campbell

Cdr. Hirshfield received awards for sinking U-606 while CO of Campbel

In 1943, while commanding officer of the *Campbell* that was on merchant vessel convoy escort duty, he engaged six submarines in the period of two days. The most significant action was when, upon sighting a German submarine on the surface, he ordered full speed to ram the U-606, a Type VIIC U-boat. While the *Campbell* was damaged in the collision and Hirshfield was seriously injured, he ordered a depth charge attack that sunk the U-boat. For this brave action he was awarded the Navy Cross with Silver Star for "Extraordinary Heroism and Distinguished Service"; one of only six such awards given to Coast Guardsmen during WW II. Hirshfield also received the Purple Heart for injuries sustained in the sinking of U-606.

Detached from *Campbell* in May 1943, he served at Headquarters and subsequently was Commander, Ninth Coast Guard District, Cleveland, from 1945-1950. LCA Directors gave Hirshfield a farewell dinner at which, LCA President John T. Hutchinson commented that Captain Hirshfield had that rare combination of talents; he was admired for his dignity and integrity, always willing to solve problems being experienced by lake transportation. Hutchinson added "Our respect and affection is even greater for Captain "Jimmy" Hirshfield as a man and a friend."

He left for Washington to become Assistant Chief, Merchant Marine Safety; and in 1951 he was appointed Rear Admiral and designated Chief, Office of Personnel. On 1 June 1954 Rear Admiral Hirshfield was sworn in as Assistant Commandant of the U. S. Coast Guard. In 1958 he was appointed Vice Admiral and confirmed in a second 4 year term as Assistant Commandant. In addition to the Navy Cross and Purple Heart, he earned many World War II campaign and service medals.

Vice Admiral Hirshfield retired from the Coast Guard on 1 February 1962 following a 39 year career. Within a few weeks he was a Vice President of LCA and the understudy to relieve outgoing LCA President Admiral Spencer with whom he had worked closely when he was Ninth District Commander.

On April 12, 1962, Hirshfield was elected as the 18th President of LCA; he retired from LCA following distinguished service in July 1970. Vice Admiral Hirshfield died on May 16, 1993.

LCA Organization

Officers

LCA Leadership team

During the entire Hirshfield presidency he was ably assisted by Oliver T. Burnham, Vice President and Secretary, Robert G. Williams, Treasurer, and Scott H. Elder, Assistant Counsel and later General Counsel. From 1926 until his death in 1968, the General Counsel was Gilbert R. Johnson. Mr.

Johnson had a distinguished career in the Great Lakes maritime industry and served as an LCA officer for over three decades; he was only the third General Counsel to the LCA having succeeded the Honorable Newton D. Baker and Harvey D. Goulder, one of the architects of the Lake Carriers' Association.

From the beginning of Hirshfield's tenure he was directed by many well-known giants of the industry including Adam E. Cornelius, T. W. Burke, C. R. Khoury, E. W. Sloan, H. G. Steinbrenner, G. M. Steinbrenner, J. S. Wilbur, H. C. Jackson, Carl B. Jacobs, Riley P. O'Brien, Day Peckinpaugh, W. F. Rapprich, John Sherwin, Fred R. White, Jr., Fayette Brown, Jr., William A. Reiss, Joseph G. Wood, H. F. Andrews, R. S. Sikes, Joseph B. Ayers, Jr., D. L. Buchanan, F. S. Sherman, E. J. Andberg, M. E. Kingsbury, D. A. Groh, John J. Boland III, R. P. Eide, Sidney E. Smith, Jr., C. F. Beukema, J. J. Dwyer and many more shipowner representatives. It is not surprising that many of the leaders listed above had vessels that bore their name.

The 1967 Articles of Incorporation and By-Laws indicated that the LCA was incorporated in the State of West Virginia and that the principal offices were at 614 Superior Avenue, Cleveland. LCA was reincorporated in the State of Ohio on 23 March 1970, at which time the stock certificates held by each member for the registered vessels had to be exchanged for new certificates.

Advisory Committee

The Committee was made up from members of the Board who were empowered to make decisions for the Board between the Annual Board meetings. The members were the senior representatives of the largest companies holding membership in LCA. The Advisory Committee received the recommendations from the other committees and authorized necessary action.

LCA Tonnage and Carrying Capacity

When Hirshfield became President in 1962, LCA members had 248 vessels with 1.9 million gross tons capacity; in December 1970, the year of his departure, there were 194 vessels with 1.6 million gross tons capacity. The carrying capacity was smaller but many of the ships could carry more cargo in a year due to increased vessel capacity, quicker turnaround time because of faster loads and self-unloading discharge and, to a lesser extent, due to a longer navigation season. The ships that were withdrawn from service primarily were scrapped but some were sold to the Canadian fleets.

Summary of Objectives and Accomplishments

Hirshfield personally worked hard on key objectives of the LCA through legislative testimony in Washington and Michigan. The primary objective was to obtain federal assistance for the Great Lakes shipping industry in order that members could compete with the Canadians in the Seaway trade and to improve productivity of the American ships in the domestic Great Lakes trade. These initiatives stemmed from the belief that the U.S. merchant marine missed out on the benefits expected from the opening of the St. Lawrence Seaway. American ships lost the grain trade transshipped at Buffalo and iron ore came into the Lakes to American steel mills from Labrador mines on Canadian ships. Newer larger efficient Canadian ships also took an increased share of the intra-lake bi-national trade. While LCA request for construction subsidy was rejected, Great Lakes shipowners benefited when the Merchant Marine Act of 1970, signed by President

Nixon on October 21, 1970, authorized Great Lakes shipowners to use tax exempt funds to build and/or rebuild ships.

Hirshfield was instrumental in obtaining appropriations to build the new Poe lock and was able to get the lock dimension increased to handle 1,000 foot vessels. Authorizations were passed directing the Corps to construct dredge spoil disposal facilities at full federal expense to receive dredge material from the connecting channels. He strongly opposed any changes to the cabotage laws and he opposed user charges, even on the Welland Canal. He stressed the importance of uniform water pollution regulations particularly with regard to marine sanitation devices. He opposed transfer of the Coast Guard to NOAA, and supported the transfer of the USCG to the Department of Transportation (DOT). In the last few years of his watch, he supported the call for a longer navigation season.

During his tenure he saw the changeover to new radio communication systems on the Lakes; the conversion of coal fired plants to diesel; the construction of the first of the super-sized vessels; and, in order to reduce crew costs, the conversion of self-propelled vessels to barges; the transition of training ship's officers at LCA schools to the establishment of officer training at the new Great Lakes Maritime Academy (GLMA) at Northwestern Michigan College.

LCA Committees

Legislative Committee

H. C. Jackson, Pickands Mather, Chair in 1962 retired; he had been a member since inception in 1944. Dave Buchanan, U.S. Steel was on the Committee. J. J. Dwyer, Oglebay Norton Company was appointed chair in 1963 and he served through 1969. In 1970, J. S. Abdnor, Pickands Mather, who had been a member since 1964, assumed the chair.

Washington Representation

In 1951, the Advisory Committee discussed the need for employing public relations counsel in Washington but decided against this action. The Committee agreed to watch the need for such legislative assistance carefully and to consider that engagement if warranted. In 1960 Admiral Spencer actively pursued the appointment of full time legal representation in Washington but that action was not taken.

Committee Actions

This Committee worked very closely with the President and the Advisory Committee to carry out the necessary lobbying in Washington or in state capitals on the governmental policy objectives approved for action. Many of the approved actions were the recommendations of the technical committees—Shore Captains, Fleet Engineers, Air and Water Conservation, Welfare, Electronics and other ad hoc committees. However, a significant part of the Legislative Committee work was to review hundreds of proposed federal and state laws and regulations that impacted Great Lakes shipping and to oppose those deemed detrimental—as well as to initiate favorable legislation or regulations benefiting the industry.

Some of the most successful achievements during the Hirshfield tenure included: congressional approval of load line legislation; many river and harbors improvements; reasonable and uniform federal waste treatment control standards to preclude the adoption of myriad of differing state laws; and the Merchant Marine Act of 1970 that gave Great Lakes ship operators the right to establish tax deferred construction reserve funds applicable to new construction and reconstruction of existing vessels.

The Omnibus Rivers and Harbors Bill of 1970 was very significant for LCA in that it authorized the Corps to construct and maintain dredge spoil disposal facilities of sufficient capacity for a period not to exceed ten years. The bill also required local governments to furnish all land, easements and rights of way and to contribute 25% of the construction cost. Fortunately for the Great Lakes, the disposal of spoil from the connecting channels would be borne at full cost by the federal government.

However, not all the legislation LCA achieved worked out as anticipated. The Water Quality Improvement Act of 1970 supported by LCA required EPA to promulgate standards for shipboard waste treatment systems and directed the Coast Guard to certify compliance. Industry supported the bill in the hopes that a federal standard would prevent the proliferation of state standards. Unfortunately, Michigan passed the Watercraft Pollution Control Act in 1970 that required vessels to install holding tanks or incineration devices. LCA and 19 member companies challenged the Michigan law in federal court.

The committee successfully opposed many attempts to enact waterway user charges, to amend the Jones Act, to extend the liability of the ship owner in cases of personal injury and death and to restrict shipowner's warranty of seaworthiness, to enact tax law changes that would have disallowed tax credits for payments into the Ohio Unemployment Compensation Fund, to enact physical standards for seamen, to require compulsory arbitration of maritime labor disputes, and to authorize the U.S. to recover by civil action the cost of removal of a wrecked vessel or other obstruction.

Since many members were impacted by the Interstate Commerce Commission (ICC) decisions with respect to the railroad rates, LCA lobbied to retain the Great Lakes bulk commodity exemption in the legislation modifying the ICC Mixing Rule, and opposed many efforts to deregulate the railroads in transportation of bulk commodities and to repeal exemptions granted to water carriers and bring bulk commodities under full regulation. LCA also testified in a number of ICC rate cases such as the coal rate case ICC Docket No. 34822 that was very important to LCA members as it sought an equitable rate for coal destined for lake transshipment.

In the state capitals, the Committee, with the help of outside Counsel at times, worked on such issues as: in Ohio where the legislature was attempting to rescind the seasonal limitations on payment of unemployment compensation to mariners; in Michigan and Wisconsin where navigation and sanitary regulation particularly regarding waste treatment systems were proposed; in Illinois where the prohibition of the deposit of dredge spoil in state waters was advocated; and, in Michigan when the state tried to impose an income tax on corporations doing business in the State including vessels passing through Michigan waters.

LCA recognized that there could be regional organizations that could help achieve uniformity, and preferably federal preemption on legislation impacting ships. One such organization was the Great Lakes Commission and when the Ohio legislators agreed on becoming members of this multi-state compact, LCA was pleased to note that the Toledo Port Director and a representative from U.S. Steel were appointed as commissions along with three Ohio state personnel.

Ohio Bureau of Unemployment Compensation

With respect to the legislation in Ohio that had been of ongoing concern for LCA for over a decade, in 1967 Mel Pelfrey, Vice President, MEBA, seriously and unambiguously challenged the LCA to cease attempting to eliminate the season unemployment compensation paid to seamen during the winter months. In letters to Admiral Hirshfield he asked for LCA support for pending legislation that would make Great Lakes seamen eligible for unemployment compensation during the winter months. He argued that part of the reason for the shortage of manpower was the fact that seamen were forced to seek non-marine employment in the winter months and then did not return to the ships. Pelfrey noted that tug and dredge operators, grain elevator operators, and other dock labor received unemployment compensation after the navigation season ended. When it came to Pelfrey's attention that LCA was lobbying the Ohio legislature against the house bill 427, he threatened to deal with the matter over the bargaining table with the MEBA contracted members of LCA demanding that company unemployment paid benefits be paid in lieu of State benefits. He said that other lake unions agreed with this position. He ended that letter stating "I do not wish any misunderstanding." As would be expected all members of LCA received copies of this last letter.

Welfare Committee

John Horton, Cleveland Cliffs Iron Company, Chaired the committee all during the Hirshfield period.

John Horton, Cleveland Cliffs

Assembly Rooms

The committee operated five Assembly Rooms in Buffalo, Cleveland, Toledo, Chicago, and Duluth; except that the Buffalo facility was closed for the period 6/29/63 until 1965. It was reopened in order to aid in recruiting. The cost of operating five centers in 1963 was about $77,000, at which time there had been a less than unanimous vote on keeping them all open. The Rooms were open during the day for the seaman but the placement service was 24/7 by phone by the company or Captains to the commissioners.

In 1963 2,057 persons were referred compared to 1,581 in 1962. G. M. Steinbrenner III emphasized the importance of training firemen, particularly for the hand-fired vessels.

In August 1954, D. C. Potts, Pittsburgh Steamship, advised LCA that they were in the process of laying up 40% of their shipping capacity and thus the Assembly room operation should be cut back. He noted that in the 1954 season up to August 19, 1954 only 3,299 men were shipped to vessels whereas in the previous year 12,339 men were shipped.

In 1965, 4,078 individuals were shipped to vessels from Buffalo, Cleveland, Toledo, Chicago and Duluth; in 1964 the aggregate total was 2,915. Buffalo was closed on June 29, 1963 and was reopened at the request of G. M. Steinbrenner III on May 3, 1965.

In 1966, Assembly rooms were open in five ports, two of which had assistant supervisors. Russ Plumb reported that the number of seamen dispatched in 1966 would be the largest since 1959. Through newspaper ads and other active recruiting, the number of men registered had increased. Steinbrenner recommended concentration of recruitment in chronically depressed areas and to look into government programs for training.

George M. Steinbrenner III

Over a period of time in the early 1960s the five Assembly Rooms dispatched/referred over 5,000 seamen each year.

In July 1968, Oliver Burnham brought to the attention of the members his concerns over the placement of college students on the ships during the summer months. He stated that in June of each year there are high school graduates and others of equal caliber who were available and interested in working on the ships for the remainder of the year and perhaps in making a career on the ships. Jobs were not available to them when company officials shipped college students in the entry ratings; and then when the college students returned to school in the fall, those other men who looked for jobs in June were no longer available. He pointed out that the Assembly Hall placement of entry rating in June fell to 44% of those placed in April and May. Mr. Burnham believed that difference was due to the placement of college students. To prove the point further, statistics on the placement of able bodied seamen, oilers and firemen in June were 11% in excess of those dispatched in May. He asked for a revision of the current hiring practice of college students in favor of greater employment stability in the unskilled ratings.

Cold War Planning and the Selective Service

As an indicator of the Cold War planning on the Lakes, in the LCA Minutes, February 15, 1962, there was a notation "...on activity of the Subcommittee on Manpower during period of the Berlin crisis at the fall of 1961. It was said that an industry survey was made to determine the number of the men in the age group 18-25 years. Responses from all of the companies in the Association... indicated that there were 663 single men and 154 married men in that age group employed at the time of the survey in August. Only three were licensed. It was indicated that contacts with lake state Selective Service officials were renewed with the result that cooperation was proffered had the situation developed unfavorably."

In summer 1965, Oliver Burnham approached each of the directors of the Selective Service in the Great Lakes area to reestablish cooperative linkages when individual cases seeking deferment arose. In all cases the directors were in place for a number of years and were familiar with the needs of Great Lakes shipping, continuous contact having been made with them by LCA since the Korean War when the Subcommittee on Manpower provided a centralized agency to request deferments. Members reported that there was an increase in the number of inductions into the military because of the Vietnam War. Members were advised that each company should file the applications for occupational deferments, sending a copy to LCA should there be a need for later LCA action. The Subcommittee on Manpower was inactive but staffed; if needed the Board could reactivate it.

In 1966 some members asked if LCA could seek occupational deferments for men in unskilled ratings. In all past communications with Selective Service officials, LCA policy was to consistently limit such requests to officers and skilled ratings, LCA decided to retain that policy.

Integration of Crews on Great Lakes Vessels

LCA was not unaware of the turmoil in the nation over the need to improve the economic, legal and social life of minorities, in particular Black Americans. On December 2, 1964 LCA officials attended a meeting at the Cleveland Cliffs Iron Company along with other member executives from Hanna, Pickands Mather and Oglebay Norton to discuss the PLAN FOR PROGRESS, an effort to racially integrate the crews on lake vessels. These companies were determined to initiate this effort and LCA attended as an observer.

It was recognized that a pool of new 'colored' sailors would have to initially receive a letter of commitment to take to the Coast Guard in order to obtain a Coast Guard entry rating document. While companies could issue the letter of commitment, LCA, through the Assembly Rooms, often issued the letter. It was recognized by LCA that they would have to furnish the necessary letter to the Coast Guard without discrimination as to race or color. Further, LCA recognized that the biggest problem would be to acquaint the vessels' officers and crew of the fact that in the future the crews of the vessels would be integrated. The companies present believed they would have to initiate this plan at the 1965 spring officer meetings; and that LCA would need to acquaint the membership with the effect that integration would have on the operation of the assembly rooms and to determine if any policy changes were necessary. I was unable to find any other correspondence relating to the integration of crews in the LCA files.

The Need for Improved Officer Education at a Maritime Academy; would it be in Toledo, Lorain, Traverse City or the MEBA/SIU facility in Brooklyn, NY?

Bertram Lewis was directed by the LCA Education subcommittee to study the LCA educational needs and to recommend an enhanced program. The preliminary annual cost estimate of the proposal was $25-28,000 as it would be directed by a full time employee. The committee rejected the proposal of a full time director of education.

LCA had prepared an analysis of the cost of the LCA training programs for the period 1961-66; the average annual cost was $9,493 and, due to officer shortages, the costs were rising. Nevertheless, LCA major expense was for salaries during the winter months when the instructors were off their ships; and LCA had the ability to reduce or increase the school size and instructor load based upon the perceived need for officers. LCA had been corresponding with U.S. government agencies who administered funds for the Manpower Development and Training Act to determine if federal funds were available.

In January 1966, Raymond McKay, President of District 2 MEBA, and Paul Hall, President of the SIU, jointly announced collaboration in providing engine officer training and upgrading at the School for Marine Engineering in Brooklyn NY. The critical need for officers generated by the demand for American shipping due to the Vietnam War was the reason for this unprecedented union collaboration

Later in 1966 McKay addressed letters to all the contracted companies promoting the Union training officer programs. This solicitation was also sent to the Chairmen of the House and Senate Committees with jurisdiction over the maritime industry. LCA recommended continuance and strengthening of the LCA educational programs.

In May 1967 the Lorain Community College addressed a letter to LCA suggesting the establishment of a two year college program for the initial training and up grading of deck and engine officers; LCA reviewed the proposal and sought more details.

In June 1967 the Welfare Committee reviewed correspondence from the field coordinator of the Economic Development Administration (EDA), Department of Commerce at Traverse City. EDA suggested that there was a possibility of using Manpower Development Training Act funds for training licensed and unlicensed personnel. A little background info that was known but there is no reference to it in the LCA files is that with Les Biederman, Chairman of the Board of Trustees of Northwestern Michigan College (NMC), had a close relationship with Gerald Ford, MI, House Minority Leader. However, the LCA response was to advise EDA of the LCA training program and to ask if there would be support for coordinating with the LCA training program

In June 1967, Dave Oberlin, Manager of Trade Development, and then later in October 1967, Louis Purdey, Executive Director of the Toledo-Lucas County Port Authority, each contacted LCA to determine interest in setting up a State Maritime Academy using federal funds at the University of Toledo. The proposal was approved by the Welfare Committee and recommended to the Advisory Committee. Admiral Hirshfield advised Purdey that the Association approved in principle the establishment of a merchant marine academy in the lakes but that it was inadvisable to support a single location at that time.

The Great Lakes Maritime Academy at Northwestern Michigan College, Traverse City, Michigan, had begun operations in 1969. Admiral Hirshfield invited the Welfare Committee to board the M/V Allegheny the training ship to be used at the proposed GLMA and visit with Les Biederman, Chairman of the Board of Trustees of NMC, while the vessel was in Cleveland on April 10, 1969.

T/V Allegheny

SAVINGS PLAN was still an element of the Welfare Plan to encourage thrift among seamen; deposits were sent to the Buffalo Savings Bank, Cleveland Trust Company and Central National Bank. Crew member interest in the savings plan began to wane in 1958; this was the first year that contributions sent to the banks did not exceed $1 million. The contributions continued to decline through 1966. Annual Reports in later years did not list the savings plan contributions. The fleets contributing the most dollars into savings accounts were the Boland and Cornelius, Pittsburgh, Cleveland Cliffs and Interlake fleets.

HEALTH of the seaman was a responsibility of the Welfare Committee and one of the concerns was for the possible prevalence of tuberculosis among the crew. The Welfare plan X-Ray Survey program started in 1955 and continued most years through 1964. LCA carried out this program with the support of the USPHS and the Michigan Department of Health through 1964. Ships were boarded 24/7 usually for a two week period; in several years after testing about 3,000 seamen, usually about 50 crew members tested positive and the results were sent to the shipowner. The cost of this program to LCA was approximately $1,500-$2,000 each year.

In 1963 2,846 persons from 17 fleets were X-rayed at a cost of $1,326 in a six day period; 56 positive films were discovered, about 4%. In 1964, 2,616 persons were processed with the support of the Michigan Department of Health at a cost to LCA of $0.40/person.

In 1965 the Michigan X-ray equipment was not available and the Committee calculated that a program using private equipment the cost would be $1.50-2.00/person. Some employers required a chest X-ray during pre-employment physicals but many did not; the LCA X-ray program was not recommended for 1965. In 1967, the MI Department of Health (DOH) advised that the X-ray equipment provided in the past would not be available. The previous year the DOH had indicated to LCA that the equipment was needed more by the shoreside population; private agencies were contacted and the estimated cost using these services would be $5,000. The committee decided against the X-ray program for 1967.

TRAINING needs of all the members were managed by the Welfare Committee. Primary emphasis was in upgrading crew from lower licenses to higher deck and engine licenses, radar and Pilotage route extension to include the Seaway. Training sessions in the winter were in Cleveland for deck and engine; and in Duluth for engine students, in conjunction with the Duluth Board of Education at the Naval Armory. Non-LCA members could enroll students in these classes at cost.

Duluth Engineering Class, 1965.

When available, special engineering class was held at USMMA, Kings Point, NY. The sixth year of this training was in 1960. The classes at Kings Point could not be held when conflicts with other programs such as special training for the crew of the nuclear ship Savannah took place. Plans were made to return in 1966.

Winter lecture programs for company staff continued in the 1960s, usually in January.

Combustion engineering classes were held in Cleveland for several years and were staffed by the Bailey Meter Company.

In 1965, in part due to the Vietnam War, there was a shortage of personnel, particularly marine engineers, able bodied seamen, oilers and firemen. The Selective Service system was notified of the industry's need for personnel, some of whom were being drafted.

Captain John C. Murray, instructor at the LCA Cleveland Navigation School from 1917-1960 and supervisor of the educational programs from 1944-1960, died at age 86 on December 26, 1965. He had asked to be relieved from his responsibilities after 42 years of service; he was relieved by his principal assistant Captain William J. McSweeney.

Captain John C. Murray with Mary Jane Cerino

The LCA members were aware in 1966 that the Unions, in particular the MEBA and the SIU, were actively seeking a major role in the training of crewmembers as these unions opened a school for engineers in Brooklyn, NY.

In 1966, 131 LCA correspondence courses were sent to students on ships; in 1967, 70 crew members received the course material; in 1968 there were 68 enrolled; in 1969-114 and in 1970-136 enrolled.

LCA increased the space for the navigation school at the Rockefeller building in Cleveland, thus enlarging the 2132 West 25th Street space to accommodate engineering training. Facilities at the U.S. Naval Reserve Training Center on Cleveland lakefront were also utilized. Because of the acute shortage of ships officers in 1966 a review was made by LCA Welfare Committee members and by the Cleveland principal instructors George Rector, Engineering, and Captain McSweeney, Navigation. As a result LCA engaged Human Engineering Institute to improve the Cleveland Navigation and Marine Engineering School. Cleveland Deck and Engine officers trained at offices of the Institute using LCA instructors. This was a much better system since the Institute had teaching machines for math, electricity, rules of the road and other subjects permitting students to study independently; some companies put the teaching machines on the ships. LCA contracted the Institute to operate the program in 1967 at a cost not to exceed the cost of the operation in 1966.

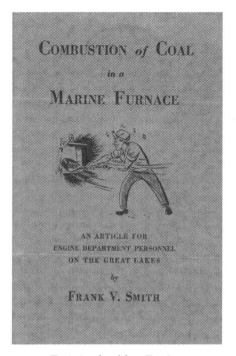

Training booklet, Engine

Capt. Hemmick (Northwestern Michigan College Archives)

LCA schools in Cleveland, Duluth and the Sturgeon Bay Vocational, Technical and Adult Education School helped 81 men to obtain licenses and 85 in 1966. At various Assembly Halls, short courses for prospective AB, fireman, and oilers were held and in 1966, 79 candidates passed their USCG exams; in 1967 110 men were successful. There is mention in the Annual Report in 1966 that the Deck license training fell off because of competition from a newly established facility of another organization. This could have been one of the officer union schools.

John Horton, in particular, and other members of the Welfare Committee were committed to improve safety onboard ship. The Great Lakes Discussion Group of the National Safety Council met 1st Tuesday of each month in Cleveland. The National Safety Council held their Great Lakes Day Luncheon in Chicago in 1967 in conjunction with the LCA and the Marine Section. Thomas Murphy and John Manning were speakers. LCA had much to showcase since 1967 was the 50th year of formal officer training by LCA. Started in 1917, license preparation was held in all years except 1932, due to the depression. In those years, the LCA helped 1,529 men obtain original Mate's licenses, and 526 received Master's license, 1,986 the original engineer license, 1,300 raised to 1st or 2nd Assistant Engineer and 569 raised to a Chief Engineer license.

In the continued effort to reduce essential crew shortages, in 1970, the committee was successful in their two year campaign with the USCG to allow the substitution of one week of shoreside training for four months of sea service. This allowed the LCA special schools to help 97 ordinary seamen obtain their Able Seaman certificate with eight months service rather than the usual twelve months. The Committee also recommended, and the USCG approved, revisions of record keeping procedures relating to engagement and discharge of Merchant Seamen on Great Lakes vessels since these procedures were different than on the oceans.

In 1970 the Committee met with NMC President James M. Davis and Captain W. M. Hemmick concerning the proposed Great Lakes Maritime Academy, Traverse City, Michigan. The Welfare Committee recommended that the LCA Board support the new officer training facility; and, to the member companies, to consider contributions to the Marine Student Loan Fund. The first group of students was matriculated in 1970 and was expected to graduate in 1973.

Death Benefits Paid

In 1962, for the first time in the history of the LCA Welfare Plan that started in 1908, there were no payments made for death or disability. In the years that followed through 1970, that was not the case as over 60 seamen died onboard Great Lakes vessels. More than half were lost on the <u>Daniel J. Morrell</u> and the <u>Cedarville.</u> The other deaths were primarily from falls into the cargo hold (9) falls from the dock into the water (2) falls from scaffolding, boarding ladders or gangplanks (3) boiler explosions (3) and unstated factors leading to drowning (9). In 1965, the Welfare Committee appointed a subcommittee to review the applicability of the death benefits but no changes were recommended.

Sault Library, as it was known, was the Soo Dispatch office of the American Merchant Marine Library Association (AMMLA) that had been placing boxes of books on the ship since 1922. In 1962, Della Wyllie was Port Representative for the 2nd year. In 1965, Mrs. Nancyann H. Sillers succeeded Mrs. Della Wyllie as dispatch agent. Generally the Library dispatch operated from April 1 through November 30.

Nancyann H. Sillers at the Soo Library

LCA continued to support this institution from the beginning, encouraging the placement of study aids and maritime professional books for the seamen to study in preparation for winter upgrade. The sailors were encouraged to contribute money to the library, and in a nine year period contributed over $15,000, an average of just under $1,700/year. In the early 60s LCA considered discontinuing cash contribution. LCA did not eliminate the payment as they were advised by USMMLA that if LCA did not continue to support financially, the Soo facility would cease operations. In 1964, the Welfare Committee surveyed the crew members and found there was 90% support for the library. LCA contributed $2,500 annually until 1969 when the contribution was increased to $3,000/year. In 1970, when the AMMLA because of financial concerns was considering closing the dispatch office, LCA gave its strong support. After a special appeal to the crews and to the marine community at the Sault the campaign was successful, the office remained open.

Navigation Committee

Members were working ship's captains who met annually with all relevant U.S. and Canadian government and industry officials in early December. Meetings were held with the Shore Captains Committee.

Prior to the meetings the Committee asked all masters in the fleets to submit meritorious proposals for the committee to consider. Among the subjects considered were: a review of the separation courses for Lake Ontario recommended by DMA; reviewed changes proposed by USCG on Aids to Navigation; reviewed and modified proposals to changes in the new Unified Rules of the Road; worked with the Weather Bureau to improve observations from ships; new anemometers (wind measuring equipment) were placed on 20 ships, as a result in the following years there was vastly improved weather reporting.

Shore Captains Committee

Captain H. C. Inches and Admiral Hirshfield

Captain H. C. Inches, who served since 1948, retired from the committee at the beginning of 1962. The Chairmanship changed as follows: in 1962-64 Captain E. H. Viall; 1965 Captain T. F. Harbottle; 1966-1970 Captain Ed Jacobsen until he was relieved by Captain John W. Rankin, U.S. Steel. In 1962, it was recognized that increasingly some companies did not have men in their shore side employment that had sailed as Captain; thus the Advisory Committee allowed the appointment of retired captains who demonstrate knowledge of current navigation matters to serve on the Committee.

In addition to dealing with the recommendations of the Navigation Committee, much of the work was to make recommendations to the Corps of Engineers for channel improvements in the connecting channels and harbors to prepare for the arrival of the thousand footers; recommendations to the fleets as to maximum drafts in the connecting channels (water levels fluctuated and there were long periods of lower than average water in 1963-65 (in 1966 water levels remarkably improved, the most abrupt change in 55 years, probably as a result of channel deepening and they stayed high from 1967-1970); to work with USCG on specific aids such as the new fog signal to replace the Huron Lightship; and, the National Navigation Plan that re-evaluated the Aids to Navigation system.

Last remaining lightship on Great Lakes.
Withdrawn from service at Port Huron, August 25, 1970.

Huron Lightship, last on Great Lakes

Other specific matters dealt with included: the recommended relocation of the Detroit River water gauge as a result of the change of status to an unmanned aid of the Detroit River light; reviewed new bridge construction plans particularly to be consistent with Seaway vertical clearance; expressed concern to the Coast Guard for speeding violations in the Port Huron-Sarnia area as the requirement of 9 MPH over the ground was too restrictive considering that at times the current was 5 MPH; and, recommended the installation of radio telephones on certain bridges in major harbors.

The Committee took steps to assure the safe operation of vessels in an extended navigation season. The Soo Locks were open for the longest period in a 115 year history, 283 days, from April 4, 1969 to January 11, 1970.

Electronics Committee

1962-63 A. S. Thaeler, Chair, Captains John Horton and Ed Jacobsen were on the Committee, 1964-1970 John Manning, Chair.

John Manning, M. A. Hanna

There were rapid changes in radio communications technology and a need for national and international regulations of frequency allocations. The consultancy relationship that LCA started with Professor Jansky in 1938 continued. In 1962 Jansky and Bailey were engaged as consultants to LCA on all electronics matters. In 1965 the LCA expenses were $11,028 and the contract with Jansky ended in 1969 when the consultancy contract was awarded to a former executive of Jansky and Baily who had formed Advanced Technology Systems, Inc.

Lorain City Radio Station, Rogers City Radio Station, RCA, Illinois Bell, Michigan Bell and a USCG representative met with the Committee. Jansky stated that the goal was universality, for all vessels to be in contact with each other and with shore stations. Committee recommended and all agreed that all vessels maintain a continuous watch on 2182 and 156.8. The Committee opposed any change in the Geneva Radio Regulations that would permit single channel operations on ships or shore stations on the Great Lakes. The United States and Canada agreed on a common code of channel designators for Radiophone in all bands, MF, HF and VHF. Hitherto these channels were designated differently in U.S. and Canada.

In 1963, Lorain County Radio Corp notified LCA that they proposed not to operate the shore stations in 1964. Radio Corporation of America planned to discontinue its shore station WBL which served the Buffalo area.

The Committee considered benefits of single side band radio telephone but did not recommend installation since it was unlikely to reduce the number of shore stations. Committee also reviewed problems relating to private owned shore stations at Buffalo, Port Washington, Lorain, and Duluth. Committee made special arrangements for the continuation of service from Lorain County Radio Corp. In 1964, over LCA objections, the FCC ruled that Single Side Band radio was to become obligatory effective January 1974. LCA planned to further object on the basis that appropriate equipment would not be available. Lorain County Radio increased its rate schedule; there was no opposition and FCC approved.

In early 1967, the Committee met to discuss installation of emergency power and/or radiotelephone equipment on member vessels seeking a solution to the communications problems raised from the loss of the <u>Daniel J. Morrell</u>. The Committee approved installation of emergency radio telephones which were installed on the majority of LCA vessels. This equipment was independent of the ship's power supply, operated by a 12 volt battery with battery charger. Committee considered what communications equipment could be taken over the side into a lifeboat but concluded there was no satisfactory equipment.

Jansky reported to the Committee that it was probable that all radio telephone equipment would have to be replaced over 5-10 years to comply with new International and U.S. regulations. They considered a possible solution to the transition would be in setting up a coordinated Great Lakes FM R/T system operated by remote control. In 1968, the Committee engaged a consultant to draft a report on the most economical and best way to proceed to have a VHF system on the Lakes; and in May 1969 the consultants outlined a number of communications systems which could be installed on the Lakes. At a 1970 meeting the participants recommended an automated VHF system to cover the entire Lakes thus eliminating the need for single side band. In that year the committee also worked on revisions to the Great Lakes Treaty that had been in effect since 1954.

It was for the Committee to decide soon about the electronic systems that needed to be installed. The Canadian government would have a VHF system in place in 1972 at government expense and the FCC was encouraging VHF as a mandatory safety and distress frequency, ultimately having a compulsory single sideband for all medium frequencies in 1977.

LCA worked with ATT, Lorain Electronics, the FCC, and the USCG to set up a 22 station remote controlled network. Committee dealt with the need for new vessel equipment and a way to deal with user charges from ATT for land line and Lorain Electronics for the stations.

Fleet Engineers Committee

From1962-1970 Dave Groh, Interlake Steamship was Chair following the 17 year term of M. E. Kingsbury, Wilson Marine Transit.

David Groh, Interlake Steamship Company

Much of the work of the committee had to do with working with the U.S. Coast Guard (USCG) and the American Bureau of Shipping (ABS) on improvements in vessel productivity by changing the Load Line regulations, developing new licensing and documentation requirements for licensed and unlicensed engineers, identifying training needed for the new main propulsion plants and automated equipment.

The concern about Coast Guard engineer officer licensing was important as new vessels with increased horsepower could not find the engineers with the higher horsepower license or with diesel endorsements. Also unlicensed crewmembers could not get initial licenses for the higher horsepower vessels since their experience was on lower horsepower ships.

Dave Groh stated that, of the 26 permanently appointed Chief Engineers in the Interlake Steamship fleet, 14 were restricted from being promoted due to their lower horsepower licenses. Another issue was the term "coal passer" that was passing on in to oblivion as newer vessels did not have need for coal passers. On older vessels the coal passer position began to be carried on the crew list as a fireman. Because of new equipment, the Committee also reviewed Certificate of Inspection (COI) manning requirements with a view to reduction of crew.

The Committee provided technical assistance to the Legislative and Air and Water Conservation Committees with respect to the use of incinerators for disposal of garbage from the galley as there were no vessel incinerator regulations in effect at that time.

When ABS relinquished the activity of providing chemists for gas freeing of shipboard tanks, LCA contributed $500 to National Fire Prevention Association for a program to certify qualified chemists for the task.

With respect to Load Lines, the committee supported an extension of the midsummer Load Line season from 5/16 to 5/31 and from 9/16 to 9/30. Later, they expressed serious concern that new vessels in excess of 750 feet would have a better draft assignment (location of Plimsoll mark) than existing vessels built since 1948. This initiated a complete load line review with U.S. and Canadian shipowners seeking a complete rewriting of the load-line regulations.

Other work of the committee included: a review of Marad reserve fleet vessels to determine potential for utilizing in the Great Lakes trades, unfortunately few were found suitable; in conjunction with SNAME, Marad and LCA, the committee conducted a vessel strength study onboard E. L. Ryerson, that was expected to be useful for planning and construction of new vessels and to a lesser extent for existing vessels; the Committee met to consider a Coast Guard Ninth District requirement for examining hatch corners of all ships 40 years or older and over 400' in length (the committee believed that, after inspecting 16 vessels and finding no structural failures, there was no justification for further examination); and they considered the age old problem regarding uniformity in application of Coast Guard regulations for Lake vessels that the Coast Guard treated at as if they were ocean going vessels (the problems usually arose with less experienced inspectors who had less than three years field service). The Committee sought more centralized control in 9th District headquarters rather than allowing a less experienced OCMI to make his own interpretation of the regulation.

Smoke Abatement Committee (in 1966 the name was changed to Air and Water Conservation Committee)

In 1962, Dave Buchanan was Chair.

Throughout the next decade there was a continued initiative among U.S. and Canadian lake port city governments to reduce smoke from vessels and shore industry, including Cook County, IL, Trenton and Detroit MI, Cleveland, OH, and Gary, IN. Considering the Canadian concerns on smoke abatement LCA collaborated with Dominion Marine Association on proposed controls. The Committee worked with the Fleet Engineers Committee to devise means to minimize undesirable emissions from vessel propulsion units.

Smoke from a vessel

By 1965, Detroit was vigorously enforcing smoke emission standards; 169 violations and 90 citations were issued, of which 56 were U.S., 32 Canadian, and two foreign. The State of Michigan sought statewide standards based upon the Detroit standard. Canada established a nationwide standard to be enforced by local authority. The International Joint Commission (IJC) Technical Advisory Board recognized the difficulty of hand-fired coal burning vessels meeting the special smoke abatement objective. At the same time, many concerns were being raised about water pollution from vessels. The committee now had to consider alleged problems of sewage, garbage, and other vessel debris and the issue of dredge spoil disposal.

LCA believed that commercial vessels on the Lakes had become a convenient target for regulations by local authorities and the regulatory measures were not necessarily related to the overall problem of pollution from all sources; the regulations proposed were not practical for shipboard installation. Garbage disposal regulations were particularly onerous in Superior, WI, and Wisconsin was considering statewide garbage regulation; Duluth was also considering garbage regulations. The Chicago City Council passed water pollution control measures. The Committee proposed language to be inserted in the federal water pollution control measure.

The IJC managed to halt the smoke abatement measurements in the Detroit River because of high levels of vessel compliance; unfortunately the special exemption for the few remaining hand fired coal burning ships was withdrawn.

In 1967 the Master of the A.T. Lawson was cited and arrested by Superior authorities for using the vessel incinerator in the port of Superior.

In 1968 the committee continued to deal with the 1967 proposed ordinances in Duluth and Superior concerning the prevention of build-up of excess garbage on deck and the removal and disposal of garbage. They encouraged the installation of incinerators on vessels. They also developed a response to proposed federal legislation on garbage disposal. LCA directed the Fleet Engineers Committee to develop a response to the Chicago Water Pollution Ordinance.

LCA continued to seek preemptive federal legislation on water pollution. LCA worked out the garbage disposal issue in Wisconsin with the intention to place more incinerators on ships; prevent excessive accumulation of garbage and refuse on vessels; and to provide for removal and disposal as needed. LCA began to work more closely with recreational boat interests who were also impacted by the water quality regulations.

In 1969 the Committee discussed a variety of proposed state legislative initiatives to reduce smoke pollution in Indiana, Duluth and Toledo

The Water Quality Improvement Act of 1970 was signed by President Nixon on April 3, 1970. There continued to be local complaints about noncompliance; the Michigan Department of Health complained of smoke emissions in the St. Clair River and the City of Cleveland adopted an Air Pollution Control Ordinance.

LCA members continued to work with local communities on the issues relating to air quality and retained special legal counsel to assist with representation to the States of Michigan and Wisconsin respecting water control laws that impacted on use of marine sanitation devices.

Public Relations Committee

In 1962-63 Loren Hammett, U.S. Steel, was Chair; from 1964-70 M.A. Bradley Chaired.

The Committee maintained an active, steady and responsive communications program through print and electronic media with the public, the members and the crew on the ships, academia and others. Primary means were through print publications such as the Annual Report that was sent to members, government officials, libraries and academia; quarterly Bulletins; LCA Soundings (initiated in 1962 to keep members informed of legislative issues); press releases, monthly tonnage statements and stories were sent to publications. Questions asked by the radio and TV stations were answered and LCA Officers and members gave speeches throughout the region. The LCA movie *Long Ships Passing* was lent out widely; extra copies were made for significant users such as the new Great Lakes Maritime Academy and revisions were made to keep the images of the vessels up to date

1962 was the 7th year of participation in the Merchant Marine Post Office Poster contest.

Thousands of brochures such as the updated *Great Lakes Shipping— the Story of the Great Lakes Vessel Industry and The Great Lakes Merchant Navy* were produced and distributed. The Committee supported the establishment of an LCA room at Great Lakes Historical Society,

Vermilion, OH. Sixteen house flags of member companies were sent to the Smithsonian Institution for use in Hall of American Shipping. A photo exhibit was developed for use at conferences and conventions and was provided to the Maritime Administration in Washington as to other venues. The Public Relations Committee worked with the Welfare Committee to make the winter lecture series a success. In 1964 the public relations committee participated in the Great Lakes Exposition held in Cleveland.

Great Lakes Shipping Brochures

1970 was the 16th year that LCA, in cooperation with the USCG, sponsored a training program about the Great Lakes shipping industry. The purpose was to introduce new Coast Guard officers being assigned to Great Lakes duties to the inner workings of the industry; the majority of member companies participated by having these officers in their offices and onboard their ships.

Vessel Construction and Modernization

Increases in vessel productivity took place in the 1960s through installation of self-unloading equipment, bow thrusters, conversions to cement self-unloaders and coal fired boilers to oil or diesel with automated boiler controls. However, there was virtually no major new construction in the Hirshfield tenure until orders were placed in 1968 for the super carriers, to be named Roger Blough and Stewart J. Cort.

M/V Stewart J. Cort

Forward and stern section of Hull #1173 Enroute
Pascagoula, Miss. to Erie, Pa., June 1970
(Subsequently christened M/V Stewart J. Cort)

M/V Stewart J. Cort as Stubby

Tank vessels and barges were constructed out of the Lakes for delivery for Lakes service; they included in 1963 M/V Sinclair Great Lakes, designed for Great Lakes service, built by Ingalls at the Decatur, Alabama, yard and delivered via the Mississippi River; in 1969 self-unloading oil barge, Toledo Sun was placed into service on the Lakes in May but after several months operation it was transferred to the Atlantic Coast; and Barge Phoenix, built in Houston, Texas, for Cleveland Tankers took its first cargo in 1969.

Several vessels were converted to cement carriers. In 1964, the tanker H. R. Schemm was converted to a self-unloading cement carrier. In 1965, J.A.W. Iglehart, the former tanker Amoco, a survivor of WWII service, was converted to the largest cement carrier on the Lakes; the work was done at the Chicago yard of American Ship Building. In 1966, the A. D. Chisholm was converted to the cement carrier Medusa Challenger.

Vessels converted from coal to oil included the Frank R. Denton, Calcite II, Myron C. Taylor, J. H. Franz, Diamond Alkali, and T.W. Lamont. The H. S. Wilkinson was converted to the unmanned barge, Wiltranco I, for the ore trade; the William A. Reiss was reconstructed by deepening of the hull 7.5 feet in order to increase draft by 4.5 feet.

Horace S. Wilkinson, renamed Wiltranco I (Roger LeLievre, Tom Manse Collection)

Many vessels including the John T. Hutchinson, Richard J. Reiss, J. H. Franz, H. L. Gobeille (renamed Nicolet), Frank Purnell, and G. A. Sloan were converted to self-unloaders. In that period over 80 vessels had bow thrusters installed and over 30 vessels had automated boiler controls installed.

Other Key Events of Period

1962

- E. L. Ryerson loaded 25,018 gross tons, a breakthrough of the 25,000 ton record in the Upper Lakes trade.
- Three vessels of Pittsburgh Steamship made 5 trips from Port Cartier to Lake Erie and Lake Michigan ports. Other U.S. flag vessels made 4 trips.
- COE stated that the new 1000' Poe Lock started in 1961 was due for completion in 1965. The lock was 10% finished and 80 % of the connecting channels improvement, 130 miles, should be at full project depth by July 1963.
- Bulletin cited a survey of shipbuilding and operating costs in U.S. and Canada noting Canadians provide 40% of construction costs for vessels built from 5/12/61 to 3/31/63; and that from 1945 through 1961 Canadian fleet expanded 80% in numbers and 194% in carrying capacity while U.S. declined 20% numerically and had increased only 6.4% in capacity. Annual Report stated that increased grain and iron ore on the Lakes benefited Canadian ships since the Seaway traffic had Canadian origins and destinations.
- Bulletin noted that the 1959 Canadian tolls for the Welland Canal were to be suspended. LCA praised the measure, not that it benefited American ships that used it little, LCA emphasized that tolls were contrary to our national interest and that canals should be free and open to navigation.
- American Ship Building Company announced closure of the 150 year old ship yard in Buffalo that in 1818 built the Walk-In-The-Water. The ship was built for the Lake Erie Steamboat Company and was the first steamer operated west of Lake Ontario. The yard predecessor ownership went back to the War of 1812. The yard also converted the Seeandbee and the Greater Buffalo to aircraft training ships in WWII.

- Deeper connecting channels in Detroit and St. Marys Rivers permitted an added draft of 2 feet 2 inches in St. Marys River and 6 inches in the lower rivers.
- William A. Reiss increased its draft by a vertical enlargement of the vessel by inserting 7' 6" of plating just below the spar deck; thus increasing draft by 4' 6".

Adding Depth Gives Steamer William A. Reiss More Cargo Capacity

- Wilson Marine Transit Company planned to convert H. S. Wilkinson into an unmanned barge. It became the first non-propelled unit in the U.S. ore trade since the barges of Buckeye Steamship terminated activity in 1955.
- Hirshfield told a Seattle audience that U.S. flag Great Lakes operators has been virtually eliminated from bulk trade between U.S. and Canada. Imports of iron ore had seriously reduced availability of domestic iron ore cargoes; overseas vessels had deprived the U.S. operator of a major portion of the grain cargo; high U.S. operating and construction costs had demolished hope of competing with overseas and Canadian vessels. Hirshfield called for the integrity of the coastwise laws or there would be no domestic trade at all. He stated that a subsidy was needed and noted that U.S. flag ships in the ocean trades could come into the Lakes with subsidy but that those U.S. flag ships in the internal lakes trade were denied subsidy.

1963

- Barge Wiltranco I (former Horace S. Wilkinson) entered service with a crew of 10 on the tug versus a crew of 36 on a steamer. It was noted that "U.S. lake fleets are watching the Wilson operation with more than ordinary interest, and it is expected there will be additional conversions of steamers to barges if the project works out well." Wilson operated Republic's fleet of nine ore vessels.
- LCA continued the call for support from the U.S. Government to permit U.S. Flag Great Lakes ships to compete with Canada. Hirshfield noted that seven new Canadian 730 foot long vessels would be added in the 1963 season.
- The Annual Report stated that a bill has been introduced in congress to amend the Merchant Marine Act of 1936 to allow credit for scrapped obsolete ships to be applied for construction or reconstruction; Construction Differential Subsidy (CDS) for Great Lakes ships; and, use of Reserve Funds of pretax dollars to be used for new ship purchase.
- The Bulletin contained the history of the Steinbrenner fleet and an announcement that George M. Steinbrenner III would become President following the retirement of Henry G. Steinbrenner in 1964. Bulletin also contained an interesting story of the near end of the hand fired coal burners.
- The Bulletin noted that Hirshfield stated that, of the 475 cargoes of Labrador and Quebec iron ore that came into the Lakes in 1961 and 1962, only 18 were moved on U.S. Flag vessels. Concerning the impact of the Seaway on U.S. flag shipping, he noted that the U.S. flag fleet had decreased from 420 vessels prior to the opening of the Seaway to 269 vessels in 1963, with a drop in carrying capacity of 460,000 tons; seven U.S operating companies had ceased business entirely; and four U.S. shipyards had gone out of business. He added that the Canadian government allows a 33 1/3% depreciation of capital costs in one year. He encouraged passage of S.1773. To that end, Hirshfield testified before the Senate Committee on Commerce asking for assistance to U.S. Flag carriers that have lost business to the Canadian fleet that now

carries 80% of the cargo between U.S. and Canada. He stated that the Canadian Vessel Construction Act of 1949 allowed for depreciation in as little as three years and the 1961 Canadian subsidy program in 1964 amounted to 35% subsidy.

1964

- Hirshfield attended a conference in Michigan called by the MI Attorney General that was looking into the problems of low water. COE nearly completed a study that looked to regulate the Lakes water; for example during low water dams would hold back the water. A Cleveland Cliffs executive called for 35' depth in the connecting channels. The IJC announced at year end that they would do a comprehensive study of Great Lakes water levels and how to stabilize levels.
- Hirshfield told the Propeller Club in NY that U.S. vessel owners want their fair share in bulk trades between U.S. and Canada and thus needed to modernize the fleet with federal assistance. He spoke of the latest efficient Canadian ship M/V Saguenay with a crew of 22, diesel engines, plastic ballast piping, lightweight high tensile steel hatch covers, etc. that had led to an extra 800 ton carrying capacity/trip.
- Hirshfield noted that although a sub-committee of the Senate Commerce Committee voted in favor of CDS and other benefits for lakers, it was too late for the full committee to take action.

1965

- In 1965, a new Senate bill 1858 was introduced with a companion bill in the House. Hirshfield wrote to Maritime Administrator Nicholas Johnson in March asking for federal action to assist the Great Lakes fleets.
- New Poe lock authorized in 1946 was to be 800' x 100'x 31'. First lock funds were appropriated in 1958 and construction started in 1961. Later, the lock dimensions were changed to 1200'x110'x 32'.

- After 6 years with no U.S. commercial vessel losses, on May 7, 1965 the Cedarville sank two miles east of the Mackinaw Bridge in the Straits of Mackinac following collision with Norwegian flag MV Topdalsfjord in heavy fog. Ten crewmembers lost their lives. The remaining crew, in 36 degree water, was rescued by the German MV Weissenburg.

1966

- There were additional ships in service and an insufficient numbers of licensed engineers. Shortage of licensed engineers caused USCG to allow applicants for third assistant engineer to sit following sailing only half of the sea time, 18 months rather than 36 months, to receive a temporary license that would become permanent following completion of the additional sea time. Also higher temporary licensed engineer ratings, such as second or first engineer, were granted after six months service in the lower rating without a license examination. The applicant could get a permanent license after completion of the additional sea service and completion of the examination process.
- Hirshfield reported that there were 10 identical bills in the House seeking to assist the domestic fleet in order to compete with Canadian vessels. The sponsors were from OH, WI, PA, NY, and CA. Tom Ashley, Waterville, OH, spearheaded the initiative to allow tax exempt reserve funds and an improved depreciation schedule—all designed to encourage new construction and modernization.
- Hirshfield opposed the increase of tolls on the St. Lawrence Seaway and the imposition of lockage fees on the Welland. He stated that the U.S. government paid for most of the improvements in the connecting channels and that the Canadian government should pay the costs of operation of the Welland since it is a connecting channel.
- Hirshfield told the American Association of Port Authorities that they were overlooking the basic importance of the Great Lakes/Seaway. It was deepened and the Seaway built and maintained to

assist in the movement of bulk raw materials. Only 9.5% of the cargo transiting the Seaway was the 'exotic cargo' from overseas. He also called upon the port industry to rally against the railroads that control the feeder routes to and from their ports since the railroads can raise the feeder rates to encourage all rail use to the east coast.

- LCA surveyed readers of the Bulletin and found that there were 5,000 people getting the Bulletin and that it was read by 12,500 including 9,000 Great Lakes sailors and virtually all the people connected to shipping as well as in libraries. The vast majority of recipients wanted to keep the Bulletin published.
- Wilson Marine announced sale of the company to Litton Industries and that Litton intended to establish a Great Lakes presence and would build a shipyard.
- Hirshfield commented that in 1966, there was an all-time record in carriage in the bulk trades, 223 million tons; 210 million of three dry bulk cargos, compared to previous record of 1953 of 200 million of dry bulk; however it was disquieting that Canadian vessels carried 28% while in 1953 that fleet carried 14.7%. Iron ore was 45% of total. It was a record grain year but U.S. ships carried only 11.3% of the trade. This change was due to the opening of the Seaway to foreign ships, Canadian carriage of grains out the Seaway, and Canadian new buildings with Canadian government assistance. The carriage in fewer vessels was in part due to the deeper channels and bigger vessels.
- Corps approved vessels of 105' beam to transit new Poe Lock versus the previous design approval for 100' beam.
- The Lake Vessel strength study started with SNAME, Marad and LCA support.
- Railroads began carrying unit train loads of iron ore in winter thus cutting into vessel winter storage. LCA began looking into proceeding against railroads for rail rate procedures that penalized rail/lake coal carriage.
- Daniel J. Morrell foundered on November 29, 1966 on Lake Huron, 28 miles north of Harbor Beach with a loss of life of 28 seamen.

1967

- Hirshfield blasted the DOT plan for the national maritime program before the Senate subcommittee on Maritime and Fisheries. Known as the Boyd Plan, he said it 'provides nothing for the Great Lakes shipping industry'. He decried the 'build abroad' proposal since it would relegate U.S. shipyards to repair only and that any vessel built abroad for the enlarged Soo Lock could not enter the Seaway.
- George M. Steinbrenner, III addressed the November Great Lakes Historical Society Annual Meeting. He announced the intention of U.S. Steel to build a Poe Class vessel at American Ship Building Company in Lorain. In October, Edwin H. Gott had announced the same news. The vessel would be the largest allowed in the new Poe Lock scheduled to open in spring 1968. The ship would be 858' long and 105' beam, with a maximum carrying capacity of 45,000 gross tons; it would have the largest horsepower of any diesel on the Lakes.
- U.S. Steel shipped the first Taconite pellets from Minntac mine, Mountain Iron, MN. The plant construction began within days of the passage of the Minnesota Taconite amendment in 1963.
- With the sale of the South American as a school ship to be utilized off the lakes, it ended the U.S. fleet of Great Lakes cruise ships.
- The Annual Report noted there was new coal handling facility at Conneaut; enlarged dockage for vessels loading at Sandusky; modernized coal handling terminal at Ashtabula; and three new iron ore pellet plants in operation, one U.S. Steel and two affiliated with Hanna Mining.

1968-1969

- In April Hirshfield testified before the House Subcommittee on Air and Water Pollution. He called for federal control not state control over vessels. It stated that there was only one seaman onboard a ship for each 6.8 square miles of lake; and that the vast majority of pollution came from shore communities.

- Hirshfield testified before a public hearing on the Study of the Extension of the Navigation Season. He stated that the average lock opening date had been April 8 and the average closing date was December 17; allowing only 254 days of navigation. He stated that it was feasible to extend by a month to January 17, giving a 10% improvement in the navigation season.
- Bethlehem Steel announced construction of a 1000' vessel in the new ship yard at Erie, PA. It would become the largest ship ever to be built on Great Lakes.
- The new Poe Lock opened to commercial traffic on October 30, 1968 with the Philip R. Clarke, down bound with iron ore. Dedication was deferred until June 1969. Contract for the new lock was let in December 1960. The first Poe lock was built in 1896 at cost of $4.7 million and was demolished in 1961. In 1962, the project was temporarily discontinued since the decision was made to build a larger lock. In summer 1964, a contract to build was awarded to MacNamara Construction Ltd.
- The largest iron ore transit was made in December 1968 and the largest tonnage of iron ore pellets was shipped in a single year. The last vessel passage was 1/11/70, making it the longest season in the 115 year history of the canal.
- An announcement was made that Northwestern Michigan College would start a course of marine instruction. The first class of about 50 students started in 1969 onboard the Allegheny. LCA stated 'The marine program at Northwestern Michigan College is applauded as timely and farsighted.' GLMA actually opened 9/23/69 with 20 men all of whom had some sailing experience.
- The new Poe Lock was officially opened and dedicated 6/26/69. The lock had been under construction since 1961 at a cost of $40.3 million. There were eight labor disputes causing a loss of 132 calendar days. VADM Hirshfield was the honorary Chairman of the event. The first upbound vessel was the Philip R. Clarke with Captain Thomas A. Small, age 95 in wheelhouse. He was wheelsman on Steamer Colgate Hoyt when it transported the first iron ore cargo through the original Poe August 4, 1896, 73 years before.

Dedication of Poe Lock 1969

1970

- The last lightship on the Lakes was removed from service on August 25, 1970. Huron lightship was the last of the vessels at that location since 1893. It was replaced by a large lighted buoy with a radar reflector and a fog signal.
- The Bulletin notes that on the Great Lakes there are 94 vessels, 43% of the fleet, equipped with bow thrusters; the first unit installed was in 1962.
- The Locks at the Soo were open until 1/29/71 when Philip R. Clarke locked down, thus ending the longest navigation season in history-- 304 days.

Chapter Seven

VADM Paul Trimble, USCG, (Ret) President 1970-1982

VADM Paul Trimble, USCG, (Ret)

Economic/Political Climate in the World and in America

The Vietnam War had spread into Cambodia and by 1973 a cease fire was called but was not observed; in 1974, South Vietnam had fallen to the Communist forces and within a few years Vietnam invaded

Cambodia. In 1972 President Nixon visited China to reestablish peaceful relations and in 1978 U.S. and China had agreed to full diplomatic relations. The U.S. and USSR had improved relations sufficient to witness a 1975 link up of their space craft in outer space but by 1980 when the Soviets invaded Afghanistan, the U.S. secretly supplied arms to the Mujahidin to fight the Soviet troops. In the middle of the decade the U.S. was in the midst of a worldwide energy crisis. At the end of the decade, the Shah of Iran was deposed and driven into exile, the U.S. Embassy was taken over and the embassy staff was captured and taken hostage.

In the U.S the Executive power was in the hands of the Republican Party led by Presidents Nixon and Ford from January 1970 until January 1977 when Jimmy Carter, a Democrat, became President. The Republicans again regained the White House when President Ronald Reagan came into office in January 1981. In the 1980 Annual Report Paul Trimble heralded the enlightened philosophy brought to Washington in January 1981; he anticipated a new era of future regulations not based upon questionable economic benefit. Democrats controlled both houses of Congress during the Trimble period except the Republicans won control of the Senate for the six-year period 1981–87.

During the 1972 election there was a break-in of the Democratic Party Headquarters at the Watergate office complex in DC. Congressional investigations embroiled the administration in public controversy in 1973 in what became known as the Watergate Scandal. During that period Vice-President Spiro Agnew was accused of extortion, tax fraud and bribery and he agreed to plead no contest for the charge of tax fraud with the proviso that he resigns as Vice-President. The House Minority Leader Gerald Ford was appointed to take his place. When Richard Nixon resigned in 1974 because of the Watergate cover up, Vice President Ford became President and the House Minority Leader Nelson Rockefeller became Vice-President.

While not connected to these political events in 1974 the U.S was in the worst economic recession in 40 years. Within a few years in 1977 the spirit of America was again lifted with the success of the first manned shuttle flight of the Enterprise. Good times did not remain long as a new economic downturn started in 1980 and the nation was considered to be in a deep recession in 1982. The streets were no longer safe even for the President; in 1981 President Reagan was shot but survived.

The first Earth Day celebrations began in 1970. Within the state governments, there was increased pressure to develop regulations apart from the federal government, particularly with regard to land, water and air pollution caused by ships and the mining industries. The states of Michigan, Wisconsin and Minnesota commanded the attention of the ship owners and the mining industry with many costly and traffic regulating proposals that would have seriously hampered vessel and mining operations.

The mood of some people in the Great Lakes region who were active in private organizations that helped shape public policy had shifted to more strident environmental protection objectives. Many of them began to question the federal expenditures for navigation projects paid for by the taxpayers. Unfortunately this anti-water carrier view was vigorously supported by many railroad interests.

The Lake Carriers' members had a full plate when Trimble took office; and there was more to be served up before his tenure would end. In 1970, Trimble's first year in office, the work of his predecessor Admiral Hirshfield came to fruition when President Nixon signed the Merchant Marine Act of 1970 which included a provision to establish tax deferred construction reserve funds to be used in the building of new ships and in major reconstruction of ships. Earlier in 1970, the President signed the Water Quality Improvement Act that included provisions to control the pollution of U. S. waters by all watercraft. In 1970, the Association asked the Corp of Engineers (COE) to keep the Soo locks open through the end of January, in an effort to extend the navigation season; the freshman class at the new Great Lakes Maritime Academy completed its first year of operation; the State of Michigan passed a Michigan Watercraft Control Act that attempted to supersede the federal laws; the Water Resources bill called for the construction of dredge spoil disposal areas to be 25% % funded by local authorities, except for the Great Lakes connecting channels which the federal government would pay 100%; testimony was given on a congressional bill to require radio-telephones on vessels and on bills dealing with Interstate Commerce Commission (ICC) regulation of vessel rates that threatened a Great Lakes bulk commodity exemption; and then there were several on-going ICC rate cases in which the Association was a party. When the Reagan Administration took office there was a serious effort to make all transportation interests pay the full cost of federal services, user fees were the order of the day, regardless of the political party in office.

Biography of Paul Trimble

Paul Trimble was born in Agenda, Kansas, in 1913. He spent his early years in Milaca, Minnesota, and graduated from the U.S. Coast Guard Academy in 1936. His first shipboard assignments were in New England. In 1940 he was selected for post graduate training at the Harvard School of Business, graduating in 1942 with an MBA with Distinction. He resumed regular military duties in New York, and in 1943 was assigned as commanding officer of the Patrol Frigate USS Hoquiam in the Pacific. He later commanded the USS Sausalito, another patrol frigate in the Pacific and wore a second hat as Commander, Escort Division 27.

In the early 1950s he commanded the Cutter Storis, stationed in Juneau, Alaska. He returned to Coast Guard Headquarters and served in various positions including Comptroller. After commanding the Cutter Duane in the North Atlantic for two years, he became Commanding Officer of the Coast Guard Base at Boston, Massachusetts. He returned to Headquarters and served as Chief of Staff before being promoted to the rank of Rear Admiral in 1964. He was appointed Vice Commandant of the Coast Guard and attained the rank of Vice Admiral.

During his Washington assignment VADM Trimble was designated as Chairman of the Interagency Task Force that developed plans for the newly enacted Department of Transportation, of which the Coast Guard would become a member. He received the Legion of Merit for his performance in this assignment. On retirement in 1970 he was presented his second Distinguished Service Medal. In July 1970 Trimble became President of the Lake Carriers' Association.

LCA Organization

In July 1970, VADM Paul Trimble relieved VADM Hirshfield as President and served until December 31, 1982. Trimble's maritime and government expertise was invaluable in dealing with Congress. Trimble was ably assisted by the long term, well known and capable Oliver T. Burnham, Vice President and Secretary, who upon retirement Burnham had served the LCA for 40 years. Roger G. Williams, Treasurer and Scott H. Elder, General Counsel were the others in the LCA leadership.

In 1973, David L. Buchanan retired from the U.S. Steel fleet and was appointed to relieve Oliver Burnham as Vice President. Dave brought with him years of valuable experience serving on many of the important LCA committees. Also in 1973, former Coast Guard officer John A. Packard joined the LCA as Secretary and Jack N. Carlson came onboard as Treasurer. In December 1980, John Packard retired and Jack Carlson died. Russ Plumb, LCA Director of Training, and Director of the Great Lakes Sailors Job Referral System (JRC), retired on January 1, 1980. On August 1,1980 Captain James A. Wilson, USCG (Ret.) became the LCA Director of Training and Job Referral Center Director, a position he held until his resignation in 1982. On January 5, 1981, Christine M. Kammer, Public Relations Director, Port of Portland, Oregon, was appointed Secretary and in the same month, William Conroy was appointed as Treasurer. In midyear 1982, Thomas O. Murphy relieved Scott Elder as General Counsel and in September 1982, George J. Ryan came on board as President-Elect.

David Buchanan

Scott Elder was Assistant General Counsel, assisting Gilbert R. Johnson, General Counsel from April 1954 to May 1965. In May 1965, he became General Counsel. Through 1972 Scott Elder was paid through the law firm of Thomson Hine and Flory; and from 1973 onward he was paid directly by LCA.

Since 1903, LCA had been incorporated under the laws of the State of West Virginia.

A reorganization of LCA took place in 1970 when, in response to IRS requirements concerning tax-exempt business leagues, the LCA Trustees reorganized as a non-profit, non-stock corporation under the laws of the State of Ohio.

LCA was governed by a Board of Trustees drawn from all the member companies. The companies with larger fleets provided more than one person to this Board, some had as many as four members. In 1970, the Board consisted of 37 men, of which four men served all during the tenure of Paul E. Trimble. They were John Dwyer, Renold Thompson and Fred R. White, Oglebay Norton, and Sid Smith, Jr., Erie Sand Steamship. Other Board leaders within the steel, mining and water transportation industries included Howard Andrews, Hanna Mining; Tom Burke, John J. Boland III and Adam E, Cornelius, Jr., American Steamship; Dick Eide, H. S. Harrison and J. S. Wilbur of Cleveland-Cliffs; Fred Sherman, Bethlehem Steel; Chris Beukema, U.S. Steel; and Henry G. Steinbrenner, Kinsman Marine Transit. The Board was the final voting body to approve new membership, dues and major actions recommended by the Advisory Committee. Paul Trimble chaired the Board and the Advisory Committee.

The Advisory Committee acted as the Executive Committee and was made up of members of the Board who monitored and directed the activities of the Association staff; they received reports and recommendations from operating committees. The members of the Advisory Committee were the top executives of the operating fleets and represented the interests of members from the steel industry, iron ore and limestone mining, cement manufacturing and larger independent ship operators. This committee approved the budget and all major expenditures not in the budget; they recommended the dues structure. Most importantly, they collectively developed positions on responses to government actions, initiatives of the Association for the good of all members and for the safety and improved productivity of the fleets in the membership.

The Committee structure changed as needed. Ad hoc committees were formed in response to concerns of members such as the Electronics

Committee to deal with VHF communications and the Air and Water Conservation Committee in response to the Michigan Watercraft Pollution Act and other environmental issues.

In the Trimble period, the leading committees were the Legislative and Government Affairs Committee (Chaired by J. S. Abdnor, Pickands Mather (he was the brother of Republican South Dakota Representative and later Senator James Abdnor); the Shore Captains Committee; the Welfare Committee (later the Vessel Personnel and Safety Committee); the Engineering Committee; the Ice Committee (later merged into the Navigation Committee); the International Joint Conference Committee; and the two previously mentioned ad hoc committees.

Paul Trimble brought to the presidency many years of experience in the Coast Guard in Washington at the highest levels. As a Vice-Admiral, he was called upon to draft the structure for the new Department of Transportation. He had close working relations with all the Flag officers in the Coast Guard and many of the new leaders in the Department of Transportation that included the Coast Guard, the St. Lawrence Seaway Development Corporation and the Maritime Administration. He was very familiar with the workings of Congress and with many congressmen, senators and staff. He knew the economic, political, regulatory and environmental issues that the Lake Carriers' Association members faced.

Recap of LCA Tonnage and Carrying Capacity

When Trimble took office in 1970 the 18 members of LCA owned 194 ships having a gross tonnage of 1,595,698 tons and in that year they carried 209.5 million tons. When Trimble left office in 1982, during the 1980s economic recession, the 15 members owned 120 ships, of which 13 were 1,000 footers, having a gross tonnage of 1,529,442; however tonnage carried had fallen to 128.1 million tons.

Traffic on the Great Lakes

The lake shipping industry primary purpose has been the carriage of bulk raw materials within the Great Lakes, the St. Lawrence Seaway, and the New York State Barge Canal; this remained its primary purpose during the Trimble period. The major commodities were: iron ore, coal, stone, grain, and petroleum products. A few major changes occurred during Trimble's watch.

- Western Coal moved by rail from Montana to Superior, Wisconsin, commenced, starting at 125,000 net tons in 1973 and by the end of the Trimble period in 1982 it was 6,005,296 tons. Shipments had reached 6.8 million tons in 1980.
- There was a decrease in grain traffic. U.S. flag ships were not the major transporters of grain in the Great Lakes during the Trimble period or in later years. During 1970, U.S. flag ships carried 197 cargoes of 80,497,035 bushels and in 1982, U.S. flag vessels carried 101 cargoes of 51,702,645 bushels. Canadian and third flag ships during 1970 carried only 1,377 cargoes of 790,577,995 bushels; and in 1982, carried 510 cargoes of 365,252,605 bushels. During these years, third flag Seaway vessels increased their share of the carriage. Within the U.S. and Canada, railroads increased their share of the market as grain elevators were built closer to consuming populations that could be served directly by rail.
- There was a major decrease in the New York State Barge Canal traffic from 1970-1981. The cargo carried was primarily petroleum products. In 1970, 2,734,963 tons were carried in the canal; and in 1981 it was 807,925 tons. Statistics for the Barge Canal were published in the LCA annual report for decades but were discontinued in 1982.

Steamer Edgewater, Lake-Barge Canal Type, Owned by Ford Motor Co.

Major Accomplishments and Disappointments

Accomplishments

Paul Trimble's achievements on behalf of the Association were numerous. In the LCA Bulletin of October-November 1982, the "Hail and Farewell" article only listed a few: the winter navigation demonstration program began and ended during his term; he was instrumental in advocating development of a new type of the Coast Guard Bay-class icebreaker and in 1976 USCG ordered four 140' icebreaking tugs; Great Lakes fleets modernization took place in his 12 years, including delivery of all thirteen 1,000 footers; he obtained recognition from the Corps of Engineers that vessels of 1,100 feet could lock through the Soo although that length ultimately would not be approved; he participated in efforts to improve shipboard survival systems; helped to develop the Great Lakes wide VHF telephone network; and, he was relentless in opposing user charges that could cripple the carriage of vital low cost raw materials. These objectives and many more will be described later.

Disappointments

- In 1980 and onward the nation was in a deep recession and many ships saw short service in those years; tonnage shipped fell off for all members
- U.S. Supreme Court declined to hear the LCA appeal of the Michigan Watercraft Pollution Act

The loss of the Steamer *Edmund Fitzgerald*

The most devastating event of the Trimble leadership period was the tragic sinking of the Edmund Fitzgerald on November 10, 1975 in Lake Superior with the loss of all hands—29 men. This catastrophic loss led to many government and industry investigations; this subject occupied the time and skill of Paul Trimble and other members of the LCA for several years as industry and government agencies worked hard to prevent another such loss. Fortunately, since 1975 there has not been another American flag Great Lakes vessel lost in a storm; unfortunately there have been several American flag vessels lost in ocean storms.

There have been many books, articles, and short news stories written about the loss of the Edmund Fitzgerald. The USCG investigation report and that of the National Transportation Safety Board are available as are the congressional records of the hearings that were held over several years. The loss has become a legend in the minds of many in North America and around the world due to the song written and sung by Gordon Lightfoot. I will not attempt to relate the events leading up to and following the loss. Unfortunately, LCA had to strongly disagree with the government findings as to the proximate cause of the sinking of the Edmund Fitzgerald. The interested reader has the opportunity to do extensive research.

The lake shipping industry and the LCA deeply felt and lamented the loss of so many good men. Their families suffered greatly.

LCA Committees

In addition to the following committees there were short lived committees formed for specific missions and then disbanded such as the Energy Utilization Committee in 1973 to consider fuel allocations, energy conservation and impacts of new regulations. The Budget Committee chaired by David Groh, Pickands Mather, did the staff work on the financial needs of LCA and submitted it to the Finance Committee. The Finance Committee included senior members of the major members (Samuel Scovil, Cleveland-Cliffs, Chris Beukema, U.S. Steel, and John Dwyer, Oglebay Norton) met annually to review and approve the budget and to recommend assessments.

Legislative and Government Affairs Committee
(Until 1971 this committee was known
as the Legislative Committee)

In 1975 there was also a Taxation Committee Chaired by J.R. Greenlee, Hanna Mining.

In the mid-1970's, government affairs work, previously carried out by other committees e.g. Shore Captains; Electronics; Fleet Engineers, Air and Water Conservation was included in the aegis of the Legislative and Government Affairs Committee.

Chair: John J. Dwyer, Oglebay Norton; 1971-1981 James Abdnor, Pickands Mather (brother of Senator Abdnor); and in 1982 Thomas J. Manthy, Pickands Mather. Other members included Michael Doyle, Hanna Mining; D. Ward Fuller, American Steamship; and R. A. Thomas, Oglebay Norton.

Legislation of major significance
Various Environmental Laws and the Water Quality Improvement Act of 1970 (WQIA)

LCA supported WQIA since it appeared that there would be federal preemption of state regulations on vessels in interstate commerce. Unfortunately, since EPA was tasked with implementation of the WQIA but Coast Guard was responsible for approval of equipment onboard and the operation of vessels, there was no consistent federal action with respect to shipboard treatment of sewage wastes. The several Great Lakes states began to take state regulatory action to control sewage from ships; the most significant was the Michigan Watercraft Pollution Control Act that became effective January 1971. Wisconsin and Minnesota also drafted state regulations prohibiting discharge of treated and untreated sewage. LCA opposed the proposed State of Wisconsin law outlawing the discharge of vessel wastes and assisted in redrafting the Milwaukee County, WI, air pollution proposed regulations.

The Committee reviewed the Great Lakes Water Quality Agreement between U.S. and Canada in order to seek federal preemptions on water quality issues particularly relating to a bi-national agreement on sewage treatment. In the April May 1971 Bulletin, on page 4, there was a cartoon titled 'Legislative Squall' showing a laker in heavy seas with dark clouds and lightning labeled Chicago, Indiana, Michigan, Wisconsin, Minnesota, New York and MWPCA. Clearly LCA was feeling the pressure from the environmental agencies on many fronts.

LEGISLATIVE SQUALL

In 1972, LCA petitioned the Minnesota Pollution Control Agency to not require the installation of sewage holding tanks on Great Lakes vessels. The U.S. Environmental Protection Agency was petitioned by Minnesota, Wisconsin and Michigan to make a finding that there were adequate sewage water reception facilities available in Lakes Michigan and Superior. EPA ruled that these facilities were available in Lake Michigan and that there were inadequate facilities in Lake Superior ports. LCA assessed the availability or lack of sewage discharge facilities in various Great Lakes ports, and in 1973 LCA appealed the finding that these facilities were available for vessels in Lake Michigan ports in Wisconsin and Michigan. Several cities also took action to unilaterally impose regulations on ship discharges. LCA hired special legal counsel to assist in affirming federal preemption.

On March 16, 1971, LCA and its members filed an action in the federal district court for the eastern district of Michigan to assert federal preemption and the voiding of the Michigan statute by seeking a temporary restraining order on the State of Michigan. The order was issued and a series of hearings and appeals including to the Supreme Court of the United States took place for years. Finally on June 21, 1982, the petition by LCA to the Supreme Court of the U.S. was denied, thus affirming the judgment of the U.S. District Court, a judgment adverse to LCA members and all vessel operators on the Great Lakes. LCA offered to continue to work with the State of Michigan to solve this very contentious issue.

This long standing opposition to the State of Michigan regarding vessel waste disposal was extremely vexing because of the anomalies governing state regulation of ships versus municipalities. Ships were to retain all black and grey water and discharge to shoreside reception facilities that in most ports did not exist; and where they did exist could only be used in non-freezing weather and then the discharged liquid would be was sent to shore facilities that did not treat the effluent to the standard capable of being achieved with shipboard treatment systems.

Another aspect of WQIA 70 dealt with oil pollution. Members had to assure they had sufficient financial responsibility for cleaning up of oil spills. In the case of negligence, liability would be unlimited. States such as Michigan tried to preempt federal regulations regarding oil spill. Air pollution concerns continued in various states particularly in Minnesota and in separate cities.

In 1978, the Legislative Committee recommended that the Air and Water Conservation Committee be reconstituted as an Environmental Committee in order to assist in furnishing factual information for the ever increasing number of public involvement meetings.

User Charges

In 1971, the Indiana Port Commission attempted to assess harbor services charges, based upon gross tonnage, for vessels entering Burns Harbor. Bethlehem Steel Company instituted an action before the Federal Maritime Commission with LCA as an intervener to test validity of the charges.

In 1973, the issue of user charges was brought up by the National Water Commission but no proposed legislation was submitted. LCA opposed federal user taxes on value of water transportation, a proposed fuel tax in Illinois, a proposed Michigan business privilege tax on industry, and, a proposed Ohio tax on transportation within the state. This effort continued for several years.

In 1975, Marine User Charges were included in the DOT National Transportation Policy.

Faced with the prospects of a federal user charge on Great Lakes vessels, LCA engaged former Minnesota Congressman John A. Blatnik as a special consultant to assist in combating these charges.

In 1978, Congress passed a fuel tax on vessels in the inland waterways when they authorized a new inland lock and dam 26 in Alton, IL; this would be a forerunner for more user taxes on transportation. LCA continued opposition to user charges; testified before DOT and DOC and a National Transportation Policy Study Commission; and, carefully studied proposals for the deregulation of the railroads to determine if railroads would unfairly take economic advantage over the water carriers. LCA unsuccessfully opposed the increase in Seaway tolls; particularly with respect to iron ore, LCA decided not to appeal the fees on iron ore since it was deemed LCA did not have a clear legal basis.

In 1979, the Committee expressed concern for imposition of Coast Guard User Charges for Navigation Aids. In 1980, the inland waters fuel tax came close to application on the Great Lakes. As the 1978 Inland Waterways User Fee legislation required payment of a fuel tax, there were efforts by the government to collect the fuel tax on lake vessels using the Calumet River, IL, until LCA petitioned that the river was not a part of the Illinois Waterway. In 1980, this tax had been raised to 10 cents/gallon although the Reagan Administration had asked for 30 cents/gallon.

In 1981, despite a continued slump in the American economy, user charges, harbor use and USCG fees were again raised in Congress. In the Burns Harbor case, after a lower court supported the Indiana Port Commission, and another court opposed the charge; the case ultimately was appealed to the Supreme Court. In other federal testimony, LCA stated that should user charges be imposed then there should be a provision for user say as well as user pay. LCA also advocated that a portion of the custom duty collected should be used for harbor maintenance.

Jones Act

LCA opposed the request by Canada Steamship Line to operate a ferry shuttle topping off service for coal from Chesapeake Bay to a large foreign flag vessel in deeper water inside the waters of the U.S. This violated the Jones Act and the CSL request was denied.

Interstate Commerce Commission (ICC) Cases

In 1970, LCA continued to engage in Interstate Commerce Commission 'Ex Parte' cases relating to the movement of product by rail to and from vessels. This was particularly important in grain and coal movements.

In 1973, LCA agreed to continue to contest the Essexville Case, costs of $17,500 to be divided among members "in same manner as in the past"; however LCA decided not to contest a proposed increase in Toledo dock transfer charges at a cost of $10,000. In 1974, the ICC Essexville case was concluded favorably for LCA after eight years of litigation.

In 1974, LCA opposed potential federal regulation to require unregulated water carriers to file rates with the ICC on presently unregulated dry bulk commodities.

Other Major Legislative Actions and Concerns

In 1970, the Merchant Marine Act of 1970 was passed that allowed Great Lakes operators to set up tax deferred construction reserve funds for the construction or reconstruction of Great Lakes ships. In the same year, the Omnibus Rivers and Harbors Act 1970 passed Congress; and, while LCA supported the bill, it required local port projects to raise 25% of the cost of containment facilities in ports. Fortunately, dredge spoil disposal and containment for connecting channels remained federal responsibility. The same law directed the various government agencies to demonstrate the practicability of extending the navigation season. One of the most far reaching and troubling aspects of the Act was the prohibition against open lake disposal of dredged material. This would sharply increase the cost of each maintenance dredging project as local ports would need to provide land, easements and rights of way to the shore based disposal facility as well as a share of the dredging costs.

In 1972, LCA opposed the proposed Buffalo ordinance requiring the engaging of tugs while passing through bridges.

In 1973, LCA successfully opposed amendment of the Ohio unemployment compensation law that had a section repealing the Seamen's Seasonal Provision that restricted benefits to those who were in seasonal employment. LCA also successfully opposed an Ohio Department of Taxation franchise tax on property based upon percentage of time in the state. In 1973, the Department of Labor OSHA inspectors attempted to board vessels inspected by Coast Guard and this action was opposed by LCA.

In 1977, LCA opposed onerous Coast Guard regulations particularly related to issuance and renewal of Pilot's licenses.

In 1977, the Committee continued efforts to amend the Merchant Marine Act of 1936 with respect to lake vessels seeking mortgage insurance. The law required owners to build vessels with at least a 14 knot speed, almost 16 mph, a speed originally intended to stimulate construction of vessels capable of achieving wartime convoy speed. This speed was uneconomical for lake vessels. In 1978 LCA was successful in obtaining legislation to remove the 14 knot speed requirement for vessels to be eligible to qualify for the Marad mortgage insurance program.

In 1977, considerable attention was given to proposed Coast Guard regulations, some drafted in part as a well-intentioned response to the sinking of the Edmund Fitzgerald.

In 1978, LCA expressed concerns for court ruling that State of Washington had the right to require tug assistance for tankers in Puget Sound since the federal government had no tug requirements; the concern was that the same condition existed on the Great Lakes. LCA also considered appealing the court decision that maintained that a three watch system was necessary even in a certified unattended engine room, but chose not to appeal as the time was not deemed to be apropos.

In 1979, in a letter from Trimble to the USACOE, LCA continued efforts to obtain authorization and appropriations for a second Poe size lock. LCA petitioned the Commandant of the Coast Guard to review a ruling that officers were not members of the crew. It appears that the

Coast Guard was ruling that a vessel could not commence a voyage under any circumstances if an officer required by the Certificate of Inspection (COI) was missing. The Commandant ruled favorably that officers were members of the crew and that, as long as the shortage was not the fault of the master or owner, and that the master determined that the shortage did not affect the seaworthiness of the vessel, it could proceed on the voyage. Unfortunately, the definition of a voyage was still not clear.

In 1980, LCA opposed proposed regulations pertaining to the licensing of pilots that came about following the concerns about Pilotage in the Puget Sound that were included in the Transport and Tanker Safety Act of 1978.

In 1982, USCG attempted to decommission the Mackinaw but through the vigorous efforts of LCA the icebreaker remained in service. The same policy change also called for increased industry responsibility for icebreaking through use of commercial tugs or reimbursement of the government for USCG services.

Maritime Union Positions on Legislation and Communications with LCA

Communications with the unions, primarily the MEBA, occurred frequently in the 1960s and 1970s. There were many issues where the union had a different policy position and these positions were clarified in letters from Melvin Pelfrey, Vice President, and Raymond T. McKay MEBA President, to the LCA President and/or General Counsel.

In 1967, MEBA outlined a 20 point national policy to save the U.S. Merchant Marine, in this effort they were joined by Paul Hall, President of the SIU and President of the AFL-CIO Maritime Trades Department, who transmitted the policy letter to members of Congress and to the President. One letter in the LCA files is from George Steinbrenner III, Kinsman Marine Transit, calling upon Admiral Hirshfield to take a positive and active approach to McKay's initiative.

In that same year Mel Pelfrey seriously and unambiguously challenged the LCA to cease attempting to eliminate the season unemployment compensation paid to seamen during the winter months. More details of this issue are included later in this book.

In June 1972, Paul Trimble responded to an earlier telegram and letter from Raymond McKay, President MEBA-AMO, asking LCA to discontinue officer training. After full consultation with the Advisory Committee and the Board, Trimble stated that LCA would continue the educational program. He included several reasons for this decision including:

1. A long history of high achievement in training and obtaining original licenses,
2. The cost per license was low; there was not a potential for savings using the union school,
3. LCA afforded alternative license prep sources in many geographical area; thus meeting officer needs and individual choice.

In 1973, McKay addressed a letter to Scott Elder, LCA General Counsel, enclosing a pamphlet describing the U.S. Steel domination of LCA from its earliest days to the present. McKay threatened to publish another pamphlet describing how LCA and U.S. Steel failed to control pollution, avoided taxes and how all steel companies dominated the smaller shipping companies. He reiterated that for LCA, Big Steel's vote was the only one that counted.

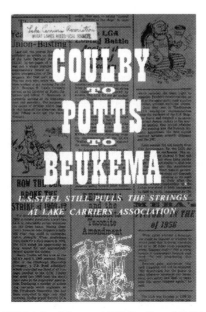

MEBA booklet anti US Steel and LCA

In December 1973, McKay addressed a telegram to Trimble questioning in detail the need for operating the ships during the winter navigation demonstration program given the energy crisis. Trimble in great detail refuted that blatant effort to stop winter sailing. Concerning Winter Navigation, Pelfrey always called for a cautious approach to late season sailing.

In 1976, following the disastrous sinking of the Edmund Fitzgerald in November 1975, Pelfrey and an official of the United Steelworkers, Local 5000, called for major improvements in life saving equipment, major changes in large vessel storm warnings, USCG regulation of the operation of vessels in November, and improved USCG watertight compartment regulations. Pelfrey called for an end to thinking of sailing as a romanticized ideal.

Welfare Committee; in 1980 the Vessel Personnel and Safety Committee

Chairman John Horton, Cleveland Cliffs, was Chair until 1980; William B. Satterness, U.S. Steel, then assumed the chair.

The Welfare Committee continued to be one of the most important decision making operating committees of the Association as it had been since 1909. Captain John Horton assumed a strong leadership position in directing the work of this group. John was honored with the title of "Mr. Safety" in his work with the National Safety Council. Every accident was scrutinized to determine cause and how to prevent reoccurrences. Training of licensed and unlicensed seamen was a major mission in the work of the Committee. The management of the Assembly Halls in Duluth, Chicago, Toledo, Cleveland and Buffalo required continuous attention in order that qualified sailors would be dispatched to the ships. The establishment and growth of the Great Lakes Maritime Academy, Traverse City was essential to the industry to provide qualified career officers and to prevent officer crew shortages.

Assembly Rooms

In 1970, Assembly rooms were in Duluth, Chicago, Toledo, Cleveland and Buffalo and they were operated 24/7 through use of telephones to the homes of the supervisors. There began to be a decline in referrals from 4,294 in 1970 to 1,993 in 1974. A five year average from 1970-1974 of the sailors referred was 2,652/year. The ten year average for sailors referred in the 1970s was 2,537.

Paul Trimble stated in the Annual Report that one of the stipulations of the 1974 United Steelworkers Union (USW), Local 5000 Management/Labor Agreements was that the Assembly Room operation, previously known as shipping offices, dating back to 1880, would be union operated as "hiring halls." In 1974, the Advisory Committee minutes indicated that the USW, Local 5000, was interested in taking over the Assembly Halls in order to operate them just as all the other seafaring unions did. Union leadership looked into leasing the building spaces where assembly rooms were located in Duluth, Chicago, Toledo and Cleveland. The expression of interest indicated the union would hire the personnel and buy fittings and fixtures. The USW had no interest in a Buffalo assembly room but the others were to be operational January 1975.

The USW desire to run the hiring halls proved unworkable; thus in 1975 LCA re-opened the Job Referral Centers (JRC) that continued to be operated by the same LCA employees who operated the Assembly Halls. Expenses were to be paid for only by the members who used them under the direction of a Mutual Study Committee, exclusively members who had union contracts with USW Local 5000. The Centers continued to be located in Duluth, Chicago, Toledo, Cleveland and Buffalo. The Duluth JRC was operated by Jack Saunders. In 1981, the Cleveland JRC superintendent Harold J. Robinson died and Jack Rose was appointed superintendent. David Hudson, the assistant superintendent in Cleveland, was transferred to head the Chicago Office in 1981. Effective May 31, 1982 the Toledo JRC was closed and the head of that JRC, William Kishel, was assigned to Chicago to relieve David Hudson whose position was terminated; Hudson went deep sea and ultimately earned his Master's license. The average number of sailors referred from 1980-1986 was only 264. The time had come to terminate the operation of the Assembly Halls known also as Job Referral Centers.

LCA Navigation and Engineering schools

In the Trimble tenure, LCA had three schools for licenses in Cleveland, Duluth and Sturgeon Bay. In the winter of 1971-72, no students were enrolled in at the Sturgeon Bay Vocational, Educational, and Adult Education School. In Cleveland, training for both deck and engine licenses was at the Naval Reserve training center. Captain H. W. (Bud) Zeber was chief instructor of the navigation school in Cleveland following resignation of Captain William J. McSweeney who served as principal since 1960 and an instructor since 1941. Mr. Arthur Urdall was the chief engineering instructor. In Duluth, Captain C. Gil Porter was in charge of the Duluth navigation school and classes were supported by the Duluth Board of Education.

Captain William J. McSweeney

In 1970, 47 students obtained licenses; 35 were from the Cleveland school. Licenses were both deck and engine, original and upgrade. Summer correspondence courses were provided to 136 seamen interested in obtaining a license; this was 22 more than in 1969. LCA also received assistance from Marad in teaching Radar at the licensing school. Consideration was being given to accepting a Marad marine radar simulator and an instructor in Cleveland; later it was decided to locate the facility in Toledo.

In 1971, 43 students received licenses. Classes for Able Bodied seamen (AB) helped 40 men gain certificates. In 1972, 31 students received licenses, 77 men received AB certificates and 15 men earned a Qualified Member of the Engine Department (QMED) certificate. In 1973, there were 23 licenses, 147 AB certificates, 28 Fireman and water tender (FWT) certificates and 94 summer correspondence course kits were sent out.

The Welfare Committee took many steps to try to alleviate the crew shortages. Considering that the experience on lower horsepower (HP) vessels was stopping the engineers from moving up in grade for higher HP licenses, USCG agreed to allow upgrades for men with lesser HP experience. The Committee appealed to Maine Maritime Academy to place cadets on Great Lakes vessels and to establish a Great Lakes curriculum. They met with the USCG seeking approval for ocean mates to sign on with a pilot's endorsement for open waters after passing a Great Lakes Rules of the Road exam.

In 1974, nine licenses were issued and 33 correspondence courses were sent out to prospective license candidates. There were 150 successful AB applicants and 23 Oiler, FWT certificates earned. In 1975, there were two licenses (both from Duluth), 142 AB certificates and 36 students received Oiler and FWT certificates. In 1975 the officer's union contract called for increased vacation time, 20 vacation days after 60 days work; thus a shortage of officer relief in the summer increased. In 1976 there was one new officer's license from Duluth, 73 AB, 7 Oiler, and FWT. In 1977, there were 4 licenses from Duluth, 18 AB, and 5 Oiler, and FWT. This was the third year when officers worked 60 days and earned 20 days paid vacation.

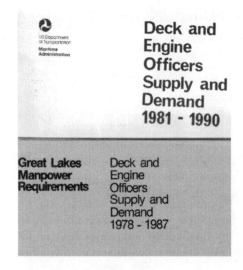

    In 1978 crew shortages were severe and LCA asked Marad to conduct a Great Lakes Vessel Officer Need survey due to the drastic shortages of officer personnel. In 1978, there were 14 licenses from Duluth, 40 AB, and 41 Oiler, Fireman and Watertender documents. Committee arranged with USCG to hold a special Oiler class onboard the Cleveland Public School ship <u>Woodbine</u>. Seven students with 90 days experience received emergency certificates to use in case of crew shortage, and then a permanent certificates was issued after another 90 days of service as Oiler. In 1979, there were 21 licenses from Duluth (training took place at the Naval Reserve Training Center), 56 AB and 32 Oiler, Fireman and Watertender certificates.

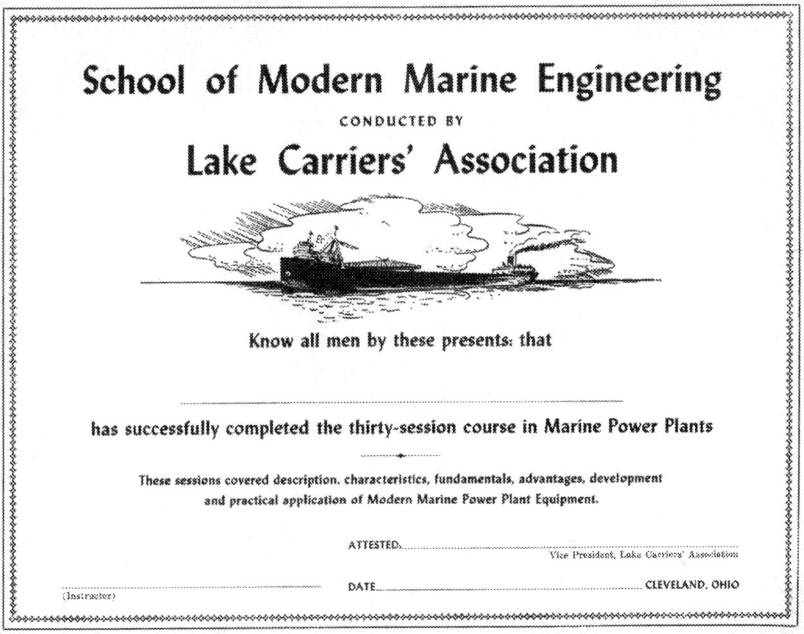

School of Modern Marine Engineering
CONDUCTED BY
Lake Carriers' Association

Know all men by these presents: that

_____

has successfully completed the thirty-session course in Marine Power Plants

These sessions covered description, characteristics, fundamentals, advantages, development and practical application of Modern Marine Power Plant Equipment.

ATTESTED:_____
Vice President, Lake Carriers' Association

(Instructor) _____ DATE _____ CLEVELAND, OHIO

LCA Engineering Certificate

Admiral Rae at graduation ceremony

LCA recognized that there was need to attract as many licensed officers to the Lakes as possible using many training institutions. While the Great Lakes Maritime Academy effort was growing with LCA and federal government support, and the LCA schools seemed to be maxed out, it was important to call for help from the other Academies such as the U.S. Merchant Marine Academy, Kings Point, and the Maine Maritime Academy. Several members had good relations with the Maine Maritime leadership and had attracted a number of Maine graduates to the Lakes in past years. LCA was asked to establish a Chair at the Maine Maritime Academy in 1979 for a period of three to five years with a contribution of $25,000/year. The LCA 1979-80 budgets included a line item to support Maritime Academies. The question was what the allocation would be between GLMA and Maine. In 1979 $25,000 was allocated by LCA to Maine Maritime Academy.

In the 1980-81-82 Annual Reports, there was no record of the numbers of officer or unlicensed training; although unlicensed training did take place. Officer training continued at the Duluth Navigation School in conjunction with the Board of Education at the Naval Reserve Center. There was an effort to set up a radar school in Duluth in 1980. In 1982, wire splicing classes for AB's were held at Samsel Supply offices, Cleveland, and there was a pump school at GLMA for oilers. In 1982 the Marad Firefighting School opened near Toledo, Ohio.

Welfare Committee Death Benefits Paid

In 1909 the Lake Carriers Association members formed a Welfare committee, in part to improve safety onboard ship through improved training and placement of improved equipment onboard ship. In the Trimble period the LCA safety messages to the crew continued to be placed in the Bulletin; they supplemented the safety and health programs administered by member companies. Other LCA safety training was included in the classes for upgrade of licensed and unlicensed crew.

One of the duties of the members of the Welfare Committee was to process applications for a stipend payment to survivors of deceased seamen or to those permanently disabled. The stipend was small and was intended to provide a small amount of cash to allow burial arrangements to be made.

In 1970 the benefits were: Master, $600; Chief Engineer, $500; 1st Mate and 1st Assistant Engineer $400; 2nd Mate and 2nd Assistant Engineer, $350; 3rd Mate and 3rd Assistant Engineer, other Assistant Engineers, First Cook, $300; and, all unlicensed men, $200.

In 1970, $1,500 was paid to six wives or mothers. Causes of death were: three seamen fell in a hold, one was scalded in a boiler explosion; and one man fell from the dock into the water, and one gateman was fatally injured. In 1971, $600 was paid out due to three deaths caused by drowning on three separate ships. In 1972, no payments were made for the first time since 1962; this was only the 2nd annual interval without payment since the establishment of the benefit in 1909. In 1973, three payments were made due to two drowning and one unexplained accident. In 1974, no payments were made but two applications were being processed. In 1975, thirty three payments were made, of which 32 were due to death and one person was a permanent disability. Twenty nine people died while onboard the Edmund Fitzgerald, of whom twenty seven had signed beneficiary cards, two drowned and one had a fatal fall at a location not recorded.

A recap of the fatalities indicated that, aside from the payments to 27 next of kin after the tragic sinking of the Edmund Fitzgerald, the majority of the deaths were due to drowning, followed by falling into the cargo hold.

The Lake Carriers Association made a decision to eliminate the Welfare Committee payment for death and disability effective March 1, 1976, the expiration date of current beneficiary designations. The time had come to eliminate this very small token payment for many reasons. The committee believed that the members Insurance Plans were adequately covering the need. Since inception in 1909, the Association paid out $153,123 to dependents or disabled persons. During the Trimble period there is no mention in the Annual Reports of the Savings Plan.

Health Benefits and Officer Training Become Union Benefits

As the economy improved in the 1970-80's, so did the power of the maritime unions. The maritime unions were stronger and they negotiated improved wages, vacation and health benefits for members. On October 1, 1981, the Reagan Administration eliminated appropriations for the U.S.

Public Health Service assistance to merchant seaman at Marine Hospitals throughout the USA; this was a service authorized by Congress since 1798. There was no longer a need for a government health care system for merchant seamen that started in a period when seamen were treated poorly by shipowners and were considered wards of the court, a citizen group that needed special protection.

USPHS hospital nurse with crew patients

LCA had regularly published the lists of USPHS services in the Bulletin and in separate handouts. In 1981 there were four USPHS Outpatients Clinics in Buffalo, Chicago, Cleveland and Detroit. There were USPHS contracted hospitals in 18 cities in Michigan; three in Ohio and one each in Minnesota and Pennsylvania. There were contract Physician Offices in Illinois, Indiana, Michigan, Minnesota, Ohio, Pennsylvania and Wisconsin. LCA members needed to create lists of physicians throughout the Lakes for consultation in case of emergency. The USPHS had a concern for the maintenance of seamen's records, continuation of care and the availability of medical advice at sea.

In the same period international maritime codes and regulations took hold and the U.S. Coast Guard was tasked with improving the safety of foreign flag ships that entered U.S. waters in order to prevent oil pollution and collisions. Improved training was required of U.S. mariners. Individual companies could not adequate perform this training function and for years depended upon the LCA to provide training for upgrade of licenses and documents as well as in new technology.

LCA turned to the new GLMA at Traverse City for improved officer training and in some cases for the unlicensed crew training. The unions, both licensed and unlicensed (except for USW 5000), grasped the opportunity during negotiations to take on the training functions with contributions from the companies. Union officials were wary of institutions such as the federal and state maritime academies that could produce an oversupply of qualified persons. Gradually LCA discontinued officer training, first in Cleveland and then in Duluth.

One training function that the companies and the unions could not provide because of liability considerations was hands-on firefighting training. Jointly, LCA and the unions supported the establishment in the Great Lakes area, a firefighting and damage control school run by the Marad. On August 11, 1982, a Firefighting School was dedicated near Toledo. The location was strongly supported by Mel Pelfrey, MEBA District II, since the union offered officer training in Toledo.

Firefighting Training Facility Toledo

Great Lakes Maritime Academy

Great Lakes Maritime Academy was officially founded in 1970. There was a shortage of officers in 1970 reaching as many as 30 officers in both the deck and engine departments. Shortages at any one time in the summer of 1973 varied from 60 to 100 mates and engineers; and seamen shortages were from 40-65 on the 127 ships surveyed. One of the causes of the shortage of officers was the fact that fewer unlicensed sailors were upgrading to officer licenses and the shortages in the summer months increased as the union vacation plan called for 20 vacation days after 60 days of work.

Scott Elder, LCA General Counsel, attended the GLMA Board of Visitors meeting at Traverse City in 1970. The Board at that time consisted of many federal, state, union and academic officials; only Elder and Art Zuehlke, Manitowoc Shipbuilding, represented industry management. From the federal government were Marad and USCG; the union officials were from MMP and MEBA; from the State of Michigan there were staff from the Commerce and Transportation Departments, and from the University of Michigan and Northwestern Michigan College.

When the school was first mentioned in the LCA records, it was referred to as the Merchant Marine Training Program at Northwestern Michigan College (NMC). Later it was usually referred to as Great Lakes Maritime Academy (GLMA). In 1971 two LCA companies contributed to a GLMA student loan fund. On August 15, 1971, in the second year of operation of GLMA, former USCG Commandant, Admiral Willard J. Smith, became Assistant to the President for Maritime Affairs.

GLMA Board of Visitors meeting 1974 (Northwestern Michigan College Archives)

In 1971 the Welfare Committee, chaired by John Horton, was concerned about the shortage of officers on Great Lakes vessels. A study by the Upper Great Lakes Commission determined that the existing pool of Great Lakes Officers had a ratio of 1.22 for deck and 1.45 for engine officers, far lower than the pool for ocean going officers. While the committee maintained support for seamen moving up the hawsepipe as the primary source of officers, they supported establishment of Great Lakes Maritime Academy as a supplemental source. At that time there were 32 students enrolled. The committee recommended that the Advisory Committee support placement of cadets onboard their ships and to pay them a daily wage similar to that of Kings Point, $5.72/day. The Committee also considered the need for a Revolving Loan Fund based on LCA contributions that would be used to make loans to deserving students. The Fund concept was not recommended to the Advisory Committee since not all members were in support of the establishment of GLMA and the LCA By-Laws did not allow the use of LCA contributions to inure to the benefit of private individuals.

In 1972, Raymond T. McKay, President, District 2, MEBA-AMO, addressed a telegram to Paul Trimble advocating the discontinuance of LCA schools. A delicately worded response cited the need for more consultation with members and recommended that LCA would consider "a consolidation of efforts."

The first graduating class to join the fleets was at vessel fit-out 1973. Graduates obtained an Associate of Science degree and the USCG license as a deck or engine officer. Half of the class took their training onboard the 110 foot training ship Hudson, a former Coast Guard utility tug; other vessels used for training included the 143 foot long Allegheny, a former U.S. Navy fleet tug, a smaller harbor tug, Anchor Bay, a LCM and several work barges. Other cadets were assigned to LCA vessels.

GLMA T/V Hudson

In 1974, the Advisory Committee declared that "GLMA should be encouraged and supported." In 1975 there was an enrollment of 80, all of whom needed shipboard assignments in 1976. In 1975, 13 students received licenses and in 1976, 16 wrote for their licenses. The Annual Report notes that in 1975, 33 deck and engine graduates, 80% of total graduates, were working on Great Lakes ships. At that time the annual school expenses for each student was $3,400.

In 1976, GLMA had an enrollment of 78 with 50 new students expected in July 1977. In 1976, 23 graduates received licenses; and 17 from the class of 1977 were writing for their licenses. Annual school fees had climbed to $4,000/year. In 1976, LCA was considering requests for funds for a navigation simulator for GLMA. In 1977 there was an enrollment of 99, 21 more than the previous year. In 1977, 19 received licenses. USCG sent inspectors to GLMA to conduct the exam instead of requiring students to go to a distant Coast Guard exam center. School fees in 1978 were $4,200; and in 1979 $4,640.

In 1978 the Upper Great Lakes Commission provided $90,000 to GLMA for recruitment and instruction; and in 1979, the grant was renewed and increased to $100,000. LCA contributed $20,000 toward the $100,000 needed for an electronics lab. LCA Welfare committee recommended major LCA contributions for the new GLMA buildings since industry's new goal for GLMA was to have an entry class of 150 students each year, which after attrition, there would be an anticipated 100 officers graduating with licenses. The Great Lakes shipping industry, based upon the Marad study to which industry provided data, foresaw a need for 200 officer replacements/year and thus needed to get 100 new employees from GLMA and the remainder from the other Academies and the hawsepipe. LCA supported a cadet corps of 300 in the three year program. GLMA asked the State of Michigan for $2.4 million.

In 1978, enrollment was 103; an additional 75 were to enter in July 1979. Coast Guard held license exams at St. Ignace due to CG officer shortages. In that year, 105 GLMA deck and engine officers were serving on Great Lakes vessels; that was 85% of the total graduates. In 1979, the enrollment was 150 and 100 were expected to enter in June 1980. Thirty-four students were expected to write for their license and the exams were held at the Academy. In 1979, 127 officers were working on Great Lakes ships; again that was 85% of graduates.

In order to get the word out to the public about the crew needs, LCA sent representatives to all the coastal academies, prepared brochures, TV spots, slide shows for museums and encouraged all officers to promote recruitment. Serious shortage of crew led to many Coast Guard citations against the vessels for inadequate manning. LCA recommended that GLMA become a regional Academy in order to garner broad Great Lakes region support

GLMA was expanded with the addition of 17,500 square feet of space for classrooms, labs offices and a conference room was built in honor of John L. Horton, long time chair of the Vessel Personnel and Safety Committee.

In 1979, expansion of the Academy was in part financed by a $900,000 grant from the U.S. Department of Commerce, Economic Development

Administration (EDA), for construction and $370,000 from private funding for equipment. In 1979, following some serious GLMA personnel turmoil with NMC, the GLMA was granted some autonomy from the NMC. GLMA became an independent branch of the college and could develop a separate budget from NMC; the Academy had a direct connection to the Michigan statehouse; the Governor's 1980 budget recommendation was $355,000, double that of the previous year. In 1979, LCA provided $50,000 to GLMA for the additional operating expenses and was considering an additional $15,000 to pay for architectural renderings for the new GLMA Center. In 1980, RADM George Rector, Director, GLMA, asked LCA to pay for $535,000 of the $1,600,000 expansion and equipment requirements. Efforts were underway to make GLMA a regional academy. In 1981, there appeared to be support for this concept by all Great Lakes state governors.

As fate would have it the next major American economic recession befell the steel industry in the Great Lakes. The anticipated demand for mariners fell off rapidly just as the increased supply of mariners needing training was in the educational pipeline.

In 1981 and 1982, due to the recession and the reduced level of shipping, it was difficult to find berths for the cadets at GLMA. Concern was also expressed by the LCA members for the insurance coverage for cadets while serving on the ships. In 1982, a new system of cadet pay was developed to separate pay from ship board berths and to establish a funding pool at the academy. Due to the shortage of berths for cadets there was an effort to set up a payment system that was made by the vessel owner to the Academy and then GLMA paid the cadet the stipend each month. This in part was considered in order to reduce potential liability caused by having a cadet on the ship's articles. The legal question was; is the cadet an employee or an observer?

Cadet monthly stipend in the beginning of the program was: $250/month; in 1976 it was increased to $300; 1977 increased to $345; 1979 increased to $351 plus travel expenses of $105 each way.

Shore Captains, Navigation and Ice Committee

In 1980, Committee activities were absorbed into the Navigation Committee as it took over the work of the Ice Committee and the Shore Captains Committee

Shore Captains Chairman: Captain Ed Jacobsen, Columbia Transportation until end of 1970; Captain John Rankin, U.S. Steel 1971-1979; Captain Ed Jacobsen 1980.

Navigation Committee Chairman 1975 Captain Wm. Simonds, U.S. Steel.

Ice Committee Chairman: 1975 Captain Ed Jacobsen.

Captain Ed Jacobsen

Major Initiatives
Rules of the Road Changes on the Great Lakes

In 1976, Paul Trimble received commendations for serving on the Rules of the Road Advisory Committee. On July 15, 1977, the International Regulations for Preventing Collisions at Sea (COLREGS) came into force but it was contested in the USA. LCA believed it would be some time before they would be acceptable on the Lakes by the Americans and Canadians. In 1979, the Legislative and Navigation Committees came to agreements with the International communities on amendments to the

Great Lakes Rules of the Road to bring them into substantial conformity with the International Regulations for Prevention of Collisions at Sea (COLREGS). LCA and DMA asked that the new rules for the Lakes go in effect at opening of navigation April 1, 1982 rather than December 24, 1981. After more negotiations, the new unified rules became effective on all U.S. inland waters except the Great Lakes on 24 December 1981 and on the Great Lakes on 1 March 1983, to match the effective date of Canada's revised rules.

Navigation Season Extension Winter Navigation

Several LCA members, in particular U.S. Steel, lobbied for government support to extend the Great Lakes navigation season that normally ended when economic conditions no longer warranted continued stockpile build ups or when ice formations were too heavy for the vessels. LCA also lobbied for assistance from the U.S. Coast Guard, to safely and efficiently complete their voyages. U.S. Steel, in 1968 ran vessels until January 3; in 1969 until January 8; and in 1970 until January 14.

After successful lobbying for this season extension, the Omnibus Rivers and Harbors Act 1970 was passed and one provision directed the Secretary of the Army to work with other departments, agencies, public and private interests to undertake a program to demonstrate the practicability of extending the navigation season of the Great Lakes and St. Lawrence Seaway. The LCA Bulletin stated in 1970 that Year 'round navigation was sought for Lakes.

In the 1970 LCA Annual Report "It was announced in late fall that some vessels in the iron ore trade would continue between Lake Superior and the Chicago area through the month of January, if operating conditions were conducive to such an extension of the season." The Philip R. Clarke made that last trip loading iron ore at Two Harbors on January 27 and transited the Soo Locks on January 29, thus marking a new record for continuous opening of the lock at the Soo. The Clarke was escorted through the Straits by the Mackinaw on January 30, again setting a record for such a late transit.

The 1970 navigation season became the longest in the Soo canal 116 year history-304 days. The next year, the locks operated until February 8, 1973 thus the 1972 season lasted 305 days.

Vessels operating in ice with USCG assistance

In 1971 LCA reported that the polar icebreaker USCG Cutter Edisto, a polar icebreaker and one other vessel would come to the lakes to help extend the season. The Edisto had a draft of 29'; thus she was less help in the connecting rivers but could work in the Straits. In 1972 the Edisto was returned to ocean duty and the Southwind was sent to the lakes.

USCG Cutter Edisto

In 1972, Trimble called for a replacement of the 110 foot USCG vessels on the lakes with 160', 10,000 HP vessels capable of working ice in the connecting channels. In 1973 LCA called for an extension of the Demonstration program that was to cease on June 30, 1974 and asked for additional appropriations. A 2 ½ year extension was authorized plus an additional $3 million.

The ability to keep the locks open was not the most serious problem for retaining support for the extended season. The St. Marys River has a number of inhabited islands that depended upon ferry service until the ice froze solid enough for snow mobiles and light trucks to cross. Children needed to get to school particularly from Sugar Island. Ship passages not only delayed fast ice formation but also caused large chunks of broken ice to float downstream causing damage to the ferry and/or docks. A major problem was keeping the channel open in order for the ferry to operate at the Little Rapids Cut to Sugar Island. Ice booms had to be installed above the island and more icebreakers were needed. Vessel traffic had to stop on February 7, 1974 because of the ferry transit problem. Trimble reiterated a request for additional small icebreakers.

In order to assure more precise navigation in the rivers when floating buoys were removed, better navigation systems were needed, Trimble heralded the adoption of Loran-C as the national long range navigation system and called for a mini chain of Loran-C in the St. Marys River to allow for a 25' accuracy in all weather; once developed through the Lakes it would eliminate the RDF equipment.

In 1974 the Advisory Committee approved expenditure of $30,000 to further the Winter Navigation Demonstration program. Several members indicated a desire to operate as long as possible. In 1975 Trimble reported that while no Coast Guard vessels were under construction for the Lakes at that time, they could look forward to delivery of small river class icebreaking tugs, single screw, with 12 foot draft in 1978 or 1979. Clearly he was disappointed in the smaller vessels but was pleased with some additional USCG vessel assistance. In 1976 the USCG placed an order for four vessels of 140' x 37' with a 12' draft and 2,500 SHP; LCA asked for a fleet of seven vessels.

In 1975 Trimble noted that the Winter Navigation Board was making an interim recommendation that the upper four lakes be open to navigation until January 31; and for extending for two years beyond the planned end of the program that would shut the locks on December 31, 1976. 1975-76 was the first year of year round navigation on the upper four Great Lakes.

In 1977 Trimble called upon Congress to replace the USCG cutter Westwind with the Finnish ORHO class icebreaker that was available for $55 million. He also recommended consideration of the Finnish ALE class as a general purpose USCG vessel for the lakes. In 1978 Trimble testified before Congress again asking for an additional vessel to support Mackinaw. He contended that the operation of the ocean cutters did not work because of the deep draft. When they operated at dual draft by having minimum bunkers and water, they needed to go in to port for bunkers and water every 2-3 days. The Westwind in December 1977 was disabled due to grounding and no Great Lakes shipyard could dry dock her. He again reiterated the availability of Finnish icebreakers.

1978 was the third year of year round navigation but significant opposition to Winter Navigation was then being raised by the State of Michigan due to concerns of the St. Marys River island residents and some of the environmental groups.

The Winter Navigation Demonstration program ended September 1979 with the expiration of COE appropriations. LCA contended that winter navigation was now a fact, thus there was no need for further demonstration; but Michigan environmentalists opposed this recognition. It was uncertain if navigation would continue after December 15, 1979; but, LCA operated beyond that date with the understanding that the Soo lock closing date was January 8 plus or minus one week. Island transportation on the St. Marys River continued to be a concern of island residents.

In 1978, the Commandant of the Coast Guard published an instruction on Domestic Icebreaking Policy that called for the local Coast Guard units to not interfere with the commercial icebreakers unless they were not available or if available but had declined, or they were inadequate and unsuccessful in the attempt to assist. Unfortunately the definitions of availability and adequacy caused many subjective judgments by local Coast Guard units that led to complaints to Congress from the commercial tug operators. Another difficult point in the instruction was that the service should only be provided to maintain 'traditional' seasons of navigation.

In 1979, the State of Michigan attempted to stop all navigation through the Soo Locks after December 15. Many environmental groups raised unsubstantiated and invalid issues concerning navigation. There was a palpable concern that essential coal and oil deliveries to Michigan and other states would cease. Likewise, the iron ore cargos to the steel mills and the late grain harvest shipments would cease. The COE declared that since the funding for the winter navigation demonstration program ended, it lacked authority to install ice booms. Congressmen Oberstar and Bonier brought about an agreement that navigation could continue to January 31, plus or minus two weeks for the next two years and that the locks would close on December 30, 1981 to monitor the environment. LCA opposed these limitations as "repugnant to the industry" since the Office of Management and Budget ruled that the COE needed no further authorization to undertake the needed action regarding the ice booms. The House bill passed and was pending in the Senate. An agreement was reached with the COE to operate the locks until January 8 plus or minus one week, allowing raw materials delivery planning to proceed.

In 1980 the COE acquiesced to the OMB opinion and LCA was pleased that there was no restrictive closing date mandated; LCA operated on the belief that the locks would remain open until January 31 plus or minus two weeks if weather conditions permitted. In 1980 the locks closed on December 31. The LCA position in 1980 was that industry should determine the extent of winter navigation based on economic justification, weather conditions and environmental impact and that for planning purposes the locks should remain open until January 31 plus or minus two weeks if weather conditions permitted.

Other work of the Navigation Committee

- Conducted the Ice Committee Meetings with U.S. and Canadian operators and the federal agencies, in particular the USCG, COE, and NWS at the beginning and end of the seasons.
- Emphasized the priority for dredging in connecting channels to accommodate the new larger vessels.
- Recommended new or modified separate courses.
- Worked with the USCG on survival systems as part of the Extended Season Demonstration.
- Called for the installation of radio telephone equipment on bridges over important channels.
- Recommend removal of abandoned and disused bridges that were a menace to navigation, such as the interstate bridge in Duluth Harbor.

- In 1973, worked on problems with dredge spoil disposal in Saginaw, MI, and the Cuyahoga River, Cleveland.
- Combated the USCG effort to decommission icebreaker <u>Mackinaw.</u>
- Worked with the National Ocean Survey to have the separate courses approved by the LCA and DMA printed on all Great Lakes charts.
- In1973 LCA petitioned for an additional Poe size lock; asks the COE to determine if vessels larger than 1000' can pass through the Poe; and for connecting channels be deepened to 32', the control depth at the Poe.

Electronics Committee, Merged with Navigation Committee in 1983

Chairman: John W. Manning, M.A. Hanna; 1980 Louis E. Ervin, American Steamship Company; 1982 Dewey Aston, Pickands Mather

- The committee worked on the revision of the Great Lakes Treaty; assisted in the setting up of a very high frequency (VHF) system of communications for safety, distress and operations as the medium frequency was to be phased out. This system needed to be compatible with Canadian systems and to meet the approval of the FCC which called for the operation of a VHF system on all the Lakes by January 1, 1974.
- Members begin to work with Lorain Electronics who made a proposal for a 22 station exclusive automated VHF radiotelephone system connected by ATT landlines. The Committee agreed upon a total of 14 stations to cover the U.S. Great Lakes. In 1973-75, a prototype system was tested with six shore stations linked with Lorain, OH. In 1975 Lorain Electronics asked for a ten year contract covering 900,000 gross tonnage of shipping in order to finance the construction of the remaining eight shore transceiver stations. In August 1977, 10 of the 14 stations were operating; the rest were in operation later that year. This was to lead to the elimination of medium frequency AM radiotelephone equipment, both single and double sideband. The advantages expected were

a far superior transmission system at lower cost with better safety and distress reporting capability, direct dialing, computerized position reporting, and the availability of facsimile service for business, weather and ice reports.
- In 1975, the Precise Navigation system in the St. Marys River system, a forerunner of a lakes wide Loran C system, leading to elimination of RDF equipment was being tested for possible installation in 1979. The Coast Guard announced the extension of LORAN C to include the Great Lakes by 1978. A mini-LORAN C system was installed in the St. Marys River to provide accuracy to 25'.
- In 1975 there was a successful testing of a lake-wide VHF radiotelephone system.
- In 1976, Scott Elder, LCA General Counsel, drafted a proposed Radiotelephone Agreement with Lorain Electronics Corporation outlining how contributions would be made by the member companies, taking into account minimum payments during curtailment of vessel operations, the gross tonnage needed to make the contract operative, and what expenses constituted operation and maintenance of the system. Each company individually entered into this operation contract with Lorain Electronics.
- In 1981 LCA asked the USCG to help with the problem of congestion on channel 16, since the FCC was not enforcing procedural violations. LCA asked that whatever was done it must be compatible with the Canadian system rather than what was used in other U.S. coastal waters. LCA was opposed to setting up a separate channel for bridge to bridge communications as that would require additional radio equipment and would be a step toward a vessel traffic control system.
- In 1982 the Committee supported the placement of Class C emergency position-indicating radio beacons (EPIRBS) in the Pilot house but opposed the placement of Class D or E EPIRBS in the lifeboats and rafts.
- The Committee reluctantly agreed to support the lifting of the Great Lakes Exemption to the Bridge-to-Bridge Radiotelephone Act in order to provide for use of an additional channel for bridge-to-bridge communications, thus relieving congestion on Channel 16.

Lake Carriers' Association History 1880-2015 | 381

Fleet Engineers Committee

Chairman: Dave Groh, Interlake Steamship Company

Dave Groh

- Engineers begin to work on systems to reduce and if possible to eliminate discharge of vessel wastes from ships. Systems considered were: containment, partial containment and incineration. Committee worked with EPA and Marad to improve technology. Working with other committees they prepared a report, "Criteria for Waste Control Systems" for the Advisory Committee.
- Committee also was concerned with the modification of the Great Lakes Load Line Regulations that came into effect in 1973.
- The committee continued efforts to meet USCG standards being developed for sewage treatment; they worked with the USCG on oil spill reporting proposals and with suppliers on oily water clean-up systems.
- Prepared a manual of instructions to be used aboard ship along with oil-transfer check off list.

Air and Water Conservation Committee

Chairman: Dave L. Buchanan, U.S. Steel until he retired from U.S. Steel and became Vice President of LCA in 1973. The Interim Chairman was J. E. Campbell, U.S. Steel.

In 1971 LCA prepared an economic evaluation of the installation of waste treatment devices onboard Great Lakes bulk cargo vessels. Alternatives considered were: first, holding tanks with ultimate disposal ashore; and second, providing secondary waste treatment onboard. A major consideration was that separate systems would be required on each end of the ship; and, that for the 155 vessels constructed before 1950, since virtually each toilet had individual outlets, they would all need to be plumbed to a holding tank. There would be a need for construction of four holding tanks inside the side tanks that would have to be pumped out every five days. Municipal waste treatment facilities would only accept treated sewage, thus the effluent would have to be aerated onboard. Last, the cargo terminals did not have the piping systems to the municipal treatment plants and if the piping existed it would have to be insulated and heated for use in the winter time.

In 1971 the State of Minnesota Pollution Control Agency proposed regulations that would treat vessels the same as shore based plants with respect to visible air contaminants.

Committee was extensively concerned with trying to get the federal government regulators to establish the technical requirements for the treatment of shipboard sewage. When the Federal Government did not act, the Committee asked all LCA members to recommend criteria for types of sewage-control systems that could reasonably be expected to perform satisfactorily under shipboard conditions. The committee reported that unfortunately a number of Great Lakes states impetuously undertook to control the discharge from vessels by unilateral action and regulation. Much of the effort was dealing with the Michigan Watercraft Pollution Control Act; the Wisconsin water pollution statutes; Milwaukee, Wisconsin, air pollution; and, Huron, Ohio, and Duluth, Minnesota pollution concerns. The Committee worked with the Great Lakes Commission to identify locations for shoreside disposal of vessel sewage; and collaborated with Marad and other government and industry organizations to develop practical vessel waste water treatment systems that were economic to operate.

In 1975, Erie County, New York, proposed extensive smoke emission standards on oil fired vessels as well as onerous regulations on the coal fired vessels that were being phased out.

Committee was relieved that the Coast Guard published regulations effective January 30, 1975 regarding certification, design and construction of marine sanitation devices. By 1980 all LCA vessels were equipped with type I, type II or type III Coast Guard certified marine sanitation devices. Nevertheless, Michigan demanded that all vessels be equipped with holding tanks.

George J. Ryan

Public Relations Committee

Chairman: Since 1964 M. A. Bradley; 1974 Floyd May; 1977 Clinton F. Goodwin

- Published the Bulletin.
- In 1973 a great deal of time was spent on countering adverse misinformation about the causes of the high water levels. Congressional hearings were held on the subject on the phenomenon of high water that lasted for over 20 years.
- In 1973 LCA agreed to share cost of a Public Relations film produced by University of Michigan promoting extended season navigation at a cost of $12,500; *An Inconceivable Commerce* in cooperation/cost share with Marad. The film was completed in 1974; it was originally planned to be 28 minutes but there was too much material and it became a one hour production. It was divided into two parts, the first for general consumption and the last half for those most interested in extended season navigation.

- In 1974 Advisory Committee approved $1,000 for a brochure promoting extended navigation season, cost shared with the Michigan Chamber of Commerce, Great Lakes Commission and Industrial Users Group.
- Continued distribution of film *Long Ships Passing*.
- Organized orientation trips on lake vessels for government officials seeking familiarization trips.
- Administered the marine industry orientation program for Coast Guard officers; 1972 was the 23rd year of sponsorship.
- Helped sponsor the National Maritime Poster program in conjunction with the National Propeller Club.
- Continued to publish *Sounding*, a periodic digest of info on legislative matters, prepared news releases, particularly rebuttals of accusations of LCA responsibility for high water.
- Prepared and distributed the pamphlet *Great Lakes Shipping: the Story of the Lake Shipping Industry*.
- When the Smithsonian Institution Hall of American Maritime Enterprise asked for assistance in creating new displays, the Advisory Committee approved $10,000 to be spent on a marine exhibit that would include Great Lakes shipping; LCA also agreed to build a model of a typical Lake freighter. It turned out that it was a model of the 1,000 footer James R. Barker.
- In response to the critical crew shortage, the committee took on a major publicity campaign in support of GLMA. The Committee cooperated with Admiral George Rector in a public relations campaign called *Come Sail With Us* to attract more students to the Academy. The program included production of TV spots, teacher's guides and brochures. An initiative to update the film *Long Ships Passing* was eliminated in order to concentrate on the Academy recruitment.
- In 1979 it was recognized that LCA needed a professional public relations program to counter the adverse public opinion, particularly in Michigan, with respect to Great Lakes shipping and specifically winter navigation. In 1980, Advisory Committee approved funding a study *Role of Lakes Shipping in the Great Lakes Economy* by Dr. Terry Monson, Michigan Technological University.

Shipbuilding, Modernizations and Ship Scraping

Shipbuilding

There were many major new ship buildings in the 1970's, some of which were assisted by the Merchant Marine Act, 1970. The decade started with the continued construction of the Roger Blough and the Stewart J. Cort. The Cleveland Tankers tank barge Phoenix, built in Texas, was delivered to the lakes in 1970. In the following years 32 vessels were delivered: Stewart J. Cort, Roger Blough, William R. Roesch, Paul Thayer, Charles E. Wilson, Roger Keys, Presque Isle, H. Lee White, Wolverine, Saturn, Sam Laud, Joseph L. Block, St. Clair, James R. Barker, Jupiter, Mesabi Miner, Belle River, Lewis Wilson Foy, Buffalo, George A. Stinson, Gemini, Edwin H. Gott, Indiana Harbor, Fred R. White, Jr., American Mariner, Burns Harbor, Edgar B. Speer, Columbia Star, William J. DeLancey, American Republic and the Tug/Barge Amoco Michigan/Amoco Great Lakes. In 1978 Cleveland-Cliffs announced an intention to build a thousand footer to carry coal for Detroit Edison under a 20 year contract; however the vessel was not built.

Modernizations

Modernizations were contracted to make the vessels more productive and safer as well as environmentally beneficial. They included:

- Conversions from coal fired boilers to oil fired boilers; Ashland, Edmund Fitzgerald, A. H. Ferbert and Frank Purnell.
- Conversions from steam to diesel propulsion occurred in several cases.
- Installation of bow thrusters took place on Armco, Reserve, Rogers City, and Paul H. Carnahan and the installation of a stern thruster on the Edward B. Greene.
- Automated boiler controls took place on Champlain, R. H. Watson, Leon Frazer, E. T. Weir, B. F. Fairless, and E. M. Voorhees.
- Lengthening of the vessels occurred on Charles M. Beeghly, John Sherwin, Armco, Reserve, Cason J. Callaway, Arthur B. Homer, Philip R. Clarke, Arthur M. Anderson, John G. Munson, Edward B. Greene, Walter S. Sterling, and William Clay Ford.
- Conversion to self-unloaders took place on J. H. Hillman, Jr.(Crispin Oglebay), Henry Ford II, J. Burton Ayers, Wilfred Sykes, Herbert C. Jackson, Walter B. Sterling, Courtney Burton,

Middletown, Sparrows Point, Edward B. Greene, Charles M. Beeghly, Elton Hoyt 2nd, Arthur M. Anderson, Cason J. Callaway, Philip R. Clarke, Armco and Middletown.

Ship Scraping

Because of the new construction of larger and more efficient vessels and the modernizations, from 1972-1981 there were 80 vessels removed from service and later scrapped, converted to a scow, storage barge or made into a dock face.

Vessel Losses

During Trimble's tenure there was the near loss of the incomplete Roger Blough in 1971 when a devastating fire occurred onboard while at the American Shipbuilding Co. yard in Lorain prior to builder's trials which resulted in the unfortunate death of four shipyard workers.

The most devastating loss was that of the Edmund Fitzgerald on November 10, 1975 in Lake Superior with the loss of all hands—29 men. This catastrophic loss led to many government and industry investigations and this subject occupied the time and skill of Paul Trimble and other members of the LCA for several years as industry and government agencies worked hard to prevent another such loss.

Fortunately since 1975 there has not been another American flag Great Lakes vessel lost in a storm; although there have been several American flag vessels lost in ocean storms.

Other losses included the constructive total loss of the Harry L. Allen, January 21, 1978, caused by a dockside fire in Duluth; and the constructive total loss of the Frontenac, November 22, 1979, following grounding near the entrance to Silver Bay, MN.

Other Key Events of the Period

- 1970 The last remaining lightship on the Great Lakes, at Port Huron, was decommissioned on August 25, 1970.
- 1971 Vice Admiral James A. Hirshfield received the Great Lakes Man of the Year award.
- Due to the national and international concerns about the U.S. pursuit of the Vietnam War, on April 30, 1971 LCA republished a booklet *Special Rules for the Protection of Great Lakes Commerce*. The purpose was to provide the lake industry, particularly vessel officers, with measures to prevent sabotage. There was concern at that time due to bombing and threats of bombing in the nation's industry. The booklet stated," This menace, attending social unrest, has been experienced with increased frequency during the past decade. Vessels have been-and may continue to be targets of such threats."
- In 1971, Westcott was advised that the Post Office was considering terminating its contract with Westcott effective July 1, 1971. In 1972, LCA negotiated an agreement for J.W. Westcott services to be for a total payment of $25,000, $4,000 less than for 1971. Negotiations had preceded this decision and options considered were for LCA to discontinue the contract and require all members to execute separate agreements for payment of a minimum annual contracted fee on the basis of vessel capacity transiting the Detroit River; other options included payment for each service such as $1.25 for each individual report, a fee of $10 for removing persons from the ship, and a minimum of $2.25 for delivery or removal of packages or freight items.
- 1972 Kinsman Marine Transit Co. acquired Wilson Marine Transit Co.; American Shipbuilding Co. acquired Great Lakes Towing Company.
- In 1972, as reported in *Youngstown Vindicator*, April 27, 1974, a group of Black investors formed a company, Maritime Enterprises, Inc., to operate Great Lakes ships hauling grain out the Seaway and iron ore inbound. They purchased a ship and had the support of George Steinbrenner; however they alleged that institutional

racism held them back. Pat Manley and Karl Fjeldstad, former employees of Wilson Marine Transit, assisted the investors who wanted to help minorities be trained in ship operations. The group had financial support from the Department of Commerce Office of Minority Business Enterprise.

- 1973 An LCA Energy Conservation Committee was formed to provide for adequate fuel allocations during fuel shortages.
- 1973 Diamond Shamrock Company completed sale of the Pickands Mather & Company division to Moore-McCormack Co. Inc.; and General American Transportation Co. (GATX) purchased American Steamship Company.
- 1974 Annual Report noted that some forward thinking LCA members advocated a new lock at the Soo accommodating 150 feet wide vessels up to 1,500 feet in length; others advocated a canal through the Upper Peninsula from Au Train Bay, through Hiawatha National Forest, Whitefish River and Little Bay De Noc. *(In 2015, as Ryan reflected on the environmental, social and economic costs of such a construction project, he disagreed with his esteemed friend and predecessor. It was Ryan's opinion that the LCA members who suggested this project were living in the past and were not forward thinking!)*
- Buoyed by the successful transit of 767 foot vessels through the MacArthur lock, LCA looked forward to passage of 1,100 foot vessels through the Poe.
- In May 1975, <u>Edward B. Greene</u> burned shale oil as part of demonstration program to determine the utility of shale oil in ship board fuel. This project was of great interest to the U.S. Navy and had the support of Cleveland Cliffs, USCG R&D and Marad region office.
- In the 1975 Annual Report it was noted that a Marad region office in Cleveland was set up under a "capable administrator." **Ryan admits proudly that the administrator to whom Trimble referred was the author of this book.**
- 1976 Lake Survey Center, located in Detroit for the past 131 years closed its doors end of June; its work was distributed to other NOAA offices. Originally established in Buffalo as an office of

the U.S. Army Corps of Engineers in 1841, it was relocated to Detroit four years later. In 1970, the COE work was transferred to the National Ocean Survey at Norfolk, VA, the NOAA HQ in Rockville, MD, and to the Environmental Research Lab at Ann Arbor, MI.

- In 1976 the Corps was authorized to study the need for a new Poe size lock and the proposed regulation for transit of 1,100' vessels at the Soo was published.
- In January 1977, Robert L. Hogle, Supervisor of the Toledo JRC, retired after nearly 40 years. He started in 1938 in the LCA Assembly Room, Toledo.
- In April 1979, the Canadian lock at the Soo was turned over to Parks Canada.
- In the October-November 1979 Bulletin, for the benefit of boat watchers, the Whistle Identification Signals for all LCA vessels and members was published.
- 1980 LCA reported that because of energy supply needs, an unidentified LCA member was considering a coal fired steam plant for a new 1,000' vessel.
- In 1980 LCA celebrated the anniversary of its 100 year history.
- In 1981 the MEBA strike started on April 16, lasted 11 days, and halted 90% of shipping.

100th Anniversary LCA art work

Chapter Eight

George J. Ryan
President 1983-2002

George J. Ryan

Political Climate in the World, Washington and State Governments

World events that impacted the nation as a whole and business on the Great Lakes during this period included the Reagan Administration support for the Contras against the Marxist Sandinistas in Nicaragua which lead to the embarrassing Iran Contra Affair. In 1985 Palestinian terrorists hijacked the cruise ship Achille Lauro and killed an American, leading to U.S. Navy F-14 fighters interception of an Egyptian airplane and the mobilization of counter-terrorist units including Delta Force and a SEAL Team. The Libyan government was involved in the bombing of a passenger airplane over Scotland in 1988. Others major events included: the 1989 military action to oust the Panamanian President; the first Gulf War in 1990 after Iraq invaded Kuwait and the successful Desert Storm operation to drive the Iraqi army out; the fall of the Soviet Union in 1991; terrorists bombing of the World Trade Center garage in New York in 1992; and in the same year the U.S. forces in the Sudan suffered humiliating losses; in 1994 the U.S. seized Haiti one more time in the history of that nation; the Federal Building in Oklahoma City was destroyed by domestic terrorists; in 1994 U.S. military operations took place in Bosnia and Yugoslavia under NATO; in 1996 a domestic terrorist bombed the Atlanta Summer Olympic games; in 1998 the U.S. Embassies in Kenya and Tanzania were bombed by Al Qaida terrorists; and then the Al Qaida attack on New York and Washington took place on September 11, 2001.

Clearly these world events showed there was still a major need for American mariners and ships that served in the Gulf war theater and that the safety of American ports was enhanced by having only Americans serving on domestic trade ships in the thousands of ports in the U.S. coastal ports and hinterlands. American cabotage laws require American mariners and thus reduce significantly the threat of foreign crew members recruited as terrorists.

The political leadership in Washington was varied during Ryan's 20 year tenure; but primarily the Republicans controlled the House and Senate. The Presidents were Ronald Reagan until 1989; George Bush until 1993; William Clinton until 2001 and George W. Bush until 2009. The Senate was Republican controlled from 1981-1987; then Democrat controlled until 1995; followed by Republican control until 2001. For the next two years there were an even number of Senators but the tie votes were cast by the Republican Vice President. In the House, Democrats had control from 1981-1995; followed by Republican control until 2007. Congress had many issues to deal with in addition to the military operations. By 1985 the U.S. became the world's largest debtor nation with debts of $130 billion and in 1989 Congress had to authorize $300 billion to overcome the Savings and

Loan Crisis. The needs of the U.S. Merchant Marine were not significantly on the agenda of many legislators.

It was essential for LCA to be nonpartisan, although many LCA members either had Washington representation or were members of other associations that contributed money to political campaign funds. LCA made no political contributions; LCA did not have a Political Action Committee (PAC) since they had too few employees and the LCA members individually or through other organizations provided financial support for political campaigns to the legislators of their choosing. It may fairly be said that LCA benefited from the identification with members and coalition allies, including unions, who had political connections that were enhanced by political campaign contributions.

Complicating the ability to obtain Great Lakes region political support was the loss of House congressional representatives in Great Lakes states. Each census showed a declining regional population and thus fewer congressmen in the Great Lakes Region. A further complication was the advent of internationalism; the call for free trade unhindered by the legislative "Buy American" provisions and nationalistic laws such as our Cabotage laws reserving carriage of goods and passengers between U.S. ports to American flag vessels (the most significant law was known as the Jones Act). And not least, there was the decline of the power of the American steel and iron ore industries.

Biography of George J. Ryan

George J. Ryan was born in Philadelphia in 1936. In 1957 following graduation from the U.S. Merchant Marine Academy, Kings Point, N.Y., he served as an Ensign on the guided missile cruiser USS Canberra (CAG-2) and in several U.S. Naval Reserve units. He was employed by the Grace Lines where, after serving in all deck officer capacities including master, he was appointed Assistant Port Captain and Manager-Supporting Services-Marine Division. During his Grace Line sailing period, Mr. Ryan was awarded a Master's Degree from the School of International Affairs, Columbia University in 1964.

He was employed by the U. S. Maritime Administration (Marad), Department of Commerce in Washington and later was appointed to the

American Embassy in London, where he served from 1971-1975 as Marad Representative for the United Kingdom and Scandinavia. In 1975 he was appointed Marad Director, Great Lakes Region when he opened the Region Office in Cleveland, Ohio. The Department of Commerce awarded him a Silver Medal for outstanding work for the Maritime Administration.

Mr. Ryan was appointed President of Lake Carriers' Association from January 1, 1983 and Executive Director of American Iron Ore Association from January 1, 1987 until his retirement on January 15, 2003. In these capacities he represented all the U. S. Flag shipowners on the Great Lakes and most of the U.S. and Canadian iron ore producers.

During the years in Cleveland, he was appointed by the Governor of Ohio to serve as a Commissioner to the Great Lakes Commission. He was a member of the American Bureau of Shipping, and was Chair of the Board of Visitors of Great Lakes Maritime Academy. In the industry-wide efforts to preserve the U.S.-Flag Merchant Marine, Mr. Ryan served as an officer of the Great Lakes Maritime Task Force, and was Vice Chairman of the Maritime Cabotage Task Force. He served by appointment of the Secretary of Transportation on the USMMA Academic Advisory Board.

The U.S. Coast Guard awarded him the Distinguished Public Service Award and the Meritorious Public Service Award. Northwestern Michigan College appointed him a Fellow of the College; and in 2006 he was named Great Lakes Man of the Year at Sault Ste. Marie, MI. He is past Chairman of the Board of the USMMA American Maritime History Project when he served as editor of the published book *Braving the Wartime Seas*. He is an Emeritus Member of the Board of the Great Lakes Historical Society.

Personal Narrative on Background of Appointment as LCA President

After several years of employment as the Marad Great Lakes Region Director in Cleveland, I wanted to find a new challenging job. I was selected as a Senior Executive Service candidate and had applied for various Marad positions including Superintendent of the U.S. Merchant Marine Academy at Kings Point and for the position of Associate Administrator for Maritime Aids in Washington. I was selected for the latter position; but due to the change in administration, the Republicans were holding back on appointments of these senior positions in order to be sure that a person with the correct conservative bent would be appointed. I was disillusioned by the waiting and began to advise the shipowners in the Cleveland area who were members of LCA of my interest in returning to the private sector.

I had worked closely with the LCA leadership on the many projects of interest to Marad; and I knew Paul and Marie Trimble as collaborators on projects and as friends. Nevertheless, I did not seek the position of President of LCA since from the little I knew Paul Trimble wasn't ready to retire. I also thought the LCA presidency was a retirement position for a retired senior executive in government, probably from the Coast Guard since the last three Presidents were retired Coast Guard Admirals. Little did I know that this would be a retirement job for me, after serving 20 years!

What a surprise it was to me when after the morning meetings of the International Joint Conference in Alabama in 1982, I was asked to meet with Paul Trimble and some of the leadership of LCA. In the room was the top leadership of LCA: Bill Buhrmann, USS Great Lakes Fleet; Rennie Thompson, Oglebay Norton; Tom Burke, American Steamship; and, Bob McInnis, Pickands Mather. After some brief preliminary conversation, I was asked if I had an interest in relieving Paul Trimble the following January. I was honored, astonished and almost speechless; instinctively I said yes; let's explore that possibility. I called my wife Cornelia and she was supportive, I think in part since we would stay in the Cleveland area.

W.B. Buhrmann

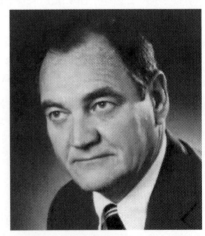
R. Thompson

R. McInnis					T. Burke

As fate would have it, after working out the details of the job offer, I notified the General Counsel of Marad so as to remove myself from any government decisions relating to the LCA member companies. A few weeks later, the Maritime Administrator, Admiral Howard Shear, USN-Retired, called me from his office late one Friday night while I was at home and told me I was selected for the Associate Administrator post; he wanted me to start ASAP in Washington. I explained to him that I was no longer available as I accepted the job as the future LCA President. Admiral Shear was a four star admiral and former Commander in Chief of allied forces in Southern Europe; he was a man who did not take rebuffs easily and he ranted on and called me a traitor to Marad. In time, he cooled down and sent me a congratulatory note and we worked together amicably during his tenure.

I joined the LCA as the President-elect on September 1, 1982 for four months learning all I could from staff, the files and the members. On January 1, 1983, I remained President-elect until the Annual Meeting, the normal time for elections. There was no contract of employment, no tenure to be expected. For the next 20 years I was annually re-elected President by the Board at the Annual Meeting. I recall that in the early years, I was concerned about retaining my job after the annual elections; there never was a performance review to know where I stood, such as we had in government. I believe the philosophy of the Board members was that the President should do the job the best way he could, keep the board informed of major policy changes and recommendations; and, if you don't hear to the contrary, proceed full speed ahead.

LCA Organization

Board of Trustees, Advisory Committee and Committee Structure

The Advisory Committee acted as the Executive Committee for the Board of Trustees and the President of LCA was the Chair of the Board and the Committee. There was a representative on the Advisory Committee only from each of the major member companies. Ryan believed that each of the 15 members should be represented on the Committee; and recommended that the unrepresented members be invited to nominate a person to represent them. The recommendation was accepted and in 1983 the following companies sent representatives: Litton Great Lakes Fleet, Amoco Oil, Cement Transit, and Erie Sand and Gravel. While these smaller members only operated a few lakers, some were large such as the Presque Isle (although some might argue that they were represented as the ship carried iron ore principally for U.S. Steel). The principle I supported was that every member be represented and participate in the deliberations.

Looking back at that decision, it was notable that there was a deep and continuing friendship between Sid Smith, Erie Sand, and Ralph Biggs, Litton. Both lived and worked in the Erie area. Ralph was a large tall man who operated a very big ship—a thousand footer, and Sid, a bit shorter and rather stout, operated some of the smaller ships. One of them drove the car from Erie and after the Committee meeting usually at the Union Club, they would meet with friends or clients, have dinner and a few drinks at Jim's Steakhouse on the Cuyahoga River and drive home to Erie. They were pleased to be among their peers, as they should have been.

Sidney E. Smith Jr.

Leadership of the Board, Advisory Committee and other Committees

The direction to LCA came from the most senior staff of the member companies. The Presidents or Chief Executive officers of the member companies served on the Advisory Committee; and, they and staff from their company, many of whom chaired the major committees, served on the Board of Trustees.

In the 20 years that Ryan served, he always had the opportunity to seek advice and direction from the leaders of the major companies: American Steamship Company, D. Ward Fuller, Ned A. Smith and Jerome (Jerry) Welsch; Pickands Mather and Interlake Steamship Company, Robert (Bob) McInnis, James R. Barker and Bob Dorn; Oglebay Norton Company, Rennie Thompson, Tom Green, Frank Castle, Stuart Theis and Mike Siragusa; Cleveland Cliffs Inc., Tom Moore; U.S. Steel (later USS Great Lakes Fleet), Bill Buhrmann, Neil Stalker and Adolph Ojard. Welcome advice and direction also came from the leadership of the smaller companies.

D. Ward Fuller

Ned A. Smith

Jerome (Jerry) Welsch

James R. Barker

Bob Dorn

Stuart Theis

Neil Stalker

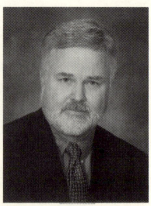
Adolph Ojard

The leadership of the Board fully recognized the vital importance of iron ore and the steel industry as the backbone of the LCA fleets; many of the ships were owned and operated by steel and iron ore companies. As that ownership changed over the years, more of the members were independents; however many of them had long term contracts of carriage or arrangements with those iron ore and steel companies. They knew never to 'bite the hand' that fed them. New leaders on the Board such as James R. Barker actively gave advice and direction that balanced the needs of all members.

Some of the major changes in membership included the loss of Cleveland-Cliffs when they sold their remaining vessel assets to Ford; and then Ford resigned when they sold their vessel assets to Interlake Steamship. In 1992 M. A. Hanna, another founding member of LCA, resigned and transferred operation of the George A. Stinson to Interlake. Litton Industry, operator of the Presque Isle since 1973, resigned when the ship was purchased in 1997 by USS Great Lakes Fleet. In 1998 Inland Steel resigned when they transferred operation and control of that fleet to Central Marine Logistics.

The technical leaders from these companies who were the backbone of the daily operations of the committees and LCA staff direction included: American Steamship Company—Tom Anderson, Gavin Sproul, Noel Bassett, and Kevin McMonagle; PM/Interlake Steamship—John Greenwood, Lou Mensen, Dewey Aston and Bob Dorn; Oglebay Norton—Ed Jacobsen, Dick Feldtz, and Dale Miller; USS Great Lakes Fleet—David VanBrunt, Fred Cummings, Ralph Bertz and Bill Satterness; Bethlehem Steel, J. H. (Duke) LeCompte. There were many others, too numerous to mention.

LCA operated on consensus of the membership; it was the President's job to submit a proposal that he thought had that consensus support. While there were votes for members of the Advisory Committee and the Board and on very few other matters as required by the by-laws, in the 20 years the votes were always unanimous; except for one time when a member of one of the smaller companies voted nay. Ryan called him up immediately and asked why; he said no one should always have a unanimous vote. Giving Ryan a lesson in humility, the member voted no!

LCA Staff, office in the Rockefeller Building, Cleveland, OH

The name Rockefeller Building was almost synonymous with LCA Headquarters for many in the lake shipping industry since the Rockefeller Building in Cleveland and the LCA were linked for almost 100 years. LCA moved into the Rockefeller Building when it opened for tenants in 1905. The LCA offices and other important lake shipping companies had offices there. When Ryan moved into the office in 1982, the Steinbrenner Company was there, and U.S. Steel had only recently vacated to move their marine operation to Duluth. LCA reduced staff during Ryan's early years; the decision was made to stay in the Rockefeller Building as long as the rent was acceptable. As LCA was one of the two longest tenants leasing space in the building, the owner wanted to accommodate LCA and an agreement was negotiated for a smaller space that met LCA needs. LCA moved into Suite 915 in 1983 and was still there when Ryan retired in 2003.

LCA Staff

Dave Buchanan was Vice President in 1982. He retired December 1984 and was relieved by Captain Gordon Hall, USCG (Ret.). Dave had been a long term employee of U. S. Steel Great Lakes Fleet whose offices were in the Rockefeller Building before the staff was moved to Duluth. Dave wanted to stay in the Cleveland area near his family, friends and church. Dave had served on and provided leadership for many LCA committees; he knew everyone in the business and was invaluable. He was a quiet and reliable man, took notes in shorthand and never revealed the secrets or confidences he held on many corporate and other issues including his three years with the FBI during World War II.

Dave Buchanan

Gordon Hall brought renewed energy and invaluable Coast Guard operational experience to the position. He had been Commanding Officer of the icebreaking cutter Mackinaw and head of Ninth District Operations. He managed the Fleet Engineers and the Navigation Committees and was the point man on the phone with the ad hoc ice operations committee at the opening and closing of the seasons. He assumed the Treasurer position when Bill Conroy had a stroke; Gordon retained that position when LCA decided not to have a full time Treasurer. Gordon was praised by the Audit Committee for his meticulous work and was well respected by those who worked with him on navigation and engineering matters.

Gordon Hall

Rick Harkins

When Gordon retired in 1994, he was relieved by Rick Harkins, a marine engineer from Interlake Steamship and a 1971 Kings Point graduate. Rick brought in a different perspective as he was a recent employee of member company Interlake Steamship, a licensed Marine Engineer and Rick had a Naval Architect degree from the University of Michigan. As a native Duluthian, he had shipped out on the lakers before he attended the U.S. Merchant Marine Academy. He more than adequately picked up on the Navigation end of the business. The staff joked about the correspondence to him titled *Captain* Harkins. He was particularly helpful in organizing systems to prevent the spread of zebra mussels and other non-indigenous species.

The Corporate Secretary in 1982 was Christine Kammer Zeber. She came to LCA with a West Coast port management background to take over from John Packard who retired. Paul Trimble met Chris at a Propeller Club Convention. She also managed LCA Public Relations and the LCA publications. Shortly after joining LCA, she married Captain Bud Zeber, an experienced Captain with Cleveland Cliffs. When she resigned, the duties of corporate secretary were transferred to William Conroy, (Bill assumed the duties of Jack N. Carlson who died on December 18, 1980); Bill was an experienced accountant who came with recommendations from Hanna Mining. Bill did a great job but unfortunately suffered a stroke that precluded his continued employment with LCA. At that time, the Corporate Secretary function was assigned to Carol Ann Lane and the Treasurer function to Gordon Hall.

The work of the LCA, the activities, the statistics, the very history of the LCA over the years has always been found in the LCA Blue Book, the Annual Report of the LCA. The task of preparing the Annual Report, Press Releases and all other statistics was the responsibility of the Corporate Secretary/Public Relations person. When Christine Zeber departed, LCA was fortunate to engage Glen Nekvasil, a young man who was with Pickands Mather and who was recommended by Bob McInnes, a PM senior executive. Glen took on the challenging job of Public Relations/Communications Director and later manager of a much reduced Job Referral Center.

Glen Nekvasil

The Secretary to the President of LCA was a key position. The lady who had the position with Admiral Trimble was uncertain about the change of leadership. Ryan had made it clear to the staff that LCA had to modernize by getting word processors and later computers to replace the mimeograph machine and the electric typewriters with the attendant carbon copies to be circulated and filed. She chose to retire and when Ryan asked her to stay and go to school for the new technology; he said to her you are only 56 years of age according to the personnel file. She announced that she was really 66 years old and eligible for social security! She was concerned about age discrimination when she applied for the job with LCA, so she just knocked 10 years off the resume. Ryan laughed and agreed that she had every right to seek and enjoy retirement.

Fortunately, Carol Ann Lane, an employee from Cleveland Cliffs marine department applied and was hired as Secretary. She was one of the most energetic and talented employees hired during Ryan's tenure; Carol Ann could tackle any job and did it well; particularly dealing with all levels of people who interacted with LCA. Carol took on many new assignments, first the managing of the Lake Carriers' Association Annual Conference with the Dominion Marine Association, a task that hitherto was managed by the Corporate Secretary/Public Relations person. Carol later became the Corporate Secretary and then the Treasurer while still performing the clerical end of being secretary to the President. Of course, by that time the entire staff had word processor/computers at each desk to reduce the demand for secretarial assistance.

Carol Ann Lane at LCA booth

The position of General Counsel of the Association was in a state of flux in 1982. Scott Elder had served for many years. He was partner in a local maritime law firm but he maintained his primary office at LCA. The Board of Trustees engaged Thomas O. Murphy, of the firm of Thomson, Hine and Flory, to become General Counsel at the time Ryan became President. Tom maintained his office at his firm and was always available for consultation and to attend any meeting of the Advisory Committee or the Board. At those meetings it was a primary concern to work together to assure that no member while on LCA business would ever violate the Anti-Trust laws. Tom was always available for good advice based upon a lifetime of experience in marine law. He was Counsel for Oglebay Norton at the time of the sinking of the Edmund Fitzgerald; he settled all the claims of the families of the lost crew members without the need for any to go to court.

Tom Murphy   Hal Henderson

In 1991, Tom Murphy began retirement planning; he recommended to the Board another member of his firm, Harold Henderson, to become General Counsel. Hal was appointed Associate Counsel and at the 1992 Board meeting Hal was elected as General Counsel.

The Manager of the Sailors Job Referral Center (JRC) who managed the Supervisors in the centers in various ports and conducted training had his office in the LCA offices in the Rockefeller Building. For many years Russ Plumb directed the Supervisors and he organized the training programs for licensed and unlicensed personnel. Russ retired shortly before Ryan came on board and Paul Trimble hired Captain James A. Wilson, USCG, (Ret.) as Director of Training starting August 1, 1980. Jim resigned shortly after Ryan came on board as LCA had to reduce the cost of the JRC during the early 1980s recession; Wilson told Ryan that he didn't want others to be laid off as he had the security of a USCG pension. Ryan assumed the duties of manager of that function until the Advisory Committee authorized the hiring of Mary Paul, an experienced marine manager from Gulf Oil Company in Houston, TX, for the management of those offices and to organize all of the LCA training and the Vessel Personnel Committee. When Mary left LCA in 1986, management of JRC fell on the shoulders of Glen Nekvasil. John T. Saunders managed the JRC in Duluth and assisted in officer training until his death in 1986. Jack Rose managed the Cleveland JRC and William Kishel managed the Toledo center. LCA consolidated all referrals in Cleveland under William Kishel who left LCA in 1992 when the last of the centers were closed.

Mary Paul

Russ Plumb

LCA had a staff of two or three other clerical employees including Daisy Fazekas and Donna Abbott to handle filing, typing, mimeographing, and later photo copying, and receptionist duties. With the advent of individual telephones for each person, answering machines, elimination of large file systems of Great Lakes seamen, transition to photocopy from mimeograph, the personal computer, e-mail and the need to reduce expenditures, gradually the clerical staff was reduced to one other person, who periodically was replaced when she departed. Carol Lane was often alone to carry the administrative load. Staff learned to type; filing was drastically reduced and when help was needed, the call went out to Carol to help. For the majority of the Ryan years LCA relied upon a small cadre of employees to manage the functions of the Association. Of the original secretarial staff, Daisy Fazekas, receptionist, was the last to retire. LCA often had the assistance of Eileen Hout Naughton to work with Carol. They all did a great job!

Carol Ann Lane at IJC

Major changes in the operation of the LCA in the period 1983-2002

- The loss of member companies who were primarily in the business of iron ore mining, steel production, cement manufacture or national fuel oil production; they were replaced by independent ship owners. The impact of this was the loss of the manufacturing and mining base that supported the Cabotage and the Buy American laws. In fact, some of the raw material companies were owned by foreign corporations. Only the Jones Act prevented foreign firms from owning/operating domestic trade ships.
- The need for the LCA President to become the lobbyist for the U.S. Flag ship owners without the consistent staff support and backing of the primary customers of our members. LCA developed a greater reliance on Washington legal/lobbying assistance rather than from the LCA general counsel.
- The formation of coalitions from within other elements of the U.S. flag maritime industry to further LCA objectives. Greater cooperation with the leaders of the maritime unions was essential to achieve common objectives.
- Operated with a smaller staff; the elimination of the once powerful Legislative Committee, establishment of a Captains Committee;

elimination of the Job Referral Centers; termination of the LCA being repository for members crew illness and injury records.

Recap of LCA Tonnage and Carrying Capacity 1983-2002

In 1983 there were 15 LCA members with 111 vessels enrolled in the Association; they had a gross registered tonnage (GRT) of 1,458,227 tons. At that time LCA did not maintain a record of tonnage carried by American carriers alone. Tonnage of the principal commodities of iron ore, coal, stone, cement potash and grain carried by U.S. and Canadian vessels in 1983 was 147 million net tons. In 1985, the first year of record keeping of tonnage in U.S. flag vessels, the tonnage carried was 96.1 million net tons while the combined U.S. and Canadian carriage was 145 million tons.

In 1986 it was clearly recognized that the carriage of grain by LCA members had decreased over the decades since the Seaway opened in 1959. The 1986 annual report discontinued significant analysis of the grain trade. The GRT enrolled in LCA dropped rapidly as the more efficient thousand footers came on line and the older less efficient boats were scrapped. In 1980 the average carrying capacity for the LCA ships was 23,000 tons; by 1990 it was 31,500 tons and the ships had a faster turnaround time since well over 90% of the LCA vessels were self-unloaders. By 1991 the GRT was less than one million tons in 62 vessels and the U.S. fleet carried 104 million tons. The highest tonnage carried by LCA in the Ryan tenure period was 125 million tons in 1997, carried by 11 members who enrolled 58 ships and eight other smaller vessels of non-members. By 2002 another recession began to take its toll on Great Lakes industries. In 2002, LCA had 12 members with 58 vessels enrolled and the U.S. fleet carried 101.5 million tons.

Lobbying Washington

When Ryan became LCA President, most of the active lobbying in Washington and in state capitols was carried out by LCA members who were leaders in the iron ore mining or steel industries and employers of many workers in Great Lakes states. These members provided staff to serve on the LCA Legislative and Government Affairs Committee. As these companies either sold their vessels to independent ship owners or concentrated their lobbying efforts on the core business—steel or iron ore—the shipowners needs for federal assistance or opposition to unacceptable proposed legislation had to be communicated separately and/or with different partners of common interest. By 1991 the Legislative Committee ceased to function as George Ryan undertook the lobbying actions approved by the Advisory Committee. His efforts would not be sufficient; LCA needed to find other allies to effectively lobby Congress.

Typically, one might look toward the well-organized powerful port interests for common support; but LCA quickly learned that internationalism and free trade dominated their thinking. The port interests were flag blind, and for the most part were opposed to the U.S. Cabotage laws and the many Buy American laws, particularly relating to steel. Port leadership objected to the efforts of LCA with regards to Cabotage laws and the steel companies trying to stop the dumping of imported steel.

The groups that shared common interests with LCA were the powerful maritime labor organizations and the other American maritime associations of non-Lakes steamship companies who each had significant and effective lobbying offices in Washington. They wanted to keep American maritime jobs; and that meant they also supported the basic industries that required maritime transportation--steel and iron ore mining. Most of the successful lobbying that happened in the last ten years of Ryan's LCA leadership came about through working closely with maritime labor leaders and other maritime associations. The unions were not ideologically wedded to either political party; they contributed their members' money to candidates and incumbents who supported labor views. Typically the party in power might receive 60% of the contributions; but labor recognized that the tide always turned and they maintained friends on both sides of the aisle. In that respect, many industry lobbyists did the same. Ryan was always grateful for the friendship and assistance given to him by comrades in Washington including: Charles Crangle, Lobbyist Extraordinaire for AMO; Jim Henry, Chairman, Transportation Institute; Tom Allegretti, American Waterways Operators; Mark Ruge, Preston Gates; and so many others. Within the Lakes, the union leadership with whom he worked very closely were Mel

Pelfrey, Tim Mohler and Dan Smith of the AMO; Byron Kelley, SIU; and the ILA leadership Patrick Sullivan, Buffalo and John Baker, Cleveland.

MCTF Award to Congressman Steve LaTourette

Economic Conditions Impacting Traffic

In any twenty year period there are many factors that impact any particular sector of the economy. For Great Lakes shipping two predominate, one negative--Dumped foreign made steel caused the dismantling of over 40 million tons of American steelmaking capacity; and one positive--the environmental benefit of using low sulfur western coal brought about a major new movement of cargo on the Great Lakes, almost exclusively on LCA vessels.

Major Accomplishments and Disappointments in the 1983-2002 Period

Accomplishments

- Protecting the Jones Act; maintenance of the Cabotage laws against assaults from private interests inside and outside the USA; from other governments through treaties; and from our own government

officials. Combined efforts effectively removed Cabotage from the U.S./Canada FTA Agreement and the North American Free Trade Area Agreement.
- Formed and worked with effective coalitions such as the Great Lakes Maritime Task Force (GLMTF) and the Maritime Cabotage Task Force (MCTF) to accomplish our goals.
- Fighting off various user charges for services from various federal agencies; most importantly icebreaking charges and the negotiation of a value based, rather than tonnage based, harbor service fee paid by the owner of the cargo not the carrier.
- Establishing a longer navigation season by negotiating a fixed open and close dates for the Locks at the Soo.
- Maintaining the 1944 Mackinaw in service and getting appropriations for a new Mackinaw and getting assurance of Coast Guard icebreaking services in the main channels as long as the locks were open.
- Obtained a six year drydocking and tail shaft interval for many Great Lakes vessels.
- Worked successfully with the federal and state agencies to permit cargo residue washdown under clearly defined conditions.
- Succeeded in avoiding state laws restricting laker ballast exchange by working with the environmental groups and state officials to test filtration technology.
- Developed a vessel security plans for all U.S. and Canadian ships on the Great Lakes very shortly after the terrorist attacks on September 11, 2001.
- Keeping the membership support for LCA as the vital lake shipping trade association, particularly those companies that had representation in Washington through other trade associations. There were accountants (bean-counters) who wanted to cut costs of "non-producing expenses" that in their minds included trade associations. Staff had to lay out the workload LCA had on the plate that impacted member's bottom line and show that none of that work was being done by other organizations and that it could not be done by existing company staff.

Major Disappointments

- Despite 20 years of effort Congress did not provide the necessary appropriations to build a new Poe size lock at the Soo; fortunately there were appropriations to keep the project alive and the ground breaking took place during Jim Weakley's term.

Soo Locks Ground Breaking Ceremony
U.S. Army Corps of Engineers, Detroit District • Sault Ste. Marie, Michigan

- LCA and members tried their best to limit the spread of the non-indigenous fish species that entered the lakes on salt water vessels but we were not successful in getting public authorities to recognize that stopping the introductions had to begin with serious constraints on the ballast operations of the salt water vessels.

LCA, George Ryan and the Maritime Unions

The LCA had a very long history of opposition to Labor Unions. The Cleveland Shipowners Association (CSA) was founded in 1880 in large part to thwart the influence of labor unions. When the Buffalo LCA merged with the CSA in 1892, the avowed purpose was to retain open shop employment and to actively discourage employees from joining organized labor. While for a brief period, from 1901-1908, some of the LCA members signed some labor contracts with unlicensed unions and thus agreed to a closed shop, the contracts were rarely fully honored by the shipowner. By 1908, all the LCA members refused to renew any contracts with labor and demanded an open shop. For all the years between 1883 and the 1940s the LCA set the wages for all personnel, including officers. While there were attempts by labor organizations, such as the Marine Engineers Beneficial Association (MEBA) and the Masters, Mates and Pilots Union (MMP) to unionize ship's crews, deck officers were not generally unionized until the 1940s. As late as 1990, one member company still resisted hiring union deck officers.

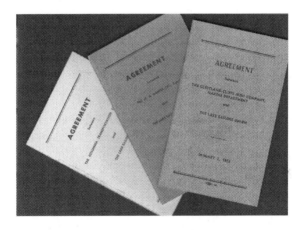

UNION-BUSTING
M. A. HANNA STYLE

Ten Steps to Bust a
Marine Officers Union

*(HOW HANNA IS TRYING TO BREAK THE
MARINE ENGINEERS BENEFICIAL ASSOCIATION)*

For Further Detailed Instructions, see the following:

→

George Ryan came to LCA with government and industry experience with the Maritime Administration and the Grace Line, an east coast company in the Caribbean and South America passengers and freight trade. He served as a deck officer on the Grace Line ships and ultimately was appointed as captain until he came ashore in management of the fleet. In the LCA presidency interviews there were no questions dealing with Ryan's political affiliation or his union connections. Ryan was and is a registered Democrat who was called upon to represent big business toward the government in either Democrat or Republican administrations. While sailing with the Grace Line he was a member of the Masters, Mates and Pilots Union, Local 88 in New York City, paid his dues regularly and he walked the picket line put up in front of the Grace Line piers in Manhattan when called upon during a strike call period. Ryan believed in the need for workers, including officers, to have union representation. In those days the maritime industry management was incapable of gratuitously improving wages, hours, benefits or vacations without being forced into change by strong economic pressures. There were too many years of management considering seamen as not needing as much income as shore side workers since they lived 24/7 on a ship where food and lodging was provided free; and that as long as the seamen were captive to the ship, they might as well work as many hours as they could.

Ryan was never asked to enunciate any of these views during his consideration for the appointment as President. Of course, since the Board of Trustees met annually to elect officers, including the President, and since there never was any employment contract or golden parachute provision for the President, his actions were always open to scrutiny and employment action.

During Ryan's 5 years as Marad Great Lakes Region Director in Cleveland, he had many opportunities to meet with marine industry union officials in his official dealing on training, Great Lakes Maritime Academy (GLMA), winter navigation, establishment of a marine industry firefighting school, and conferences to assist the Great Lakes marine industry. There had been sufficient time for members of LCA to witness his dealing with all maritime and government factions including labor union officials. Apparently there was no need to question his judgment with respect to fair minded dealing with any group impacting LCA, and in particular with the labor unions.

There is another important set of factors to acknowledge. Times were changing rapidly. Practically all the member companies had labor agreements with unions representing licensed and unlicensed personnel. Maritime training, with the exception of new officer training at GLMA, had almost completely been turned over to labor managed schools with management funding and trustees. Labor unions had the funding from members that was needed to lobby in Washington for matters of benefit to the marine industry. Many labor leaders in Washington were powerful lobbyists for maritime industry government assistance and they supported leaders in either political party who could help them reach their goals. It was essential for shipowners to work closely with maritime labor in order to get anything positive done in Washington.

The LCA Welfare Plan was essentially moribund and it eventually was abolished after the sinking of the Edmund Fitzgerald. The only vestiges of the past Welfare Plan activities were the publishing of the Bulletin, an industry wide magazine primarily for men on the ships dealing with safety, LCA lobbying efforts and general marine news; the organization of training programs for unlicensed personnel in the deck and engine departments, primarily for fleets contracted with USW 5000, and some officer development not yet taken over by the MMP and the MEBA; and Assembly Rooms, known later as the Sailors' Job Referral Centers (JRC) used by members contracted to USW 5000. The JRC was the last element of the LCA hiring halls.

Yes, times had changed and that fact was not yet fully recognized during the Trimble period when the LCA leadership decided to not become a member of the Great Lakes Task Force, a lobby group led by Mel Pelfrey, VP-MEBA, with members from most of the other unions and a few port authorities. After Pelfrey's death, that organization atrophied and George Ryan was able to initiate a new Great Lakes Maritime Task Force (GLMTF) composed of many LCA members, all the Great Lakes unions and a few major shipbuilders. There were no port authority members since a condition of membership was to be a strong supporter of the U.S. Cabotage laws; primarily support for the Jones Act. The LCA Trustees were advised of this development of a unified lobby group and they approved wholeheartedly. Times had changed and perhaps having a President who once held a union book membership and who walked the picket line was then of value.

American Iron Ore Association

The American Iron Ore Association, located in Cleveland, had several members who were also LCA members. They included Cleveland-Cliff, Hanna Mining, Oglebay Norton and U.S. Steel. In 1986 when AIOA Director Larry Turnock retired, Ryan suggested to the LCA Board that he could reduce the cost of operation of the two Associations if Carol Ann Lane and Ryan would take on the additional duties of managing AIOA. The AIOA and LCA Boards approved. Two AIOA staff members including Joy Earlywine, Statistician, co-located within LCA offices. The arrangement worked out very well for a number of years until 2002 when the AIOA Board decided to reduce the operation further and moved the remaining statistical functions to Duluth. In addition to cost savings, it was invaluable for LCA to have AIOA positions shaped by LCA and often enunciated to Washington leadership as a joint position.

Coalition Building--Great Lakes Maritime Task Force

Aside from the shipboard maritime unions, there were other organizations who shared the vision and objectives of the Lake Carriers' Association. They included the ship building and ship repair industry and to some extent the International Longshoremen Association (ILA). The latter group is and always has been very pro-American; and despite the fact that their jobs were primarily as a result of international trade, they supported other American workers on the ships and in the shipyards.

Before Ryan came to the LCA in 1982, there was an organization of Great Lakes maritime unions that lobbied Washington. It was the Great Lakes Task Force (GLTF) and it was organized primarily by the MEBA District 2, American Maritime Officers (AMO) Vice-President Mel Pelfrey. They wanted to include management among their membership but because of labor relations issues, invitations to LCA and to its members were declined. For a short period of time American Steamship Company, under the leadership of D. Ward Fuller, a progressive executive from GATX, cooperated with the unions and attended their meetings. When Mel Pelfrey died, the organization became moribund.

When Ryan was in Washington in 1992, riding the Metro going between meetings on the Hill and in the Departments, he felt like a lone wolf howling alone in the wilderness. He remembered what Congressman Phil Ruppe, MI, said to him on that trip "... everyone who sees me says they represent the Great Lakes maritime interests and when that person leaves, another person comes in and says he represents the maritime interests; can't you guys get together?" Something needed to be done soon if the maritime interests were to get the combined message across in Washington. Ryan began to identify the groups that supported key LCA objectives: protection of the Cabotage Laws; improved navigation systems; improved Coast Guard ice-breaking services; a longer navigation season; a new lock at the Soo; improved weather forecasting and more. It was the very maritime unions that were part of the old GLTF, the ILA and the shipyards.

When Ryan returned to Cleveland, he asked for advice from the larger members of LCA and asked if they would become part of a larger organization that included the unions, shipyards and others who supported LCA. The time was right. Old animosities had dampened; the need for solidarity was recognized. Invitations were sent out to all those groups to meet and to form a consolidated group that could face Washington with a united front.

Tim Mohler, MEBA-AMO, Byron Kelley, SIU, and Pat Sullivan, ILA, were very supportive of the idea. When they met in Toledo in November 1992, they agreed that no one interest group would be dominant. Four categories of membership in the Great Lakes Maritime Task Force (GLMTF) were set up: Ship Owners, Shipboard Labor Unions, Ship Builders, and Dockside Labor Unions. In short order, 30 Great Lakes area companies, Associations, unions and councils became members with the common objective to promote a strong U.S. Flag merchant marine on the Lakes. Annually each group would assume the President position and the others would be 1st, 2nd, and 3rd Vice Presidents. LCA offered to perform the secretariat function through Glen Nekvasil. From that day forward LCA communicated their common agenda to members of congress and achieved a high level of success.

LCA Officials Present Award to Senator Mike DeWine

The interest group that could not be included in GLMTF was the Great Lakes port leadership because they could not support the Cabotage laws. Some Port Directors, either in praise or disparagement, called Ryan 'Jones Act George' because of the single minded litmus test that bound LCA with its principal collaborators.

Nevertheless, LCA worked with port leaders such as Davis Helberg, Duluth; Jim Hartung, Toledo; Noel Painchaud, Cleveland; American Great Lakes Port director Steve Fisher, and others collaboratively on issues of joint interest such as improved icebreaking services, a longer navigation system and a new lock at the Soo. Later, we found another issue arose that LCA tried to collaborate on but eventually had to deal with separately. That was the issue of nuisance non-indigenous species—the zebra and quagga muscle, the Ruffe and other species that came into the lakes in the ballast tanks of vessels in the overseas trades. Once those species were in the Lakes, all ships in the Great Lakes trade transported the species around through necessary and essential ballast water exchange. LCA had to part ways with the port industry on the remedy since the port industry wanted the same remedy for all ships—domestic and international. In essence, LCA maintained that the foreign ships brought them into the lakes and they must find a technology to stop the introductions. LCA strongly believed that the domestic trade should not be penalized as a result of the actions of the foreign flag ships in the international trade.

LCA Committees

Vessel Security Committee

This was an emergency committee Chaired by Bob Dorn, Interlake Steamship Company, that quickly formed following the 9/11 attack on America.
The tragic attack on the United States by terrorists on September 11, 2001 caused LCA and its members, working jointly with the Canadian Shipowners Association, to develop a vessel security plan. The plan was directed at the protection of their ships, the terminals in which they traded, the bridge infrastructure under which they navigated and the locks they passed through. Within days the plan was in place, operational and was praised by the Coast Guard and other federal agencies. LCA had gone through national security times before in the two world wars and other conflicts. It was not hard to call up the old proven plans, bring them up to date and circulate them to all U.S. and Canadian shipowners for their input and approval within a very short period of time before giving the plan to the U.S. Coast Guard.

Bob Dorn, Ian Sharp, Mark Barker Interlake Steamship Company

Public Relations and Publications

While in the past this work was part of a committee effort, gradually it all fell upon LCA staff. Glen Nekvasil did an outstanding job in media and public relations, in particular the publications, press releases and other visual media. One of the major efforts was to publish the Annual Report that was recognized by industry, government and academia as the 'Bible' of Great Lakes shipping in the domestic trade. As Alexander T. Wood, LCA President, in his Annual Report of 1939, stated concerning the Annual Reports: "Persons employed in Great Lakes Commerce and a widespread public have benefited by the data. I believe these annual reports have been and will continue to be a careful historic treatment of this vital industry."

The Annual Report stated LCA accomplishments, membership, committee reports, the positions held by LCA on all important issues and the objectives for the year ahead. Improvements to the Annual Report were made gradually over the years. LCA strove to continue to publish the familiar blue cover perfect with a binding showing the year on the spine, only resorting to drastically reduce the number of pages for the 1982 Report because of the recession when all costs were cut. That brought a bit of a howl from some members since the bookcases in various offices appeared to not have the 1982 report. It didn't have sufficient pages to print a perfect binding and thus there was no title on the spine. Also, Nekvasil began to provide more useful information such as including vessel rosters in 1983; a color map showing lake ports and the commodities moved through those ports in 1986; and in 1986, in recognition of the decline of the grain trade, he reduced the detailed reporting of the grain trade, concentrating statistics on the big three cargos -- iron ore, coal and stone. In 1989 LCA turned to printing in the 8 1/2" x 11" format since we could do layout in house using computer software and easily pull position papers on any subject from the report. Later all of this data, statistics, and positions were also carried on the LCA web site.

Lake Carriers' Association History 1880-2015 | 423

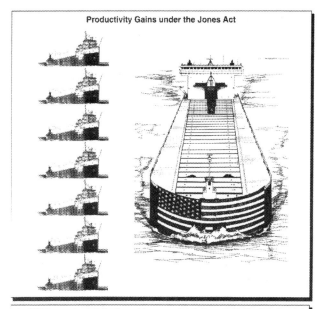

Productivity Gains under the Jones Act

In 1920, the year in which the Jones Act was enacted, the largest U.S.-Flag "laker" carried 462,498 tons of cargo during the season. In 1996, the longest laker hauled 3,244,780 tons. With a level playing field provided by our nation's Cabotage laws, American carriers and investors have continually modernized the U.S.-Flag Lakes fleet to the point where today the largest vessels are equal to the hauling power of seven 1920-vintage ships.

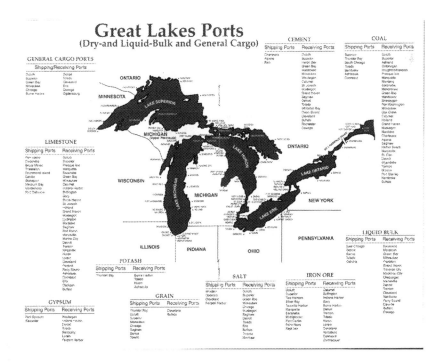

Great Lakes Ports
(Dry-and Liquid-Bulk and General Cargo)

The LCA Bulletin was first published in 1912; and, the last issue was Vol.73, No. 3 July 1986. In the beginning the Bulletin was for members only, advising shore and shipboard managers of changes in regulations, navigation aids, safety programs and other vital information. Gradually the distribution was wider and was sent to many persons on the ships and many others in industry ashore, even to libraries and government officials. At the end of its day, the purpose was to advise this broader audience of changes in Association and member management, major issues impacting the Great Lakes industry such as user charges, water levels, dumped imported steel, the need for new port, channel and lock infrastructure and Coast Guard assistance. As many member companies and some of the unions covered these issues in their newsletters and newspapers and, since we were always under pressure to reduce expenses, we decided to discontinue publication of the Bulletin after nearly 75 years of service.

The Advisor was a periodic publication, generally monthly, that kept all the members, particularly the committee members, up to date on what the Association was doing. Press Releases were published and sent to the media and to members on major issues and reports on monthly tonnage movements. By 1995 LCA had its own web site that contained the press releases, statistics and other vital information for members and the public.

Other publications such as the LCA List of Members and Vessels Enrolled also were recognized as redundant since the data was in *Greenwood's Guide*, in government publications and later in the LCA Annual Report and website. Some forms and publications were just no longer needed, such as vessel crew and officer passes, crew list blank forms and envelopes to send to the Coast Guard, the *Declaration of Inspection Before Fuel Bunkering* form, as well as the Separate Courses, Port Information and Whistle Signals booklet. Yes, every company and every ship had a distinctive Morse code sound signal and even one for the class of ship. While at anchor or waiting in the outer harbor or anchorage, the shore staff and other vessels would know what ship was out there. Radiophone changed the need for whistle signal identification.

LCA staff produced many other publications and media to promote Great Lakes shipping and videos for crew training and for the public and the government to visually understand industry issues. This included separate brochures on the Benefits of Great Lakes Shipping in Ohio and Michigan, graphics on the numbers of railroad cars that it takes to load a laker, comparisons of tons of cargo carried per extra inch of draft as well as large posters showing Great Lakes ports served and commodities carried. All of these products were designed to influence legislators and the public about the importance of Great Lakes shipping.

International Joint Conference

The Dominion Marine Association, later the Canadian Shipowners Association, and the Lake Carriers' Association had been holding an International Joint Conference (IJC) in February for many years; during which government officials, academics, economists and technical experts would meet with representatives of American and Canadian shipowners staff over a several day conference that included business meetings, banquets, golf, tennis and other convivial relations. The only Great Lakes maritime interest group leadership not invited was the union leaders. Many of the attendees would have their spouses and in some cases their children in attendance. Each association would alternately host the conference; in the early years the location was in the host country. However for the most part, as years went on, there was a desire to enjoy warmer climates in the southern part of the USA in the winter, particularly in Alabama and Florida. In poor economic times, the conference was cut back to reduce expenses and the meetings were of shorter duration in Toronto, Ottawa or Washington.

IJC, Admiral James Gracey at Podium, John Greenwood at table

After Fred White, Oglebay Norton, chaired the IJC for many years, the responsibilities were transferred to John Greenwood, Interlake Steamship. Several other companies served on the committee and the chairmanship was rotated among them for two year cycles.

Maintaining a lively and continuous cooperation between the shipowners on the U.S. and Canadian side of the Lakes was extremely important for safety of navigation and joint actions toward the respective governments. Fortunately or unfortunately, there was little competition for cargo between the Americans and Canadians. Each country had cabotage laws reserving the carriage of cargo between ports to the ships registered, crewed and owned by each respective country. The Canadians generally offered lower freight rates so the Canadians had a cost advantage on the cargo going between the two nations. This meant that there was little concern for getting shipowners together at conferences whereat they might collude over freight rates; the Canadians had the edge, except when American thousand footers could deliver.

Fred White   John Greenwood

While Ryan was LCA President, Chris Zeber, Corporate Secretary, Glen Nekvasil and, later for many years, Carol Ann Lane, and he tried very hard to have very professional conference sessions with high ranking executive and legislative official present to address the joint conference.

While they succeeded in that endeavor and always had very high attendance at the conference that started at 8 AM, it was recognized that many of the participants had their eye on the warm weather opportunity to have a golf tee off at 1 pm or a tennis match! Participants learned a lot and played hard in their respective athletic activities. For those who didn't play golf or tennis LCA arranged entertaining outdoor games they called 'Mini-Olympics' that brought many together.

Ryan was not then and never has been a golfer; so in the spare time, his wife Cornelia and he would go bird watching, do walking trails and photography in the afternoons. When in the right location, they organized canoe rentals through the mangrove swamps, in the company of large alligators and some wonderful birding. These conferences were invaluable in getting to know the many government officials in Washington or Ottawa with whom industry had to interact during the rest of the year. Good solid friendships and mutual understandings developed.

LCA General Counsels

The General Counsels over the years were essential leaders in the Association. They not only provided advice on the impact of changing state and federal laws regarding trade association organization, in particular the Anti-Trust laws, they guided the Association through reorganizations to assure compliance with the laws. They attended all major meetings with the senior leadership of the Association, providing invaluable advice on the substance of discussions including those relating to lobbying for improvements to navigation and personnel safety onboard Great Lakes vessels and in port. In the early years, the General Counsels engaged directly in lobbying activity in Washington and the state capitols. From the very beginning of the Association in the 1880s, the LCA leadership was asked to engage and fund permanent lobbying organizations in Washington, but did not do so. The Board, at times, did approve engagement of outside counsel to lobby on behalf of LCA on specific projects but did not engage a firm to represent the LCA on all issues before the U.S. Congress. Over time, the LCA President or Vice President began to spend more time directly lobbying Congress for necessary navigation and safety legislation instead of the LCA General Counsel.

Gradually, as the demands upon the LCA President grew, the Board recognized the complexity of what it took to convince members of Congress to support necessary authorizations or the appropriations needed for improved Great Lakes vessel productivity or safety. Washington D.C. law firms that specialized in the areas of our interest were engaged directly or through coalitions in which LCA was a leading member. The Law firm of Preston Gates Ellis & Rouvelas Meeds was the principal firm LCA engaged, being assisted by many attorneys but principally by Mark Ruge who knew Capitol Hill intimately. This relationship continues as this book is written and the firm is known today as K & L Gates LLP. During my tenure, I can attest to the professionalism and notable success of the work carried out by Mark Ruge who I consider a trusted friend.

Mark Ruge

The LCA General Counsel continues to carry out all the legal duties needed by the Association with the exception of Lobbying. General Counsel and outside Counsel in Washington continue to immeasurably enhance the work of the Association.

Lake Carriers' Association History 1880-2015

Harvey D. Goulder,
1885-1925

Newton D. Baker
1925-1937

Gilbert R. Johnson,
1938-1968

Scott H. Elder,
1968-1982

Thomas O. Murphy,
1982-1992

Harold W. Henderson,
1992-Present

Legislative Committee

In 1982, the Legislative Committee was one of the most important LCA committees; it included members who knew the politics of the Washington and of state governments; they knew personally many key officials. The leadership came from the members who owned iron ore mines and/or operated steel mills. These individuals represented their company at high level government meetings in Washington and state capitals and served on other trade association legislative committees within the American Iron Ore Association, the American Iron and Steel Institute and others. These members testified in Washington on behalf of LCA as needed. As the membership of LCA changed, with the loss of Cleveland Cliffs Iron Company, Pickands Mather and M. A. Hanna, the legislative committee relied upon capable members who spoke for their company but who themselves did not have the hands-on legislative experience of those who served in the past. Gradually, the President of LCA made the trips to Washington, Lansing, and Columbus to represent LCA. By 1990, the work of the Legislative Committee ended as the President contacted the Advisory Committee for direction.

Chaired by: Tom Manthey, Pickands Mather; Mike Scheidt, American Steamship through 1990

Taxes and Fees

Cost recovery for government services by many administrations over the years had to be opposed since these taxes raised the costs of maritime operations. Lower costs were essential to the farmers, the mining and steel interests, the employees and, of course, LCA members. The arguments used against all new taxes and fees were;

1. an economic analysis must be performed by the government to determine the impact upon the industries LCA served;
2. consideration must be given to the principle that the maritime industry must be maintained since it is an arm of national defense;
3. fees, if imposed, must be federal not by states or local authority because of the regional and national scope of marine transportation;

4. if users of the services are to be charged they must have a significant say on what services are needed and how they are provided (User Pay-User Say);
5. if fees were to be charged on the marine mode for federal services, they must also be imposed on competing transportation services, particularly the railroads.

Harbor Maintenance Tax

The Harbor Maintenance Tax (HMT) challenge to Great Lakes shipping was on the agenda for LCA when Ryan became President. It was brought about by the Indiana Port Commission in 1970 through a regulation to collect a Harbor Service Charge from all vessels entering/leaving Burns Harbor, a federal harbor. While the major company to be impacted would have been Bethlehem Steel, clearly the success of this port authority fund raiser would not have been lost on the rest of the port industry, in the Lakes and elsewhere. LCA joined the case in an *Amicus* status. Lower courts supported the imposition of the fee. Finally in 1987, after 17 years of litigation, two higher courts rejected the imposition of the charge and the Indiana Port Commission announced it would not appeal to the Supreme Court.

The Reagan Administration, while supportive of the maritime industry in principle, had a policy of seeking user fees from every sector, including maritime. In the Reagan Administration's initial budgets, they asked Congress to legislate port use fees, a Harbor Maintenance Tax, to pay for the cost of maintenance dredging of channels and ports nationwide; as well as to require a local cost share of the cost for new navigation projects. The maritime industry had no friend in the Office of Management and Budget; director David Stockman was quoted as saying the maritime interests maritime interests were "…one of the seven sobbing sisters of subsidy."

Nevertheless, the Great Lakes port industry saw this as a potential opportunity to eliminate St. Lawrence Seaway tolls and worked with the administration to eliminate the tolls; they argued that if the tolls were eliminated, the port industry could support a HMT that would be based upon tonnage rather than value of cargo. Initially, LCA recommended use of Customs duties to pay for port maintenance dredging. The Customs revenues option was decidedly opposed by the Administration since the government sought increased revenue not diversion of existing revenue. LCA and the dry bulk shippers they served leaned toward a cargo value based HMT, should a tax be imposed. LCA also privately did not favor the reduction in Seaway tolls since that action would reduce the costs of imported steel and iron ore; publicly LCA strongly opposed the concept that the carrier would pay the fee instead of the shipper. These were delicate issues since several LCA members were shippers and carriers and some of those members had iron ore reserves in Canada that entered the Lakes via the Seaway. For years, LCA worked with other maritime associations and the American Iron and Steel Institute (AISI) to shape legislation LCA could support.

In 1986, LCA was able to support a HMT to be paid by the shipper not the carrier; and, that the fee would be based on the value of the cargo. Effective April 1, 1987, the charge of .04% of the value would be paid by the shipper. By accepting this formula for the tax, the low cost raw materials moved in large volumes on the Lakes were saved an enormous amount of money; for example the value tax per ton of iron ore would be $0.018 and the actual tax per ton would have been about $0.60! An additional nuance for the carrier was that if the carrier had to pay it, the added cost would have to be included in the overall negotiation of the freight rate, an uncontrollable cost that the carrier would be absorbing along with controllable costs and some reserve for profit and capital charges; in essence the shipper could be getting a free ride. Further, LCA wanted the fees to go into a national Harbor Maintenance Trust Fund so as there would not be a clear connection between the small amounts of money collected on the Lakes compared to the high cost of maintenance of the many lake ports and connecting channels.

Proposals for a new and enlarged Harbor Services User Fee (HSUF) were presented by the Administration in 1989. How fortunate LCA was in fighting for the value tax, since in 1990 there was a budget deficit that called for increased tax income; and, without any meaningful Congressional hearings, the tax was tripled to 0.125% of value. Unfortunately for the federal treasury, the Supreme Court struck down the HMT as it applied to exports.

Coast Guard Fees--Another job for a Coalition

The Reagan Administration had a policy of seeking user fees from users of other government provided services. In 1987 the Administration called for nationwide Coast Guard User Charges of $355 million in FY 88 and $474 million annually thereafter. These charges, directly imposed upon ship owners, could not be easily passed on to the owners of the cargo; it would have hurt the U.S. maritime industry nationwide. Congress listened to the marine industry and rejected these taxes in the budget. Unfortunately, the budgeters looked at other elements of the Coast Guard service provided, such as icebreaking, and attempted to reduce the availability of these services.

LCA challenged all those fee proposals; but finally in 1990 the Coast Guard was ordered by Congress to collect some fees. The Coast Guard decided to collect fees from the shipowners for vessel inspections and from the seamen in the form of fees for obtaining, renewing and upgrading documents and licenses. In 1998, OMB came back with a Navigation Assistance Tax (NAT) for Aids to Navigation and to be later expanded to icebreaking. LCA was instrumental in forming a national coalition to oppose the NAT charges and Congress listened again and rejected these taxes in the budget. When LCA met with Congressmen they wore lapel stickers that graphically stated NO NAT! LCA thanked Congressman Jim Oberstar (MN) for the language prohibiting collection of NAT.

U.S. Customs Fee

In 1986 a Customs Fee of $397 was to be charged for every entry of a vessel into a Customs district. The AISI and many other shippers of iron ore and other bulk materials on the Lakes petitioned congress to reduce this fee and the attendant paperwork. Industry managed to get the fee reduced to $100 per entry payable for only the first 15 entries in a calendar year.

Imported Steel and Iron Ore, Impact on Great Lakes Shipping

The steel industry in the United States was seriously hurt by the large tonnage of 'dumped' imported steel landed in our sea ports (dumped steel was sold in U.S. markets at less than the cost of production and transportation). In 1970 the U.S. percentage of consumption of imported steel was 13.8% and by 1984 it was 26.4%. In that period, iron ore shipments from Great Lakes ports fell by 30 million net tons. Working with other trade associations, in particular the American Iron and Steel Institute (AISI) and the American Iron Ore Association (AIOA), LCA supported a Fair Trade in Steel Act that was rejected by the Administration since that would mean setting quotas by country. Ultimately industry had to accept a Voluntary Restraint Agreement on imports that tried to limit the amount of 'dumped' steel to about 20% of consumption. In 1986, imported steel came into the USA at 23.1% of the domestic market; and, as imported goods made from steel increased, the American steel and iron ore industry continued to suffer. In 1987, imports accounted for 21.1% of the U.S. market and the American steel industry returned to profitability. The tonnage moved on the Great Lakes was up nearly 21% from the previous year and efforts turned to the VRA program that was to expire in 1989. A modest extension of the program was worked out.

However, by 1998 steel imports had reached a new all-time high. From 1997-2003, 35 U.S. steel companies and processors had filed for bankruptcy protection; some closed their doors forever. Many iron ore miners and steel workers were laid off; and of course the reduced demand for iron ore caused many lakers to layup early. In 2002, the Bush Administration did impose a tariff on many types of steel imports. In 2003, legislators were still seeking a long term solution to dumping of steel into the USA. Steel imports would be a problem that will plague the nation for many years to come from an economics and a national defense viewpoint, as well as a major problem for Great Lakes shipping.

Cabotage Laws- the Jones Act

The Cabotage Laws of the United States go back to the earliest history of the nation. The term stems from the French verb *caboter* meaning to sail by the capes or coastwise. Many nations reserved the right to restrict carriage of cargo and passengers to the ships built and/or owned by their own citizens. Over the years the laws in the USA have been amended and the most relevant laws were the Passenger Vessel Services Act of 1886 as amended and Section 27 of the Merchant Marine Act of 1936, known as the Jones Act.

As in the past, the challenges to the Jones Act on the Great Lakes often come from the Canadian ship owners through their government. In 1982, there was a major world demand for export of American Great Lakes area origin coal due to political issues worldwide that restricted normal world coal supply. Canada Steamship Line wanted to use some of their larger self-unloading vessels loaded with coal from American lake ports to top off very large bulk carriers within the coastal waters of the east coast of the USA. While it was not going to reduce demand for American Great Lakes vessels, it was clear that this would be a dangerous precedent. With the help of others in the U.S. flag merchant marine, LCA opposed the granting of a waiver of the Jones Act to permit these top off operations. The waiver was not granted but that did not end Canadian interests to break the Jones Act. Working together with other maritime interests on this issue helped LCA fight later challenges to the Cabotage laws long term through a coalition of American ship owners called the Maritime Cabotage Task Force (MCTF).

U.S./Canada Free Trade Area Agreement; the Jones Act and other Cabotage Laws

The Canadian Government in 1987, with the support of Canadian ship builders and Canadian carriers, viewed the U.S./Canada Free Trade Area Agreement as a new opportunity to break into the coastal trade of the United States, first in the Great Lakes and then ultimately on the other coasts and the inland waterways. That threat became very apparent to the U.S. maritime industry nationwide. A few years earlier, the Canadian Government had provided construction subsidies to rebuild the Canadian fleet; thus in 1987, the Canadian operating costs were lower than that of the United States; and if it were not for the Jones Act, within a short period of time, Canadian carriers could capture the U.S. domestic trade. American carriers and those they employed as well as American shipbuilders, ship repairers and shipboard and shore side staff would be negatively impacted. The maritime industry knew that within a matter of time, all other Trade Agreements, such as the upcoming North American Free Trade Agreement (NAFTA) with Mexico and Canada and the Uruguay Round of the General Agreement on Tariffs and Trade (GATT), would open the doors for foreign flag vessels to operate on all coasts and inland waters. In 1987, Mel Pelfrey, Ryan and others met with Ambassador Peter O'Murphy, Chief Negotiator, Office of the U.S. Trade Representative, to press our case to exclude Cabotage from the negotiations. But this was not enough; it was time for a national coalition to be formed to fight the inclusion of Cabotage Laws in the U.S.-Canada Free Trade Area Agreement. This was a battle that the American maritime industry had to win. No efforts or expense was spared.

Another Coalition-- Maritime Cabotage Task Force (MCTF)

The MCTF was formed to combat the threat posed by the Trade agreements. It included LCA, all the major Washington based water carrier trade associations, the major maritime labor organizations and their Washington based lobbyists. The group engaged a prominent law firm, Preston Gates Ellis & Rouvelas Meeds LLP, to coordinate efforts. The strategy started with the invaluable help of a staff attorney, Mark Ruge. In the end, MCTF succeeded by having a Joint Resolution of the House of Representatives signed by an overwhelming majority, 235 of the 435 House members of Congress and 56 Senators calling for the removal of Cabotage from the trade agreement. After this very strong challenge to a relatively small element of the Trade Agreement, the Administration withdrew Cabotage from the negotiating table. These efforts were further enhanced by the inclusion of support for Cabotage Laws in the December 1987 report of the President's Commission on Merchant Marine and Defense. The report recommended that the government "... should support the existing

Cabotage Laws and should resist any attempt either to weaken or eliminate them." Then, in the 1988 Presidential Campaign, both candidates issued statements supporting the Jones Act!

The Free Trade Area Agreement between the U.S.A., Canada and Mexico became another opportunity to challenge the Jones Act. Due to the combined efforts of the maritime industry through the MCTF, that policy change did not see the light of day. At the 1994 International Joint Conference between the LCA and our Canadian counterpart, the Canadian Shipowners Association, with tongue in cheek, Ryan gave his opening address in Spanish congratulating everyone for bringing about the passage of the U.S./Canada Free Trade Area Agreement without any change in U.S. Cabotage Laws. He emphasized that had this trade agreement gone through as the Reagan Administration supported, it would be necessary to extend the rights to our Cabotage trade to Mexico and then to other countries with whom we had 'most favored nation' treaties. He said that future IJC meetings would not be conducted in English but in Spanish or another language since the ships would be built overseas and owned by many foreign nationals, and the crews would be the lowest cost foreign crews available.

Given the dangerous terrorist potential of having non-citizens from anywhere in the world onboard vessels in every major port and coastal or inland population center, it remains essential to national security to not allow ships that could never be adequately inspected to assure there were no weapons of mass destruction onboard. Without the Cabotage laws America would have significantly greater national security problems.

Clearly one of the most significant LCA efforts in decades was to go all out to defend the Cabotage Laws. To have lost that battle would have led to the demise of American Flag Great Lakes shipping and the LCA; and more significantly it would be a national security nightmare.

Strangely enough the next challenge to the Cabotage laws, and in fact all of the programs benefiting the Merchant Marine, came in 1993 in the form of a study instituted by Vice President Al Gore to study government efficiency. It was called the National Performance Review (NPR). Industry initially viewed the NPR study as potentially beneficial in that it could eliminate regulatory and tax burdens. Fortunately a draft set of recommendations were leaked; and the maritime industry found that it called for a total abandonment of current government policies supporting the Merchant Marine, including the Jones Act. Swiftly the same broad U.S. Maritime Coalition came together again and lobbied Congress to table those NPR recommendations.

Then in 1994 Canadian shipowners, noting that there had been a 15 or more year decline in St. Lawrence Seaway tonnage transits, sought more help from their government. In the guise of recommendation from a subcommittee of the Canadian Parliament, they recommended a combining of the Seaway authorities and a suspension of the U.S. and Canadian cabotage laws as a way to encourage more tonnage to be moved on all flags transiting the Seaway. The threat had to be dealt with quickly to nip this radical policy change early on. LCA strongly stated that this was a bad idea and should be tabled, as it was.

Challenges to the Jones Act seemed like an annual event just as wild mushrooms raise themselves from the detritus of the woodland. In 1995, North Carolina chicken farmers and one of the Great Lakes grain houses with the leadership of Rob Quartel lobbied congress to jettison the Jones Act. They claimed that mid-west grains could be moved cheaper from Toledo to the North Carolina chicken farmers at a lower price than the railroads could deliver the chicken feed. They clearly wanted to see this vital American maritime industry turned over to cheap foreign labor. They called themselves the Jones Act Reform Coalition (JARC) and caused legislation to be introduced in the House by Nick Smith, a Michigan Republican and farmer, and in the Senate by Republican Senator Jesse Helms, North Carolina. They called the bill the Coastal Competitive Shipping Act. In the House the bill had 14 co-sponsors. The MCTF went to work; and by early 1998, 240 House members co-signed the House Continuing Resolution 65 supporting American cabotage laws. JARC was dead in the water.

Periodically other challenges to the Jones Act arose that had to be challenged, such as from Hawaii when certain interests wanted more foreign flag cruise ships to be in intra-island trade; from Alaska when some claimed Alaskan coal was penalized since foreign ships couldn't carry coal to the lower 48; from America's Pacific islands—Guam, Samoa, Midway and others—that claimed higher costs of using American ships, and closer to home, from the Mayor of Milwaukee who called for the end of Cabotage at meetings of American Mayors and at Governors conference. All had to be refuted and were done so.

Environmental Issues

Great Lakes Commission

The Great Lakes Commission (GLC) was established by joint legislative action of the Great Lakes states in 1955 and granted congressional consent in 1968. The purpose of the Commission "... is to carry out the terms and requirements of the Great Lakes Basin Compact: To promote the orderly, integrated, and comprehensive development, use, and conservation of the water resources of the Great Lakes Basin. The Commission addresses a range of issues involving environmental protection, resource management, transportation and economic development." However from the experience of LCA, the GLC was primarily interested in environmental matters and the state appointees came from state agencies with that focus. The federal agencies and not for profit agencies who were granted observer status also appeared to have a strong environmental focus. There were representatives from the COE, USCG, Departments of Transportation and Commerce but they were outnumbered by the states that often sent staff with strong environmental protection credentials and little economic background.

Fortunately on some of the state delegations there were people who had transportation and economic development interests. LCA member Sid Smith, Erie Sand and Gravel, was on the Pennsylvania delegation and the Port of Duluth always had someone on the Minnesota delegation who spoke up for the Seaway water transportation interests. Ryan attended many meetings as a guest, but had little authority with the Ohio delegation or with the group as a whole. He knew that LCA needed a stronger representation on the GLC since they were a powerful player on legislation of interest to LCA. Ryan explained this to the LCA Advisory Committee. Rennie Thompson, Oglebay Norton, called Governor George Voinovich's office in Columbus and shortly after Ryan was appointed by the Governor to the Ohio delegation. That appointment lasted through later Governors' tenures and he was better able to explain the LCA position to the various delegations.

Michigan Watercraft Pollution Control Act

Michigan passed legislation that superseded the federal legislation on use of Coast Guard approved shipboard waste water treatment systems and the discharge of the treated water into Michigan waters. LCA appealed these regulations to the federal courts that ruled in favor of the state of Michigan. LCA then appealed to the Supreme Court and on May 24, 1982 the Supreme Court affirmed the judgment of the U.S. District Court; LCA petitioned for a rehearing that was denied. LCA asked the EPA to review and rescind findings that allowed Michigan to take the legal action cited; EPA believed that would require Michigan to provide new data. LCA considered that it was futile to continue; members and LCA proceeded to work with state officials to achieve a satisfactory solution.

Non-indigenous species

In 1989, there was environmental concern about the negative impact of zebra mussels discharged into the Great Lakes by ocean going salt water vessels and then transferred around the lakes by all commercial vessels that required ballast water to maintain stability and by recreational boats in hull wells. It was a major issue of concern. The passage of the Nonindigenous Aquatic Nuisance Prevention and Control Act of 1990 called for control of ballast water on lake and salt water vessels. In 1993 LCA developed a Voluntary Ballast Water Management Plan for vessels trading in the Duluth/Superior harbors to stem the spread of the European River Ruffe. Congress in that year held hearings on a Ballast Water Control Act at which LCA was a leading witness.

LCA Ballast treatment system was installed on SS Algonorth

In 1996-97, LCA joined with the Northeast Midwest Institute in a $1.3 million grant from the Great Lakes Protection Fund to test technology to stop transfer of non-indigenous species in ballast water. With the cooperation of a Canadian carrier, Algoma Central Marine, the Algonorth was used as a platform to test filtration systems. Rick Harkins, LCA, was the principal engineer working on this project. When the Algonorth was laid up for lack of grain business, the equipment was transferred to a barge in Duluth and for a time in Two Harbors to continue the ultraviolet filtration testing. The study helped many policy makers understand the magnitude of the problem; it also affirmed that filtration with state of the art equipment was only one technology that needed to be used in conjunction with thermal heating, ultraviolet radiation or other technologies not yet known. In 2000, secondary treatment tests were conducted using cyclonic separation and ultraviolet irradiation. In some quarters the use of biocide chemicals was suggested but for valid environmental reasons Great Lakes maritime industry and the states rejected the use of chemicals.

By 2000 the concern for the introduction and spread of nuisance non-indigenous species by ships had reached worldwide proportions; and, in the USA, many states sought solutions that could not be limited to the state's waters. In 2001, a Michigan bill was introduced that called for the sterilization of all ballast water discharged; it was modified after LCA testimony called for the testing of new technologies on ocean going vessels and a code of best practices on all vessels calling in Michigan waters.

The bottom line LCA position was that any requirements for treating of ballast water must be confined to the ocean going vessels that had introduced the non-indigenous species in their ballast water. LCA believed that the various non-indigenous species in the lakes would naturally migrate unless some indigenous species killed them. LCA contended that there was no conceivable technology that could treat the 15 million gallons of water that is pumped out of many large lakers at a rate up to 80,000 gallons/minute.

Cargo Residue Washdown

In 1988, the U.S. signed an international agreement to 'Prevent the Pollution by Garbage from Ships'. The Great Lakes had been protected from discharge by ship of garbage since 1899 by Federal statute; but the international definition of garbage included cargo waste or residue that was prohibited from being discharged from vessels. From the earliest days of lakes shipping, vessels carrying inert cargos, such as iron ore, coal, and stone as well as grains were washed down from decks and hold. It was necessary to wash down the decks and cargo holds for crew safety and sanitation in crew quarters. It was particularly important to wash down a cargo hold to prepare for another type of cargo, as when an ore or coal carrier was booked to carry grains for its next trip. The cargo residue was washed down over the side in areas away from water intakes and dredged channels. In 1994 LCA developed a policy that would allow the wash down of non-hazardous cargo residue only in clearly defined areas thus excluding sensitive environmental areas. This met the requirements of Annex V of MARPOL. A major effort was undertaken by the carriers to minimize spillage on deck and to discharge all the cargo in the holds.

Washdown on deck

Jim Traficant's Lake Erie Ohio River Canal attempts to revive Kirwan's Ditch

Representative Kirwan (OH) was an effective 17 term congressman first elected in 1936, a leader in the Democratic Party with close friendships with Presidents and other leaders. Kirwan envisioned the cheap waterborne transportation of goods into the American heartland, as well as the creation of a connecting link between the Atlantic Ocean (via the St. Lawrence Seaway) with the Gulf of Mexico (by way of the Ohio and Mississippi Rivers). Unfortunately, many port interests on the coasts did not share his vision and a few detractors called it Kirwan's Ditch! He was unable to see his vision of a Lake Erie-Ohio River Inter-Connecting Waterway fulfilled.

Then in 1985, out of the blue without any consultation with industry, Congressman James Traficant, Youngstown, OH, revived the call made some 20 years earlier by Congressman Kirwan to build a canal from Fairport, OH to East Liverpool, OH. While Traficant said it could be done with private financing, the COE estimated it would probably cost over $3 billion. LCA chose not to publicly oppose this project of personal interest to a powerful local congressman who supported maritime interests on many Cabotage issues. For many reasons including economic and environmental, LCA did not support canal construction. Fortunately the issue died without legislative hearings.

Other Legislative Issues handled by the Legislative Affairs Committee

- Supported legislation to prohibit diversion of water from the Great Lakes.
- Opposed ownership of water carriers by railroads.
- Opposed bills in the House increasing the limits of liability for seamen's death and injury.
- Lobbied congress to reinstate the full deductibility of crew meals for tax purposes.
- Lobbied Congress to correct a 1986 law that required all marine users to pay a $0.15/gallon tax on diesel fuel that was to be applied only to highway users. While marine users could file a claim for refund, this was a loss of cash flow and a bureaucratic burden. Eventually LCA was successful.
- Opposed onerous Washington legislation stemming from the oil spill from the Exxon Valdez relating to shipowner liability and a requirement to have a four person navigation crew on the bridge of all tankers when a state pilot was not onboard; and, opposed other onerous proposed Michigan tanker regulations.
- Lobbied Congress to assure that an Immigration Bill did not define longshoremen work as the work crew members performed discharging cargo from self-unloading (SUL) vessels. Had a broad definition of longshoreman work passed, it would have prohibited Canadian crew members from discharging the SUL vessels in U.S. ports; LCA was concerned there would have been a reciprocal impact on American SUL ships discharging in Canadian ports.
- LCA opposed a requirement to have all domestic vessels repaired in U.S. yards or face a 50% duty; at the same time LCA opposed the loss of Jones Act privileges if a "major rebuild" were done in a foreign yard, as the definition of 'rebuild' was being redefined.

- LCA worked with Marad, Customs and Department of Energy to clarify that coal would not be included in a provision to waive the Jones Act during an energy shortage.

Navigation and Electronics Committees

These committees merged in 1982.
Initially chaired by: Ed Jacobsen, Oglebay Norton; Members included Dewey Aston, Pickands Mather; Mike Elson, American Steamship; Gene Stafford, Inland Lakes Management; Dan Cornillie, Inland Steel; David Van Brunt, USS Great Lakes Fleet; Fred Cummings, USS Great Lakes Fleet; Tom Anderson, American Steamship Company

The principle objectives of this committee were in obtaining navigation improvements and navigation safety. Principal among these action were to extend the Navigation Season, maintain and or replace the <u>Mackinaw</u> and lobby for a new Poe sized lock. This Committee, working with Canadian counterparts, served as the Ice Operating Committee at the beginning and the end of every season communicating the industry needs for icebreaking services to the U.S. and Canadian Coast Guards.

Establish Extended Navigation Season; from March 25 until January 15

The congressionally authorized eight year Winter Navigation Demonstration Program demonstrated the practicality of keeping the Soo locks open later than the tradition of a December 15 closing date and of opening the locks no earlier than April 1. Unfortunately, the effort also brought out many opponents of the season extension from within the environmental communities. LCA also had to counter the efforts by some congressmen who wanted to authorize year round navigation, in part stimulated by some in the port communities who wanted the Seaway opened year round. LCA recognized that the environmental impact as well as the technological difficulties by ship owners and on government facilities and services involved with year-round navigation were overwhelming. This tangential debate caused even more opposition from some in the environmental community who saw LCA efforts to achieve a limited season extension as merely 'the foot in the door'.

In order to meet the needs of the steel industry, the LCA petitioned the COE and the USCG to provide necessary services so as member vessels could transit the St. Marys River and the Sault locks early in the season and later in the season. In 1987 the locks opened on March 22, the earliest date on record; and the locks stayed open until January 15, 1988, the latest since 1979 when the Winter Navigation Demonstration Program authorized that late operation. LCA initially supported a rule that, under certain environmental and economic conditions, the Soo Locks would remain open until January 8, plus or minus one week.

Neebish Island Ferry

Getting the locks to stay open later and open sooner and getting the best icebreakers possible would not have been sufficient unless LCA solved the nagging problem caused by the political power of a small number of people who resided year round on various islands in the St. Marys River, in particular the residents on Neebish Island. They demanded that the deep draft down bound West Neebish Channel be closed when ice formed. These residents used a public ferry until the ice froze, at which time the ferry had difficulty getting to the island dock. The residents believed it was economical to use their own vehicles to cross the ice and they were less constrained by ferry schedules. Vessel traffic not only made it impossible to use the snow mobiles but also caused ice flows to jam up at the ferry dock. In 1985, Ryan made contacts with Cliff Tyner, the operator of the Neebish Island Ferry and the owner of the island dock that was on his property, and the Eastern Upper Peninsula Transportation Authority (EUPTA) to discuss relocation of the island ferry dock to a location where ice formations would not deter ferry traffic during the extended navigation season period. This would permit the opening of the West Neebish Channel for longer periods of time. In 1986-87, LCA, Tyner and EUPTA determined that the best location for the island dock was directly across from the mainland dock. After many public hearings and voiced opposition from residents and environmental interests, LCA finally reached a consensus to move ahead. This required a joint action of the EUPTA and State of Michigan (including MI DNR who opposed for fear that it would lead to year round navigation) to build a new dock; for the Corps of Engineers to allow the use of previously dredged rock stored on the island to be used to build the road to the ferry dock. The rock was to be only used for navigation purposes and LCA argued that this was appropriate use and for the LCA Board to agree in 1988 to privately fund the relocation of the ferry dock access road to link with the main island road. All the players cooperated and the project moved ahead. In the history of the LCA this was the only road construction that LCA partially paid for. The new ferry dock was opened on November 26, 1990.

New dock and road Neebish Island

Impact of Domestic Icebreaking on Extended Navigation Season
Icebreaking, a Responsibility of the U.S. Coast Guard

Ice forms a solid blockade of the channels in the connecting rivers of the St. Marys, St. Clair and Detroit and in the harbors as well as portions of the open lakes. For decades, vessels operated in the channels below the locks and in the lower lakes long before the locks at the Soo opened and after the locks closed. During the Winter Navigation Demonstration Program the U.S. and Canadian Coast Guards operated to keep the locks and channels open, even year round.

The Great Lakes shipping industry depended upon the Coast Guard to provide icebreaking services just as they had since the 1940's and at times before. Coast Guard, for budget reasons, frequently attempted to reduce that service. In 1983 Coast Guard declared that after the locks closed they would refer all calls for assistance to commercial operators and that Coast Guard would only respond in emergencies. LCA considered this policy as a gift to the small commercial tug operators whose tugs were inadequate to the task; and when they failed, but were paid, the Coast Guard was called to assist.

The Reagan Administration philosophy was to discourage the use of government services such as icebreaking in order to allow commercial interests to provide services. In the Great Lakes there were inadequate commercial ice breaking tugs. After extensive lobbying, in 1984 LCA was able to get an agreement with the Coast Guard that whenever the Soo Locks were open, the Coast Guard icebreakers would keep the channels open. This solution was not adequate but it was a half a loaf.

In 1986, there were a number of Congressmen who were concerned for potential environmental damage caused by icebreakers operating after January 15. This came to a head when the Corps of Engineers was ready to commence a feasibility study that would consider a scenario when the Soo Locks could be open until January 31, plus or minus two weeks. LCA had previously supported this initiative in order to determine and document what safety considerations there would be if a national economic emergency called for navigating after 15 January. A Congressional Resolution was prepared and passed that called for ending all Coast Guard icebreaking anywhere on the Lakes after January 15. This would have created havoc in the movement of liquid fuels, cement and coal in the lower lakes. As all of these movements impacted Michigan shippers and ports, LCA successfully petitioned a few Michigan legislators to amend the resolution so as the prohibition only applied to vessels passing through the Soo Locks after January 15.

In spring 1987, the St. Clair River was ice clogged so much that navigation was stopped for three days. The LCA Navigation committee worked with the Coast Guard to reopen the channel in the most expeditious and safe manner.

In 1986, because of the need to clarify industry's specific navigation season needs, LCA began to publicly call for a fixed navigation season through the Locks, without unnecessary environmental constraints. The final rule setting the closing date at midnight January 15 was effective March 1992. In 1989, LCA began to focus on a fixed opening date of March 21, but after much consultation with various federal agencies and the State of Michigan, a 1993 agreement ultimately led to a fixed opening date of March 25. LCA agreed to abide by that agreement and not to challenge it unless there was a national emergency that required a change. This 10 year agreement affirming those dates was signed by USCG, COE, U.S. Fish and Wildlife and Michigan DNR.

Meanwhile, every year at the end and beginning of the navigation seasons when heavy ice was a navigation obstacle, it was necessary to form a LCA sub-committee to coordinate with the U.S. and Canadian Coast Guards and the operators of U.S. and Canadian vessels to assure that the vessel traffic moved as efficiently as possible. The men who worked on this project were on the job 24/7. Typically communications coordination fell to Gordon Hall and later Rick Harkins. The LCA membership team generally was led by Bob Dorn, Interlake Steamship, and Fred Cummings, USS Great Lakes Fleet.

Save the Old Mackinaw; Build a new large Icebreaker

Due to a $105 million budget shortfall in 1987, the USCG announced it would permanently lay up the heavy icebreaker Mackinaw after the spring 1988 break out. This alleged saving of $3.7 million would cost the nation significantly more since the five Bay class icebreaking tugs could not keep the channels open. In 1988, LCA successfully spearheaded the formation of a coalition of Great Lakes interests called the MACKINAW 2020 Task Force to convince Congress of the need not only to save the Mackinaw but to modernize and/or replace it. Through the support and leadership of Michigan Congressman Bob Davis, Congress listened and directed the Commandant to get the ship ready for opening of the 1989 season and in that year funds were appropriated to modernize the Mackinaw. The Coast Guard was slow to move ahead on the modernization and merely studied it.

By 1993, the next challenge came because of a federal deficit – the Mackinaw was to be decommissioned after the spring breakout in 1994. LCA and their allies in the several coalitions mounted a vigorous "Save the Mackinaw" campaign that ended on March 24, 1994 when Admiral Kime, Commandant of the Coast Guard, Senator John Glenn, (OH), Congressman Bob Carr (MI) and George J. Ryan, President of the LCA, sat around a table in Senator John Glenn's office and heard the Commandant agreed to delay decommissioning of the Mackinaw.

George Ryan and Senator John Glenn

In 1997 Fred Cummings and Ryan flew to the Saguenay River to make an inspection trip on the Canadian icebreaker Des Grossiers. In 1998 Commandant Admiral Kramack supported keeping the Mackinaw operational until 2006.

Fred Cummings on inspection trip of the Canadian ice breaker Des Grossiers

Canadian ice breaker Des Grossiers

Eventually, the Mackinaw modernization study came in with a price tag of $92 million, far in excess of what anyone expected or could support for a single mission vessel. LCA believed it was the time to call for a new multi-mission vessel with the icebreaking capability of the Mackinaw. Fortunately the new Commandant, Admiral Loy, was a supporter of heavy icebreaking on the Lakes. We now needed appropriations for the Coast Guard to solicit construction proposals from American shipyards. In 2001 the Coast Guard contracted with Marinette Marine, Wisconsin, to build a new multi-purpose vessel. After much consideration of names for the new vessel, it was decided to continue the historic name Mackinaw for the new heavy icebreaker on the lakes

New ice breaker Mackinaw WLBB 30

452 | George J. Ryan

Admiral Loy, Commandant, USCG

The Office of Management and Budget (OMB) decided this was the time to propose icebreaker user fees amounting to $0.63/ton for all cargo carried between December 15 and April 15. Fortunately two of the consistent champions of Great Lakes commerce, Jim Oberstar, MN, and Dave Obey, WI, were quick to gather signatures from 48 other legislators telling OMB that this proposal was dead in the water.

James Oberstar, Jim Weakley, Mark Barker

Congressman Dave Obey

New Poe-Sized Lock

In 1983, LCA began an effort to obtain authorization and appropriations to build a new large lock at the Soo. The Poe Lock opened in 1968, and in the years that followed, American flag lake carriers had thirteen 1,000 foot self-unloaders and other vessels were lengthened; thus, of the 92 vessels registered with LCA in 1986, 31 vessels were restricted to the Poe lock for transit; additionally the four LCA registered tankers were restricted to the Poe by safety regulation. In 1984 LCA had a preview of what might happen if there were to be a shutdown of the Poe in the operating season. The International Railroad Bridge that spanned the locks had a casualty and blocked the downbound approach to the Poe and the MacArthur locks for 41 hours, thus delaying 12 U.S. flag vessels carrying over 225,000 net tons of iron ore and coal. In record time, Corps emergency action waived the time consuming contracting procedures and the requirement to use only U.S. corporations in order to get the bridge raised to allow vessels to transit. Another wakeup call concerning lock failures came when the wall at lock seven in the Welland Canal collapsed in 1985, closing the locks for 23 days and delaying the transit of 125 vessels. This closure impacted the U.S. and Canadian economies and in particular grain and iron ore shipments.

LCA argued that for National Defense, coal energy supply and the economics of the steel industry, a duplicate Poe sized lock must be built. LCA recognized that this effort was in the same time frame when the Reagan Administration was calling for local sponsors to pay a major portion of new projects. LCA argued that this was a national need that no local city, such as the city of Sault Ste. Marie could sponsor and pay for the local share of the lock; and neither could the State of Michigan. LCA enlisted the aid of the Great Lakes Commission, the port industry, the maritime unions, the American Iron and Steel Institute, the American Iron Ore Association and others to contact legislators to support this appeal.

In 1986, the Water Resources Development Act authorized construction of the new lock and directed the Corps to study the appropriate way to fund the lock; in 1990, LCA lobbied to have the authorization extended for five years. In 1999, after the Great Lakes states, with the help of the Great Lakes Commission, agreed in principle to fund the local cost share over

50 years without interest and agreed to a formula to reduce that share by deducting the Canadian/Canadian and Canadian/International trade that transited the lock. Only the imagination and dedicated support of Congressmen Jim Oberstar, MN, and Dave Obey, WI, could have conceived of this solution! However, the appropriations to build the lock had to wait for the next leadership of LCA to bring about.

Christening Honorable James L. Oberstar, 2011

Great Lakes Water Levels

The LCA tracked water levels for its members and communicated those water levels in various channels for decades. The reason remains simple. For each inch of added draft a vessel can load to, there is additional cargo and revenue. Each vessel has a relationship at certain drafts as to how many tons it takes to immerse the vessel by one inch. This is called the TPI or tons per inch immersion, which ranges from a 70 TPI for a small vessel to 270 TPI for the large 1,000 foot vessels. Before the vessel was loaded the Captain had to know water depth and the water under the keel wherever the vessel was to be safely navigated.

IMPACT OF LAKE LEVELS ON VESSEL CARRYING CAPACITY
(net tons)

Great Lakes Bulk Carriers	Vessel Length (feet)	Per-Trip Carrying Capacity	Capacity Per Inch Of Draft*
	1,000	69,654	267
	806	34,720	146
	767	28,336	127
	635	22,064	107
	501	13,776	71

*Capacity per inch of draft reflects the incremental tonnage carried at normal loaded draft.

In 1983, water levels were above the long term averages and high water levels continued for many years. LCA was challenged many times by riparian land owners, marina operators, environmentalists and others to work with the government to lower the water levels. Public hearings were held, particularly in Michigan and in Illinois. At one such meeting where Ryan testified, he was challenged by a concerned citizen who claimed that LCA was the culprit since LCA members benefited from high waters as they carried more cargo; he stated that LCA controlled the COE and the water levels and that the President of LCA had the key that controlled the valves. Ryan was flattered and wished that the association had the powerful image and control that was imagined.

Clearly high water levels benefited about half of the vessel owners whose load line permitted deeper loadings. However, not all was good for the ship owner as some vessels had difficulty getting under loading rigs, some older docks were awash and masters had to be concerned for vertical bridge clearances. The issue of high water levels became a major issue in the 1980s as riparian shoreline owners were losing their beaches and storm tossed waters did greater damage. There were many complaints about ship wakes damaging the shore structures. Speeds had to be reduced in some of the connecting channels; at times extra tugs had to be engaged to overcome stronger currents in harbors; as ships were higher in the water, the loading and unloading rigs were in danger of being struck thus causing the ships to add more ballast and then adjust more ballast during cargo operations.

Shore residents were legitimately concerned with wake damages; environmentalists were concerned with habitat damage by ship transit wakes; and marinas upstream from fixed bridges could not move boats with tall structures under the bridge. The IJC ordered the outflow from Lake Superior reduced in 1986 since the lower lakes were too high. Higher than average precipitation then brought new record high levels to Lake Superior.

As to be expected, over the years ahead there were lower levels of precipitation and thus lower than average water levels causing many vessels to reduce loading and to be even more diligent in navigating in shallow channels. LCA called for increased surveys and additional dredging. Then some new marinas that were built during the high water periods had another problem; the recreational boats were mired in mud just short of the marina.

In 1988, water level concerns changed drastically as the nation faced a long drought. Mississippi River barge interests even called for diversion of water from the Great Lakes. LCA counseled against that action although that diversion would not be permitted since the U.S. Supreme Court was still the Court of last resort on water diversion, and a subject carefully watched by government officials in Michigan and Wisconsin and by LCA. Water levels continued to fluctuate and by June 1998 regional drought conditions were recognized and low water challenged the navigators. By 2002, all of the lakes were below long term averages.

Removal of Hazards to Navigation

In order to keep the waterways safe, the Navigation Committee annually petitioned the USCG and the COE to improve the ports and channels. One such effort that ended successfully in 1985 was the removal of the Canal Street abutments in Indiana Harbor; and, in 1987 LCA succeeded in the removal of derelict bridges including the Central Furnace Bridge in the Cuyahoga River, the Conrail Bridge in the Maumee and the Burlington Northern Bridge in Duluth-Superior harbor. LCA continually asked for the rehabilitation of Rock Cut, West Neebish Channel in the St. Marys River since boulders and channel wall rocks were falling into the channel. The Corps did sweeps and hauled out large rocks that were discovered.

Dredging of Harbors and Channels

Improvements to the authorized depths of connecting channels and key harbors are very difficult to bring about because of the limitations in the maintenance dredging budget of the COE. LCA always attempted to help set priority for the most essential work to be done. Authorizing new depths, widths and reaches of channels required Congressional authorization and appropriations and LCA testified in support of these projects. Despite the new harbor taxes to pay for operation and maintenance dredging, Congress continued to under appropriate the needed funds for dredging ports and channels in the Great Lakes. Annually LCA and their allies lobbied for additional funds.

Standard practice in the past was to deposit clean dredged material from the harbors and channels into the open lake or into confined disposal facilities. Environmental concerns for the toxins and contaminants in dredged material led local authorities to ban open lake dumping of all dredged material in the lakes. This led to a higher cost and a shortage of confined disposal facilities on land to accept all these dredged materials. To no avail, LCA continued to lobby that much of this material was clean and should have been allowed to be deposited in areas of the lakes that were not environmentally sensitive.

LCA lobbied key Great Lakes area legislators in 1992 to authorize deeper dredging of the Vidal Shoals section of the Upper St. Marys River, Duluth/Superior Harbor and several turns in the lower St. Marys River near Little Rapids and the St. Clair River high spots near Sans Souci. The LCA Board agreed to cosponsor the cost of dredging the Vidal Shoals area since the State of Michigan and the City of Sault Ste. Marie could not do so. The City of Duluth cosponsored the Duluth dredging.

After lobbying for years to improve the overall authorized depth of the Great Lakes connecting channels, the Corps was authorized in 2001 to undertake a Great Lakes Navigation Review. LCA advocated a new project depth of 30 feet to replace the current 25.5 feet depth.

Conflict between commercial vessels and recreational boats and marinas

Artwork Conflict large ships and pleasure craft (Sandusky Register, Cartoon copyright Don Lee, used by permission)

LCA reviewed every application for approval of plans to locate marinas near commercial channels and opposed these applications if there was a potential for danger to the small boaters and marina docks if they were near vessel wake and bow or stern thruster action.

Recreational boats too close to large vessels Cuyahoga River

In order to help local public officials understand the conflicts that could arise between recreational boats and lake freighters in close quarters near marinas in the rivers, LCA frequently testified against approval of marinas in certain locations. In 1986, at the request of the City of Cleveland, the Committee mapped the Cuyahoga River and indicated the spots in the river where marinas would not be a hazard to navigation; LCA called for safety zones where recreational boats could not moor. In 1987, LCA arranged for Lorain City Council officials to ride the <u>Cason J. Calloway</u> from the mouth of the Black River up to the USX mill so they could understand first-hand the safety problems that would arise if they approved proposals for certain marinas in the Black River. LCA produced an educational video tape to visually illustrate the dangers in order to educate local government officials.

LCA successfully opposed the 360 feet extension of Cobo Hall, Detroit, into the Detroit River, arguing that recreational boats would be diverted into the navigation channels.

Safety Equipment

The LCA position on the many proposed regulations for new equipment onboard lake ships was to clarify to the Coast Guard that LCA would support the regulation if it was of a demonstrative need on the Great Lakes. LCA frequently successfully opposed new regulations for equipment to be placed on all U.S. flag vessels regardless of the area of service. Great Lakes ships operated with First Class Pilots in fresh not salt water, followed recommended course lines in open water and were in traffic information systems in confined waters, were usually close to a port and often in shallow water. LCA argued that when a new piece of equipment such as automatic radar plotting devices and satellite positioning needed in the deep sea trade proved their value in lake navigation, then, as in the past, LCA members would install them without regulatory mandates.

New Communications systems

With the advent of improved radio communication equipment onboard ships, there was a need to improve communications regulations such as bridge to bridge navigation communications. In part, this was due to excessive use of radio channels, such as Channel 16. What was needed was to establish Channel 13 as the Bridge to Bridge Channel. In the beginning, LCA opposed establishing a new channel but after much study and discussion, in 1982 LCA supported a new channel for bridge to bridge communications. This effort was complicated by the international nature of the Lakes that had separate U.S. and Canadian communications regulations; and there was different equipment on the salt water ships. Solutions had to be worked out with the American and Canadian mariners and government agencies as well as the Pilots navigating the salties. The Coast Guard approach was to mandate vessel traffic management systems in the connecting channels. The policy of LCA was to work with the Canadian Shipowners to oppose government controls but supported vessel information systems without the need to install mandatory new radio equipment and accept unnecessary government control of traffic.

Weather Communications and Centralized Marine Weather Forecasting Center

Ever since the loss of the Edmund Fitzgerald in the violent November 1975 storm, there were renewed efforts to improve weather forecasting and communications to the officers onboard the lakers. LCA members had contracts with Lorain Electronics to transmit weather and business correspondence and a network of radio towers were installed up by Lorain Electronics for that purpose.

In 1983 LCA supported a Centralized Marine Weather Forecasting Center and worked with the National Weather Service (NWS) to improve weather data transmissions. The NWS was not supportive of the LCA recommendations since NWS offices and functions served many users besides maritime; and forecasts were based upon broader geographic areas than just the Great Lakes. Buffalo, Cleveland and Chicago all reported to different NWS regional offices. The NWS believed coordination was adequate. LCA wanted a centralized office for all the Great Lakes to be in Cleveland. Finally in 1986 the NWS agreed to enhance weather forecasting for commercial vessels from the Cleveland office. In 1986, the NWS developed a Computerized Marine Weather Data System (CMAWDS) and asked the advice of LCA members as to what the system should contain. The system concept was that ship's officers could choose what data they needed for their area of operation.

Complicating this issue was the movement toward privatization of government services. There was a significant lobby effort by commercial marine forecasting companies advocating that they alone should provide forecasts to the marine industry. They maintained that this private industry should receive all the government meteorological data from the NWS who would then manipulate it and sell it to the marine industry. It was argued that commercial forecasting services were used by the agricultural industry to help with planting and harvesting decisions and by ocean shipping for long ocean voyage routing around bad weather. In the Great Lakes, ship owners didn't need a burden of added operating cost for a service that the government could provide using tax dollars. LCA allied with recreational boating and successfully lobbied to maintain NWS direct forecasting of lakes weather to the ships in an improved format.

Another complication was the rapid change in communication technology. New radio communications systems were developing rapidly in the 1980s and after. MF/HF usage continued to decline and the SSB operation was discontinued after a very short time. Soon it was realized by the contracted companies that the need for Lorain Electronics, WMI, after nearly 47 years of HF service to the lakers was coming to an end. The VHF system was operated until 1984 when it was sold to WJG Maritel. In 1985, the remaining contents of 2307 Leavitt Rd. were sold and Lorain Electronics closed its doors. Maritel operated the VHF system until 1990 and then shut it down for lack of business.

Other efforts of the committee

- The Navigation Committee and LCA staff was active in the transfer of timely navigation traffic information to the Coast Guard and the COE at the beginning and end of each season. Daily telephone conference calls with U.S. and Canadian Coast Guard shore staff and vessel operators and the U.S. and Canadian ship owners kept the traffic flowing through the ice covered waters.
- Succeeded in obtaining permission from the Coast Guard to allow vessels carrying coal from Toledo to Detroit River terminals to

travel this short distance with hatch covers off, thus increasing coal tonnage carried and valuable crew time closing and opening hatch covers. LCA rationale was that the practice did not negatively impact stability and, recognizing that the ships traveled in very shallow water and in the extreme chance that the hull might be penetrated, the vessel would quickly and safely rest on the bottom.

- Worked with the U.S. and Canadian Coast Guards to implement a workable Vessel Traffic Information System for the Detroit and St. Clair Rivers.
- Worked with the National Ocean Survey on revisions to Great Lakes Charts to include the LCA/DMA recommended course lines.
- Successfully obtained improvements in obtaining water level data at Buffalo, Toledo and Duluth.
- Frequently communicated to municipal authorities the need to improve fenders on bridge abutments and to reduce the number of delays caused by restrictive bridge opening hours.
- Committee reviewed the effectiveness, use of and if there was a continued need for LORAN C navigation system.
- Pilotage regulations were always on the agenda of the Navigation Committee including opposing use of non-licensed pilots on the open waters of the Great Lakes. LCA also opposed the proposal for recent re-familiarization trips on all the Great Lakes by licensed pilots.
- Succeeded in getting an amendment in a water resources bill requiring the Corps at the Soo Locks to reduce the requirement to land three seamen down to two seamen from the vessel to the dock to handle lines.
- Convinced the National Ocean Service, publisher of Great Lakes Charts, to retain polyconic projections on charts so as the scales could be in feet, fathoms and nautical miles until all the charts were converted to metric, at which time Mercator projections might be acceptable.
- Provided data to the Coast Guard in response to a proposal to provide special limited Load Line Certificates to river barges in the Chicago/Milwaukee trade.

- Committee began to explore the navigational improvements that could be brought about by use of the differential global positioning system (DGPS) and electronic charts (ECDIS) and the Automated Identification System (AIS) in the St. Marys River.
- Successfully argued against a Coast Guard proposal to mandate a national standard for under keel clearance in that the shallow Great Lakes and channels were well surveyed, pilots were familiar with the routes that they crossed frequently and that such a concept would negatively impact productivity without measurable benefit.
- Coordinated with the Canadian shipowners and the Canadian Coast Guard about the reduction of the number of Canadian aids to navigation required for commercial navigation. This was brought about by industry attempting to reduce operations they believed were not needed and were being paid for through the Canadian government Marine Services Fee.
- In addition to the major task of assuring that the Mackinaw stay in service, the committee petitioned for additional icebreaking capable vessels to replace the buoy tenders built in 1944. LCA had to constantly make the argument that these vessels were to supplement the Mackinaw, not to replace her.
- In 1980 published a new separate courses booklet in conjunction with the Canadian Shipowners Association to replace the last publication in 1959.
- As the year 2000 approached there was world-wide concern that the computers used in communications, electronics, navigation and engineering systems might fail. This was called the Y2K crisis. All the LCA committees spent much time, effort and money to assure that the shipboard systems would not malfunction. Fortunately the Y2K crisis was a non-event.

Captains Committee

When Ryan became president of LCA, he realized there were a comprehensive number of working and ad hoc committees that met and advised or directed the activities of the Association. Only one sector was missing and that was the voice of the experienced Captains in each of the member companies. Years before, LCA had the benefit of a Captains group called the Navigation Committee made up of working captains from many of the fleets; this group was disbanded in 1980. It also had been the practice for member companies to bring experienced Captains ashore as Port Captains to direct the ship's officers on navigation matters and they served on the Shore Captains Committee. As years went on, more of the shore management was in the hands of engineers, accountants and managers with little hands-on shipboard experience, thus the Shore Captains Committee was disbanded and their mission turned over to a newly established Navigation Committee. While the ship board Captains passed along their concerns to the shore staff, the Captains had little opportunity, in any formal way, to develop joint recommendations to improve navigational safety except through the Shipmasters' Association.

Captain Edgar Jacobsen, Oglebay Norton Company, was the Chair of the Navigation Committee and the last of the Shore Captains representing the larger companies in LCA. When Captain Jacobsen retired in 1983, Ryan asked the Advisory Committee to formally create the Captains Committee, a sub-committee of the Navigation Committee. They agreed and, on January 19, 1984, the first meeting of the Captains Committee took place. They were charged with making recommendations on navigation issues such as aids to navigation, courses, depths of channels, charts, vessel information services and other related navigational concerns. The Captains elected their own Chair to develop the agenda and conduct the meeting.

At many times later, this voice of experienced Masters helped the U.S. and Canadian Coast Guards understand the navigation issues more clearly; particularly when more narrowly focused Coast Guard members, or the groups or individuals representing vendors, the Shipmasters Association or the maritime unions might have held a different view. LCA invited all who had a stake in navigation issues to the annual Captains Committee meeting. The meetings were held at a convenient time in January prior to the annual Coast Guard Industry Day meetings. Both U.S. and Canadian officials attended the meetings, including the USCG, COE and the National Weather Service. Each of the member companies and many Canadian shipowners attended these informative meetings. Recommendations were passed to the Navigation Committee for action during the upcoming season.

Members of the Captains Committee included: Captains Daleski (Huron), Toreki (Columbia), Elson (ASC), Fitch (Bethlehem), Peacock (USS), Casper (Columbia), Dayton (Interlake), and Vandogen (ASC)

Ryan consider the re-establishment of a Captains Committee as one of the most fruitful accomplishments during his tenure as President of LCA.

Captains Committee Meeting

Fleet Engineers Committee

Chaired by: Ralph Bertz, USS Great Lakes Fleet; members included Gavin Sproul, American Steamship, and Dale Miller, Oglebay Norton

This committee focused on the improvement of the operations of the engineering plant and the modification of Coast Guard regulations that had become unnecessary, onerous and expensive.

Some of these actions included:

- Improvements to the Damage Stability Regulations by contracting with Marine Consultants and Designers to conduct a study of Great Lakes vessel casualties in order to comment on proposed regulations. The Coast Guard accepted the findings of the LCA

study. The final regulations on stability, flooding protection, and subdivision were suitable for Great Lakes vessels.
- Requested an extension of the dry dock period for vessels that had been in long term layup.
- In 1983 requested an extension of the dry dock period and tail shaft inspection period from five years to six years for newer larger vessels that would be compatible with the ABS requirements. When the Coast Guard did not concur, LCA gathered information supporting the position from records of 37 five year drydockings. In order to support the use of underwater surveys in lieu of drydocking, LCA documented the underwater survey of the Mesabi Miner in 1987. Finally in 1996, the Coast Guard agreed to a case-by-case one year extension of the load line drydocking following an in-water survey.
- Requested continuous delegation of authority from the Coast Guard to the American Bureau of Shipping to conduct and approve certain inspections.
- Requested modification of proposed Coast Guard regulations on marking of ships, the installation of new lifeboats and davits on all ships (the government did not make the case that the installation was essential for safety of crew; plus the cost of these unnecessary requirements exceeded the value of the older vessels).
- Successfully convinced the American Bureau of Shipping to retain a technical office and staff in Cleveland.
- Commented to the EPA that used lubricating oil was not a hazardous waste thus avoiding the need to adhere to costly regulations for storage and disposal.
- Worked with the Coast Guard to develop safe procedures for the transportation of coal; this stemmed from serious accidents where methane gas was ignited, one of which occurred on the Middletown that had a serious explosion in 1986 killing two crew members. Clearly there was a need for improved venting and equipment modifications were made on all coal carrying lake vessels.
- Responded to the EPA on a draft study on controlling diesel emissions.
- Compiled a list of company owned oil spill and recovery equipment that could be shared and a Directory of Oil Spill Contractors in

oil spill recovery. Increased shipboard and shoreside training with seminars to enhance assurance of a no spill policy. LCA staff in 1994 prepared a prototype draft of an Oil Spill Response Plan to be used by members in preparation of a plan for each ship that became a requirement of the Oil Pollution Act of 1990 (OPA90).
- Through the joint efforts of this committee and the Navigation committee, developed a policy on confined space entry specific to Great Lakes vessels that was acceptable to the Coast Guard. The previous CG policy was based on conditions prevalent on ocean going vessels. Developed procedures acceptable to the Coast Guard in training a crew member as a Shipyard Qualified person.
- The committee in 1994 began development of a Simplified Inspection Program (SIP) as part of the USCG Alternate Inspection Compliance Program. The purpose for this initiative was to reduce the delays at fit out caused by an insufficient number of qualified Coast Guard inspectors. The plan was to have the crew and owners inspect the vessel in accord with approved Coast Guard standards and to record the results. The Coast Guard then would audit the procedures and records to assure compliance. In 1996 a pilot program with several vessels began operations without a Coast Guard fit out inspection.
- Developed a Marine Sanitation Device (MSD) testing and monitoring program in conjunction with the Coast Guard and Seaway authorities that would be uniform for all vessels to assure satisfactory operational compliance.
- Succeeded in modifying USCG requirement to post garbage disposal placards on Great Lakes ships since the placard was only relevant to ocean vessels.

Vessel Personnel and Safety Committee

Chaired by: Bill Satterness, USS Great Lakes Fleet; over time members included Bob Dorn, Dewey Aston, James A. Stiegel, Jim Weakley, James A. Barker Interlake Steamship; Bill Bolton Oglebay Norton; Tom Wiater, Central Marine Logistics; David A. Schultze, Tom Anderson American

Steamship Company; Peter Collins, John Townley Cleveland-Cliffs; Jim Gaskell National Gypsum; Margaret Kane, Gerald Grammenos Cleveland Tankers; Bill Lippy, Cal Durham Bethlehem Steel; Bob Wright, Dean Noonan Hanna Mining; J. (Red) Williams, Daniel J. Cornillie Inland Steel, and many others.

The Vessel Personnel and Safety (VP&S) Committee dealt with all personnel and safety matters, often stemming from Coast Guard proposed rulemaking. The members who were from companies with labor contracts with USW Local 5000 also served on the Job Referral Center (JRC) Committee. Some of the issues and agenda items of VP&S committee overlapped with the JRC. When issues relating to JRC came up, only those JRC members dealt with it. Cooperation and joint action came on issues relating to training.

For a short period of time there was a separate Safety and Health Committee that worked closely with the Vessel Personnel Committee and it was chaired by Thomas S. Anderson, American Steamship Company. This was a time when OSHA sought jurisdiction over American mariners and there was a concentrated effort to define Permissible Exposure Limits (PEL) for marine asbestos hazards.

Officer Training

Officer shortages were a continuous concern of all members as there was a need for technologically prepared officers. This was one reason that LCA operated winter schools to help the crew study for the USCG exams. Eventually the Great Lakes Maritime Academy (GLMA) more than adequately filled that need. In the engineering department, this need was heightened as main engines were converted from triple expansion steam reciprocating and other steam engines to diesel; and more ships were self-unloaders, equipped with bow and stern thrusters, air conditioned quarters and computers. In the deck department, LORAN and RDF were replaced by GPS navigation systems; communication systems went from single side band to cell phones; radars were integrated into sophisticated navigation systems that would almost allow a navigator to operate safely in zero visibility, often without lookouts on the bow.

The MEBA-AMO and the MMP officer unions had their own officer original license and upgrade training facilities paid for by the shipowners through the labor contract. However, occasionally there were courses that were of short duration and Great Lakes ship specific that the committee would arrange for the training to be in the Great Lakes area, at times in Cleveland or at GLMA in Traverse City. Unlicensed training for all the members of Local 5000 union was handled by the JRC Committee and was open to other seamen at times. Training included marlinspike seamanship and rigging for ABs and self-unloader maintenance for QMEDs. This training was held in various cities from Duluth to Traverse City to Cleveland. As needed, video training courses and training texts were prepared by LCA for use onboard ship.

QMED Training with GLMA Instructors

Great Lakes Maritime Academy

The founding and operation of the Great Lakes Maritime Academy (GLMA) deserves a separate book. Suffice it to say that the long term professional training of deck and engine officers was needed to supplement the private study of sailors 'going up through the hawse pipe'. Support for the GLMA was consistent by LCA even during the recessions since it was clear that the officer population was aging. Only in one instance did LCA decide to cut back on financial support for the school; that was in the deep recession of the early 1980s when Ryan was directed to advise the GLMA leadership that LCA would not be able to contribute a substantial financial commitment that was made during the boon days in the late 1970s. However the members were committed to assisting the school in many other ways including payment of a monthly stipend to the cadets while they were in training aboard LCA ships. In 1983 the members paid the cadet stipend into a fund administered by GLMA; thus Cadets received the stipend when they completed the work study requirements.

Each of the GLMA Superintendents and the instructors brought new talents to enrich the education and future success of the students; none were cut from the same mold. It was a great pleasure to know and to work with those who served during my tenure. I did not have a chance to work with Captain Mike Hemmick (1969-1974), Willard Smith (1974) Interim Superintendent or the present leader RADM Gerard "Jerry" Achenbach.

George Rector (Northwestern Michigan College Archives)

RADM James McNulty, Superintendent 1984-1991, (Northwestern Michigan College Archives)

RADM David C. Brown
Superintendent 1992- 1995,
(sunymaritime archives)

RADM John Tanner,
Superintendent
(Northwestern Michigan
College Archives)

The Committee authorized an Officer Supply and Demand Analysis for a period of 5 years and updated it as needed; LCA worked with Marad on these officer shortage studies. Many new officers from Kings Point, New York State Maritime College, Maine and Massachusetts Maritime Academies who landed jobs on Great Lakes ships often did not stay long in the profession. Also the deck officers from those academies needed Great Lakes Pilotage training before they could take a watch. GLMA became the primary source for Great Lakes deck and engine officers. The LCA President chaired the GLMA Board of Visitors and members of the VP&S committee often were on the Board. They advised the school on the curriculum and what future enrollment was projected, a difficult task when it was a three year program and a near impossible task when it became a 4 year fully accredited baccalaureate program. During the recessions it was difficult to place all the cadets onboard the smaller number of operating ships and fit that training time within the GLMA shoreside academic curriculum.

During the Reagan Administration in 1986, the OMB called for the elimination of the annual $100,000 grant to each of the state maritime academies; and the Student Incentive Program (SIP) for students in the

Naval Reserve training was to be cut out. This would have been a critical harm to GLMA; LCA weighed in to support continued payment on the grounds that the graduates served the nation. LCA supported the need for simulators at GLMA that could reduce the shipboard training days required to sit for a license.

Management did not want to exclusively depend upon the union schools that were set up under union contract, and paid for by management. As business conditions changed and the rates of retirements fluctuated, there were apt to be shortages of or an oversupply of officers. Even though the training program at GLMA was three years and later four years, through the advice of the GLMA Board of Visitors, some adjustments of enrollment and course contents could be made. In 1992 LCA, through the Board of Visitors, recommended that GLMA enroll 50 students annually

GLMA Lifeboat training

The GLMA Board of Visitors consisted of marine industry, officer union and government officials. When Ryan took over as President of LCA, his predecessor, Admiral Paul Trimble, was Chairman of the Board. Ryan was immediately elected to succeed Trimble and was reelected for 20 years. The members and GLMA wanted to reduce potential tensions between separate shipping company and union officials and wanted someone such as the LCA President, who was not only a lobbyist for the good of the whole industry but who also did not have a union/management contractual relationship that might influence actions. There were times of tension between the AMO and MMP union officials on the Board and with the company representatives but they always worked disagreements out amicably. Toward the end of his tenure, Ryan advocated that GLMA graduates with industry stature and experience should be on the Board and be considered for the chairmanship.

Other issues that confronted the VP&S committee were:

- The discontinuation of the historic care of merchant seamen by the Marine Hospitals, U.S. Public Health Service, was ordered by the Reagan Administration in 1981. The committee had to establish entry rating physical standards in 1982 that were provided to private medical offices since the Master needed to know that newly employed seaman were fit for duty. The transition for some seamen was smoother where the labor unions had already contracted for medical coverage; although it became much more costly for the ship owners.
- Communicated to the Coast Guard the need to improve the regulations on the Licensing of Pilots in order to consider the Great Lakes as a single extended Pilotage route; the need to allow First Class Pilots to obtain an annual physical anytime in the calendar year rather than within 30 days of the expiration of the pilot's license.
- After the grounding and oil spill on the Exxon Valdez, there were new regulations concerning drug use and alcohol use. These regulations requiring the Captain to conduct testing and to delay the vessel in certain cases were onerous; there were also issues concerning constitutionality of the tests. Commenting on proposed regulations consumed considerable time and expense over a number of years.
- Convinced the Coast Guard to recognize that ships no longer employed 'wipers' but rather employed crew with other job titles such as utility/maintenance or wiper/gateman; these positions had become the engine entry rating for time in grade to qualify for the Oiler or QMED tests. The Coast Guard accepted a fraction of the time in the new job descriptions to allow sailors to take the tests to move up in grade.

- In 1984 LCA recognized that the time had passed for LCA to collect injury and illness reports for all seamen working on LCA vessels, as well as the monthly crew lists. Some illness and accident records were sent to the Marine Index Bureau in New York; the remaining records were destroyed. For a short period a minimal annual report on seamen employed by members was sent to LCA.
- Supported the establishment of a merchant marine training program at Cuyahoga County Community College, Cleveland, and the acquisition of a retired USCG tug for hands on training. This program was only marginally successful and eventually was terminated.

- Worked with the U.S. Customs to amend regulations calling for the seizure of vessels when small quantities of "personal use" drugs were found onboard. Negotiated with the USCG to require drug testing only for new hires, not regular crew members returning to their vessels.

- Communicated to the Departments of State and Labor and the Immigration and Naturalization Service the LCA concerns for the possible redefinition of the work done by seamen in loading and unloading cargo and line-handling to be classified as 'longshore work'.
- Petitioned the Coast Guard to develop minimum physical standards for seamen in light of the passage of the Americans with Disabilities Act. Committee began a study of Bona Fide Occupational Qualifications for all seamen. After detailing essential job functions for 29 shipboard positions, LCA engaged a team of doctors and ergonomics specialists to make trips onboard ships to determine physical force required to perform tasks.
- Opposed the draft legislation that would have assigned vessel personnel safety to the Occupational Safety and Health Administration (OSHA).
- LCA sponsored a Sexual Harassment Seminar and advocated a sexual harassment policy be put in place by each member.
- Through the Safety and Health Committee, LCA opposed the proposed rulemaking of the Coast Guard with respect to Permissible Exposure Limits (PEL) to the marine asbestos hazard. The PEL was much higher than required by OSHA in a shoreside environment.
- Delays in processing crew members' documents by the Coast Guard in Toledo were a factor in crew shortages. Committee petitioned CG Headquarters to increase Toledo staff and to improve their processing equipment. Many of these delays were caused by the need to process Merchant Mariner Documents (MMD) for the casino boats.
- The Soo Library, a branch office of the American Merchant Marine Library Association, was financially supported by the LCA Welfare Plan since 1909 and LCA promoted the use of the library by crew members. However, by 1984 times had changed significantly as to what the crew members wanted in the form of recreation in their time off. The LCA Board decided to discontinue financial support to the Soo Library in 1984 and requested members to support the library unilaterally.
- As needed organized training sessions at GLMA and elsewhere to help mariners upgrade to AB and Oiler. LCA assisted GLMA

in getting USCG approval to not only train seamen but to test and certify eligibility for a MMD.

Great Lakes Job Referral Centers

Dan Cornillie, Inland Steel, chaired.

The Association members, in the early days of the LCA, jealously guarded the prerogative as ship owners to hire and discharge shipboard employees. The history of the late 1800s and the first half of the 1900s were fraught with labor strife as maritime unions attempted to organize the sailors and officers on the Great Lakes ships. Fortunately for Ryan, for the most part major labor strife was in the past for members. All of the companies had labor agreements with one of the unlicensed seamen's unions. What started as the LCA members' hiring hall known as Assembly Rooms went through many name and management changes until it became the Sailors Job Referral Center (JRC). Management membership and funding came only from the companies with labor contracts with the United Steelworkers Union, Local 5000. Only those sailors who wanted jobs on those ships enrolled at the JRC offices in Cleveland, Duluth and Toledo. All other sailors who were members of the officer unions (American Maritime Officers, MEBA District II and Masters, Mates and Pilots) and the unlicensed sailor unions (Seafarers International Union and National Maritime Union) received their shipboard assignments as the union contracts outlined.

The United Steelworkers Union did not wish to set up hiring halls or training centers as the other unions preferred. LCA JRC organized the training needed to meet shortages of certain ratings, such as Able Bodied Seaman (AB) or Qualified Member of the Engine Department (QMED).

In 1983 there were only three JRCs open; Duluth, Jack Saunders; Toledo, Bill Kishel and Cleveland, Jack Rose. Jack Rose died in 1985 and John (Jack) Saunders, died in 1986. Bill Kishel took over the Cleveland office when Jack Rose retired and the Toledo JRC was closed. When Jack Saunders died, the Duluth JRC was closed and all JRC activities were consolidated under Bill Kishel in Cleveland. When the JRC operations were discontinued in April 1992, Bill, who had served JRC for 17 years, returned to sailing on the Lakes. LCA staff continued to coordinate the phasing out of the files and training with the help of LCA staff Eileen Hout and AIOA staff Joy Earlywine and Jeff Gordon.

Vessel Construction and Conversions 1983-2002

During the period 1983-2002 there were no new vessel deliveries to U.S. flag Great Lakes shipowners. The last major deliveries were in 1981 when two thousand footers, Columbia Star and William J. DeLancey and the very efficient river class boat the American Republic and the Amoco Oil Company Integrated Tug Barge M/V Amoco Michigan/Amoco Great Lakes were delivered in 1982.

During this period there were conversions of a number of vessels to self-unloaders and the repowering from coal to oil, steam to diesel; automated boiler controls; lengthening and conversion to self-unloaders; and the installation of bow and stern thrusters continued as needed. Older ships no longer needed were scrapped or sold to Canadian interests; the Cliffs Victory was sold to Chinese interests.

In the 20 year period only one LCA member vessel was lost. On September 16, 1990 the tanker Jupiter, while unloading in the Saginaw River, suffered an explosion during which one crew member died when he jumped into the river. The vessel was a total loss and was scrapped.

MV Jupiter fire 1990

Chapter Nine

By James H. I. Weakley, President, 2003-Present

James H. I. Weakley

The Lake Carriers' Association continues serving the needs of the American Flag ship owners on the Great Lakes. The challenges are many.

On January 15, 2003, I was fortunate to follow in the wake of great men, master mariners and leaders of industry, serving as the next president of Lake Carriers' Association. Many of George's accomplishments continue to pay dividends today. His vision and ability to lead the association through challenging times serves as a guiding example for me and other maritime professionals. As gracious in retirement as he was during the transition, George Ryan asked me to provide a summary of the issues and challenges faced during my twelve years at "at the helm."

My review will take a topical approach, since most of LCA's goals take years of effort. Before I begin, I must note that while LCA's role is to take the lead in addressing the challenges faced by our industry, our success reflects the involvement of our member companies, collaboration with other organizations and the support of our legislators and their capable staff. Policy decisions, funding allocation and prioritization all take place in our nation's Capital. Vital to our success has been the Great Lakes Congressional delegation, most notably Senator Carl Levin, (D-MI, retired), Congressman Dave Obey (D-WI, retired), Congressman Jim Oberstar (D-MN, deceased), Congresswoman Marcy Kaptur (D-OH) and Congresswoman Candice Miller (R-MI, retired). Without them and the dedicated support of such talented and brilliant staffers as John Cullather (retired Democratic staff director of the House Coast Guard Subcommittee), Paul Carver (retired from Congressman Obey's personal office) and Alice Yates (Senator Levin's personal office until his retirement) very little of our work would have produced significant results. A sincere Great Lakes Salute is also due to Mark Ruge, lobbyist with the law firm K&L Gates. A native of Menominee, MI, he has a passion for the Great Lakes and remains grounded in the Midwest ethos and work ethic. His relationships on Capitol Hill and understanding of the inner workings of government proved invaluable to furthering the goals of the Lake Carriers' Association, promoting the U.S. Merchant Marine and defending the Jones Act.

Much of LCA's time and resources have focused on the Great Lakes dredging crisis. Decades of inadequate funding for the Army Corps of Engineers' (ACOE) dredging program on the Lakes reached a crisis point in the late 1990s. Previously high water levels plunged so low that they no longer masked the lack of maintenance dredging. For every inch of navigational depth lost, a thousand-footer forfeits 250 tons of cargo. For some trades, vessels had lost well over a foot of water. Starting in 2005, increasing the Corps' Lakes dredging budget has been a top LCA priority. Historically, the Great Lakes Port Authorities had advocated for their needs; however, there was no advocate for the connecting channels, ports or docks not represented by a port authority, or the overall system. After the Lakes and Rivers Division (LRD) was formed in 1995, the President's budget for the Great Lakes operations and maintenance (O&M), which includes dredging, remained flat through 2012. In fact, in nominal dollars (not adjusted for inflation), the President's proposed budget for Great Lakes O&M for 2012 was only 5% higher than it was in 1995. This was not the case for the national ACOE budget or for O&M for other parts of the country.

Recognizing the Great Lakes Navigation System was in a death spiral, we knew something had to be done. LCA implemented a multifaceted approach to solving the crisis. At the national level, LCA's focus was on expanding the ACOE budget for O&M. LCA immediately recognized that the best chance for the Great Lakes to receive more of the budgetary pie was to increase the size of the total pie and this could best be achieved by working with other vested interests. We reached out to other maritime trade associations, labor unions, manufacturers, shippers, and port authorities in the Great Lakes region and in other parts of the country. We found many interested and willing partners who also saw the need to address our failing navigational infrastructure. To help support our efforts, LCA was one of the founding members of an organization called Restore America's Maritime Promise (RAMP). Working with other organizations, LCA sought additional funding from the Harbor Maintenance Trust Fund (HMTF), a user fee collected by the Federal government to maintain our coastal waterways. At the time, the HMTF had a surplus of over $3 billion (currently, it is approaching $10 billion). Through a series of proposed laws (I testified before Congress several time on the subject), LCA and RAMP put pressure on the Office of Management and Budget (OMB) and Congressional Appropriators to spend more of the money collected on the purpose for which it was collected. As a result of these efforts the ACOE's Navigation Business Line continues to see significant increases. The goal is to increase spending the annual revenues from the HMTF from 50% to 100% by the year 2025, a significant increase. The size of the national navigation budget pie has increased and should continue on that trend.

The next step in addressing the dredging crisis was to increase the funding for the Great Lakes Navigation System. Recognizing that claiming a larger slice of the available pie was a task greater than the resources of

LCA, we enlisted the support of the Great Lakes Maritime Task Force (GLMTF) a labor/management coalition representing broader interests than LCA. Expanding their focus from defending the Jones Act to include infrastructure maintenance allowed the GLMTF to expand and include shippers and port authorities so that it could truly speak for the entire navigation system. Fortunately, shippers and port authorities needed little convincing that the status quo was negating the efficiencies of Great Lakes shipping and within a remarkably short time, GLMTF's membership had more than doubled.

Engaging the Great Lakes delegation in Washington was critical to our effort to add regional funding and earmarks for specific projects. Using this approach, in 2008, the Corps dredging budget for the Lakes had increased to a level which allowed the Corps for the first time to both remove the sediment that builds up over the course of a year (about 3.3 million cubic yards), and, begin to whittle away at the backlog, which then stood at 18 million cubic yards. However, the Lakes dredging budget for FY09 was cut by nearly $50 million. It was clear ending the dredging crisis would be a long-term effort and demanded an additional strategy for the President's budget process. LCA hired a lobbying firm specializing in the ACOE to help increase the frequency and scope of our work on the budget process at the Corps District, Division, Headquarters, Assistant Secretary of the Army for Civil Works, and OMB, while continuing our efforts on the Hill.

The Water Resources Reform and Development Act (WRRDA) of 2014 resulted in two major achievements. One of those milestones had national implications and the other regional. That bill sets the stage to adequately fund our national navigational infrastructure by setting targets for the Federal government to incrementally increase expenditures from the HMTF until they reach 100 percent of annual receipts in 2025. Another key element of WRRDA14 was the provision designating the "Great Lakes Navigation System." Up until that point, the Great Lakes and connecting channels were not considered a navigation system and the 60 Federally maintained ports on the Great Lakes were pitted against one another, other coastal ports and river systems in the battle for maintenance dollars, whereas the inland river ports were treated as systems (Mississippi and Ohio River for example). The lack of a system designation has been a significant disadvantage to the Great Lakes. For example, the Ohio River, because it was viewed as a system and not treated as a series of individual ports, received twice as much funding per ton of cargo than the Great Lakes Navigation System did.

This decade long fight resulted in significant benefits for the Great Lakes. In FY14 and FY15, the Corps received dredging dollars to reduce the backlog in both years. There's much to be done; more than 17 million cubic yards of sediment still choke our Great Lakes ports and waterways. If the Federal government keeps incrementally increasing expenditures from the HMTF, the dredging crisis could be a thing of the past. The FY16 President's budget for Great Lakes Navigation is the largest we have ever seen (tracking back to 1995). In fact, the President's proposed budget for Great Lakes O&M for 2016 was 40% higher than it was for 2012 (46% higher than it was for 1995).

Efforts to build a second Poe-sized lock began during George Ryan's tenure and remain a priority for LCA. George was instrumental in getting the project authorized in the Water Resources Development Act of 1986, which required local sponsors to share in the cost of new construction. LCA hoped to have that requirement removed and in 2007 Congress authorized it at full Federal expense. Yet, another hurdle has to be cleared, namely the lock's benefit/cost (B/C) ratio. When the Corps conducted its study on the need for the lock, it mistakenly assumed that the railroads could step in and move the cargo (at no increased cost) if the Poe Lock was incapacitated for a lengthy period of time. Today, our nation's railroads are straining to meet current demand. It would not be possible for the railroads to handle the 60 million tons that typically move through the Poe Lock. Furthermore, many steel mills and some power plants lack rail access. It is no exaggeration to say the Soo Locks are the single point of failure that threatens the future of Great Lakes shipping and North American manufacturing. The Corps also projected significantly lower cargo volumes and that all new vessels built would be able to transit the MacArthur lock (implicit in this assumption was that the Poe-restricted vessels would become less important and perhaps even replaced by MacArthur sized vessels).

The above assumptions led to a B/C ratio below 1.0, which makes the project not fundable in the President's Budget request. After years of LCA objecting to the flawed B/C ratio, the Corps yielded to Congressional pressure and agreed to do a "sensitivity analysis" of the B/C ratio. While the results of that analysis are not known at this time, given the effort and the amount of time since the B/C ratio was calculated, the Corps is seeking funding for an "Economic Re-evaluation Report" (ERR). Fortuitously, the Department of Homeland Security is currently completing a report on the importance of the Soo Locks from a national security perspective. That study is not yet finalized either; however, I do believe that we are moving in the right direction. Suffice it to say that the prospects for building a second Poe-sized lock have never been better.

Promoting adequate Coast Guard icebreaking resources has been another constant over the past twelve years. In 2003, we made an official request for the USCG to transfer an additional 140' icebreaking tug from the East Coast to the Great Lakes. Ten years later, the USCGC MORRO BAY (WTG-106) was transferred from New London, CT, to Cleveland, OH. The following summer the ship sailed to the Coast Guard Yard in Baltimore, MD to become the first of its class to undergo a major rehabilitation and life extension program. This program has been another of our goals as that class of vessel has aged and become significantly less reliable.

The winters of 2013/2014 and 2014/2015 have been so severe that it is clear that the U.S. Coast Guard lacks adequate icebreaking resources on the Lakes. Voyages that should have taken 62 hours stretched out to 11 days. Cargos that should have been loaded in 6 hours took days. Total cargo movement plunged and in the winter of 2013/2014, LCA members suffered more than $6 million in ice-related damage to their vessels.

Given the impacts of the past two winters and the questionable reliability of the current Coast Guard icebreaking fleet, LCA undertook the mission of advocating for a second heavy icebreaker as capable as the USCGC MACKINAW (WLBB-30). Fortunately, the House's Coast Guard Authorization Act of 2015 includes a provision that authorizes the Commandant to design and build a new icebreaker for the Great Lakes fleet. The Senate must concur, and then the difficult appropriation process must begin. It is estimated that the vessel will cost more than $150 million. That's a lot of money in this fiscal environment, but the cost of not building the vessel could be even greater. It is estimated that the cargo that did not move during the winter of 2013/2014 cost the economy more than $700 million in business revenue and 3,800 jobs. The delays suffered in the winter of 2014/2015 cost another 2,000 jobs and $356 million in economic activity.

Ballast water regulation remains complicated and confusing. Under the current Transport Canada, Coast Guard and EPA regulations oceangoing vessels entering the Great Lakes have to conduct ballast water exchange and will eventually have to install ballast water treatment systems. Those regulations also exempt lakers (vessels operating west of Anticosti Island in the Gulf of St. Lawrence) from installing ballast water treatment systems. However, it is worth noting that EPA regulations do not grant laker status to vessels built after 2009 (this currently applies to one U.S.-flag laker). It is also worth noting that two Great Lakes states require lakers to treat their ballast water, by 2018, if there is a USCG approved system available. Currently there are no USCG approved systems that will work on lakers and it is unlikely there will be by 2018. Lakers are required to continue to employ the current Best Management Practices.

The EPA's Vessel General Permit (VGP) is renewed every five years and the next iteration (in 2019) could expand the treatment requirement to all LCA vessels. The states have the right to do that now under the VGP rulemaking process. The regulatory process is so complicated that every five years we must monitor and participate in at least one federal and ten state ballast water rulemakings (MN and WI have two regulations and permits that must be renewed). One state published a proposed rule the Wednesday before Thanksgiving and closed the comment period the Monday after Thanksgiving. We often find ourselves challenging a final rule in court or just as often defending the regulator against a legal challenge brought by someone else. In some cases we have done both simultaneously. This regulatory patchwork quilt is the reason we support a single federal rule regulating ballast water. The legislation has been proposed during this and three previous Congresses. We continue to work this issue hard and hope for a reasonable resolution in the near future.

Canada has further muddied the waters by proposing that its implementation of the International Maritime Organization's Ballast Water Convention impose a transit standard, i.e., that they intend to apply the IMO discharge standard to all vessels entering Canadian waters, not just those ballasting/deballasting in Canadian waters. We believe Canada is the only country in the world requiring the installation of equipment on vessels with no intention of using the equipment in its waters. What's frustrating is that when New York proposed a transit standard, Canada objected vehemently and we actively supported Canada's objection. New York eventually withdrew its transit standard, but as of this writing, Canada's plan is to implement a transit standard, and since U.S.-flag lakers transit Canadian waters while moving cargo between U.S. ports, Canadian regulations could well spell the end for the American Great Lakes fleet. There is no way for our vessels to physically comply with the requirement. It is the equivalent of a regulatory blockage of U.S. Great Lakes ports by the Government of Canada. We are actively working this issue on both sides of the border and will continue to do so.

Defense of the Jones Act consumed much of George's time in the mid and late-1990s. Our national defense policy, and that of many other maritime nations, requires domestic cargo to be moved on vessels owned by Americans, built in America and crewed by Americans. There are, and always will be people willing to sell out our long-term security for their short-term economic gain, but the most active of the recent or current threats have not been specifically related to the Jones Act trades on the Lakes. In defense of the Jones Act, I serve on the Board of the American Maritime Partnership, the Washington, DC-based national coalition that protects our cabotage laws and moves in lockstep with the other segments of the U.S. merchant marine.

Many new issues have surfaced in my twelve years at LCA. The last minute addition of the Great Lakes to the "North American Emissions Control Area" (ECA) by the EPA would have retired all the U.S.-flag steamships by 2012. The EPA's 2009 proposed rule, during the depths of the Great Recession, would have required steamships to repower with internal combustion engines or use a type of fuel that would have made them prone to boiler explosions. At a cost of $20 million per vessel to repower, most, if not all of those vessels would have been scrapped with little time or capital to replace the carrying capacity. Implementation of the ECA on the Great Lakes would have also required internal combustion vessels using a medium grade fuel to switch to a more expensive lower sulfur diesel. Given the short time for implementation and limited distribution of that type of diesel in the Great Lakes vessels would have been idled due to a lack of fuel. At the last possible minute, an "appropriations rider" prevented the

EPA from implementing the requirement on the steamers. Once the dust settled, LCA and the EPA negotiated a temporary fuel availability waiver for those vessels taking on fuel in a port where the lower sulfur grade was not available. We also developed an innovative program to provide incentives to convert steamships to internal combustion engines. During a limited window of opportunity, any of those thirteen steamers in use on the Great Lakes could repower to internal combustion and be allowed to burn the higher sulfur fuel for a limited amount of time. The cost savings in fuel help justify the project. The environmental benefits of the conversion began immediately and they significantly increased when the repowered vessels were eventually required to burn only the lower sulfur fuel. Several of the steamers have since repowered under this program and several others plan on it.

We still have plenty of challenges to deal with. Many of our Congressional champions are no longer in office. Foreign steel dumping is once again threatening our industry. The U.S. and Canada are moving away from coal for power generation and that has had a major impact on that cargo. Still, I believe more than ever that Great Lakes shipping is here to stay. The Corps estimates waterborne commerce on the Lakes saves its customers $3.6 billion per year in transportation costs compared to rail and truck. That's no exaggeration or accident. Great Lakes shipping is safe, efficient and the greenest mode of transportation and despite the many challenges, there is much to look forward to.

Very respectfully,

James H. I. Weakley
President

Detailed Acknowledgements of those who supported the author and the LCA

I am in debt to all those who helped me and the LCA during my tenure. LCA members worked closely with each other solving technical and operating problems even to the extent that they shared spare parts; they were very trustworthy. Their word was their bond. They negotiated, concluded with a handshake and a minimum of paperwork, even trading cargos at times. I can never remember all of them; I include names as follows of some of these people in no particular order of importance. As I have prepared this history of LCA, their names surfaced and I was pleased to recall our interactions and friendships.

American Steamship Company
Ward Fuller, Ned Smith, Jerry Welsch, Tom Anderson, David Schultz, Mike Scheidt, Captain Mike Elson, Jim Wager, Lou Ervin
Bethlehem Steel
Duke LeCompte, Cal Durham, Jim O'Carroll
Cleveland Cliffs
C. Tom Moore, John Horton, John Townley, Jim Peters, Pete Collins, Dana Byrne, John Kelley
Cleveland Tankers
Gerry Grammenos
Erie Sand
Sid Smith, Dan Mania
Ford
Jim Comerford

Inland Steel
Riley O'Brien, Dan Cornillie
Hanna Mining
John Manning, Mike Travis, Bob Wright
Huron Cement/Inland Lakes Management
Jim Gaskell, Wally Watkins, Captain Jim Daleski
Interlake/Pickands Mather
James R. Barker, Bob McInnis, Bob Dorn, Dewey Aston, Dave Groh, John Hopkins, Lou Mensen, Jim Stiegel, Dave Anderson, Mark Barker
Litton
Ralph Biggs
Oglebay Norton
Rennie Thompson, Fred White, Stu Theis, Frank Castle, Ed Jacobsen, Dick Feldtz, Tom Green, Mike Siragusa, Dale Miller, Mark Rohn,
USS Great Lakes Fleet
Bill Buhrmann, Neil Stalker, Fred Cummings, Ralph Bertz, Bill Satterness, Dave Van Brunt
American Bureau of Shipping
George Palmer, Bob Nash, Tom Stewart

Dominion Marine Association, later named Canadian Shipowners Association
Admiral Bob Timbrell, T. Norman Hall, Don Morrison, Rejean (Reggie) Lanteigne
Canadian Shipowners
Jack Leitch, Peter Cresswell, Rob Paterson, Ray Johnston
Senators and Representatives

There were many elected officials whose understanding of our maritime industry needs and their subsequent legislative help was essential. The list would be too long to note them all. Not unexpected, the most attentive ears and help came from the Minnesota, Michigan, Wisconsin and Ohio delegations and in particular their staff. Some of those who were always there to listen included the following:

Senators John Glenn, Mike DeWine, George Voinovich, Carl Levin, and Debbie Stabenow
Representatives Jim Oberstar, Dave Obey, Walter B. Jones, Bob Davis, Bart Stupak, Vern Ehlers, Pete Visclosky, Marcy Kaptur, David Bonier, Steve LaTourette, Mary Rose Oakar

Congressional staff that provided the most assistance included John Cullather (Oberstar), Paul Carver (Obey), Joy Mulinex (Senator Levin), Carl Bentzel (Senate Commerce and Transportation Staff). There were many others, too numerous to mention.

United States Coast Guard

I was fortunate to arrive in Cleveland to open the Marad Great Lakes Region office when Admiral Jim Gracey was the Ninth District Commander. I worked with him on the Winter Navigation Demonstration Program; thus began my utmost respect for all the District Commanders that followed. We became good friends with many of them including, Jim Gracey, Bob Scarborough (a Kings Point graduate), Tony Fugaro, Henry Bell, 'Dan' Danielsen, Dick Applebaum, Rudy Peschel, Gerry Woolever, and Jim Hull. Cornelia and I got to know their wives and often shared meals at each other's home. Some retired from the Ninth while others went on to higher positions including Commandant as did Jim Gracey. Fortunately I had the opportunity to know other Admirals, some also who made it to become Commandant. Regardless of their assignment they were great leaders. Some included Bill Rae, Mike Benkert, Jim Card, Bill Kime, and Jim Loy.

Reunion of previous 9th District Commanders, Back row Admirals Applebaum, Gracey, Peschel, McGowan, front row Admirals Bell, Hull, Fugaro

I also gained the utmost respect for the many men in the Coast Guard who made it to Captain; not everyone could make it to Flag rank, and those who made it to Captain had already proven themselves as leaders of men and specialists in their field. Many of them had served in several of the Great Lakes ports. It was wonderful to work with these experienced leaders when they came to the District office. I will only name a few of the Captains and I won't even try to list those other dedicated officers and enlisted men who served on the Great Lakes—in particular on the Cutters breaking ice and performing buoy operations in all weather.

U.S. Coast Guard Officers who served as Captain
Captains Dave Freeborn, Pat Gerrity, Gordon Peche, Jerry Foley, Randy Helland, Jimmy Hobaugh, Arnold Litteken, Tom Daley, Jon Nickerson, Rich Goodchild, Rick Rooth, John Bastic, Chuck Millradt, John Bruce (who later served on Capitol Hill), Carl Swedberg, John Mihlbauer, Lorne Thomas, Kurt Carlson, Paul Pluta and many others. The civilian Captain who worked for the USCG and who understood the navigation system on the Great Lakes the most was Captain Skip Skuggen.

Corps of Engineers

In the Great Lakes there were many Corps officers and civilians doing a magnificent job as long as they had the congressional appropriations to carry out the studies and to operate dredges and locks and contract for other necessary work to keep the ports and channels open for commercial navigation. The main Corps offices were in Buffalo, Detroit, Chicago and the Soo with many other offices in ports. While they all reported up to the General in Chicago, my work was generally with the Colonels in Buffalo, Chicago and in particular in Detroit and the Area Engineer at the Soo.

Detroit District Engineers in particular who I recall were Colonels Mel Remus, Ray Beurket, Jr., John Glass, Dick Kandra, Brian Ohlinger, Randy Buck and the Area Engineer in charge at the Soo, Harold Lawson. There were so many Corps civilians who did a great job I hesitate to mention any of them.

Memberships in Organizations and Coalitions that Helped the LCA Mission

There were many in which was I was a member or an officer. They included: American Bureau of Shipping, American Iron Ore Association, GLMA Board of Visitors, Great Lakes Maritime Task Force, Maritime Cabotage Task Force, National Cargo Bureau, National Waterways Conference, Seaway Review, Propeller Club, and USMMA Advisory Board.

Organizations with whom LCA Needed to Confer/Coalesce/Coordinate.

American Association of Port Authorities, American Great Lakes Ports, American Iron and Steel Institute, American Petroleum Institute, American Shipbuilding Association, American Waterways Operators, Chamber of Shipping of America, Dredging Contractors Association, Maritime Institute of Research and Development, National Waterways Conference, Northeast-Midwest Institute, Transportation Institute and Great Lakes Towing.

Ports Executives

I developed cordial working relationships with all the port directors and in some cases real friendship. Those I remember most vividly are Davis

Helberg, Ray Skelton, Jim Hartung, John McWilliams, John Sulpizio, Noel Painchaud, and Steve Pfeiffer; there were many others whose company I enjoyed and who worked closely with LCA.

Maritime Administration

As I had a background working in the maritime industry and for Marad, I had a wonderful rapport and working relationship with all of the Administrators and many of the staff; in particular Andrew E. Gibson, later Assistant Secretary of Commerce for Maritime Affairs (who incidentally appointed me captain of a ship while I was with Grace Line), Warren Leback, Maritime Administrator (who gave me my first job as 3rd Mate with the Grace Line following my graduation from Kings Point), and many others including Al Herberger, John Graykowski, Howard Waters, Admiral Harold Shear, John Gaughan, Bill Schubert, James Saari, Gary Misch, Ron Rasmus and Al Ames.

St. Lawrence Seaway Development Corp. and St. Lawrence Seaway Authority

Dave Oberlin, Albert Jacquez and Bill O'Neil were great administrators who worked with LCA on common objectives.

Seaway Review Harbor House Publishers

Jacques LesStrang, Michelle Cortright, David Knight

Great Lakes Commission

Colonel Hank Goodsell, Mike Donahue, David Knight, and Steve Thorp

Unions

Charlie Crangle, Mel Pelfrey, Tim Mohler, Dan Smith, Karen Myers, Tom Bethel, John Baker, Jack Duff and Byron Kelly

USMMA

Admirals Tom King and Joseph Stewart

GLMA

George Rector, Jim McNulty, John Tanner, Dave Brown, Mike Hochscheidt, Jerry Williams, Bob Mason, Louise Wilkes

So Many Others

Paul C. LaMarre was the man we relied upon to graphically depict the ships on the Great Lakes; thanks PC for all you did. John Wellington at the Soo was the man to turn to when there were any problems at the Soo or in the St. Marys River. John was always a good friend to many. I shall not forget the help and friendship of Mark Ruge our lobbyist in Washington; he opened many doors.

Please forgive me as I stop here without mentioning other organizations and the people who operated them so well. There were many great people who worked tirelessly in government agencies doing jobs authorized by congress, too frequently without adequate recognition and praise. They deserved accolades not discouraging words.

Photograph Acknowledgements and Recognition of Support in writing this book

I thank Michelle Cortright, Harbor House Publishing, for her continued support and encouragement to find a publisher to complete this work.

I also give gratitude to those who reviewed the book, some of whom sent comments to be included in the front section of this book.

My very sincere thanks are extended to the many people and organizations who took the time to help me obtain the photos and other information in this book. I hope I don't overlook someone but this is my list. They include: Lake Carriers' Association, Al Hart, Bob Graham, Historical Collections of the Great Lakes, Bowling Green State University, Roger LeLievre and BoatNerd, Jerome Welsch, Peter Groh, Lurene Buhrmann, Davis Helberg, Wes Harkins, Richard Bibby, Gil Porter, Jane McNulty Cook, Hal Henderson; Mark Barker and Kathy Feketik Interlake-Steamship Company, Diane Tokarczyk, American Steamship Company, Carrie Sowden, National Museum of the Great Lakes, Jerry Achenbach and Ann Swaney, Great Lakes Maritime Academy, Canada Parks, Library and Archives Canada, Chippewa County Historical Society, Lighthouse Friends, Michael Schwartz Library Cleveland State University, Don Lee Sandusky Register, Wikipedia Commons, the U.S. Coast Guard and the Corps of Engineers, and the Library of Congress Archives.

Appendix 1

Obituaries

Since the founding of the Association, the tradition of honoring the many leaders in Great Lakes shipping, and in particular, those who led the LCA and its committees, by placement of a special recognition or an obituary of their life in the Annual Report lasted until 1985. After 1985 the members were informed of the death of many of the past leaders through a notation in the Advisor; however the notice was hardly a lasting tribute sufficient to honor their contribution to LCA and to the industry. It was an action Ryan later regretted as he reflected on the contributions to maritime history that these men created. Cutting back on expenses, concentrating on the essentials, the 'bean counter' mentality prevailed and another tradition passed.

Since all of the LCA Presidents witnessed the passing of the many giants who built Great Lakes shipping and the raw material mines that provided them with the cargo to build America, I believed it essential to include a few words about each man and the three women: Anna C. Minch, Sophia Minch Steinbrenner and Ruth E. Webster. Most of their names are well known to Great Lakes history buffs. These leaders impacted the policies and action of the LCA leadership in direct and indirect ways. The full history of each of these leaders will need to wait for another time; only their names and a few words are possible here.

Obituaries as contained in the LCA Annual Reports

The 1900 Annual Report laments the death of **Captain Thomas Wilson** of Cleveland, one of the founders of the Lake Carriers' Association and a former President. Also noted were the deaths of **David Whitney** of Detroit and **F. N. La Salle** of Duluth.

The 1901 Annual Report notes the deaths of two of its most prominent members, **David Carter** and **William E. Fitzgerald**.

The 1902 Annual Report notes the deaths of **William H. Mack, Patrick Smith and Captain J. T. Hutchinson**, a member since organization of LCA. A special note and long and flowery tribute was included recognizing the death of **Senator James McMillan** "... His untimely death robs this association of one of its strongest and most loyal members."

The 1903 Annual Report has no mention of deaths during the year.

The 1904 Annual Report stated that "With grateful hearts and thanks to Divine Province we are happy to report that there were no deaths among our members for the entire year 1904"

The 1905 Annual Report stated "A Divine Providence has seen fit, during the year just closed, to take unto Himself the President of one of our constituent companies, **Mrs. Anna C. Minch**, President of the Kinsman Transit Company... at the ripe age of eighty-six years." The article continues with the history of her becoming President and notes that '... with the assistance of her son-in-law, Mr. Henry Steinbrenner, as manager of her interests...' she gave personal attention to the business.

1906 Annual Report has no mention of deaths during the year.

In the 1907 Annual Report there is a section labeled Deaths wherein there is note of the deaths of **Thomas Adams and Captain Marcus M. Drake**. **Adams** built a steamer, the Tom Adams, in 1879 that was the largest steamer on the lakes. **Drake**, born in 1835, began sailing at the age of sixteen. When the Civil War broke out he was sailing as Captain but enlisted in the army as a private and rose to the rank of first lieutenant. Both men were members of LCA.

In the 1908 Annual report there is a section memorializing the **Honorable Peter White**, a man whose life accomplishments, particularly in the Upper Peninsula, filled at least one book. Another section of the report is titled Obituary and it details the lives of **James Corrigan and Frank L. Vance**. **Corrigan** was a member of the Cleveland Vessel Owners' Association and was instrumental in the consolidation of CVOA into the Lake Carriers' Association in which he became President in 1894 and later a long-term member of the Executive Committee. He was remembered as a captain of industry whose character was plain, blunt, straightforward and intensely loyal to his friends. **Vance** had an enviable reputation for honesty and square dealing; many LCA members received their training while in his employment.

The 1909 Annual Report notes the deaths of three members; **Gibson L. Douglass**, Vice President, Western Transit Company, Buffalo; **Lafayette S. Sullivan**, Toledo, owner and manager of some of the largest steamships and a self-made man, modest, retiring, of strict integrity, a friend of the poor, a man whom the world was better for his living in it; and, **Abram W. Colton**, Toledo, former President of the Toledo Board of Trade, manager and director of the Detroit & Toledo Steamboat Line—it was said that the community lost a pattern of Christian manhood, the poor a steadfast friend, and a delightful companion.

1910 Annual Report has no mention of deaths during the year.

The 1911 Annual Report contains an obituary for **Thomas T. Morford**, Buffalo, a member of LCA and in addition to his transportation industry achievements, it was said that he was genial, and while strong, gentle, and a loving man, kindly in every impulse, wholly sincere, generous and just; **Michael J. Cummings**, Oswego, who was born in Ireland and became owner of many canalers, barks, schooners, and at the end he built steamships. He was praised as a man of high ideals, modest and retiring in disposition, a firm believer in the teaching of his church and much more. Others noted in death were **John C. Shaw**, Detroit Admiralty lawyer connected with many lake lines; **F.M. Osborne** who was president of a dozen large corporations and a director of as many more including steamship, coal mining, and dock and banking companies.

The Association noted in the 1912 Annual Report that five members passed away. Most prominent was **Captain J.J.H. Brown**, originally from Buffalo, who was a member of the Executive Committee and past President of LCA. In his youth he sailed around the world on whalers and merchant ships before coming to Cleveland at age 20. On the lakes he became a sailor, mate, master and owner of schooners. As a member of LCA he made frequent trips to Washington to lobby for the betterment of lake navigation. He was a half-brother of Harvey D. Goulder. Others who died in 1912 included **Frank W. Gilchrist**, a principle in the lumbering business and the Gilchrist Transportation Company and three term mayor of Alpena, MI; **Captain David Vance**, one of the youngest masters on the lakes, operator of vessel brokerage firms and was instrumental in building steel steamships; **Captain J.J. Rardon** who shipped out as sailor, mate and master and was manager of a lake freighter at the time of his death; and, **W. B. Davock** who started his career in the pig iron and iron ore industry and later he managed the Shenango Steamship Company.

Separate attention in the 1912 Annual Report was given to the deaths of **Charles T. Harvey**, builder of the first lock at the Sault, and **Franklin J. Firth**, Philadelphia, President of LCA in 1899. In 1852, after Congress authorized a grant of land for the person who would build a canal around the falls of the St. Marys River, **Harvey** was recuperating from an illness in the Upper Peninsula. He appreciated the wealth of the land around Lake Superior and the benefit of a canal to the lower lakes. While not an engineer he was placed in charge of construction and the lock was built within two years. **Firth** drafted the constitution for the Lake Carriers' Association and in 1899 became the President of the consolidated Cleveland Shipowner's Association and LCA. He did not remain an active member of LCA since his home and business interests were in the Philadelphia area.

The 1913 Annual Report included the obituaries of **Captain John W. Westcott**, Captain **Edward Morton** and **Captain John G. Keith**. **Westcott** was drawn to the water in his youth and he received his master's papers when he was 20; in 1870 he was considered the youngest Master of a vessel on the Great Lakes. He established range lights at Grosse Point and the first lightship in Lake St. Clair and he created the Detroit Marine Reporting Station and the present day mail boat. **Morton** was a pioneer navigator on the lakes, as a lad he enlisted in the Navy to serve during the Civil War. He went deep sea sailing all around the globe until upon returning to the Lakes he sailed schooners as master and came ashore in management where he became Vice President of Wilson Transit Company, a Director of LCA and a member of the Welfare Committee. **Keith** also sailed on the lakes early and received his master papers at the age of 22.

After sailing in all capacities including master, he came ashore in the insurance and lake transportation business in Chicago, and in 1900 he was one of the LCA Vice Presidents.

The 1914 Annual Report Obituary section reports the deaths of **Captain Joseph Sellwood, Alfred Noble** and **General Garrett J. Lydecker**. **Captain Sellwood**, Duluth, was born in Wales, worked the tin mines, and immigrated to Michigan where he worked the copper mines and then moved into managing iron ore mines, banks and ultimately became a ship owner. **Noble** was a civil engineer who was in charge of improvements in the St. Marys Fall Canal and St. Marys River. He was a man of rugged simplicity and adverse to any form of ostentation. **Lydecker**, a graduate of West Point served in the Civil War and at the Military Academy; his contributions to the Great Lakes navigation infrastructure started in 1869 and continued as District Engineer in Detroit when he helped design the Livingstone Channel and was superintendent for the completion of the Poe Lock. He retired in 1907.

The 1915 Annual Report honored the lives of **Edward Smith, Captain John Manson** and **Hugh Ross**. **Smith** was a member of the LCA Executive Committee and President of the Great Lakes Towing Company and the American Shipbuilding Company. It was said that he was genial, kindly and courteous as well as respected for his knowledge of Great Lakes shipping. **Captain John Manson**, Amherstburg, Canada, was keeper of the Canadian lighthouse at Colchester Reef. Upon his retirement he received the Imperial gold service medal from the British government. Ross was born in Scotland and served in the British Navy before immigrating to Canada where he worked in the department of fisheries; later he aided the survivors of the Johnstown flood and sought gold in the Yukon. Ross was employed as an LCA commissioner helping the Welfare Plan place men on the ships.

In the 1916 Annual Report there is a photograph and a special page as a memorial for LCA Vice President **Jasper Holmes Sheadle**. In 1890 Sheadle was employed by the Cleveland Cliffs Iron Co. as Secretary and was in charge of ore sales and lake transportation; and as the years went on he assumed many other responsibilities with Cleveland Cliffs. He was elected LCA Vice President in 1901; and was a member of the Executive Committee since 1907 and Chairman of the Welfare Committee since inception in 1909. The obituary continues noting his private life was unspotted and unselfish and he was a warm hearted and public spirited citizen.

The 1916 Obituary section honors the life of **John P. Reiss, James Chase Wallace, Ralph D. Williams** and **William H. Hill. Reiss** was an LCA member who died at his desk at the age of 41. Born in Sheboygan he spent his entire working career in the coal and vessel business becoming Vice President of the C. Reiss Coal Company, Vice President and Treasurer of the Reiss Steamship Co. and later VP of Peavey Steamship Company. **Wallace** became a pioneer among shipbuilders, just as his father had been. He worked for Globe Iron Works, Cleveland and when the iron steamer Onoko began operation he sailed on her as first assistant engineer. Later, he and his father organized the Cleveland Shipbuilding Company and he also became President of American Shipbuilding Company and a director of steamship companies. **Williams**, the author of *The Hon. Peter White* worked his way up to managing Editor of the *Plain Dealer* and later editor of the *Marine Review*. Due to ill health he chose to spend the remainder of his career assisting the LCA with publishing the *Bulletin*, doing the statistical work of the Association and the details in connection with the LCA schools. **Hill** raised in Buffalo became a machinist and later a ship engineer. He became fleet engineer of the W.H. Becker Fleet; he was a valuable member of the Fleet Engineers' Association.

The 1917 Annual Report honored the lives of five men connected with Great Lakes shipping; **Roy A. Williams, Otto M. Reiss, Frank S. Masten, Captain Alfred Mitchell** and **William E. Lloyd. Williams**, Cleveland, spent most of his early life working for Carnegie Steel Company and United States Steel Corporation. He was assigned to the traffic department of the Pittsburgh Steamship Company and later branched out on his own and formed the North American Steamship Company. He was elected to the LCA Advisory Committee and later a LCA Director. **Reiss** died at age 25 after an operation for appendicitis. He was the Secretary of the C. Reiss Coal Company and connected with the Reiss Steamship Company. **Masten** was an attorney who entered the office of the LCA General Counsel in 1893 and was admitted to the firm of Goulder, Holding and Masten in 1898. His specialty was maritime law and marine insurance and was identified with the work of organizing LCA in 1903. He was president of the American Interlake Steamship Company at the time of his death. **Captain Mitchell** was born in Canada and was considered the oldest and best known marine man on the Great Lakes at the time of his death. His career started at age 12 as a hand on a logging barge; by age 17 he and his brother owned a lumber barge. Over time after he had served as master, he and his brother owned and managed vessels on the Great Lakes for 26 years. Lloyd was the Buffalo agent of the Great Lakes Transit Corp. and was an active LCA member and served on the Welfare Committee. He was known to be in good humor and was known for his perennial unselfishness. His untiring energy and zeal for the Association were of great value.

The 1918 Annual Report lamented the deaths of **Captain George Perry McKay, Captain Denis Sullivan, Captain Charles H. Westcott** and **Charles F. Eddy.**

Captain McKay, LCA treasurer and pioneer of the Lake Superior trade, started sailing as a boy on his father's ships. He served on a schooner that had to be hauled over the portage at the Sault in 1839. He commanded many large steel ships until he came ashore as General Manager of the Cleveland Transportation Company fleet in 1883. He became secretary and Treasurer of the Cleveland Vessel Owners' Association in 1882 and remained in that capacity until the LCA was formed, at which time he became the Treasurer until his death. He was very much respected and universally liked. In his business life he was the embodiment of honor. **Captain Sullivan** was born in Dublin, Ireland and after his parents settled in Ontario, he began working on vessels in the Welland Canal and moved up rapidly to command schooners before he had a steamer built that he commanded. He was a member of the LCA Executive Committee. His friends knew him as he was—a big hearted, noble man. He was generous, helped others help themselves, and was always hopeful, busy and cheerful. **Captain Westcott** was Supervising Inspector of Steamboat Inspection Service for 27 years. He performed his duties carefully and thoughtfully. His concern was always for the safety of life of the passengers and crew and thus was highly esteemed and respected. **Charles Eddy** of Bay City, MI was a director and the treasurer of the Lake Transit Company. It was noted that he was always of a retiring nature and was one of the most charitable men Bay City had ever known.

The 1919 Annual Report noted the deaths of **Captain Wesley C. Richardson, Joseph C. Gilchrist** and the **Honorable James A. Tawney**. **Captain Richardson** was actively connected with Great Lakes shipping for a half a century. After sailing before the mast on a schooner he studied for his Chief Mate's license and along with his brother purchased a schooner onboard which he served as Chief Mate. In 1880 he came ashore and held many positions in industry including management of bulk freighters. He was a member of the Executive Committee of LCA. **Gilchrist** began his sailing career as a steward on a lake steamer and when he moved to Vermilion he was associated with the owner of a few wooden vessels. Upon moving to Cleveland he organized the Gilchrist Transportation Company and by 1909 his fleet consisted of 30 steel and 28 wooden steamers. He was a former member of the Executive Committee and Board of Directors of LCA. **Tawney** was not a member of the LCA but was well respected as a member of the International Joint Commission (IJC) to settle disputes between the United States and Canada. As a youth he was near the military action at the battle of Gettysburg and proudly walked with the soldiers. He became a blacksmith and a machinist before he began the study of law. He was elected to the State Senate of Minnesota and later to the Congress of the United States and served until President Taft appointed him to the IJC.

The 1920 Annual Report laments the death of **Captain John Mitchell** who was a member of the Board of Directors since its inception. He started sailing at age 14 and in a few years, in company with his brother, he purchased a barge and later a steamer. He was primarily engaged in the lumber trade, but about 1888 he disposed of the fleet of lumber vessels and build ships for the carriage of coal and iron ore. He was one of the strongest and most useful members of LCA. It was noted that he was genial, kindly and courteous and he had the respect and affection of his friends; was an indulgent father and loving husband.

In the 1921 Annual Report, while **William H. Becker** and **Albert R. Rumsey** are highlighted, there are also paragraphs on former members of LCA who died in 1920 including **William P. Snyder, H.M. Hanna, L.C. Waldo** and **Harvey L. Brown**. **Becker** was a self-made man who started out with a small tug. At the time of his death he was the driving force behind the operation of seventeen steel steamers serving as President of Valley Steamship Company and manager of Interstate Steamship Company. He was an LCA director and was noted as big hearted and broad minded.

Alfred Rumsey was hired by the Cleveland Shipowner's Association to supply crews to vessels and in 1892 was appointed Chief Commissioner for the Lake Carriers' Association, serving both organizations for 40 years. He was raised in the Vermilion area and passed away there. He worked on fish boats at age 12 and at 16 years of age he left to work the schooners; over time he obtained a pilot's license and served as 2nd Mate. He was a large man and was said to have an aggressive spirit tempered by a mild and generous heart. He established all of the assembly halls around the lakes that were necessary to get the crews at a moment's notice and he selected all the assistants to operate them. His work was admired so much that the members contributed to a purse to allow him to make a round-the-world trip in 1895.

William P. Snyder was not a LCA director but he was identified closely with the Shenango fleet that he established as well as his mining and furnace interests. He believed in the control of the industrial process from raw material to the finished product thus he needed ships as part of the chain. At the time of his death the two largest vessels in the Great Lakes fleets bore Shenango stacks, the Col. J. M. Schoonmaker and Wm. P. Snyder, Jr. **H.M. Hanna** was a moving spirit behind the Cleveland Vessel Owners' Association and an active LCA leader. He was president of the Globe Iron Works when the first iron hull bulk freighter the Onoko was built and when the first steel steamer the Spokane was built. **L.C. Waldo** was an LCA director and was president of one steamship company and the secretary of the Northwestern Steamship Company. **Harvey L. Brown**, the son of Captain J.J.H. Brown, became a lawyer specializing in admiralty and practiced in the office of his uncle Harvey D. Goulder. In 1903, Brown was secretary of LCA.

The 1922 Annual Report has no notations of deaths.

In the 1923 Annual Report the deaths of **William H. Smith, Harvey H. Brown** and **Sydney C. McLouth** are recorded. **Smith** was general manager of the Canada Atlantic Transit Company, operator of package freighters on the upper lakes. He had a long career in the railroad business and also managed the Ontario Car Ferry Company. He is remembered as a man of great frankness and sincerity and a sunny disposition and was remembered by his friends as a genial, courteous and unpretentious gentleman.

Brown, the son of Fayette Brown was a pioneer vessel owner and helped to develop the iron ore industry in the lakes. He managed 32 lake vessels among them was the R.J. Hackett, the first modern bulk vessel. He was an active officer in the Brown Hoisting Machinery Company that revolutionized unloading of ships. His brother Alexander E. Brown developed the cable-wired rig that hoisted the bucket from the hold and conveyed it to the shore storage. In 1898 he was a member of the Board of managers of LCA. **McLouth** started working life at 14 as a chore boy in a Michigan lumber camp, became a fireman on a tug, and at 21 a chief engineer. Ultimately he owned a fleet of wooden steamers in the coal trade and other larger steamers. He was an LCA member, served on the Welfare Committee and took an active interest in LCA schools in Marine City where he lived.

The 1924 Annual Report has no obituaries.

In the 1925 Annual Report, there were no Obituaries but there was section titled Memoriam for the late **William Livingstone** who died on October 17, 1925.

In 1926, **Peter Reiss** died; he was the founder of one of the largest coal shipping companies on the Great Lakes. While not an officer of LCA, this self-made man became a prominent ship owner and a shipper of coal cargo on many more LCA vessels.

In that year **Earl W. Oglebay** died; he was not connected with LCA but was a senior partner of the Oglebay, Norton and Company, a major producer of Lake Superior iron ore and the operator of the Columbia Steamship Company.

In 1927, **A. (Archie) W. Thomson** died; he was the President of Wilson Transit Company and a nephew of Captain Thomas Wilson. He served on the LCA Board and on the Welfare Plan Committee.

In 1928, **David Z. Norton** died; he was not connected with LCA but was a senior partner of the Oglebay, Norton and Company, a major producer of Lake Superior iron ore and the operator of the Columbia Steamship Company. In that year several other giants of the industry died. **Carl D. Bradley**, President of Michigan Limestone and Chemical Company and the Bradley Transportation Company died. **Harvey D. Goulder**, LCA General Counsel for over 25 years also died in 1928. Flags on all LCA ships were directed to fly the American flag at half-staff honoring Goulder.

In 1929, **Harry Coulby** died in London, England; he was President of the Interlake Steamship Company and a founding member of LCA and the Great Lakes Protective Association. He was one of the most effective leaders in these associations and served on the most important committees. For a period of time he was also the President of the Pittsburgh Steamship Company. His lifetime achievements in Great Lakes shipping are too extensive to be covered in this text.

In 1929, **Henry Steinbrenner** died; he was President of Kinsman Transit Company. He was a member of LCA from its inception. In that year **Henry C. Pickands**, a principal of Pickands, Mather and Company died. He was not directly connected with LCA since his major work was in the development of the company steel interests, he was also a Director of Interlake Steamship Company.

In 1930, **Joseph B. Rodgers** of Buffalo died; he was President of Brown Steamship and a Director of LCA from 1912-1929.

In 1931, **James Carey Evans** of Buffalo died; he was President of the Anchor Line and a leader on the LCA Board and the Executive Committee. **Samuel Mather** died at age 80 in 1931; he was a distinguished philanthropist and pioneer in the developing the iron ore ranges. This industry giant was a leader in the iron ore, steel and ship operating industries.

In 1932, **James A. Paisley** died; he was prominent in coal mining, coal shipping and U.S. and Canadian vessel operations. While not active in LCA membership, his vessels were enrolled in the Association. As President of Valley Camp Coal Company he was active in the management of 23 subsidiaries. In the same year **Captain Walter J. Stewart** died; he was a member of the LCA Board and Executive Committee and was the youngest shipmaster in his time. He served as fleet superintendent for Gilchrist Transportation Company and for Interlake Steamship Company.

In 1933, **Herbert K. Oakes** died; he was a valuable member of the LCA Board, the Executive Committee and the Welfare Plan Committee. He was the Vice President of Bethlehem Transportation Company and the Mahoning and Cambria steamship companies. **William P. Schaufele** of M. A. Hanna also died in 1933; he was a member of the LCA Board and the Welfare Plan Committee, he was a strong advocate of Safety Committees and had them on the ships under his control. **Mrs. Henry Steinbrenner (nee Sophia Minch)** died at age 79 in 1933; Sophia was the daughter of Philip Minch, a pioneer in the operation of sailing vessels and wooden steam ships from Vermilion, OH. Her father brought out the Onoko in 1882, the first iron bulk freight steamer on the lakes. After his death her mother took over the company and she had built the Western Reserve, one of the first ten steamers of steel construction on the lakes. Following the death of her mother, Sophia Steinbrenner took an active part in the development of the Kinsman Transit Company and assumed the presidency in 1905.

In 1936, **James A. Armstrong** died after being struck by a Cleveland street car. He began employment in 1909 with LCA and GLPA as chief clerk and in later years also served as assistant treasurer of the GLPA.

Newton D. Baker died on Christmas Day at age 67; he was the General Counsel of LCA from 1926 until his death. Baker was one of the giants of his time. He had a distinguished law career prior to his role in LCA serving as the Cleveland City Solicitor for Mayor Tom L. Johnson, as Mayor of Cleveland, OH, as Secretary of War in 1916 for President Woodrow Wilson, and a leader in the Democratic Party where he was considered a potential Presidential candidate. (Time magazine honored Baker on the cover in 1927.) **Horace S. Wilkinson**, a director of LCA since its inception, died in 1937. He was a leader in the steel and shipping industries; he organized the United States Transportation Company, later known as the Great Lakes Steamship Company, that became the largest independent fleet in Great Lakes service.

In 1939, **Henry G. Dalton** died; he was a Board member of the earlier Lake Carriers' Association and later a Board member of the reorganized LCA. He was a senior partner in Pickands, Mather & Company, President of Interlake Steamship Company, and many other companies including Chairman of the Board of Youngstown Sheet and Tube. He was called upon by Presidents Wilson, Coolidge and Hoover to assist on major boards and committees during World War One and after. He was the last surviving member of the leaders who built Pickands, Mather including James Pickands, Samuel Mather, Jay Morse, and Harry Coulby among others. He truly was one of the giants of Great Lakes shipping. In 1939, two other long serving members of the LCA Board died; they were **John T. Kelly**; Board member from 1921-1937 and **Calvert C. Canfield,** Board member from 1914-1935. Kelly had been President of Columbia Steamship Company and Canfield managed the vessel department of Pickands, Mather and Company. In 1939 **Richard A. Harrison** also died; for 28 years he was a traveling Shipping Commissioner for LCA and in 1921, upon the death of Alfred Rumsey, he assumed the duties of the Chief Commissioner serving with distinction on the Welfare Plan Committee.

In 1940, **Walton H. McGean** died; he had been a LCA Director since 1909. He was the partner of Charles Hutchinson in the formation of the Hutchinson & Company. In World War One he was a member of a Committee of three who mobilized and allocated vessels to move iron ore, coal and grain. In that year **Frank J. Sullivan** also died; he had been a member of the LCA Executive Committee, and an officer in the Fleet and the Gartland Steamship Company

In 1941, **John Stanley Ashley** died; he was LCA President for six years starting in 1925 following the death of William Livingstone; he was Chairman of GLPA from its inception in 1909 until February 1, 1939. He was a marine manager for M. A. Hanna Company when he directed the operation of the 3rd largest fleet of ore carriers on the Lakes during World War I; served on the LCA Board since 1909, the Executive Committee in 1915 and was elected Vice President in 1916. In 1941 **Allyn Fitch Harvey** died; he had served Pickands, Mather & Company and upon the formation of the Pittsburgh Steamship Company joined the firm as an assistant to the president and upon the death of Harry Coulby, Harvey was elected President of Pittsburgh Steamship Company.

Charles Hallam Keep died in 1941; he was the Secretary of the Buffalo based Lake Carriers' Association in 1891; he continued as Secretary under the reorganized LCA in 1893 with M.A. Bradley, President. He was a practicing lawyer in Buffalo and accepted an appointment from President Theodore Roosevelt to head a federal commission; later he served as Superintendent of Banks in New York before becoming a member of the New York Public Service Commission. **Clemens A. Reiss** died in 1941; he was Vice President of Reiss Steamship Company and his career was primarily centered on the management of the C. Reiss Coal Company. In

1941 **George Ashley Tomlinson** died; he was the last surviving member of the LCA Board of 1905 and the executive Committee of 1906 that included Coulby, Wolvin and Gilchrist. He was the driving force behind the formation of the Tomlinson fleet.

In 1943 **George A. Marr**, a foundation of the LCA, died. He was integrally connected with the Welfare Plan—the savings plans, the schools, the safety program, sanitation on the ships and the Soo Library. He was a bitter foe of any legislation that he thought hindered the flow of commerce on the lakes; he was an ardent foe of the maritime unions. In 1904 William Livingstone selected Marr to be the LCA Secretary, a position he held until 1936; in 1919 Marr added the duties of Treasurer, a post he held until his death in 1943. In 1929, by a special amendment of the by-laws, he was elected Vice-President. From 1909 he was also the Secretary and Attorney in fact for the GLPA until his death. He was appointed LCA Vice President in 1936, a position he held until he resigned in 1939. For nearly 40 years the name of George Marr, this giant of a leader, was associated with LCA and the Welfare Plan.

Charles L. Hutchinson died in 1943; he was the last survivor of the vessel owners who organized the current LCA. From deck hand at age 16 to earning a master's license at age 20, he went on to command many ships until he operated the Buckeye Steamship Company and later formed the Hutchinson & Company fleet and the Pioneer Steamship Company.

In 1945, **George H. Warner** died; he was a member of the LCA Executive Committee from 1931 until his death in 1945. He had been the successor to J. S. Ashley at M. A. Hanna and Company where he managed the vessel and dock departments. In 1945 **James E. McAlpine** died; he was a LCA Board member since 1929 and a member of the Advisory Committee of the GLPA. After joining Brown and Company as an office boy in 1896, ultimately he was elected President of Brown Steamship Company.

In 1947, **Frank C. Oakes** died; he was a member of the LCA Board and the Executive Committee and served Bethlehem Transportation Corp. as vessels manager. **Frank Armstrong** died that year; he was another previous member of the Board and Executive Committee. He served with the Pickands, Mather and Company from 1899 until 1943.

In 1948, **R. C. Allen** died; he served as a member of the LCA Board and Executive Committee. He was a prominent metallurgical and mining engineer and served as Executive Vice President of Oglebay-Norton. He was also the President of the Battelle Memorial Institute. **A. H. Ferbert** also died in 1948; he was a member of the LCA Board and Executive Committee. His entire life was devoted to Great Lakes shipping joining the Pittsburgh Steamship Company in 1904 and was elected President in 1940. In 1948 **Arthur C. Sullivan** died, he was a member of the LCA board from 1914 until his death. He directed the D. Sullivan and Company and the Gartland Steamship Company since 1917. The third President of LCA since 1903 reorganization was **Captain Joseph S. Wood** who died in 1948. He also served as a member of the LCA Board from 1926 until his death. He held his first command at age 24 and continued with Wilson Transit Company for 54 years, serving as President from 1928-1948. **Crispin Oglebay** died in 1948; he was President of Oglebay-Norton and later Chairman of the Board. While not active in the LCA, in early years he did serve on the Board and Executive Committee from 1935-1941. **George M. Steinbrenner** died in 1948, he was President, Kinsman Transit Company; his grandfather was Captain Philip Minch, builder of wooden schooners and steam vessels. In 1901 he went into business with his father to form Kinsman. Steinbrenner was a Director of LCA for 35 years and Chair of the Welfare Committee from 1922-1941.

In 1949 **Fred I. Kennedy** died; he was associated with Great Lakes shipping for 50 years serving as the Cleveland representative for Reiss Coal and was on the Board of LCA from 1918-1944 and the Executive Committee from 1935 until retirement. That same year the patriarch of the Lake grain trade **T. W. Kennedy** died; he was the manager of the Grain Handling Corporation at Buffalo from 1920-1938; prior to that from 1900-1920 he was the LCA superintendent supervising the unloading of grain in Buffalo.

In 1950, **Harry J. Sullivan** died; he was a member of the LCA Board and was President of Gartland Steamship Company. In 1950, **Louis Carlton Sabin** died; he was active in the industry for sixty years and was the LCA Vice President from 1925-1948. He served as General Superintendent of the St. Marys Falls Canal from 1906-1925, during which time he supervised the construction of the Third (Davis) and Fourth (named Sabin in 1943) locks. During WWII although a civilian he was appointed District Commander of the COE District office.

William J. Conners, Jr. died in 1951; he was an LCA Executive Committee and Board member from 1931-38. Prior to his operation of the government requisitioned Great Lakes Transit Corporation fleet during WWII, he directed the largest package freight operation and a group of passenger vessels on the Great Lakes.

William G. Mather died in 1951; he was active in the iron ore and Great Lakes shipping industries since 1878. He was President of Cleveland-Cliffs Iron Company from 1890-1933. Many of his executives served on the LCA Board and Executive Committee during that time.

In 1952, four men who served as members of the LCA Board died, they were **Water C. Hemingway**, President of Pittsburgh Steamship Company, **Charles O. Jenkins**, founder of the Jenkins Steamship Company in 1904, **Robert J. Paisley**, President of J.A. Paisley Steamship Company and Morrow Steamship Company, and **Captain Warren C. Jones** a member of the LCA Board and Executive Committee; he commenced his career on sailing vessels. He was President of the Tomlinson Fleet. **John G. Munson** died in 1952; he was President of Bradley Transportation and Michigan Limestone and later Vice President, Raw Materials, United States Steel.

In 1953, **Adam E. Cornelius, Sr.** died; he served on the Board of LCA since 1927 and the LCA Executive Committee and the GLPA Advisory Committee. He was Chairman of the Board of American Steamship Company and a partner in Boland and Cornelius.

In 1954 **George J. Dietrich** died; he was an employee of LCA from 1916 until 1948 where he served as statistician and editor of the Bulletin. In the same year two past members of the LCA Board died; they were **Captain Richard W. England,** who after sailing as master on cargo and passenger ships, became manager of the District 9, U.S. Emergency Fleet Corp. during WWI, and marine manager of Interstate Steamship Company; and **Charles F. Platz**, Vice President of Michigan Limestone.

In 1954, **Albert E. R. Schneider** died; he served on the LCA Board for forty years, from 1914 until his death, and on the LCA Executive Committee and the GLPA Advisory Committee. He was associated with Cleveland-Cliffs from 1903 and served as marine department manager from 1916-1945. He also operated the Schneider Transportation Company fleet of two vessels.

In 1955, **Elton Hoyt, 2nd** died; he was a member of the LCA Board and Advisory Committee since 1934. He was President of Interlake Steamship Company, Mather Iron Company and Erie Mining Company.

In 1956, **John J. Boland** died; he was Senior Director of LCA serving since 1912 and a member of the Advisory-Executive Committee since 1920. With his partner Adam E. Cornelius he established the firm of Boland and Cornelius in 1904. He served as the Chairman of American Steamship Company until the day of his death.

In 1957, **Edward B. Greene** died; he was a member of the LCA Board and Advisory Committee. He was an officer of the Cleveland Trust Company serving as Chairman of the Executive Committee from 1926-1933; and in 1933 he became President of Cleveland-Cliffs Iron Company and then Chairman of the Board in 1947.

In 1958, **John T. Hutchinson** died; he served as LCA President from 1947-52 and served on the LCA Board and Executive Committee from 1935 until his death. He was in Great Lakes shipping for 50 years starting in 1908. He was the third generation of his family operating the Hutchinson and Company shipping interests, including the Buckeye Steamship Company and the Pioneer Steamship Company. In 1958, **Harrold L. Gobeille** died; he served on the LCA Board since 1945 until his death. He was associated with Cleveland Cliffs Iron Company since 1916 and served as Vice President of the Marine Department. During that time he arranged for the conversion of the Notre Dame Victory that was renamed the Cliffs Victory.

In 1959, **William A. Reiss** died; he served as a member of the LCA Board from 1942-1958. He was President and later Chairman of the Board of Reiss Steamship Company.

In 1959 **Harry W. Warley** died; he was an LCA Board member from 1942-1958. He was in charge of ocean and Great Lakes vessel transportation for Bethlehem Steel. He was an advisor in the formulation of the Merchant Marine Act, 1936.

In 1960, **Alexander T. Wood**, age 57 and his wife died of drowning caused by sudden water turbulence while on vacation in the Bahamas on December 8, 1960. Alexander T. Wood was Vice President of Wilson Marine Transit Company when he was elected President of LCA from 1938-1947 and was a Director since 1934; he served on the Legislative and Advisory Committees. He served as President of LCA all during the World War II years as well as the Director, Great Lakes Division, Office of Defense Transportation. He assumed the Presidency of Wilson Marine Transit Company in 1948, succeeding his father Captain Joseph S. Wood. He was truly one of the giants of Great Lakes shipping. In 1960 **Walborn W. Newcomet** died; he served on the LCA Board from 1934 until his death. He was Vice President of Reiss, Rockport and Red Arrow Steamship Companies.

In 1961, **Timothy J. McCarthy, Sr.** died; he was a pioneer in the automobile carrying trade first with Nicholson Transit Company and later with the Detroit and Cleveland Navigation Company. For a short period in 1958-1960, he was a member of LCA when his company expanded into the bulk commodity trade. When he died he was Chairman of the T. J. McCarthy Steamship Company, a company he formed in 1935.

In 1962, **John J. Boland, Jr.** died; he was a member of the LCA Board and Advisory Committee. He was Chairman of American Steamship Company and a senior partner in Boland and Cornelius Company. In 1962 **J. Burton Ayers** died; he was a member of the LCA Board for 43 years – the longest tenure for any Board member. He was Chairman of the Great Lakes Steamship Company and for a period of time he was President of Toledo Ship Building Company when the USCG Cutter Mackinaw was built.

In 1963 Captain **R. Scott Misener** died at age 85; he was the founder of Scott Misener Steamships, at one time the third largest company in the lake trade. He rose from deckhand to Captain and shipowner.

In 1964, **Alexander C. Brown** died: he had been a member of the LCA Board from 1939-1957 and a member of the Advisory Committee. He was President of Cleveland Cliffs Iron Company from 1947-1955. During WWI he served on the War Industry Board and in WWII he served on the War Production Board. In 1964, **Henry J. Lester** died; he was a member of the LCA Board from 1956-1963. He was connected with the Tomlinson Fleet for 50 years starting in 1913. In 1964 **Ruth E. Webster** died; she had been Assistant Secretary of Kinsman Marine Transit Company having worked with four generations of Steinbrenners. In 1964, the former E.H. Gary was named R.E. Webster, only one of two U.S. flag vessels named after women at that time.

In 1965, **Captain John C. Murray** died at age 86; he was the principal instructor at the LCA Cleveland navigation school from 1917 through 1960 and a member of the shore captains' committee from 1949 until his death. He was a master of 14 vessels in the Pittsburgh Steamship Fleet. An epoch accomplishment was to pilot the British Royal Yacht Britannia during a portion of the vessel's Great Lakes voyage following opening of the Seaway.

In 1965, **Herman C. Strom** died; he served on the LCA Board from 1926-1948. He was a Vice President of the Pittsburgh Steamship Company and was affiliated with the War Shipping Administration during WWII.

In 1966, **Joseph G. Wood** died; he had been a member of the LCA Board from 1948 until his death. He was Vice President of Wilson Marine Transit Company.

In 1967, **G. C. Hutchinson** died; he was a member of the LCA Board and Advisory Committee from 1940-1962 as well as other LCA Committees. He served as President of Pioneer Steamship and Buckeye Steamship Companies and was active in the Great Lakes Historical Society. In 1967 **William P. Snyder, Jr.** died; he was a member of the LCA Board for 37 years from 1914-1950. He served as Chairman of Shenango Furnace Company and President of Crucible Steel Company.

In 1968, **Gilbert R. Johnson**, LCA General Counsel for thirty years died. He affiliated with LCA in 1936, was Secretary, Counsel and then General Counsel until his death. He was the third General Counsel of LCA following the Honorable Newton D. Baker and Harvey D. Goulder. He was the senior partner and founder of the Admiralty law firm of Johnson, Branand and Jaeger. In his youth he sailed as an unlicensed seaman on the Lakes and his three brothers sailed until they were Masters with the Hutchinson fleet.

In 1968, **Robert G. McCreary**, dean of the Great Lakes admiralty bar died. He was Chair Great Lakes Protective Association from 1945-1966 and he served as GLPA Counsel from 1928-1966. In 1968, **Joseph H. Thompson** died; he was President of M. A. Hanna Company and the Chief Executive of the Iron Ore Company of Canada. He served on the LCA Board and Advisory Committee from 1946-1952.

Merle M. McCurdy died in 1968; he was the first black U.S. attorney in Cleveland. He was born in Conneaut in 1912 and put himself through the Western Reserve University Law School by working a variety of jobs, including on Great Lakes ore boats and as a hotel bellhop. He began his career as a criminal defense lawyer. He later worked as an assistant Cuyahoga County prosecutor. In 1960, he became the county's first public defender. He was engaged by George M. Steinbrenner as legal counsel at Kinsman Marine. After his death, Mr. Steinbrenner named a Great Lakes freighter the SS Merle M. McCurdy, possibly the only Great Lakes freighter named after a black man.

In 1969, **D. R. Gairing** died; he served on the Board of LCA from 1960 until his death. He was manager of the Cleveland office of the C. Reiss Coal Company. In 1969 **H. Lee White** died; he was Chairman of American Steamship Company and a senior partner in the New York City law firm Cadwalader, Wickersham and Taft. He was also President of Marine Transport Lines, a fleet of ocean vessels. He served as Assistant Secretary of the Air Force for President Eisenhower during 1953-1954.

In 1970, **George M. Humphrey** died; he was a member of the LCA Board from 1934-1945, President of M.A. Hanna Company from1929-1952, and he served as the 55th Secretary of the United States Treasury from 1953-57. He pioneered the development of Iron Ore Company of Canada. In 1970 **Claude Peck** died; he was a member of the LCA Board from 1919-1957 and a member of the Advisory Committee from 1952-1957 and served on the GLPA from 1929-1958. He served as Vice President of Shenango Furnace Company. In 1970 **Captain John Roen**, Roen Steamship Company died. He organized and served as President of Roen Steamship Company. A hallmark of his career was in 1944 when, in the middle of WWII and when every vessel was needed to haul iron ore, he organized the raising of the sunken George M. Humphrey in the Straits of Mackinaw.

In 1971, **Joseph B. Ayers, Jr.** died; he was a member of the LCA Board during the periods 1946-1958 and 1965-1969. He served as President of the Great Lakes Steamship Company and of the Buckeye Steamship Company; later he was an official with the Kinsman Marine Transit Company. In 1971, **George W. Callahan** died; he was a member of the LCA Board from 1945-63 and served on many other LCA Committees. He retired as Vice President of Interlake Steamship Company. In 1971, **Henri P. Junod** died; he had been a member of the LCA Board Advisory

Committee from 1960-1965. He served as Executive Vice President of Pickands Mather and Company and Interlake Steamship Company. In 1971, **Donald C. Potts** died; he served on the LCA Board and Advisory Committee from 1941-1956 as well as many other committees. He joined U.S. Steel in 1913 and retired as President of the Pittsburgh Steamship Company.

In 1972, **Harrie S. Taylor** died; he served as a member of the LCA Board and Advisory Committee and other committees including as Chair of the Legislative Committee from 1944-1960. He was an admiralty attorney who joined Oglebay Norton as general counsel until he assumed the position as president; he was instrumental in the development of the Reserve Mining taconite facility in Silver Bay, MN.

In 1975, **Professor C. Moreau Jansky, Jr.** died; he was the LCA Consultant for 32 years on the development and implementation of the use of Radio Telephone on the lakes.

In 1976, **John F. Wedow, III** died; he was a member of the LCA Board and Advisory Committee from 1967 until his death. He was President of Cleveland Tankers. In 1976 **John J. Boland, III** died he was a member of the LCA Board. He served as Vice President of American Steamship Company.

In 1977, **Floyd May** died; he was member of the LCA Board and Advisory Committee. He served as President of Cleveland Tankers. In 1977 **Captain Chesley H. Inches** died at age 95; he started his sailing career in 1901 and was appointed Master in 1925 and was in command of many vessels for Interlake Steamship Company. He was a member of the shore Captain's Committee and during his retirement devoted his life as Curator of the Great Lakes Historical Society.

In 1978, **Day Peckinpaugh** died; he was a member of the LCA Board from 1962-1967. He retired as President and Chairman of the Board of Buckeye Steamship Company. He started in Great Lakes Shipping in 1900 and was one of the early members of the Ore and Coal Exchange during the First World War. In 1978 **Steward W. Sexsmith** died; he served on the LCA Board from 1959-1970. He served in the fleet dispatch office of M. A. Hanna Company, was the shipyard liaison for the construction and conversion of many Hanna ships and retired as Vice President of Hansand Steamship Corp. and Carryore Ltd.

In 1978 **Walter C. Dressler** died; he was a member of the LCA Board and the Advisory Committee of the GLPA. He retired as Vice President of Oglebay Norton.

In 1980, **Jack N. Carlson** died; he was LCA Treasurer since 1971 until his death. In 1980 **Albert B. Cozzens** died; he was on the LCA Board and was Senior Vice President of Oglebay Norton. In 1980 **Walter A. Marting** died; he was a member of the LCA Board and upon retirement was President, Hanna Mining Company. In 1980 **Walter A. Sterling** died; he was a member of the LCA Board and had retired as Chairman and CEO of Cleveland- Cliffs.

In 1981, **Herbert C. Jackson** died; he was a member of the LCA Board and served on the Legislative and Government Affairs Committee from its inception in 1944 until he retired in 1962. He was Executive Vice President of Pickands Mather and Vice President of Interlake Steamship Company.

·In 1981, **VADM Lyndon Spencer** died; he was the first full time President of LCA. He joined LCA in 1946, was named President in 1952 and retired from LCA in 1962. He had a distinguished career in the Coast Guard during WWII including commanding a naval assault transport ship in the Normandy invasion on D-Day. He had been the USCG chief of the office of merchant marine safety from 1941-1943.

In 1982, **Russell H. Plumb** died; he was an LCA employee for 34 years retiring January 1980 as Superintendent of the Job Referral Centers and LCA Director of training.

In 1983 **John Manning** died; he was general manager of marine at Hanna Mining. He had a sterling career sailing on the lakes and oceans, including experiencing a torpedo attack to his ship and surviving in an open lifeboat on the North Atlantic. When the Stinson was ordered he made certain it would have a covered lifeboat. He went on to become a highly respected and tough marine manager who served on many LCA committees. **Henry G. Steinbrenner** also died in 1983. He had served as President and Chairman of the board at Kinsman Transit Company. He was a Trustee of LCA since 1941 and a member of the Advisory Committee for many years.

In 1984 **Glen V. Evans** died. He had been a founding member of many LCA Committees including the Legislative and Public Relations

Committees formed in 1944. He served on the Board since 1945 and on the Advisory Committee since 1959 until he retired. **Baird R. Tewksbury** was the retired President of Midland Steamship; he died at age 97 in 1984. He served on the Executive (Advisory) Committee from 1937-1947 and on the Board from 1930 until 1960.

In 1985 **John (Jack) Rose** died; he was one of the last Assembly Hall managers.

In 1986 **Oliver T. Burnham** died at age 79. Oliver was a long term employee who in his 40 years of service worked for all the presidents from Captain Joseph Wood through part of Admiral Trimble's tenure. His positions included Assistant Secretary, Secretary and Vice President. **Jack Saunders** died in 1986; a Great Lakes sailor who worked for Pickands Mather afloat and ashore. He helped teach navigation at the Duluth LCA School and in 1969 he became the LCA Job Referral Center manager until his death.

In 1989 **Melvin H. Pelfrey** died. He was an International Vice-President of MEBA-AMO; a strong Great Lakes labor leader. As his memorial service pamphlet stated, he was "The Voice of Reason." While not everyone on the LCA Board would have agreed with that assessment, Ryan found him to be a friend and mentor following their first meetings in 1975.

In 1993 **VADM James Hirshfield** died at the age of 90. Hirshfield was elected as the 18th President of LCA in 1962; he retired from LCA following distinguished service in July 1970. Vice Admiral Hirshfield died on May 16, 1993. He served for over 39 years in the USCG retiring as Assistant Commandant. While on WWII service in command of a Coast Guard vessel in the North Atlantic, he engaged six submarines in the period of two days, ultimately sinking a German submarine U-606. For this brave action he was awarded the Navy Cross with Silver Star for "Extraordinary Heroism and Distinguished Service"; one of only six such awards given to Coast Guardsmen during WW II. Hirshfield also received the Purple Heart for injuries sustained in the sinking of U-606.

In 1995 **Fred R. White, Jr.** died at age of 82, he was born in Cleveland and after graduating from Yale University in 1935, he joined Oglebay Norton Company which had been co- founded by his grandfather, David Z. Norton. During WWII, as a member of the Ohio National Guard, he was stationed in both North Africa and Italy, rising to the rank of Lieutenant Colonel. Following the War, he returned to Oglebay Norton where he went on to become Vice Chairman of the Board and Chairman of the Executive Committee until retirement. His primary interest was always Great Lakes shipping. In recognition of this fact, in 1979, a 636 foot self-unloading, lake freighter was christened Fred R. White, Jr

In 1997 **Renold Thompson** died at age 70. He joined Oglebay Norton in 1952, was elected president and chief executive officer in 1982 and retired at age 65. He served on the LCA Board of Directors and Advisory Committee.

There were several leaders who died after Ryan retired; some are listed below.

John O. Greenwood died in 2004. He was a Vice-President with Interlake Steamship a Great Lakes historian and a publisher and author of many invaluable Great Lakes books.

David L. Buchanan died in 2005. He served with the FBI during WWII, with Pittsburgh Steamship Company and the LCA until his retirement in 1985.

Vice Admiral Paul E. Trimble died in 2005. Following a distinguished career in the U.S. Coast Guard, Paul Trimble became President of LCA. His accomplishments were extensive; his friends were numerous. He was Ryan's mentor and a very dear friend.

Rear Admiral Robert Timbrell, R. C. N. (Ret) died in 2006. Following a distinguished Naval Career in WWII he survived vessel sinkings and much enemy action including at Dunkirk evacuating British troops from France. He was the first Canadian naval officer to be awarded the Distinguished Service Cross in WWII. His last sea going naval command was Commanding Officer of the Aircraft Carrier HMSC Bonaventure. In 1973, he became President of the Dominion Marine Association until his retirement in 1985.

John L. Horton died in 2006. He was the first recipient of the Shepheard Award for Marine Safety. He was a retired Master Mariner, Cleveland-Cliffs executive and a dear friend. John served in WWII aboard hospital and troop ships in North Africa, Italy and Normandy. He was Mr. Safety on the Great Lakes.

George M. Steinbrenner III died in 2010 at the age of 80. He was named after his grandfather, a prominent member of LCA. Steinbrenner joined Kinsman Marine Transit in 1957, a company he later purchased from his family. He became chairman and chief executive officer of American Shipbuilding Company, of which he was part owner. While well known for his sports franchise career he was closely involved with Great Lakes shipping and served on important LCA committees. Less noted he named one of his ships after a woman, Ruth Webster, and a Black man, Merle McCurdy.

Captain C. Gil Porter died in 2015. Gil was a retired USCG officer having been CO on the USCG cutter Woodrush, a former Great Lakes Pilot and an avid supporter of Great Lakes shipping. He was in charge of the LCA Duluth navigation school.

There is a major error in all the index pages! All are off by 18 pages. In order to find anything on a page listed in the index for a subject you have to subtract 18. Examples: Abdnor, James listed at 316 is actually 298 and Coulby, Harry 29-30 is 11-12. New printing of book will have corrected index.

Index

A

AB (able bodied) seamen. *See* seamen, AB (able bodied)
Abdnor, James S., 316, 361, 366
ABS (American Bureau of Shipping), 337, 413, 486, 508, 511
accidents, 47, 69, 71–72, 106, 117, 122, 124, 132, 134, 211, 272, 274, 277, 288, 374, 486
Adam E. Cornelius, 220, 306
Advisory Committee, 54, 71, 182, 233, 239, 247, 268, 278, 295, 297, 315, 317, 325, 333, 360, 373, 386–87, 394, 400, 402–3, 416–17, 419, 424–25, 429, 448, 484, 528, 532, 534, 536–37
Aids to Navigation Committee, 33, 44, 47, 65, 167
AIOA (American Iron Ore Association), 436, 448, 452, 472, 511
AISI (American Iron and Steel Institute), 448, 450–52, 472, 511
American Bureau of Shipping. *See* ABS (American Bureau of Shipping)
American Iron and Steel Institute. *See* AISI (American Iron and Steel Institute)
American Iron Ore Association. *See* AIOA (American Iron Ore Association)
American Maritime Officers. *See* AMO (American Maritime Officers)
American Merchant Marine Library Association. *See* AMMLA (American Merchant Marine Library Association)
American Steamship Company, 222, 408
AMMLA (American Merchant Marine Library Association), 160, 212, 331–32, 495
AMO (American Maritime Officers), 430, 436, 496
Andberg, E. J., 314
Anderson, Dave, 508
Anderson, Thomas S., 419, 463, 488, 507
Ashley, John Stanley, 63–65, 71, 80, 139–40, 143–44, 146, 528
Assembly Halls, 78, 83–84, 116, 120, 127–30, 135, 154, 157, 166, 266–67, 276, 321, 330, 375, 523
Assembly Rooms, 63, 126–27, 132–33, 153–55, 186, 203–4, 211, 265–67, 320–21, 323, 375, 435, 496
Aston, Dewey, 397, 419, 487, 508
Ayers, Joseph B., Jr., 289, 314, 534

B

Baker, John, 430, 512
Baker, Newton D., 139, 144–45, 182, 314, 447, 526, 533
ballast water, 458–60, 504
banks. *See* savings plan
barges, 51, 72–73, 152, 170, 188, 199, 316, 344, 346–47, 459, 522
Barker, James R., 417–19, 508
Barker, Mark, 439, 471, 508, 513
Beukema, Chris F., 120, 314, 360, 365
Biggs, Ralph, 416, 508
Board of Directors, 65, 119, 144, 146, 183, 522
Board of Managers, 30, 36, 44, 47
Board of Trustees, 360, 416–17, 424, 434
Boland, John J., 55, 146, 184, 531
Boland, John J., III, 314, 360, 535
Bradley, M. A., 30, 34–35, 401, 527
bridges, 25, 27, 38, 89, 213, 249, 287–88, 293, 334, 371, 396, 398, 462, 472, 475, 479–80
Brown, Fayette, Jr., 314
Brown, J. J. H., 37–38, 517, 523
Buchanan, David L., 200, 240, 297, 314, 316, 339, 359, 400, 420–21, 538
Buhrmann, Bill, 414, 417, 508
Bulletin, The, 69, 78, 97, 119, 122, 124, 134, 149, 153, 155–56, 163, 165–67, 169, 174, 178–79, 188, 195–96, 199, 203, 208–9, 211, 214–15, 221, 225–26, 233, 272, 295, 299–301, 303–4, 307, 345, 347, 350, 354, 366, 381, 383, 402, 409, 435, 442, 520, 530
Burke, Tom W., 314, 360, 414–15
Burnham, Oliver T., 182, 233, 240, 249, 265, 307, 313, 321–22, 359, 537

C

cabotage, 199, 427, 454, 456
cabotage laws, 236, 255–56, 316, 412, 429–30, 435, 437–38, 444, 453–55, 505
cadets, 377, 387, 389, 490
Caldwell, S. D., 23–24, 30, 33
Canadian government, 30, 32, 36, 38, 67, 89, 95, 100, 102–3, 109, 169, 187, 236, 253, 262, 332, 336, 347, 349, 453
Canadian vessels, 24, 152, 199, 214, 236, 247, 249, 251–52, 255–56, 263, 285–86, 301, 346, 349–50, 428, 467
Captain's Committee, 427, 483–85
Carver, Paul, 499, 509
Castle, Frank, 417, 508
CDS (Construction Differential Subsidy), 347–48
channels, 31, 35–36, 38–39, 45, 66–67, 71, 76, 94, 97, 102, 104, 106–7, 113, 151, 170–71, 186–87, 215, 229, 232, 247, 254, 283–84, 286, 290, 294, 333, 335, 350, 393, 398, 431, 442, 449, 465–67, 473, 475–76, 480, 483–84, 511
charts, 482
Chicago Drainage Canal, 38, 59, 92, 151, 225
Chicago Sanitary District, 46, 92, 151
Claims Committee, 200–201
Cleveland Navigation and Marine Engineering School, 328
Cleveland Shipowners Association. *See* CSA (Cleveland Shipowners Association)
Cleveland Vessel Owners' Association. *See* CVOA (Cleveland Vessel Owners' Association)
coal fired vessels. *See* vessels, coal fired

coalitions, 427, 446, 451, 453–54, 467–68, 511
Coast Guard Academy, 310, 388–89, 403
Coast Guard regulations, 338, 371, 485–86
COE (Corp of Engineers), 104, 236, 345, 348, 357, 395–97, 457, 462, 464, 467, 474–76, 481, 484
Comerford, James R., 246, 507
communications, 21, 69, 114, 134, 214, 289, 291, 293, 322, 372, 397, 480, 483
Congress, 20, 30, 33, 35–36, 38, 57, 67, 98, 102, 110–11, 141–42, 151, 153, 185, 188, 199, 229, 236, 245, 250, 253, 255–56, 259, 261–62, 283, 310, 356, 358, 361, 369, 372, 383, 394–95, 411, 445–46, 449, 451, 458, 467–68, 476, 500, 502, 518, 522
Construction Differential Subsidy. *See* CDS (Construction Differential Subsidy)
continuous discharge book, 83, 155–56
conversions, 261, 316, 343, 405, 497, 506, 531, 535
Cornelius, Adam E., 146, 184, 314, 360, 530–31
Corp of Engineers. *See* COE (Corp of Engineers)
Coulby, Harry, 29–30, 61, 65, 71, 76, 82, 98, 113, 120, 146, 525–27
crew shortages, 377–79, 388, 495
CSA (Cleveland Shipowners Association), 66, 128, 432
Cummings, Fred, 419, 463, 467–69, 508
Cuyahoga River, 170, 213, 224, 397, 416, 475, 479
CVOA (Cleveland Vessel Owners' Association), 21–22, 25–26, 32–35, 517, 521, 523

D

death benefits, 82, 132–37, 150, 163, 204, 209, 276, 278, 331
Democrats, 51, 141–42, 229, 310, 356, 411, 434
depression, 142–43, 147–49, 154, 159–60, 166, 174, 181, 184, 230, 330
Detroit River Tunnel, 89
diversion of water, 93, 151, 237, 257–58, 462, 475
DMA (Dominion Marine Association), 68, 88, 236, 247, 250, 275, 290, 295, 308, 332, 339, 391, 397, 423, 443, 508, 538
Dorn, Bob, 417, 419, 439, 467, 508
draft, 32, 78–79, 94, 107, 197, 201, 203, 239, 243, 261, 288, 336, 344, 346, 361, 393–94, 443, 464, 473
draft boards, 79, 201–2, 241
draft deferments, 79, 194, 201–3, 240–42, 322
dredging, 38, 72, 102, 104, 287, 396, 476, 500
dredging crisis, 500–502
Duluth Navigation School, 271, 376, 381

E

economic/political climate, 19, 141, 180, 229, 309, 355, 410
Edmund Fitzgerald, 363, 365, 371, 374, 382, 405–6, 424, 435, 480
education, 69, 82, 124–25, 159, 268, 270, 323, 326, 376, 381, 490
Education and Public Relations Committee, 221, 268, 299
Eisenhower, Dwight D., 229, 248, 250, 256–57, 259, 262, 534
Elder, Scott H., 255, 313, 359–60, 373, 385, 398, 424, 447
Electronics Committee, 249, 286, 289, 291, 334, 397, 463

525

emissions, 294–96, 298, 339
engine officers, 129, 197, 270, 324, 328, 386–88, 489, 491
EPA (Environmental Protection Agency), 366–67, 400, 458, 486, 505–6
Escanaba, 173, 177–78
Executive Committee, 47–48, 61, 80, 88, 143, 146–47, 149, 157, 162, 182, 184, 198, 233, 255, 360, 416, 517, 519, 525, 527–29, 531, 538

F

fatalities, 122, 161, 163–65, 277, 382
FCC (Federal Communications Commission), 214, 287, 290–93, 336–37, 397–98
federal government, 61, 76, 81–82, 177, 198–99, 263, 298, 317, 357, 371, 385, 401, 500–502
Firth, Franklin J., 23, 518
fleet engineers, 294, 298
Fleet Engineers Committee, 174, 220, 250, 269, 293, 337, 339–40, 399, 485
foreign vessels, 247–48, 250, 252, 286, 292
freight rates, 68, 75, 86–87, 260, 444, 450
Fuller, D. Ward, 366, 417–18, 436, 507

G

garbage, disposal of, 287, 338, 340
George M. Humphrey, 223, 305–6, 534
Gilchrist, Joseph Clough, 30, 61, 65, 522, 528
GLC (Great Lakes Commission), 319, 401, 413, 457, 472, 512
Glenn, John, 468, 509
GLHS (Great Lakes Historical Society), 303, 341, 413, 533, 535

GLMA (Great Lakes Maritime Academy), 244, 316, 325, 330, 341, 352, 357, 374, 381, 385–89, 403, 434–35, 488–92, 495, 512–13
NMC (Northwestern Michigan College), 316, 324–25, 352, 385, 389, 413
GLMTF (Great Lakes Maritime Task Force), 413, 431, 435–38, 501, 511
GLPA (Great Lakes Protective Association), 63, 69, 71–72, 76, 103, 143, 165–66, 197, 211, 525–26, 528, 534, 536
GLTF (Great Lakes Task Force), 435–37
Goulder, Harvey D., 43–44, 61, 63–64, 71, 93, 98, 100, 102, 139, 314, 447, 518, 523, 525, 533
Government Affairs Committee, 361, 365–66, 429, 536
grain cargoes, 59, 252–53
grain shoveling, 47, 116–17
grain trade, 147–49, 173, 255, 315, 428, 440
Great Lakes Air Pollution Abatement Program, 237, 295
Great Lakes Commission. *See* GLC (Great Lakes Commission)
Great Lakes Engineering Works, 108, 222
Great Lakes Historical Society. *See* GLHS (Great Lakes Historical Society)
Great Lakes Maritime Academy. *See* GLMA (Great Lakes Maritime Academy)
Great Lakes Maritime Task Force. *See* GLMTF (Great Lakes Maritime Task Force)
Great Lakes Protective Association. *See* GLPA (Great Lakes Protective Association)
Great Lakes Task Force. *See* GLTF (Great Lakes Task Force)

Great Lakes Towing Company, 78, 84–85
Great Lakes Water Quality Agreement, 366
Greene, Edward B., 531
Groh, Dave, 337–38, 399, 508

H

Hanna, H. M., 22, 30, 65–66
Hanna, Marcus (Mark), 39–40, 44, 47, 65–67
Harbor Maintenance Tax. See HMT (Harbor Maintenance Tax)
Harbor Maintenance Trust Fund. See HMTF (Harbor Maintenance Trust Fund)
harbors of refuge, 26, 93–94
Harvey, Allyn Fitch, 143, 146, 518, 527
hearings, 152, 249, 256, 291, 365, 368, 458
Henderson, Harold, 425, 447, 513
Henry Steinbrenner, 238, 278, 280, 304
Herbert C. Jackson, 306, 405
H. G. Steinbrenner, 314
Hirshfield, James, 236, 312, 315, 346–49, 351–52, 537
HMT (Harbor Maintenance Tax), 449–50
HMTF (Harbor Maintenance Trust Fund), 500–502
Homer, Arthur B., 306, 405
Horton, John, 200, 264, 267, 319–20, 330, 386, 507
House Subcommittee on Air and Water Pollution, 351
H. S. Wilkinson, 344, 346
H. S. Wilkinson, 65, 80, 146, 344, 346
Humphrey, George M., 146, 184, 192, 534
Hutchinson, John T., 147, 183–84, 193, 215, 228–30, 233, 531

I

ICC (Interstate Commerce Commission), 318, 357, 370
ice blockades, 59, 76–77, 173, 217, 220
icebreaking vessels. See vessels, icebreaking
Ice Committee, 361, 390
ice operations, 95, 170, 215–16
IJC (International Joint Commission), 85–86, 92, 294–96, 298, 340, 348, 427, 443–44, 475, 522
Indiana Port Commission, 368–69, 449
Industrial Committee, 153, 163
injuries, 72–73, 133–34, 136, 150, 161, 164, 258, 312, 462, 494, 537
integration of crews on Great Lakes vessels, 323
Interlake Steamship Company, 29, 61, 223, 306, 337, 399, 417, 439, 521, 525–26, 531, 534–36, 539
International Joint Commission. See IJC (International Joint Commission)
International Joint Conference, 308, 361, 414, 443, 455
Interstate Commerce Commission. See ICC (Interstate Commerce Commission)
iron ore, 19, 81–82, 87, 95, 98, 118, 147–49, 174, 185, 187–88, 193, 199, 217, 223, 230, 241, 246, 248, 252, 255–56, 301, 305, 315, 345–46, 350, 352, 360, 362, 369, 407, 419, 428–29, 440, 450–52, 460, 472, 522, 525, 527, 530
iron ore mining, 244, 427–29
iron ore trade, 147–48, 391
IWW (Industrial Workers of the World), 58

527

J

Jackson, Herbert C., 255, 314, 316, 536
Jacobsen, Ed, 234, 333–34, 390, 419, 463, 508
James R. Barker, 403–4
Jansky, C. M., Jr., 168, 214, 286, 292–93, 335–36
JARC (Jones Act Reform Coalition), 456
Job Referral Centers. *See* JRC (Job Referral Centers)
Johnson, Gilbert R., 144–45, 182–84, 255, 313–14, 359, 447, 533
Jones Act, 25, 236, 255–56, 318, 370, 412, 427, 430, 435, 453–56, 463, 499, 501, 505
Jones Act Reform Coalition. *See* JARC (Jones Act Reform Coalition)
JRC (Job Referral Centers), 359, 375, 425, 428, 435, 488, 496

K

Kammer, Christine M., 359, 422
Kings Point, 270, 299, 327, 381, 386, 412–13, 422, 491, 509, 512
Kishel, Bill, 496

L

labor unrest, 119, 157, 244
Lake, Ore, Coal and Vessel Committee. *See* LOCVC (Lake, Ore, Coal and Vessel Committee)
Lake Carriers' Association. *See* LCA (Lake Carriers' Association)
lake levels, 92, 177, 288
Lake Michigan, diversion of, 257–58
Lake Survey, 110, 188
Lake Vessel Committee, 192–93, 202, 240
Lane, Carol Ann, 422–24, 427, 436, 444
LCA (Lake Carriers' Association)
    annual reports, 60, 68, 72, 75, 117, 133, 135, 152, 258, 391, 442, 516
    board, 26, 80, 82, 98, 112, 132, 143, 146, 176, 182, 214, 247, 286, 436, 465, 476, 495, 524–37
    committees, 76, 149, 197, 214, 255, 316, 365, 381–82, 420, 439, 483, 533–34, 536
    integration of crews on Great Lakes vessels, 323
    organization, 63, 81, 144, 182, 233, 313, 358, 416
    reorganized, 34, 61, 63, 225, 526–27
L. C. Sabin, 171, 174
legislation, 27, 35–36, 43–44, 47, 59, 65, 112, 198, 248, 253–54, 257, 260–61, 317–19, 366, 368, 372, 429, 456–57, 504, 528
Legislative Committee, 149, 182, 250, 254–58, 261, 283, 316, 361, 365, 368, 390, 427, 429, 448, 535
licensed engineers, 31–32, 349
Lifesaving Service, 111
Lighthouse Board, 40, 44, 47, 103, 107
lighthouses, 37, 44, 93, 107, 109, 160, 177, 217, 287
lightships, 30, 35, 47, 102–3, 109, 160, 407
Livingstone, William, 28, 30, 36–37, 43–44, 47, 50–55, 58–61, 63–64, 66, 68–69, 71, 75–77, 87, 93–94, 97–98, 100–101, 111, 113, 118, 139, 143, 176–77, 200, 524, 527–28
    memorials to, 176–77
    presidency of, 49, 60, 65, 72–73, 89, 94, 102, 126, 128, 133, 139, 149
Livingstone Channel, 55, 96–97, 101, 103, 106, 139, 170, 519
    opening of, 96–97

528

load line, 30, 113, 196, 222, 237, 242, 282, 285, 317, 337–38, 400, 474, 482, 486
LOCVC (Lake, Ore, Coal and Vessel Committee), 240, 242
Lorain Electronics, 337, 397–98, 480–81

M

Mackinaw, 217, 219–20, 284, 372, 391, 431, 463, 467–69, 483
MACKINAW 2020 Task Force, 467
Manning, John W., 330, 334–35, 397, 508, 536
Manpower Subcommittee. See Subcommittee on Manpower
Marad (U.S. Maritime Administration), 235, 338, 376, 378, 384–85, 400–402, 412, 414–15, 463, 491, 512
Marine Engineers' Beneficial Association. See MEBA (Marine Engineers' Beneficial Association)
Maritime Cabotage Task Force. See MCTF (Maritime Cabotage Task Force)
Marr, George, 144–45, 150, 166, 182–83, 528
Masters, Mates and Pilots Union. See MMP (Masters, Mates and Pilots Union)
Mather, Samuel, 138, 525–26
Mather, William G., 29–30, 166, 217, 530
McKay, Raymond, 324, 373
McMillan, James, 32, 37, 39, 44, 47, 59, 67, 516
McSweeney, William J., 271, 327–28
MCTF (Maritime Cabotage Task Force), 413, 431, 453–56, 511

MEBA (Marine Engineers' Beneficial Association), 115, 319, 324, 328, 372, 385, 433, 435
Merchant Marine Act, 261–62, 264, 315, 317, 347, 357, 370–71, 404, 453, 531
Michigan Department of Health, 326, 341
Michigan Watercraft Control Act, 357
MMP (Masters, Mates and Pilots Union), 385, 433, 435, 488, 492
Mobilization Committee, 65, 80–82, 87
Murphy, Thomas O., 330, 359, 424–25, 447, 454
Murray, John C., 158, 251, 271, 327–28, 533

N

NAT (Navigation Assistance Tax), 451
national defense, 185, 187, 193, 229, 248, 448, 472
National Industrial Recovery Act. See NIRA (National Industrial Recovery Act)
National Safety Council, 271, 330, 374
National Security Resources Board, 239
National Weather Service. See NWS (National Weather Service)
navigation
 aids to, 27, 31–32, 37, 60–61, 72, 87, 102, 104, 109, 169, 190, 213–14, 288, 332, 334, 451, 483–84
 extended season, 402
 safety of, 71, 107, 247, 444, 463
 year round, 391, 394, 464–65
Navigation Assistance Tax. See NAT (Navigation Assistance Tax)
Navigation Committee, 167, 212, 214, 248, 250, 282, 286–88, 332–33, 361, 390, 396–97, 421, 475, 482, 484–85, 487

navigation improvements, 24, 67, 87, 93, 168
navigation infrastructure, 229, 249, 282
navigation season, 69, 147–48, 170–71, 177, 185, 190, 195, 202, 215–16, 220, 237, 270, 282, 315–16, 319, 352, 357, 370, 391, 395, 431, 437, 463, 467
navigation systems, 66, 237, 241, 289, 334, 394, 438, 482, 488, 501, 510
Nekvasil, Glen, 422–23, 425, 437, 440, 444
NIRA (National Industrial Recovery Act), 150, 166
non-indigenous species, 422, 458–60
Northwestern Michigan College. *See* NMC (Northwestern Michigan College) *under* GLMA (Great Lakes Maritime Academy)
NWS (National Weather Service), 396, 480–81, 484
weather bureau, 114, 288, 332

O

Obey, Dave, 470–71, 473, 499, 509
occupational deferments, 194, 202, 241–42, 322
Occupational Safety and Health Administration. *See* OSHA (Occupational Safety and Health Administration)
ODT (Office of Defense Transportation), 182, 191–94, 202–3, 532
Office of Management and Budget. *See* OMB (Office of Management and Budget)
Ohio legislature, 198, 254, 258–59, 319
oil fired vessels. *See* vessels, oil fired

OMB (Office of Management and Budget), 395, 449, 451, 470, 491, 500–501
Open Shop policy, 116, 118, 120, 126
Ore and Coal Exchange, 81–82, 535
original licenses, 124–26, 205, 270, 488
OSHA (Occupational Safety and Health Administration), 488, 495

P

Palmer, Thomas W., 51–53
patrol boats, 102, 106, 190
Paul, Mary, 425–26
PEL (Permissible Exposure Limits), 488, 495
Pelfrey, Melvin, 319, 372, 374, 384, 430, 435–37, 454, 512, 537
Philip R. Clarke, 352, 354, 391, 405–6
Pittsburgh Steamship Company, 221–22, 234, 276, 345
Plumb, Russell H., 266–67, 321, 359, 425–26, 536
Poe, Orlando M., 28, 31
Poe Lock, 94, 225, 283, 345, 472, 502, 519
new, 236, 316, 350–52
port authorities, 349, 500–501, 511
port industry, 350, 438, 449, 472
Potts, Donald C., 120, 193, 234, 239, 261, 307, 320, 535
private lights, 26, 30, 34, 38–40, 44, 47, 103
Public Relations Committee, 221, 268, 299, 341–42, 401

Q

QMEDs (Qualified Member of the Engine Department), 377, 489, 496

R

radars, 212, 214, 236–37, 271, 282, 286–87, 289, 300, 326, 488
Radio Corporation of America. *See* RCA (Radio Corporation of America)
radio direction finders. *See* RDF (radio direction finders)
radiotelephones, 168, 213–14, 236, 290–91, 293, 334, 535
railroad bridges, 25, 89, 91, 213
RAMP (Restore America's Maritime Promise), 500
rationing, 194–95
RCA (Radio Corporation of America), 169, 215, 335
RDF (radio direction finders), 108, 166, 169, 287, 488
Reagan Administration, 357, 369, 382, 449, 451, 455, 466, 472, 491, 493
recession, 123, 130, 147, 236, 356, 363, 389, 425, 428, 440, 490–91
Recommendations for the Prevention of Accidents, 70, 162
recreational boats, 458, 475, 477–79
Rector, George B., 270–71, 328, 389, 403, 490, 512
Republicans, 20, 57, 141–42, 229, 356, 411, 414
Restore America's Maritime Promise. *See* RAMP (Restore America's Maritime Promise)
Rockefeller Building, 63, 197, 328, 420, 425
Rose, Jack, 375, 425, 496
Ruge, Mark, 429, 446, 454, 499, 513
rules of the road, 247–48, 250, 377, 390
Rumsey, Albert R., 522
Rumsey, Alfred R., 63–64, 127, 523, 527

Ryan, George J., 359, 408, 410–13, 416–17, 419–20, 423, 425–26, 428–29, 432, 434–38, 444–45, 449–50, 454–55, 457, 464, 468, 474, 483–85, 490, 492–93, 496, 499, 502, 504, 537–38

S

Sabin, Louis C., 77, 102, 139, 144–45, 183–84, 225, 233
Sabin Lock, 100, 102, 218
sabotage, 80, 185–87, 238, 407
Safety Committee, 73, 122, 153, 163, 165–66, 208, 272, 361, 374, 388, 487, 526
Sainte Marie, 171, 216–18, 284
sanitation, 69, 82, 93, 119, 122, 153, 163, 166, 316, 341, 401, 460, 528
Satterness, William B., 374, 419, 487, 508
Sault Ste. Marie, 25, 28, 91, 98, 100, 160, 170, 251, 413, 472, 476
Saunders, John T. (Jack), 375, 425, 496, 537
savings plan, 69, 123, 150, 157, 161, 166, 207, 211, 272, 325, 373, 382, 519, 527–28
schools, 24, 51, 69, 124, 126, 150, 158–59, 205, 211, 268–69, 271, 300, 321, 328, 376, 385, 393, 423, 490–91, 528
seamen, 25, 31, 61, 73, 78–79, 82–83, 112, 116, 118, 123, 126–30, 132–34, 137, 150, 153–57, 159–61, 163–65, 175, 194–95, 198–201, 203–4, 206–7, 209–10, 223, 237, 240, 258–59, 270, 272, 275–78, 318–19, 321, 325–26, 331–32, 350, 372, 376, 382–83, 386, 434, 451, 482, 489, 493–95

AB (able bodied), 112, 156, 159, 196–97, 242, 322, 327, 330, 377–79, 381, 495–96
lake, 84, 201, 239, 259
unlicensed, 267, 277, 374
seamen laws, 143, 155
Seaway, 236–38, 248–50, 252–53, 271, 291–92, 297, 299, 326, 334, 347, 349–51, 407, 428, 450, 456, 464, 533
secretary of war, 25, 39, 57, 92–93, 98, 151, 526
Selective Service, 78, 186, 194, 202, 211, 239–40, 243, 300, 322
Selective Service Boards, 240–42
Senate, 20, 25, 57, 65, 141–42, 229, 247, 250, 257–58, 261, 356, 395, 411, 456, 503
separate courses, 88, 167–68, 212, 250, 282, 286, 397, 442
Sheadle, Jasper Holmes, 30, 63–65, 71, 97, 128, 200, 519
Sheadle, J. H., 30, 63–65, 71, 97, 200, 519
Shipping Board, 81–83, 127–28
shipping offices, 22, 34–36, 47, 83, 127–28, 375
Ship Safety Committees, 122, 134, 162, 208, 237, 265
shipyards, 79, 174, 201, 240, 347, 350–51, 436–37
Shore Captains Committee, 65, 88, 144, 162, 167, 186, 212, 214, 247, 250, 282–83, 285–87, 317, 332–33, 361, 365, 390, 484, 533, 535
Sillers, Nancyann H., 331
SIP (Simplified Inspection Program), 487
Siragusa, Mike, 417, 508
Smith, Ned A., 417–18, 507
Smith, Sidney E., Jr., 314, 360, 416–17
Smith, Willard J., 244–45, 385, 490

Smoke Abatement Committee, 339
smoke emissions, 237, 294–95, 341
sobriety, 69, 123, 166, 211
Soo Locks, 59, 80, 94–95, 104, 189, 213, 275, 288, 334, 357, 391, 395, 463–64, 466, 482, 502–3
Southeast Shoal, 47, 102–3, 169
Special Rules for the Protection of Great Lakes Commerce, 185, 238, 407
Spencer, Lyndon, 183, 228, 230–33, 236, 249, 251, 253, 261–63, 283–84, 289, 295, 536
Sproul, Gavin, 419, 485
Stalker, Neil, 417–18, 508
Steamboat Inspection Service, 112–14, 126, 170
steel
 imported, 429, 450, 452
 industry, 19, 60, 66, 83, 117, 157, 229, 241, 244, 246, 251, 282, 360, 389, 419, 428, 452, 464, 472
Steinbrenner, George M., 65, 128, 153, 197, 200, 314, 351, 529, 534
Steinbrenner, George M., III, 321, 347, 539
Steinbrenner, Henry G., 347, 360, 536
St. Lawrence Seaway, 199, 229, 236, 248, 251, 253, 263, 282, 315, 349, 361, 391, 449, 456, 461
St. Lawrence Waterway, 152, 199
Story of the Soo Locks, 302
Straits, the, 76, 170, 173–74, 216–18, 220, 391, 393
strikes, 21, 59, 83–84, 115, 118–20, 185, 191, 244, 251, 272, 277
Subcommittee on Manpower, 193–94, 202, 239–41, 322
subsidy, 161, 262, 264, 346, 348, 449
Sullivan, Arthur C., 529

T

taxes, 41, 247, 262–63, 317, 357, 369–70, 448, 450–51, 462
Theis, Stuart, 417–18, 508
Thomas W. Palmer, 52–53
Thompson, Renold, 360, 414, 417, 457, 508, 538
tolls, 35–36, 41, 229, 236, 247, 249–51, 256–57, 345, 349, 428, 449
Tomlinson, George Ashley, 30, 64–65, 71, 146
TPI (tons per inch immersion), 473
training, 134, 158, 202, 205, 245, 272, 280, 321, 326–27, 376, 379, 384, 387, 389, 488–89, 494, 496–97, 517
  unlicensed, 381, 489
treaties, 24, 56, 79, 152, 430
Treaty of Washington, 24, 32
Trimble, Paul, 356–58, 360–64, 371, 373–75, 381–82, 386, 390, 393–94, 406, 408, 414, 422, 425, 435, 538
tunnels, 27, 89–90

U

unemployment compensation, 198, 258–59, 319
unions, 58–59, 82, 115, 118, 150, 155, 167, 191, 258–59, 264, 276, 328, 372, 375, 384–85, 429, 435–37, 442, 489
  officials, 117, 384–85, 492
  unlicensed, 115, 433, 496
United Steelworkers Union. *See* USW (United Steelworkers Union)
Upper Great Lakes Commission, 386, 388
U.S.-Canada Free Trade Area Agreement, 453–55
USCG (U.S. Coast Guard), 106, 169, 188, 190, 216–18, 237, 244–46, 248, 250, 282, 284–85, 288–89, 292, 298–99, 316, 330, 334–35, 337, 342, 349, 363, 372, 377–78, 383, 387, 391, 394, 396, 398, 400, 413, 439, 457, 464–65, 467, 475, 484, 494, 503–4, 510
user charges, 256–57, 337, 363, 368–69, 431, 442
user fees, 256, 284, 358, 369, 407, 448–51, 500
U.S. Maritime Administration. *See* Marad (U.S. Maritime Administration)
U.S. Merchant Marine Academy. *See* Kings Point
USPHS (U.S. Public Health Service), 112, 114, 122, 163, 209, 221, 275–76, 298, 326, 383, 493
U.S. Post Office, 161, 407
U.S. Steel (later USS Great Lakes Fleet), 58, 120, 319, 351, 359, 373, 391, 400, 416, 419–20, 436, 452, 535
U.S. Treasury, 41, 262
USW (United Steelworkers Union), 375, 384, 435, 496

V

VanBrunt, David, 419
very high frequency. *See* VHF
Vessel Manpower Subcommittee, 240
Vessel Personnel and Safety Committee. *See* VP&S (Vessel Personnel and Safety) Committee
Vessel Personnel Committee, 425, 488
vessels
  American, 24–25, 262
  capacities of, 87, 132, 242, 407
  coal fired, 305, 401
  construction and conversions of, 497

construction and modernization of, 174, 221, 343
dry docking of, 250, 299
icebreaking, 95, 218, 284
losses and crew casualties, 72, 122, 175, 223, 304, 406
obsolete, 261, 263
oil fired, 296, 305, 401, 405
productivity of, 337, 343
salt water, 247, 432, 458
traffic, 181, 290, 393, 464, 467
wastes from, 366, 400
Vessel Security Committee, 439
VHF (very high frequency), 236–37, 290–93, 335–36, 397
system, 336, 397, 481
Vidal Shoals, 94, 104–5, 476
VP&S (Vessel Personnel and Safety) Committee, 361, 374, 388, 487–88, 491, 493

W

wages, 20–21, 65, 111, 118, 123, 132, 150, 153, 157–58, 204, 244, 247, 433
waivers, 199, 236, 242, 254–56, 453
War Department, 27, 38, 91–93, 98, 225
War Production Board. *See* WPB (War Production Board)
War Shipping Administration. *See* WSA (War Shipping Administration)
Watercraft Pollution Control Act, 318, 366, 401, 458
water diversion, 257
water level gauges, 102
water pollution, 85–86, 340
Water Quality Improvement Act. *See* WQIA (Water Quality Improvement Act)
Weakley, James H. I., 246, 432, 471, 487, 498, 506

Weather Bureau Service, 114
Welfare Committee, 126, 162, 200–201, 204, 207–8, 211–12, 239, 241, 264, 268–69, 272, 274, 276–77, 299, 319, 324–26, 330–32, 342, 361, 374, 377, 381–82, 386, 518–19, 521, 524, 529
Welfare Plan, 65, 69, 72, 82–83, 120, 127–28, 132–34, 138, 156, 159–61, 163, 165–66, 204, 210, 237, 271, 325, 519, 528
Welfare Plan Committee, 128, 149, 153, 163, 200, 524–27
Welfare Plan for the Benefit of Employees of Vessels, 70
Welfare Plan Safety Committee, 72, 134
Welland Canal, 24, 32, 35, 41, 59, 67–68, 152, 185, 248–51, 316, 345, 472, 521
Welsch, Jerome (Jerry), 417–18, 507, 513
Westcott, Charles H., 521
Westcott, John W., 29–30, 161, 518
West Neebish Channel, 45, 94, 169, 171, 464, 475
White, Fred R., 242–43, 308, 314, 360, 404, 444, 508
Whitefish Bay, 76–77, 95, 170, 216–18, 284
Wilfred Sykes, 304–5, 405
Wilkinson, H. S., 65, 71, 80, 146
William E. Corey, 97
William Livingstone, 52, 55, 96–97, 101–2
Wilson, Thomas, 30, 36, 144, 516, 524
Wilson Marine Transit Company, 144, 182, 346, 531–33
winter navigation, 374, 394–96, 403, 434
Winter Navigation Demonstration Program, 363, 374, 394–95, 463–64, 466, 509

winter schools, 205, 265, 268–70, 276, 301
Wolvin, A. B., 30, 47, 528
Wood, Alexander T., 180, 182–84, 191–94, 199, 209, 224, 233, 440, 531
Wood, J. F., 220
Wood, Joseph S., 140, 143–44, 146, 167, 182, 184, 532
working conditions, 157
WPB (War Production Board), 191, 193, 201–2, 532
WQIA (Water Quality Improvement Act), 366, 368
WSA (War Shipping Administration), 188, 202, 226, 533

X

X-Ray program, 275–76, 300, 326

Z

Zeber, Christine. *See* Kammer, Christine M., 359, 422

Printed in the United States
By Bookmasters